The I

The I

NORMAN N. HOLLAND

YALE UNIVERSITY PRESS
NEW HAVEN AND LONDON

Published with assistance from
the Louis Stern Memorial Fund.

Designed by Sally Harris
and set in Times Roman type by
The Saybrook Press, Inc.
Printed in the United States of America by
Vail-Ballou Press, Binghamton, New York.

Library of Congress Cataloging in Publication Data

Holland, Norman Norwood, 1927-
  The I.

  Bibliography: p.
  Includes index.
  1. Identity (Psychology) 2. Ego (Psychology)
I. Title.
BF697.H53   1985   155.2   84-20917
ISBN 0-300-03196-3 (alk. paper)

10   9   8   7   6   5   4   3   2   1

The extract on pp. 3−6 is reprinted by permission from
The Psychopathology of Everyday Life by
S. Freud (London: Adam and Charles Black, 1901).

To my favorite I, Jane

As kingfishers catch fire, dragonflies dráw fláme;
As tumbled over rim in roundy wells
Stones ring; like each tucked string tells, each hung bell's
Bow swung finds tongue to fling out broad its name;
Each mortal thing does one thing and the same:
Deals out that being indoors each one dwells;
Selves—goes itself; *myself* it speaks and spells;
Crying *Whát I dó is me: for that I came.*
—G. M. Hopkins

Contents

Part III / A History of I

Part IV / A Science of I

Preface

In recent months, people have been asking me, "What's your new book about?" When I answer, "human nature," or "the I," they simply look at me perplexedly, not knowing how to continue the dialogue. Let me try to explain.

Not long ago, I found a journal that I kept when I was in my twenties. It ended with these words:

> I am glad to have kept this book, even as sketchily as I have. Someday I shall look back, and when I do I daresay the then-I will wonder what the now-I was like, just as the now-I wonders about the then-I. . . .

The I who at twenty-three wondered about the self wonders to find himself at fifty-six writing *The I,* in which he still wonders about the self. This essentially psychological book could not remotely have entered the thoughts of the young, passionately literary student who wrote those lines. How different those two selves of twenty-three and fifty-six are, yet we were and are ourselves in much the same way. Three decades ago this I was puzzling, reasoning, using abstractions like "self," turning even "I" into an abstraction, wanting the right figure of speech yet not finding it and using no imagery at all, left wondering, to borrow the words of the poet Hopkins, about

> my selfbeing, my consciousness and feeling of my self, that taste of myself, of *I* and *me* alone and in all things which is more distinctive than the taste of ale or alum, more distinctive than the smell of walnut leaf or camphor, and is incommunicable by any means to another man (as when I was a child I used to ask myself: what must it be to be someone else?).

No wonder I still wonder. Nothing, they say, interests one more than one's self. It is, after all, the only thing we finally have, although nothing is harder to speak about or know in any systematic way. It is impossible, I think, to make any statement in either the sciences or the humanities without making some assumptions about the I, if only that the I can make such a statement. Yet rarely do we spell those assumptions out. The I speaks, but remains unspoken, unarticulated, unexplored.

ix

I am honored to find that my wondering is like Freud's. He wrote to his friend and disciple Karl Abraham in 1924, when he was sixty-eight, "It is making unreasonable demands of the unity of the personality to think that I should feel myself identical with the author of the work [I wrote in 1878] on the spinal ganglia of Petromyzon. And yet, all the same it should be so. . . ." He saw the same unity that perplexes me in my twenty-three and fifty-six.

On January 15 in the last year of his life, Tolstoy wrote:

> I am conscious of myself in exactly the same way now, at eighty-one, as I was conscious of myself, my "I," at five or six years of age. Consciousness is immovable. Due to this alone there is the movement which we call "time." If time *moves on,* then there must be something that stands still. The consciousness of my "I" stands still.

I know that feeling. The way I am conscious of I remains the same despite the ways I have changed in age and state. That consciousness includes the knowledge of a personal history that traces unbroken connections from that bachelor student and would-be poet to the husband, father, professor, critic, theorist of today.

John Updike, commenting on that passage from Tolstoy's *Diaries,* speaks eloquently of old age as "a physical change bafflingly rung upon an immutable self," "the end stage of our adamant individuality." But is our individuality so immutable and adamant?

I know my own I, as I can never know yours, yet like a dim star, like an after-image, if I turn my vision toward it, it disappears. It is intense as long as I do not stop to name it. Once I do, it becomes not quite the same unmediated I, slightly alien, other, the subject of my intellection and inference—like your I.

Unreal, elusive as this "I" is, it is most intensely me, the innermost keep of me, yet not solitary confinement, not even a prison. "I," although it is more private than privacy itself, lies open to every sensation, every experience, every other thing from the kiss of a lover to the faintest, glimmering pinhole of the farthest star. All are immediately I. In the very moment they come into being as other, they become not-other.

Immovable, immutable, they say. I would say the self is completely paradoxical, adamant and quicksilver both, and it is the aim of this book to explore how that can be and how we can think about the paradox.

Yet we are reluctant to think about that I, "the selfless self of self, most strange, most still" (Hopkins again). To avoid "psychologism," the recognition that that changing, unchanging I is at the core of everything we do and think, philosophers make mind-wobbling phenomenological and deconstructive sidesteps. The psychologist tells us that we can talk about "I" only if we turn it into things we can count. The psychologist claims that he is being scientific in this demand, and indeed science, so they say, has wrought its prodigies precisely by leaving the I out.

If I enters in, if my eye does not see what yours does when we look through the telescope, then either I am wrong or we are not doing science. Or are we simply—and inevitably—being I's?

There is, of course, one science that tries to deal with the self, although other scientists often glance askance at it: psychoanalysis. It is the one science of subjectivity, if there can be such a thing. I find it a notably powerful explainer of I's.

A cultivated European forgets a word from a line of Virgil. Why did he forget? And why *this* word? A man finds himself unaccountably thinking of a certain six-digit number. Why *this* number? A boy who was born with his fingers joined together and his toes unseparated surprises himself by doodling the deformity of his left hand. A reclusive, self-enclosed doctor, after three years of Chinese "thought reform," becomes a compulsively open, giving person. Then, on his release, he goes back to his former style. What had happened? A man dreams a dream that enables him to sleep through the sound of church bells that wake his wife. How did the dream function to filter out the noise? Anyone can ask these questions, but, so far as I know, only psychoanalysis, that highly "subjective" discipline, offers answers.

It is the purpose of this book to understand the psychoanalytic answers to such questions as a theory of the I. Someone has said that if an idea is any good at all, you should be able to write it on the back of a calling card, like Einstein's $e=mc^2$ or Newton's $f=ma$. Were I to try for such a dramatic concision with this large, long book, I would write, I ARC or perhaps I ARC DEFTly.

Very briefly, I act forth into the world from myself as agent (A) and the world acts back onto me, so that I am a consequence (C) of what the world does both on its own and in response to my agency. My I initiates feedback but is also the consequence of the feedbacks it initiates. One can spell out those feedbacks as: expectation (E), what I am habituated to seek in the timestream of my experience; defense (D), what I will admit into myself from the world; fantasy (F), what I project out into the world; transformation (T), the meanings outside of time that I make my experience into.

The I is agency and consequence, and something more. It is a representation (R) of an I, either the I's own or somebody else's. In particular, it is some I's attempt to put an I into words, and I propose one particular form of words.

We can reconcile the adamant and the quicksilver I's by representing them as a theme and variations (adapting an idea from the psychoanalyst Heinz Lichtenstein). That is, "I" feel partly like something that changes from instant to instant and year to year, the now-I of my journal, and partly like something less changeable, "immovable" in Tolstoy's sense. Further, if "I" is a whole, each of these aspects affects or, really, defines the other. We see difference against a background of sameness, and we see sameness by seeing what does not change in a world of differences. The idea of a theme and variations provides a way of structuring such a dovetailing of change and constancy, movement and stillness, sameness and difference, the now-I and the then-I and the I that writes about them both.

It is this theory of identity that the first part of this book develops: we can look at an I as we would a work of art. From this first part the rest of the book fell more or less naturally into three more parts: the psychology, the history, and the science of I.

The first part says we can think systematically, or at least aesthetically, about an I. We can trace the persistence of, say, Norman N. Holland in the way I use words or size up situations—in general, through my use of symbols or senses or skills. We can use the theme-and-variations concept of an I to understand how the processes that psychologists study—symbolization, perception, cognition, or memory—are all ways that an I ARCs, sustaining and re-creating an I. We can use a theme-and-variations concept of identity to develop a psychology of I, and that is part II of this book.

One can put an otherwise almost ineffable I into words as the history of such a theme and variations. The word "history" preserves a necessary ambiguity. History, in one sense, is the way things actually were. History is also somebody's—some I's—story of the way things actually were. We need both, since only an I can look at an I and try to say how things were.

There is another sense in which this theory leads to a history of I. It becomes possible, by thinking of an I continually confronting new situations, to imagine the recurring patterns in human development. As the baby moves from total dependence on another, to the first stirrings of self-rule and self-control and self-direction, to standing and walking and talking to loving and resenting its parents, and on through life, we can imagine an I confronting a series of riddles. Some of them are the same for all human beings (how will you accept death?). Some are the same for many human beings (how can you depend on others in a culture that prizes the lack of dependence?). Some will be unique to this or that individual (how will you stage operas in America?). The story of how this individual or some individuals or all individuals meet these questions and answer them becomes the history of an I (as developed in part III), and that history becomes in each of us a kind of paralogic by which we unite our experiences, a logic beyond ordinary logic in which eyes are like mouths or money like excrement.

Finally, part IV addresses the question of whether there can be a science of the individual, since such a science could never be independent of the scientist—the scientist is what is being studied. Can there be a science in which the "subjectivity" of the scientist is not only not a faint contamination but the very essence of the enterprise?

The ambiguity in "history" remains essential. I cannot bend to the usual pressure to choose between what are ordinarily called "objective" and "subjective." My goal is precisely to explore the way each is the essence of the other. Objectivity and subjectivity create each other, as stillness movement and movement stillness. To explore one is to explore both. Indeed, I believe that they so interlace that it is meaningless to use either word by itself.

Can such a study be a science? I may be offering no more than a method for thinking systematically about the I: wording the I as a theme in order to understand thoughts and actions as variations on that theme; thinking of that theme and its variations as a feedback ARC of agency, consequence, and representation.

Clearly there are other modes for putting I's into words—the poet's, the philosopher's, the novelist's—and there are obviously limits to this mode. The only way I know to find those limits, or to find the point at which some other mode of thinking about the I becomes more useful, is to test this one. I want to drive the idea of an I as a theme and variations governing a hierarchy of feedbacks as far into the problem as it will go, to see if it will enable us to connect aspects of self that we are otherwise unable to connect (like subjectivity and objectivity). To do so is precisely to feed the idea out into the world and see how it ARCs back.

Since the nearest thing we have to a science of I is psychoanalysis, you could regard this book as a rethinking or rereading of psychoanalysis as a theory of the I. You can, I think, use it as an introduction to psychoanalysis in the 1980s, if you are willing to accept one man's systematizing of psychoanalysis. And that brings me to the first and greatest of my

Acknowledgments

—to Freud. His was an incredibly gifted, severe, majestic, and even sometimes puckish I. It is impossible, I find, to explore his processes of thought or the elegance of his German without acquiring awe for his genius.

I am not, however, a "Freudian." Using the discoverer's name that way, it seems to me, beggars psychoanalysis, making it less of a developed science and more the "teachings" of Freud, as though he had created a dogma, a system of interpretations, or, as some French writers have suggested, a work of fiction. "Freudian" confines and reduces Freud's great achievement to a sequence of small ones. It is with his great one that I am concerned here: the setting in motion of a whole new discipline, the systematic study of subjectivity, the science of I.

There comes a point in every new science when it divides into a present "state of the art" and a past of earlier ideas, some retained in the state of the art, some retained but changed to fit new contexts, and some put aside. Psychoanalysis has long since matured beyond that transition. One can teach a history of psychoanalysis, as of physics or biology, and it would be of use as any history is. To learn psychoanalysis or a theory of the I as it is today, however, one must judge concepts as they are, not as they once were—even for Freud. Limiting psychoanalysis to what Freud wrote (as is all too often done) curtails Freud's great achievement.

One of the great pleasures of writing this book has been working with my friend and former colleague Murray Schwartz. As we taught in each other's seminars over a period of ten years, we arrived together at many of the ideas that follow, particularly the great clarification of theory made possible by Heinz Lichtenstein's theme-and-variations concept of identity. We began this book as a joint project in the summer of 1975, and my only regret is that we did not complete it that way. As it is, in the chapters on symbolism and the first year of life, I worked from Murray's outline and notes, and throughout the writing, his comments, corrections, and suggestions have greatly enriched *The I*. It has been a constant source of reassurance for this I to draw on his encyclopedic knowledge of the psychoanalytic literature and on his remarkable sensitivity to the large implications of the smallest details.

I am indebted to my colleagues at the Center for the Psychological Study of the Arts and the Group for Applied Psychoanalysis in Buffalo who have read and listened diligently to sections of this book, offering their intelligent, helpful, and most welcome comments: Charles Bernheimer, Paul Diesing, George Hole, Claire Kahane, Paul Kugler, Theodore Mills, Robert Rogers, William Warner, David Willbern, and especially Joseph Masling, whose tact has so often calmed my fulminations about the scientific claims of psychology. Heinz Lichtenstein's ideas quite simply permeate *The I*. In many ways this book does no more than summarize my fifteen years of cheerful talk with this gifted, inspiring group.

I remember with gratitude and a pang of grief (for several have died) the warm and brilliant analysts who first introduced me to psychoanalysis and admitted me to psychoanalytic study: Joseph Michaels, Ives Hendrick, Robert Waelder, and my own analyst, Elizabeth Zetzel. I feel a very special gratitude to my uncle-in-law, Henry Katz, who made it possible for me to be analyzed. Among the present generation of analysts I am especially thankful to Otto Kernberg and Roy Schafer, who took time from their own work to read and comment on sections of this manuscript. In the same way, I am grateful to Robert Silhol and Ellie Ragland-Sullivan, who aided me greatly in thinking about Lacan, and to Richard Held, Ulric Neisser, and Keith White, who helped me avoid errors in some of the material on perception. Bernard Paris generously provided me with a detailed and subtle commentary. Obviously, the final book is my own responsibility, but *The I* would have been much more questionable than it is without the expert help of these kind people.

Over the years many research assistants have searched out the references that appear at the end of the book: Mary Childers, Ellen Golub, Patrick Hogan, Laura Keyes, Kathleen McIlugh, Judith Moses. All helped. To all I owe much, as I do to Patricia Berens of the Sterling Lord Agency and to Gladys Topkis and Lawrence Kenney of Yale University Press. Geri de Santis did her usual excellent work on HAL and the Electric Pencil, and John Bevis and Michael Pepper helped my own HAL convey the manuscript to a mainframe computer in distant New Haven. I hope they will all feel that the final version of *The I* justifies their efforts.

Three foundations, the American Council of Learned Societies, the John Simon Guggenheim Foundation, and the Research Foundation of the State University of New York, provided crucial support that made writing this book possible and even pleasurable. I have benefited also from the conferences on individual testimony organized by Paul Fussell, Peter Read, and the Social Science Research Council. I am indebted to W. H. Freeman for permission to reprint on p. 234 a diagram from T. G. R. Bower's *Development in Infancy* and to David Higham Associates for permission to reprint excerpts of Elizabeth Jenning's poem "Identity" on pp. 81–2.

This book has had a long gestation, during which I have had the opportunity to try out some of the ideas as articles. I have adapted these as well as excerpts from two previous books (*Laughing* and *5 Readers Reading*) into the argument of *The I*. To the editors of the journals and to the presses involved, *Criticism, Critical Inquiry, The International Journal of Psycho-Analysis,* and the *International Review of Psycho-Analysis,* Cornell University Press, and Yale University Press, I am grateful both for the original publication and for permission to adapt.

Similarly, a number of universities and other institutions have provided me with a lectern from which to explore these ideas: in America, the universities of Chicago, Colorado, Iowa, Kansas, and Virginia, Yale University, and Cornell University's department of psychiatry at New York Hospital; in other countries, the universities of Copenhagen, Delhi, Düsseldorf, Freiburg, Hokkaido, Rome, and Würzburg, Banaras Hindu University, the Free University of Berlin, the Hungarian Academy of Sciences, the Tavistock Clinic of London, and the Sigmund Freud-Gesellschaft of Vienna. I am indebted to my audiences for their patience and their willingness to exchange ideas, and I am grateful to my hosts for hospitality which ranged from postlecture conviviality at a *Beisel* in a time-honored quarter of Vienna to a motocab scattering pigs and chickens as Jane and I careened through the streets of the oldest city in the world. It is, of course, to her, my first and always editor, that I am most anciently and profoundly grateful.

Norman N. Holland

Part I | The Aesthetics of I

1 | Themes and Wholes

Once upon a time, perhaps during the summer of 1900, Freud chanced to meet a young man. They chatted, and the young man began eloquently to protest his position as a Jew in Vienna at the beginning of this century. He declared his regrets that Austria had passed from a period of relative liberalism to one of reaction. Now Jews (like himself and Freud) were deprived of full freedom to develop their talents.

He waxed stronger and stronger on the theme, finally ending his speech with a line from Virgil's *Aeneid* in which Dido, queen of Carthage, expresses her rage at her lover Aeneas who has abandoned her. She leaves her revenge, she says, to the Carthaginians who will follow: *Exoriare*— But then the young man could not remember the word that came next. He put together a semblance of the line by changing word order: *Exoriare ex nostris ossibus ultor*. Let an avenger arise from my bones! But at last, in some embarrassment he asked Freud for help. Freud supplied the missing word: *Exoriare* aliquis *nostris ex ossibus ultor*. Let someone (*aliquis*) arise as an avenger from my bones (1901b, 6:8–14).

At this point, the young man remembered some of Freud's psychological work and his claim that one never forgets something without a reason.

Young Man: I should be very curious to learn how I came to forget the indefinite pronoun *aliquis* in this case.

Freud: That should not take us long. I must only ask you to tell me, candidly and uncritically, whatever comes into your mind if you direct your attention to the forgotten word without any definite aim.

Young Man: Good. There springs to my mind, then, the ridiculous notion of dividing up the word like this: *a* and *liquis*.

Freud: What does that mean?

Young Man: I don't know.

Freud: And what occurs to you next?

Young Man: What comes next is *Reliquien* [relics], *liquefying, fluidity, fluid*. Have you discovered anything so far?

Freud: No. Not by any means yet. But go on.

Young Man: I am thinking [and he laughed scornfully] of *Simon of Trent*, whose relics I saw two years ago in a church at Trent. I am thinking of the accusation of ritual blood-sacrifice which is being brought against the Jews again just now, and of *Kleinpaul's* book in which he regards all these supposed victims as incarnations, one might say new editions, of the Saviour.

Freud: The notion is not entirely unrelated to the subject we were discussing before the Latin word slipped your memory.

Young Man: True. My next thoughts are about an article that I read lately in an Italian newspaper. Its title, I think, was "What St. *Augustine* Says about Women." What do you make of that?

Freud: I am waiting.

Young Man: And now comes something that is quite clearly unconnected with our subject.

Freud: Please refrain from any criticism and—

Young Man: Yes, I understand. I am thinking of a fine old gentleman I met on my travels last week. He was a real *original,* with all the appearance of a huge bird of prey. His name was *Benedict*, if it's of interest to you.

Freud: Anyhow, here are a row of saints and Fathers of the Church: St. *Simon,* St. *Augustine,* St. *Benedict.* There was, I think, a Church Father called *Origen.* Moreover, three of these names are also first names, like *Paul* in *Kleinpaul.*

Young Man: Now it's St. *Januarius* and the miracle of his blood that comes into my mind—my thoughts seem to be running on mechanically.

Freud: Just a moment: St. *Januarius* and St. *Augustine* both have to do with the calendar. But won't you remind me about the miracle of his blood?

Young Man: Surely you must have heard of that? They keep the blood of St. Januarius in a phial inside a church at Naples, and on a particular holy day it miraculously *liquefies.* The people attach great importance to this miracle and get very excited if it's delayed—as happened once at a time when the French were occupying the town. So the general in command—or have I got it wrong? was it Garibaldi?—took the reverend gentleman aside and gave him to understand, with an unmistakable gesture toward the soldiers posted outside, that he hoped the miracle would take place very soon. And in fact it did take place . . . [And he broke off.]

Freud: Well, go on. Why do you pause?

Young Man: Well, something *has* come into my mind . . . but it's too intimate to pass on . . . Besides, I don't see any connection or any necessity for saying it.

Freud: You can leave the connection to me. Of course I can't force you to talk about something that you find distasteful; but then you mustn't insist on learning from me how you came to forget your *aliquis.*

Young Man: Really? Is that what you think? Well then, I've suddenly thought of a lady from whom I might easily hear a piece of news that would be very awkward for both of us.

Freud: That her periods have stopped?

Young Man: How could you guess that?

Freud: That's not difficult any longer; you've prepared the way sufficiently. Think of *the calendar saints, the blood that starts to flow on a particular day, the disturbance when the event fails to take place, the open threats that the miracle must be vouchsafed or else. . . .* In fact, you've made use of the miracle of St. Januarius to manufacture a brilliant allusion to women's periods.

Young Man: Without being aware of it. And you really mean to say that it was this anxious expectation that made me unable to produce an unimportant word like *aliquis?*

Freud: It seems to me undeniable. You need only recall the division you made into *a-liquis* and your associations: *relics, liquefying, fluid.* St. Simon was *sacrificed as a child*—shall I go on and show how he comes in? You were led onto him by the subject of relics.

Young Man: No, I'd much rather you didn't. I hope you don't take these thoughts of mine too seriously, if indeed I really had them. In return I will confess to you that the lady is Italian and that I went to Naples with her. But mayn't all this just be a matter of chance?

That last, gently evasive question expresses the doubts and confusions that have dogged psychoanalysis for the eight decades of its existence.

Against those doubts, however, stands the striking convergence that Freud's explanation represents, two convergences, really. First, the young man *himself* became aware that something was on his mind of which he had been unaware. An unconscious idea became conscious. Second, the unconscious idea served as a centering theme around which Freud could fit the other themes of the young man's associations.

That is, his associations went: liquids—relics—Saint Simon—Jews vs. Savior(s)—Italian—St. Augustine—women—an "original"—(St.) Benedict—St. Januarius—blood flowing on a certain day. We could group these into two large themes: first, liquids, liquefying, flowing; second, relics and a series of saints. These two lines relate in form to the Latin syllable *liqu*—and in content this way:

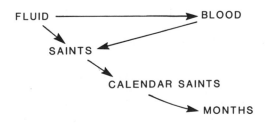

Fluid, blood, saints, calendar, and months converge toward a centering theme of monthly bleeding. As Freud states his final interpretation:

> The speaker had been deploring the fact that the present generation of his people was deprived of its full rights; a new generation, he prophesied like Dido, would inflict vengeance on the oppressors. He had in this way expressed his wish for descendants. At this moment a contrary thought intruded. "Have you really so keen a wish for descendants? That is not so. How embarrassed you would be if you were to get news just now that you were to expect descendants from the quarter you know of. No: no descendants—however much we need them for vengeance."

Freud's final formulation of the young man's thought—I wish and I don't wish for descendants—brings together not only the themes of *liquis,* liquid flowing, blood, and saints but also the particular word forgotten and the larger conversation around the theme of generations.

Freud began in the 1890s by taking seriously this kind of unifying interpretation of meaning in people's symbolic actions. At the same time, he found he could enlarge and strengthen that kind of analysis by free association, nicely defined in his first words to the young man. Each of these techniques sustains and confirms (or disconfirms) the other. Association provides evidence for interpretation to unify. That unity then becomes a source of further associations, as the young man recalls a trip to Naples with his Italian lady friend. Together, association and interpretation make up the essence of psychoanalytic insight.

In form, Freud's proof rests on probability. How many elements in the young man's talk could he bring together and how directly and easily could he connect them?

At the same time, however, the proof of his interpretation simply happened. Indeed, there was no need for a proof. The young man's sudden perception demonstrated the truth of what Freud had arrived at by reasoning alone.

In patient-therapist encounters whether face to face or across the analytic couch, I think psychoanalytic explanations usually draw on both these kinds of proof. In the first, the interpreter or explainer finds a way to create a verbal space between himself and the "other" in which they can each add and share words until they both feel convergence. "How could you guess that?" asked the young man. The second proof is less interpersonal and more formal. Eighty years after the event, I, a literary critic, can supply other themes for Freud's explanation to bring together: that the young man knew he was "no saint," that Origen castrated himself (thereby ending any possibility of descendants), or that "a-liquis" could be read as "without liquid."

Indeed, we can see Freud himself trying such hypotheses with the young man, essaying a theme of saints as first names, the notion of Origen-origin, and "Paul in *Kleinpaul*" (literally, little Paul). He was evidently reaching for a theme having to do with "first" or birth or children (who are addressed by their first names), but he got little confirmation from the young man—the first sort of proof—and dropped it.

Characteristically, a psychoanalytic explainer draws on both the creation of a shared verbal space through free association and a thematic analysis of that space. The sharing provides the basis for cure, although one can use the technique to explain other, more casual events like this young man's forgetting. The second move, thematic analysis, links psychoanalytic thought to many other disciplines. It is, however, quintessential to psychoanalysis. It deserves fuller treatment and its proper name:

Holistic Analysis

Freud imaged this kind of reasoning by a jigsaw puzzle: "If one succeeds in arranging the confused heap of fragments, each of which bears upon it an unintelligible piece of drawing, so that the picture acquires a meaning, so that there is no gap anywhere in the design and so that the whole fits into the frame," then one has solved the puzzle (1923c, 19:116, see also 1896c, 3:205). As early as 1896 he compared this kind of convergence thinking to an archaeologist confronted with half-buried ruins, fragments of inscriptions, and the garbled traditions of the local inhabitants. His task would be to dig out as many additional data as he could and make them converge into a reading.

> If his work is crowned with success, the discoveries are self-explanatory: the ruined walls are part of the ramparts of a palace or a treasure-house; the fragments of columns can be filled out into a temple; the numerous inscriptions . . . [may] yield undreamed-of information about the events of the remote past, to commemorate which the monuments were built. *Saxa loquuntur!* (1896c, 3:192; see also 1937d, 23: 259–60)

One feels that the very stones speak that theme which unifies all the data, and this is the sense one often gets that a holistic interpretation is self-evident.

We reason this way in everyday life, for example, when figuring out the function of an unknown device. Once I know that this conglomeration of clamp, crank, spikes, and blade is an apple-peeler, I understand that the clamp holds the device to a table, the spikes hold the apple, the crank turns it, and the blade shaves the skin off. In short, once I have grasped the central theme of peeling apples, I can use the theme to relate a host of otherwise baffling details.

We toy with this same kind of reasoning in detective stories. Listen to the immortal Sherlock Holmes at the end of "The Adventure of the Speckled Band."

> "Well, there is . . . a curious coincidence of dates. A ventilator is made, a cord is hung, and a lady who sleeps in the bed dies. Does that not strike you?"
>
> "I cannot as yet see any connection."
>
> "Did you observe anything very peculiar about that bed?"
>
> "No."
>
> "It was clamped to the floor. Did you ever see a bed fastened like that before?"
>
> "I cannot say that I have."
>
> "The lady could not move her bed. It must always be in the same relative position to the ventilator and to the rope—for so we may call it, since it was clearly never meant for a bell-pull."
>
> "Holmes," I cried, "I seem to see dimly what you are hitting at."

The good Dr. Watson evidently glimpses a theme: fixed physical connections leading from the stepfather's room through the ventilator down the rope onto the heiress in her immovable bed. Holmes phrases this idea later as "a bridge for something . . . coming to the bed." The idea of a bridge unifies these four details and their dates. Again and again, Holmes demonstrates this basic strategy of holistic reasoning: bringing clusters of details into mutual relevance around themes, until finally he infers that the doctor has been letting a swamp adder down the rope, hoping it will kill the heiress whose fortune he craves. The "solution" brings together both the details the distressed heiress told Holmes and Watson in London and those they have discovered "on the ground."

Holmes also demonstrates—elegantly—two criteria for judging the validity of a holistic explanation: one quantitative, coverage, the other qualitative, directness. At first, Holmes mistakenly entertained a less viperous explanation:

> When you combine the idea of whistles at night, the presence of a band of gypsies who are on intimate terms with this old doctor, the fact that we have every reason to believe that the doctor has an interest in preventing his stepdaughter's marriage, the dying allusion to a band, and finally, the fact that [the surviving sister] heard a metallic clang, which might have been caused by one of those metal bars which secured the shutters falling back into their place, I think there is good ground to think that the mystery may be cleared along those lines.

The pattern of reasoning is the same, converging details toward a centering theme: the doctor somehow let the gypsy band through the shutters to do the sister in. That would interrelate the whistle, the clang, the presence of gypsies, the doctor's finances, and the dying cry of "the band!" but not *all* the details (the ventilator or the bell-pull).

A good holistic explanation, like Holmes's second, covers the relevant data. One can compare two interpretations quantitatively in the number of details they relate and qualitatively by the relative importance of those details (which in part depends on the quantitative effectiveness of the explanation). Holmes's swamp adder explanation accounts for a great many more details than the gypsy hypothesis. Indeed, the second explanation renders the presence of gypsies relatively unimportant compared to more telling details like the ventilator linking the two rooms, the dummy bell-rope, or the heel-marked chair on which the villain stood. Having arrived at the ingenious idea of the swamp adder, Holmes comments on the earlier hypothesis: " 'I had,' said he, 'come to an entirely erroneous conclusion, which shows, my dear Watson, how dangerous it always is to reason from insufficient data.' "

Second, a holistic explanation that neatly and directly relates the details it covers satisfies us more than one that establishes only tenuous or devious connections. Holmes's gypsy explanation simply says "the band" did something. The clang was caused by some movement of the shutters. With the second explanation, however, the phrasing "the band" is explained very exactly by the appearance of the snake, and "The metallic clang heard by Miss Stoner was obviously caused by her father hastily closing the door of his safe upon its terrible occupant."

Holmes demonstrates other characteristics of holistic reasoning, notably the need to move away from categories and toward particulars. For example, the category "poisonous snake" does not account for as many details as the more particular "swamp adder" (poisonous plus speckled). The more general the category, the less it explains, like the biblical conclusion Holmes draws: "Violence does, in truth, recoil upon the violent."

Because of this need for particulars, holistic research does not proceed by counting or by the repetition of experiments but by gathering more data. Holmes has to visit the scene of the death, where, having surmised that the ventilator ran from the victim's room to the doctor's, he can now see its size and position. He can find an iron safe to explain the clang. He can discover that the victim's bed is clamped to the floor. Research leads to more data that require a stronger explanation, one that leaves no loose ends in the new, larger body of material.

To put one's own mind actually to work in this kind of interpretation, the best exercise I can think of is a rather trivial one, a children's game that was taught to me under the name of Puzzling Polly. The one who knows the game starts listing things that Puzzling Polly does or doesn't like. As the other players catch on to Puzzling Polly's secret (her identity theme, really), they join in, until the secret finally has to be explained to the last players, who may be much puzzled and annoyed by this time. For example, I might start by saying, "Puzzling Polly likes puppies but not dogs." "Puzzling Polly doesn't like flowers, but she does like blossoms." "Puzzling Polly likes trees but not shrubs." If you have caught on, you might chime in, "Puzzling Polly likes the funnies, but not the comics." "Puzzling Polly likes summer and fall but she doesn't like winter or spring."

If you have not recognized the theme behind her likes and dislikes, you are probably trying out hypotheses. Polly likes small things better than large—puppies not dogs, blossoms not flowers—but then the hypothesis fails with trees not shrubs. You might hypothesize that the pattern runs: like, dislike, dislike, like, like, dislike, dislike, like, like, and so on, based on the way the sentences are phrased. This works for the sentences I gave, but it fails on the second sentence after someone else joined in, fall but not winter. Then, too, that hypothesis doesn't seem to deal with the constancy or particularity of Polly's likes and dislikes. One could just as well say, if it were the third sentence, "Puzzling Polly likes shrubs but not trees." But, in fact, Polly does like trees and not shrubs.

For a pattern explanation, we require that the theme explain every last one of the details and that it be itself specific or precise enough to account for the specificity of the details it must explain. Most of all, we ask that we recognize that precision by a kind of "Aha!" when the answer comes, as when you realize for the first time (and this is very much harder to do when the game is spoken, not printed) that Puzzling Polly likes things with doubled letters in them, or should I say twinned? "Puzzling Polly likes summer but not spring." "Puzzling Polly likes cartoons and newsreels but not feature films." And Puzzling Polly is, of course, narcissistic.

The game is trivial but it offers one a chance to experience in one's own mind three basic characteristics of holistic thinking toward a centering theme. First, the theme works by convergence into classes, rather than by sequences of cause-effect or if-then. That is, it is not correct to relate the data by saying, "*Because* Polly likes blossoms, she doesn't like flowers." Or, "Polly's liking puppies *implies* that she doesn't like dogs." Rather, one sorts the data into themes or polarities: liking and not liking, words having similar meanings but with or without doubled letters. In the same way, we can focus the details of the young man's association to *aliquis* into a few subthemes which can then finally be stated as one central theme, (not) having descendants.

Second, such a theme states a law of a special kind: one can say whether particular outcomes obey it or not, but one cannot predict any one outcome. The law of gravity says that *if* I drop this typewriter *then* it will certainly fall at a constant rate of acceleration. We can be absolutely sure of that. A central theme, however, is more like a generative rule (as in transformational grammar). If you begin a sentence, "In the _____ . . .," I can be fairly sure a noun or a noun preceded by an adjective is coming next, but I cannot say exactly what the noun or adjective will be. If you begin, "Puzzling Polly likes cellars but not _____ . . . ," I can be quite sure the last noun will not contain a doubled letter, and I can be fairly sure it will have a class relationship to "cellars," but I cannot predict the precise word. "Basements?" "Kitchens?" In other words, we are dealing with a different kind of determinacy from that for physical objects like typewriters—but a determinacy nevertheless. In the same way, we can understand after the fact the young man's forgetting the line from Virgil. It *is* lawful, but we could not have predicted it ahead of time.

Third (and key), the theme has to come from and interrelate all the details it is supposed to account for. They may be details like the young man's associations to months, saints, and blood or the details of the murder of Miss Stoner, but the theme must deal with *all* the details. A statistical confirmation of part of the data may be adequate for an experiment in the social sciences, but there must be no loose ends in a holistic explanation.

"No loose ends" is an aesthetic criterion and this thinking-toward-wholeness has long dominated thought in the arts and humanities. The literary theorist René Wellek says this method is "the main source of knowledge in all humanistic branches of learning." The interpreter "proceeds from attention to a detail to an anticipation of the whole and back again to an interpretation of a detail" (1960). Holistic analysis or "pattern explanation" (as it is sometimes called in the social sciences) corresponds exactly to the everyday method of the literary critic, that is,

> first observing details about the superficial appearance of the particular work . . . then, grouping these details and seeking to integrate them into a creative principle . . . and, finally, making the return trip to all the other groups of observations in order to find whether the "inward form" one has tentatively constructed gives an account of the whole (Spitzer, 1948, p. 19)

A standard handbook for graduate students in literature describes the strategy as seeing "the whole design of the work as a unity. It is now a simultaneous pattern radiating out from a center, not a narrative moving in time." In other words, one arrives inductively at a central theme that can then be applied deductively to bring every detail into relation with every other and all "with the central theme . . . the unity to which everything else must be relevant" (Frye, 1963, p. 65).

The analyst of a poem or a fiction (or a painting or a symphony) usually proceeds as the archaeologist, the anthropologist, the clinical psychologist, or Sherlock Holmes does. One notices patterns of recurrence or absence. One articulates them as different themes, checking them against the evidence and fitting them together to form a model of the whole as one or more very general themes (themes of themes) at the center and a surface of lesser subthemes and variations. As a literary critic I would require of such large themes that I be able to include within them every detail of the text I am analyzing and, if there be one or more central themes of themes, that I be able to subsume all the lesser themes under them.

I should be able to trace any one detail, even the tiniest, up one or another ladder of abstractions to the very center of the thematic structure. Conversely, a central theme should serve as a kernel statement each one of whose terms can be expanded, transformed, and particularized back down the ladders until I arrive at the details of the text I am working with.

Evidently, if we credit Freud, we can use the same strategy to understand a patient. Freud spoke of the central fantasy of his patient the Wolf Man and

> how, after a certain phase of the treatment, everything seemed to converge upon it, and how later, in the synthesis, the most various and remarkable results radiated out from it; how not only the large problems but the smallest peculiarities in the history of the case were cleared up by this single assumption (1918b, 17:52).

The importance of holistic reasoning to the humanities does not, of course, imply that it is "unscientific." On the contrary, major scientific achievements of the last two centuries draw heavily on holistic analysis. Consider evolution. To give an explanation of the decline and fall of a certain species of sparrow (as Darwin did), one interrelates a host of facts about weather, grains, hawks, lice, squirrels, and the sparrow's anatomy or its eating and mating habits. The explanation will be a holistic one.

This kind of problem does not lend itself to the usual kind of laboratory experimentation. In holistic thinking, testing takes the form of getting new data to be converged around a given hypothesis or theme. Thus, astronomers study pictures from Mars or radio waves from a galaxy to acquire a variety of disparate facts. Then they reason like the evolutionist (or Sherlock Holmes) to arrive at a centering idea that will make them all fit.

It is only in the earliest forms of modern science, kinetics and statics, the physics of the eighteenth century and the freshman year in a modern university, that events are reversible and hence predictable. That kind of science can rely almost entirely on if-then, covering laws, obscuring the role of holistic reasoning. At bottom, what differentiates holistic method and the covering laws of these kinds of science, however, is their treatment of time. In a given happening, the fall of a sparrow, say, if-then reasoning looks at some events as prior to others, whereas a holistic reasoner would look at all the separate events as though they coexisted. Hence in holistic reasoning one uses more data as confirmation, while in if-then reasoning "more data" takes the specific form of a future event—prediction. The sparrow will fall at so-and-so-many inches per second.

Otherwise, however, even in statics and kinetics it is possible to regard Newton's principles or Hooke's law as "centering themes" that interrelate such disparate events as the orbiting of Jupiter and the fall of an apple, the flex of a bridge and the crack of a tooth. The confirmations of science look different from those of the holistic interpretation, but are they? Don't both systems, finally, appeal to the facts (or what the systems define as the facts)? It should be no surprise, then, that one can use, at least in part, the same reasoning to interpret a dream as to probe the origins of a galaxy. In the natural sciences, holistic and if-then reasoning overlap and work together.

In the social sciences, the situation is more problematic. In his fine study *Patterns of Discovery in the Social Sciences* (1971), Paul Diesing distinguishes four methods of exploration in common use: the formal analysis characteristic of economics or linguistics; survey methods as used in sociology; experiments, as in academic psychology; and the case-study, participant-observer method, pattern explanation, or holistic analysis used in anthropology, history, and clinical settings like psychoanalysis. Each of these four methods has different criteria for validity, confirmation, and generalization. Each is differently useful. Errors arise from confusing them or insisting that one alone can claim to be scientific—an issue I shall return to in the last part of this book.

One can think of holistic analysis, then, as the hermeneutic circle of the humanities or the pattern explanation of the social sciences or the holistic analysis of the hard sciences. However we think of it, this kind of interpretation by means of details converging into themes and themes into one centering theme plays a dominant role in psychoanalytic thinking from the very beginning, as such writers as W. W. Meissner (1966, 1971), Michael Sherwood (1969), and Erik Erikson (1958b, p. 72) have shown.

Consider, for example, Freud's analysis of the brief dream he used as the "specimen" for his short book "On Dreams."

The Table d'hôte *Dream*

"Company at table or table d'hôte . . . spinach was being eaten . . . Frau E. L. was sitting beside me; she was turning her whole attention to me and laid her hand on my knee in an intimate manner. I removed her hand unresponsively. She then said: "But you've always had such beautiful eyes." . . . I then had an indistinct picture of two eyes, as though it were a drawing or like the outline of a pair of spectacles . . .' (1901a, 5:636–40, 648–50, 655:–57, and 671–73, see also 1901b, 6:120, 136.)

Frau E. L., Freud drily comments, was not a friend, and the dream as a whole seemed without emotion, disconnected, unintelligible. To discover its meaning, Freud began to free associate, first dividing the dream into its separate elements, then associating to each separately.

Company at table or table d'hôte (Freud seems to mean a meal to be divided among a group, all paying the same fixed price and helping themselves from the same serving dishes). On the day before, Freud recalled, a friend had driven him home in a cab and the friend paid for it. He had joked that he liked a cab with a meter—it gives you something to watch. Freud continued the joke: "A cab with a taximeter always reminds me of a *table d'hôte*. It makes me avaricious and *selfish*, because it keeps on reminding me of *what I owe. My debt* seems to be growing too fast, and I'm afraid of getting the worst of the bargain; and in just the same way at a table d'hôte I can't avoid feeling in a comic way that *I'm getting too little,* and must keep an *eye* on my own interests." He had gone on to quote one of the songs of the harpist in *Wilhelm Meister:*

> Ihr führt ins Leben uns hinein,
> Ihr lasst den Armen schuldig werden (I, xiii).

Addressing the heavenly powers, the harpist says, "You lead us forth into life, / You make the poor wretch guilty." But *Armen* can mean monetarily poor and *schuldig,* in debt. Thus Freud could have been addressing a cabdriver: You lead us forth into life, / You put the poor man in debt— rather droll for so impromptu a recollection.

Freud associated something else to this first element of the dream. He and his wife had been sitting at a *table d'hôte* at a resort, and she was paying more attention to a gentleman of distinguished name across the table than to Freud. Further, Freud had reasons for not renewing his acquaintance with this man. He became irritated, impatient, and finally asked her to concern herself more with him than with these strangers. "This was again *as though I were getting the worst of the bargain at the table d'hôte."* Freud erased the disagreeable experience and expressed his wish that his wife would turn her whole attention to him by dreaming a situation exactly opposite to what had in fact occurred.

In fact, he had reproduced an episode during their courtship: after a particularly pressing loveletter Martha had responded by putting her hand on his "under the table," and he then recalled that that phrase was also represented in the dream. However, "the intimate laying of a hand on my knee belonged to a quite different context"—about which he is discreetly silent.

It is clear, nevertheless, that he had cast Frau E. L. in the role he wanted his wife to play. Associating to her, he remembered that he had once been *in debt* to her father, and at this point Freud realized that his associations were bringing out a theme not directly visible in the dream itself—money and debts.

In connection with Frau E. L.'s statement that he had beautiful eyes, he associated the phrase, "Do you suppose I"m going to do this or that for the sake of your *beaux yeux?*"—just because you're so charming? But she had said *he* had beautiful eyes. In the dream, that must have meant, "People have always done everything for you for love; you have always had everything *without paying for it*." Again, this was a reversal, Freud felt. "I had never had anything free of cost"—except that his friend had taken him home in a cab *"without my paying for it."*

Further, he remembered, on the evening of the cab ride he had felt in debt to their host—an *eye* surgeon. Freud had given him one present, an *occhiale*, an antique bowl with *eyes* painted round it, but he had let slip a more recent opportunity of repaying him. That night, Freud had inquired after a woman he had referred to the oculist for *spectacles*.

Finally, Freud asked himself "why *spinach*, of all things, was being served in the dream." Notice the form of his question. He assumes an aesthetic unity for the dream. Everything is there for a common expressive purpose.

What came to mind was the Freuds' family dinner table: precisely the son who deserved to be admired for his *beautiful eyes* refused his spinach. (Another reversal: as a child, Freud, too, had disliked spinach, but it had become one of his favorite foods.) Martha urged the boy "just to taste [*kosten*] a bit of it." (*Kosten* can mean 'to taste' or 'to cost' or 'costs.') The word, notes Freud, thus "fits into the 'table d'hôte' circle of ideas." It could be represented by the spinach. Martha had said, in the way of most mothers, "You should be glad to have spinach. There are children who would be only too pleased with spinach!" Freud now recalled Goethe's words as though they were addressed to parents: "You lead us forth into life, / You make the poor wretch guilty."

At this point, Freud stopped his associations to the dream. He had gone through one "circle of ideas" after another, each leading by association to the others until he had arrived at "certain central ideas" (I would call them themes): "the contrast between 'selfish' and 'unselfish,' and the elements 'being in debt' and 'without paying for it.' " "I might draw closer together the threads in the material revealed by the analysis, and I might then show that they converge upon a single nodal point, but considerations of a personal . . . nature prevent my doing so in public" (5:640).

In later comments on the dream, Freud introduced another element. He had recently had to come up with 300 kronen (about $200 in 1984) to help out a relative who was ill, with whom he had had several cabdrives and of whom he was quite fond. Nevertheless, he admitted, "I cannot escape the conclusion that *I regret having made that expenditure.*" Although he felt no conscious regret, he had been passing through a thin time financially. "No wonder," said the dream-thoughts, "if this person were to feel grateful to me: love of that sort would not be 'free of cost.' Love that is free of cost, however, stood in the forefront of the dream thoughts"—another reversal (5:672, 656–57).

Freud's candor and fullness of association make it possible to set out the four themes in relation to a single nodal center: as he phrases it, "a wish for once to enjoy love, love which 'costs nothing.' " That unitary idea comprises two polarities:

being in debt (schuldig, guilty)	*without paying for it*
Frau E. L.'s father	the touch of the hand
table d'hôte	*beaux yeux*
harpist's song	the free cabdrive
spinach *(kosten)*	"love that is free of cost"
child to parent	
eye doctor	
eye bowl	
the grateful relative	

selfish	*unselfish*
cabdrive with meter	friend paid for cab
table d'hôte: I'm getting too little	loving fiancée during courtship
my wife should concern herself with me, not strangers	parent to child
keep an eye on my interests	"love that is free of cost"
I regret having made that expenditure	

The themes are related to one another and to what Freud calls the "center" by a fundamental reversal: "Not until I have recognised this impulse [that *I regret having made that expenditure*] does my wish in the dream for the love which would call for *no* expenditure acquire a meaning."

As the role of money in this interpretation might suggest, holistic analysis can apply to any event that can be translated into any kind of symbols. Take, for example, a seemingly random number:

426718

During analysis, a patient of Freud's discovered a theme even in this (1901b, 6:246–48).

The patient was the youngest child in a large family, and at an early age he had lost his greatly admired father. While he was in a particularly cheerful mood the number 426718 came to his mind, and he asked himself: "What ideas occur to me in that connection? First of all, a joke I have heard: 'When a doctor treats a cold it lasts for 42 days; when it is not treated, it lasts 6 weeks.' " This corresponds to the first figures in the number ($42 = 6 \times 7$). Then the patient was silent. Freud intervened to point out that the six-figure number he had chosen contained all the first digits except for 3 and 5. The patient was immediately able to continue the interpretation. "There are 7 of us brothers and sisters, and I am the youngest. In the order of our age, 3 corresponds to my sister A., and 5 to my brother L.; they were my two enemies. As a child I used to pray to God every night for him to remove these two tormenting spirits from life. It seems to me now that in this choice of numbers I was myself fulfilling this wish; 3 and 5, the wicked brother and the hated sister, are passed over."

Freud then asked, "If the number represents the order of your brothers and sisters, what does the 8 at the end mean? There were only 7 of you after all."

"I have often thought," replied the patient, "that if my father had lived longer I should not have remained the youngest child. If there had been 1 more we should have been 8 and I should have a younger child after me to whom I should have played the elder brother."

The patient's associations had explained the whole number, but Freud still wanted to establish the connection between the first part of the interpretation and the second. He found it in the necessary precondition of the last figures: "if my father had lived longer." "$42 = 6 \times 7$" symbolized the patient's derision and anger at the doctors who had not been able to help his father. Therefore it expressed his wish for his father to go on living.

The whole number, 426718, thus worked out the fulfillment of his two infantile wishes about his family, that the brother and sister he disliked should die and that the baby should be born after him. He expressed his wish in the shortest form: "If only those two had died instead of my beloved father." The numbers, including one after 7, were all there, except for 3 and 5.

The themes that interrelate the numbers form polar opposites:

42 days of doctoring	6 weeks of no doctoring
all 7 sibs, except—	numbers 3 and 5
a loving father and 1 more child	the missing 8th child

The terms on the left represent various forms of presence, those on the right, absence, but my abstract words "presence" and "absence" have for the patient the more concrete meaning of living a longer or shorter time, finally, of living, of not having ever lived, or of dying. The theme of the numbers, so to speak, is: I wish the loved ones had lived and the bad ones had not.

For this patient, for the young man who forgot *aliquis,* and for the dreaming Freud, the relations among the themes and numbers and words are established *by these individuals,* and they have highly individual meanings. Like an electrical engineer examining signals or a literary critic interpreting a text, I might arrive at an extraordinarily coherent holistic interrelation of symbols, but the usual psychoanalytic interpretation draws on an additional source of persuasiveness, the personal witness of the person whose symbols are being interpreted, the interpretee.

The symbols being interpreted form a verbal space which both interpreter and interpretee enter. The act of interpretation makes it possible for both of them to own the symbols between them, but differently, the interpreter by thinking, the interpretee by his actual experience. These two different ways to experience symbols can come together. If I associate to and interpret my own dream (as in the psychoanalytic setting), I explicitly fuse the active, intellectual effort of understanding with the more passive, emotional creation of the symbols I seek to understand. If interpreter and interpretee are one person, the act of interpreting makes it possible for that one person explicitly to join two intellectual stances that in disciplines like electrical engineering or literary criticism we believe we keep separate.

Nowhere is this shared symbolic space more visible than in the "squiggle" technique developed by D.W. Winnicott for the analysis of children. Consider

Iiro

whose case has long seemed to me one of the most moving in the psychoanalytic literature (1971b, pp. 12–7).

Winnicott had been invited to present a case to the staff of a children's hospital in Finland. So as to discuss someone the staff knew, he interviewed (through an interpreter) Iiro, a nine-year-old boy who was in the hospital not for psychiatry but for hand surgery. He had been born with his fingers joined together and unseparated toes (syndactyly).

Winnicott asked the boy to take turns with him in "the squiggle game." One of them would shut his eyes and scribble with a pencil on a piece of drawing paper. Then the other would take the pencil and turn it into something, saying what it had become. In effect, the drawings elicit free associations from the child.

Winnicott went first, and Iiro quickly said, "It's a duck's foot." Winnicott realized that Iiro wanted to talk about his own webbed hands, and he offered the boy a second squiggle, even more explicit. Iiro in turn drew his own version of a duck's foot. Winnicott concluded that "we were firmly entrenched on the subject of webbed feet."

Then, given Winnicott's next, open squiggle, Iiro drew a line that closed it off and said it was a duck swimming in a lake. Finland being a land of lakes, Iiro being like all Finnish boys involved in swimming and boating, Winnicott concluded that Iiro was expressing a positive feeling about ducks and swimming and lakes, hence a positive feeling about his own webbed hands.

Iiro turned his own next squiggle into a horn, and began to talk about music, the way his little brother played the cornet. "I can play the piano a little," he said. Iiro said he was fond of music and would like to play the flute—a manifest impossibility. Winnicott then made his first reference to the material as it related to Iiro's hands. Knowing that Iiro was a healthy, happy boy with a sense of humor, Winnicott remarked that it would be difficult for a duck to play the flute. Iiro was amused.

After some intervening squiggles, Winnicott turned one of Iiro's into a swan, asking Iiro if he could swim. " Yes," he said, warmly. Winnicott's next squiggle Iiro said was a shoe. He said it did not need anything done to it. Winnicott's made his squiggle half-consciously into a kind of hand. Iiro turned it into a flower. From this sequence Winnicott inferred that Iiro was unwilling to look at his own hands.

Iiro, however, did a more deliberate drawing that looked like a drawing of a deformed hand. When Winnicott asked him what he was thinking of, he said, "It just happened," and he seemed to have surprised himself.

Winnicott wanted to let things rest a bit and asked about dreams. Iiro said, "I sleep with my eyes closed so I don't see anything." His dreams, he said, were "mostly nice." "I have not had a nasty dream for a long time." I sense, from Winnicott's presentation, that Iiro was saying he could look away from the unpleasant reality of his hands. In technical terms, he was able to deny or disavow them.

Iiro's next drawing put an arc around an angle like the angle between the two prominent fingers of his left hand, which was a few inches away on the table. Winnicott commented, "It is like your left hand, isn't it!" and Iiro replied, "Oh yes, a bit." Winnicott felt that Iiro had become, perhaps for the first time in his life, objective about his hands. He said that he had had a lot of operations and would have more and that his feet were the same way (hence the shoe in his earlier drawing). Winnicott commented, "It is rather like the duck, isn't it!"

At this point, Winnicott made something of an interpretation: "The surgeons are trying to alter what you were like when you were born." Iiro talked about his hope to play the flute and about future operations. When he grew up, he said, he wanted to be like his father, a contractor, or perhaps the man who taught handicrafts at school. When Winnicott asked him if it ever made him cross to be operated on, he brushed the idea aside. "I am never cross." "I choose to be operated on." "It is better for work to have two fingers than it was when I had four all joined together." Winnicott felt that Iiro was both refusing to acknowledge his problem and reaching out toward the therapist, trying to put his problem into words.

Returning to the squiggle game, Iiro turned Winnicott's scribble into the hilt of a sword, and then provided his own drawing, an eel (although Winnicott took it to be the sword for the hilt). Playing with the idea of an eel, Winnicott asked, "Shall we put it back in the lake or cook it and eat it?" to which Iiro replied, "We will let it go back and swim in the lake because it is so small."

Winnicott concluded that Iiro had identified himself with the eel, in a sort of prebirth imagining, and ventured on an interpetation:

> If we think of you as small, you would like to swim in the lake or swim on the lake like the duck. You are telling me that you are fond of yourself with your webbed hands and feet and that you need people to love you that way as you were when you were born. Growing up, you begin to want to play the piano and the flute and to do handicrafts, and so you agree to be operated on, but the first thing is to be loved as you are and as you were born.

Iiro's answer seems to say that he and Winnicott were truly communicating, no matter how obliquely: "Mother has the same thing that I have got." One of his subsequent squiggles accurately copied his deformed left hand, and he was surprised by it. "It's the same again!"

By way of relief, Winnicott asked about his family and home, and Iiro was positive about both, particularly about new babies. "One knows if one is sad."

Winnicott made Iiro's next squiggle into feet and shoes. Iiro turned Winnicott's last drawing into a duck again. He was restating, Winnicott felt, both his love of himself and his need to be loved in the state in which he was born, without any alteration.

Between them, Winnicott and Iiro made a record of Winnicott's extraordinary tenderness and intuition as well as a tribute to the boy's trusting candor in dealing with the cruel inheritance fate had dealt him. The case shows psychoanalytic method at its best, the combination of a search for the emotionally telling detail with the search for themes about which to focus those details.

Obviously, it is easier (in some ways) for me, thinking through this printed transcript for the umpteenth time, to outline themes and themes of themes than it was for Winnicott. He had to respond in real time, to the boy sitting there in front of him, waiting, while I write in the timeless time of literary criticism. Nevertheless, I think it is useful to spell out Winnicott's sensitive thematic analysis.

In effect, he grouped Iiro's associations to the drawings into three themes. First, there were swimming and the ducks (they appear in four squiggles). These Winnicott identified with Iiro's feeling that he could love himself and had been loved with his webbed feet and hands. The water suggested to Winnicott an Iiro at or before birth. Second were horn, cornet, flute, and carpentry. All involve abilities of the hand (which were so problematic for Iiro) and the relation of those abilities to Iiro's growing up to be a man like his father or his teacher.

Third were Iiro's images for his real situation: shoe, hand, sword hilt, sword, and eel, and his remarks on his father and mother. The shoe and hand imaged the way Iiro's hand and feet then were. The eel had to do with swimming, but it was also a sword, something a boy Iiro's age might use to play martial, masculine games, an emblem for his ability to become a man like his father. In this symbolic sequence, the sword hilt, which resembled his deformed hand, became an eel or a sword blade.

Then, in talking about his parents, Iiro noted that his mother shared his deformity. He declared his acceptance of his father, and his father precisely as a source of new babies. It seems to me that these remarks combine with the other clusters of images to say, "In order for me to grow up and become a man, I need to be loved as I am now, handicapped like my mother." Winnicott had broached this theme to Iiro, that he needed to be loved as he was, webbed feet and all, like a little duck. By returning to the theme of the ducks, the two of them brought this exquisite interpretation round to its beginning and a natural close.

Conclusion

Winnicott's interview, like the other three instances in this chapter, shows two basic characteristics of psychoanalytic thought. First, analyst and analysand create a space between them pregnant with symbols they each own. In a way, this is what we do in any ordinary conversation, even if we are not so learned as to include quotations from Virgil. What is especially psychoanalytic, however, is the deliberate enlarging of this symbolic field through the technique of free association. Thus Freud asked the young man (in the classic psychoanalytic method) to tell him, "*candidly* and *uncritically,* whatever comes into your mind." Thus Winnicott and Iiro each drew random squiggles for the other to "turn into something."

Psychoanalysis, then, offers a mode of analysis for that shared space. We can call it the hermeneutic circle of the humanist, the pattern explanation of the social scientist, or (best, I think) holistic analysis. An interpreter groups details together into similar or contrasting themes, then brings those themes together toward a still more central theme so as to structure the symbolic space into a focal generalization and peripheries of detail. The interpreter interrelates the details and makes them mutually meaningful in the light of that central focus.

Psychoanalytic method usually operates in a therapeutic context where one party in the dialogue is creating a verbal space in order to remedy something perceived as wrong or sick (as the young man wanted to understand his forgetting). Yet as Holmes and the apple peeler show, holistic analysis and theme or pattern explanation apply just as well when the motive is simply a wish to understand—as when Winnicott wanted to present a case to his Finnish colleagues or Freud to demonstrate his methods through an "obscure and meaningless" dream.

Often, in finding a centering theme, especially in a therapeutic setting, the interpreter or interpretee will suddenly become aware of some thought that was formerly unconscious, but this is not necessarily the case with all holistic analyses. Holistic method serves in geology, astronomy, evolutionary biology, and many other disciplines where what is revealed by the analysis may be hidden without being unconscious. In these contexts, the success of a holistic interpretation, its validity or accuracy or satisfactoriness, does not depend on a cure or sudden perception. The more details from its discourse a holistic analysis interrelates, and the more directly it interrelates them, the more valid it is—for any purpose.

In all these settings we make a holistic analysis stronger by creating more data, more symbolic entities in the space between the interpreter and the interpreted. In this need for ever more data, holistic interpretation differs from other kinds of analysis, notably the "if this, then that" hypotheses one tests by experiments. An experimenter needs to define the *this* and the *that* quite narrowly and to exclude or control for data outside the definitions, an altogether different procedure.

Holistic analysis becomes more persuasive as the humans involved in that analysis bring in more and more symbols for the centering theme to unify. Hence the intellectual form of psychoanalytic thought—its holism—meshes with the classic psychoanalytic procedure—free association. To think psychoanalytically, as one must to think about the I, is to blend the creation of new symbols, spaces, and interactions with their analysis so that association and analysis, whole and theme, each will actively sustain the other in what another kind of scientist might call a positive feedback.

2 | The Idea of Identity

Iiro's story differs from dreaming about a *table d'hôte* or thinking of 426718. They are isolated incidents that one can think through holistically (as a whole "fitting" around a center). They yield to psychoanalytic explanations that contrast unconscious and conscious motives. Winnicott's theme for Iiro's drawings and associations, however (the boy's need to be loved in the state in which he was born), suggests something far more pervasive: a *style* that permeates much of what Iiro thinks and does.

I mean "style" just exactly in the literary sense: as someone's characteristic choices of words, sentence structures, and perhaps even ideas. In effect, such a concept of style extends the traditional psychoanalytic method of holistic interpretation from particular acts (or "behaviors," one particular dream or symptom or slip of the tongue) to a whole life.

To construct someone's style in this general sense, you would draw out essentials from the many, many manifestations of that style, just as you would abstract a musical theme from its variations—or just as the young man's associations to *aliquis* led to a single worry underlying them all or just as Sherlock Holmes could fit many puzzling details into one coherent scheme by the hypothesis of a swamp adder.

Perhaps because it is a literary concept, writers are particularly good for instancing style, because in every work they leave behind hundreds of choices from which one can state holistic patterns of sameness and difference. Consider a man I think of as—

The "Promising" Writer

F. Scott Fitzgerald left in his letters an unusually full account of his choices and opinions about life in general.* For example, he wrote of his talent as a

---

* All but a few of the biographical quotations come from Andrew Turnbull, *Scott Fitzgerald: A Biography* (New York: Scribner's, 1962). The remainder appear in *The Crack-Up*, ed. Edmund Wilson (New York: New Directions, 1945), *The Letters of F. Scott Fitzgerald*, ed. Andrew Turnbull (New York: Scribner's, 1963), or *Scott Fitzgerald: Letters to His Daughter*, ed. Andrew Turnbull (New York: Scribner's, 1965). These also contain, of course, many of the passages quoted from Turnbull's splendid biography. My quotations from *The Great Gatsby*

writer, and indeed of everything else he had, as a fluctuating store of supplies. "We feel so damned secure," he wrote of himself and others like him, "as long as there's enough in the bank to buy the next meal, and enough moral stuff in reserve to take us through the next ordeal. Our danger is imagining that we have resources—material and moral—which we haven't got. . . . Wiser people seem to manage to pile up a reserve." He described a period of depression as "an overextension of the flank, a burning of the candle at both ends; a call upon physical resources that I did not command, like a man overdrawing at his bank . . . a feeling that I was standing at twilight on a deserted range, with an empty rifle in my hands and the targets down. No problem set—simply a silence with only the sound of my own breathing." Indeed, his last words were cast in these terms of supply and resources: "Everything has started to go." "Everything has started to fade." He left in his typewriter a final bit of doggerel:

> There was a flutter from the wings of God and you lay dead.
> Your books were in your desk
> I guess some unfinished chaos in your head
> Was dumped to nothing by the great janitress of destinies.

When, however, Fitzgerald felt that he had the necessary supplies, he felt confident, even omnipotent. "Poetry is either something that lives like fire inside you—like music to the musician or Marxism to the Communist—or else it is nothing, an empty formalized bore." "All good writing is *swimming under water* and holding your breath." "You know," he wrote to another writer, "I used to have a beautiful talent once. . . . It used to be a wonderful feeling to know it was there, and it isn't all gone yet. I think I have enough left to stretch out over two more novels. I may have to stretch it a little thin, so maybe they won't be as good as the best things I've ever done. But they won't be completely bad either, because nothing I ever write can be completely bad." The self-confidence a sense of inner supplies gave him could all too easily shade off into arrogance, as in those sentences or in something he said of himself: "As long as I'm unknown I'm a pretty nice fellow, but give me a little notoriety and I swell up like a poison toad."

Fitzgerald was much aware of the material and spiritual supplies he was given and how he responded, but he was much more aware of what he gave and what it cost him. As he half-laughingly wrote, "I am not a great man, but sometimes I think the impersonal and objective quality of my talent and the sacrifices of it, in pieces, to preserve its essential value has some sort of epic grandeur. Anyhow after hours I nurse myself with delusions of that sort." In a more somber vein, "Often I think writing is a sheer paring away of oneself

---

occur near the ends of chaps. 6 and 9, *The Portable F. Scott Fitzgerald* (New York: Viking, 1945), pp. 163, 103, and 167.

leaving always something thinner, barer, more meager." And so it was that when Scott Fitzgerald felt rejected and unknown at the end of his career, his words for it were "to die so completely and unjustly after having given so much."

The imagery he uses—buying the next meal, holding his breath, nursing himself, hearing only the sound of his own breathing, giving of a body substance (or something that lives inside him), and being destroyed by "the great janitress of destinies"—these images echo to me a version of the early relation between feeding mother and dependent child. It was perhaps because of the style of that early experience that Fitzgerald tended to see the giving and withholding of inner supplies in terms of greater and lesser forces. Perhaps. We can never know, of course.

Fitzgerald did, however, interpret situations in terms of greater and lesser forces. It was this way of polarizing experience that lay behind what he called his "wise and tragic sense of life." "My view of life," he wrote, is "that life is too strong and remorseless for the sons of men." "The thing that lies behind all great careers," he said, is "the sense that life is essentially a cheat and its conditions are those of defeat, and that the redeeming things are not 'happiness and pleasure' but the deeper satisfactions that come out of struggle."

"There was a book," he remembered from his childhood, "that was I think one of the great sensations of my life. . . . It filled me with the saddest and most yearning emotion. It was about a fight the large animals, like the elephant, had with the small animals, like the fox. The small animals won the first battle; but the elephants and lions and tigers finally overcame them. . . . My sentiment was all with the small ones. I wonder if even then I had a sense of the wearing-down power of big, respectable people. I can almost weep now when I think of that poor fox, the leader—the fox has somehow typified innocence to me ever since." As a teenager, Fitzgerald chose Princeton for his college because it always just lost the football championship, nosed "out in the last quarter by superior 'stamina' as the newspapers called it. It was to me a repetition of the story of the foxes and the big animals in the child's book."

In the same vein he idolized a man who came back from the Great War already a hero and the greatest polo player in the world, yet had the "humility to ask himself 'Do I know anything?' " and enter Princeton as a mere freshman.

Fitzgerald interpreted the advent of the movies in the same way, as a confrontation of greater and lesser forces. "There was a rankling indignity, that to me had become almost an obsession, in seeing the power of the written word subordinated to another power, a more glittering, a grosser power." "I saw that the novel, which at my maturity was the strongest and supplest medium for conveying thought and emotion from one human being to another, was becoming subordinated to a mechanical and communal art that . . . was capable of reflecting only the tritest thought, the most obvious emotion. It was an art in which words were subordinate to images, where personality was worn down to the inevitable low gear of collaboration." Yet it was typical of Fitzgerald that he found it necessary to identify with that grosser power and, in fact, to go to work for Hollywood himself.

All his life he identified with that greater power by molding, manipulating, and cajoling the human material around him, getting people to perform in one way or another. When, for example, there was a fire in Fitzgerald's house, he took command of the firemen. His chauffeur had a speech defect in which he substituted *s* for *th*. Fitzgerald composed a sentence full of *th*s which he then made the poor man repeat over and over. Late in life he set himself up as a tutor to his mistress, Sheilah Graham, as, much earlier, in his college years, he had written his sister long instructions on how to be a coquette, how to get boys to talk about themselves to her, how to flirt and tease, and how to have a good laugh and a charming smile. During his daughter's college years, he advised her on which books to read, men to date, and invitations to accept. He had something to say about every single course she took.

Although Fitzgerald kept trying to make himself into a superior power, he seems to have thought of himself as a lesser force, being given to by that power—or being withheld from. As he said about democracy, "The strong are too strong for us and the weak too weak." He particularly saw his own creativity this way. Sometimes he gave. Sometimes he was given to. "I don't know what it is in me or that comes to me when I start to write. I am half feminine—at least my mind is."

These extremes showed strikingly in the famous image of the crack-up with which Fitzgerald described himself during a depressed period: "his realization that what he had before him was not the dish he had ordered for his forties. In fact—since he and the dish were one, he described himself as a cracked plate, the kind that one wonders whether it is worth preserving." Again there is the duality, this time based on the double meaning of the word *dish*: "dish" as the food he hungered for; "dish" as the cracked container; and "he and the dish were one," the eater, the eaten, and the empty worthlessness.

He saw his marriage to Zelda as creating the same duality between his being filled or his being depleted so as to fill someone else. As a young bachelor, he said, "I lived with a great dream. The dream grew and I learned how to speak of it and make people listen. Then the dream divided one day when I decided to marry. . . . I was a man divided—she wanted me to work too much for *her* and not enough for my dream." Before the situation became totally hopeless, he said, "I had spent most of my resources, spiritual and material, on her."

In writing, he created by being given unto and then by giving again himself. As a boy, in a prototype of his later career, he would attend the old Teck Theatre in Buffalo and take in long sections of dialogue and then, with his prodigious memory, repeat the performance to the other children in the neighborhood. Essential to Fitzgerald's idea of writing was giving something to the reader: "I believe that the important thing about a work of fiction is that the essential reaction shall be profound and enduring." "I would rather impress my image (even though an image the size of a nickel) upon the soul of a people than be known"—that is, than receive personal recognition. "The purpose of a work of fiction is to appeal to the lingering after-effects in the reader's mind."

One could only give something to the reader, though, if one had first taken it into oneself. The artist's purpose, Fitzgerald thought, should be to express in some palatable disguise emotions he had himself lived through. In this sense, Fitzgerald saw the purpose of fiction as "to recapture the exact feel of a moment in time and space, exemplified by people rather than by things . . . an attempt at a mature memory of a deep experience." "It was necessary for Dickens," he said, "to put into *Oliver Twist* the child's passionate resentment at being abused and starved that had haunted his whole childhood. Ernest Hemingway's first stories, *In Our Time,* went right down to the bottom of all that he had ever felt and known." The idea turns up in one of Fitzgerald's own early stories, set in Elizabethan times. A fugitive rushes in to hide in his friend's quarters. The guards come looking for him and tell the friend that a lady has been raped, but they do not find the fugitive. The friend remonstrates, but the fugitive insists that he is responsible only to himself for what he does. Then, after his friend has gone to sleep, he sits down and writes *The Rape of Lucrece.*

The same giving and being given to, Fitzgerald felt, applied to character as to content. "It takes half a dozen people," he maintained, "to make a synthesis strong enough to create a fiction character." And also to style. "A good style simply doesn't form unless you absorb half a dozen top-flight authors every year." Your style should be "a subconscious amalgam of all that you have admired."

His creativity consisted of being given to by the world and giving in turn to his readers. Fitzgerald had an extraordinary flair for sizing people up as well as a remarkable ability to incorporate and reproduce vocabulary. Finally, he had a sense of himself as an actor, absorbing a part given him, making it part of himself, and then giving it to his public. He was greatly concerned with when and how his books would appear, with autographing them, for example, and otherwise making himself a public figure. Give unto others as you would have them give unto you. In effect, Fitzgerald was playing out his version of the Golden Rule on a public stage, and he was very, very good at it.

Yet there was a failure built in simply because of the magnitude of the demands he made. At the beginning of his career he saw himself entering a world of "ineffable toploftiness and promise," and he himself having "a sense of infinite possibilities that was always with me whether vanity or shame was my mood." Not to have that relation to infinity was to be fatally flawed—as he described a woman who he felt had failed, "She didn't have the strength for the big stage." As for himself, however, being inspired gave him an infinite power: "I can be so tender and kind to people in even little things, but once I get a pen in my hand I can do *anything.*"

Writing would balance the books between the real and the fantastic, the finite and the infinite, the loving and the aggressive. For example, Fitzgerald advised a fellow writer, "Try and find more 'bright' characters; if the women are plain make them millionairesses or nymphomaniacs, if they're scrub-women, give them hot sex attraction and charm. This is such a good trick I don't see why it's not more used—I always use it just as I like to balance a beautiful word with a barbed one." "Reporting the extreme things as if they were the average things," he once noted, "will start you on the art of fiction." Thus, his writings are full of marvelous aphorisms achieved by moving from human details to the grand scale, for example, "The faces of most American women over thirty are relief maps of petulant and bewildered unhappiness." Or moving from planetary forces to the helpless human, as in this closing of a letter: "Pray gravity to move your bowels. It's little we get done for us in this world."

Yet these attempts to get from the finite to the infinite were, inevitably, doomed from the start; and the deepest strain in Fitzgerald's life and works is the sense of inevitable loss and failure. "The utter synthesis between what we want and what we can have," he wrote, "is so rare that I look back with a sort of wonder on those days of my youth when I had it, or thought I did." "Again and again in my books I have tried to imagize my regret that I have never been as good as I intended to be." It was this sense of inevitable loss that gave rise to his "tragic" sense of life and a feeling for the chanciness of existence: "You have got to make all the right changes at the main corners—the price for losing your way once is years of unhappiness."

This sense of an unanswerable demand from the infinite could give Fitzgerald as stern an artistic conscience as any writer ever had. This work ethic could also, however, make loss and depression dominant themes in his work and life. As he said, "It is from the failures of life, and not its successes that we learn most." Once, simply from hearing someone recite Horace's *Integer vitae* ode, he sadly thought, "I knew in my heart that I had missed something by being a poor Latin scholar, like a blessed evening with a lovely girl." His sense of loss could yield this extraordinary image for the succession of the generations: "We are creatures bounding from each other's shoulders, feeling already the feet of new creatures upon our backs bounding again toward an invisible and illusory trapeze."

The same sense of reaching toward a vanishing security gave rise, I think, to Fitzgerald's special, magical feeling about money and being rich. It was as though those who had money proved they were in touch with the infinite by spending it, and he had to try to identify himself with them by his own spendthrift ways. "All big men have spent money freely," he wrote. "I hate avarice or even caution." "That was always my experience," he wrote near the end of his life, "—a poor boy in a rich town; a poor boy in a rich boy's school; a poor boy in a rich man's club. . . . I have never been able to forgive the rich for being rich, and it has colored my entire life and works." He told a friend that the whole idea of *The Great Gatsby* was "the unfairness of a poor young man not being able to marry a girl with money. This theme comes up again and again because I lived it."

The way out of Fitzgerald's doomed effort to climb into the infinite was to separate himself from it. Thus, breaking up an affair with a married woman, he wrote her: "The harshness of this letter will have served its purpose if on reading it over you see that I have an existence outside you—and in doing so remind you that you have an existence outside me." It is in this sense, I think, that we have to take his artistic conscience as represented in such statements as, "Work was dignity and the only dignity." "To me," Fitzgerald wrote, "the conditions of an artistically creative life are so arduous that I can only compare to them the duties of a soldier in war-time." And, in this context, I think of his image for himself in failure, standing at twilight on a deserted firing range with an empty rifle and the targets down.

The image of the soldier suggests some of the violence he felt in being separate from that infinitely giving source. A word he used even more for such catastrophes was "broken." Thus, of Zelda, he said, "She broke and is broken forever." And in still another style, his sense that being separated from the giver was a breaking could let him arrive at an aphorism like, "The insane are always mere guests on earth, eternal strangers carrying around broken decalogues that they cannot read." He advised a would-be writer, "If you want to be a top-notcher, you have to break with everyone. You have to show up your own father." And indeed, his father's being fired seems to have laid down for this man the prototype of the loss of inner resources as a breaking: "That morning he had gone out a comparatively young man, a man full of strength, full of confidence. He came home that evening an old man, a completely broken man." Then he in turn as a father conveyed all kinds of "breaking" messages to his own daughter.

If she went to the wrong kind of parties with the wrong kind of people, he said, he would have a "broken neurotic" "on my hands . . . for the rest of my life." At one point, he threatened to send her to work in a canning factory: "It would have made you or broken you (i.e., made you run away)." Again, to be separate is to be "broken." The line was a fine one, as when he wrote her about a social fiasco. "I don't want it to be so bad that it will break your self-confidence, which . . . is fine [if] founded on . . . work, courage, etc., but if you are selfish it had better be broken early." In a more playful vein, he threatened to change her nickname to "Egg, which implies that you belong to a very rudimentary state of life and that I could break you up and crack you open at my will."

How can I phrase Fitzgerald's life style? I see three basic polarities within which he interpreted his world. First, I think, he saw situations in terms of bigger powers and lesser powers, in particular, his own self and the much bigger world he resolved to conquer. Second, he tended to divide things into those which were magical and infinite as against those which were separate and broken. The most important such dualism involved himself and the world: either he magically participated in the world, or he was his stoically resolute, separate self at the risk of being emptied and broken by it. Third, actions for him took the shape of giving and being given unto as against not giving, not being given unto, and therefore being—in that word which he came back to over and over again—"broken." His great imaginative gift was that he could project all these inner ups and downs onto an infinite plane outside, as a child might.

If I try to put into a single sentence a Fitzgerald-ness based on these three complex polarities—giving and being given to, big and small powers, being part of a magical world and having a separate, broken self—I come out with this: *By giving myself, I show I am part of a world that magically gives me infinite supplies of talent and grace; but by not giving I show I can stand alone, even at the risk of being broken.*

Obviously, there are many ways of talking about a style besides trying to phrase it into a single sentence. I like the sentence method, though, because it allows me to state both the key terms I see and the relations I see among them. A noun like "supplies" can serve as a theme summarizing a variety of traits: Fitzgerald's perception of his own and others' talent; his preoccupation with wealth; or his drinking. Each of these words in turn, "talent," "wealth," "drinking," can serve as themes for grouping particular behaviors: this or that writing, a certain party, some advice to his daughter. "Supplies" in turn becomes the object of giving or not giving, being given to or not being given to. These verbs can be unfolded into diverse traits and the traits in turn into particular behaviors. In other words, such a sentence functions like a theme in a piece of music or a kernel sentence in the early transformational grammars. One can unfold it and transform it into an infinity of variations, each new and different, yet all echoing the original.

By giving myself, I show I am part of a world that magically gives me infinite supplies of talent and grace; but by not giving I show I can stand alone, even at the risk of being broken. In other words, Fitzgerald always headed in two directions at once: to give infinitely and so prove he himself had been infinitely given to; to withhold and so show that he had not been given to, that therefore he had a right to be angry and to break into that magical source or to be broken himself. In his own words, "I have no patience and when I want something I *want* it. I break people. I am part of the break-up of the times."

Thus, he was always involved in one of two cycles, giving or withholding. He was driven from one to the other as it became apparent that he was not going to receive infinitely (after all, none of us does), or as he needed to assert his own separate identity apart from the era in which he lived. He always created expectations but only sometimes did he live up to them. One word that (for me) might unify him or the way he saw his world is *promising*.

In his life, he worked—and played—very hard at making himself into a legend. As one way of uniting himself with a larger past he insisted that he was descended from Francis Scott Key. In another mode, he became the very embodiment of the Jazz Age. He carried on fabulous parties and debauches, many of them marked by recklessness and violence. At one party, for instance, when Zelda lay down in front of their car and told him to drive over her, he had released the brake before their friends could restrain him. Sober, Fitzgerald was the picture of grace, gentility, and generosity. Drunk, out came a mean streak of rudeness and cruelty that appeared in his sober self mostly as a liking for boxing and other contact sports and a persistent hobby of military history. But perhaps this violence was implicit in his sense of the conflict between the giver and the receiver—as in his imagery of breaking and cracking. He could say, for example, of Zelda's career, that she was working "under a greenhouse which is my money and my name and my love. . . . She is willing to use the greenhouse to protect her in every way . . . and at the same time she feels no responsibility about the greenhouse and feels that she can reach up and knock a piece of glass out of the roof any moment."

Finally, however, what interests me more about Fitzgerald than his wife or his life is his literary achievement. If what I have said about his having a style of choices is correct, then I should be able to trace in the ego choices his work embodies the same style as in the ego choices expressed in his opinions and his life. Consider, then, three of the passages I like best from my favorite among Fitzgerald's novels, *Gatsby*.

This, for example, is a single sentence describing college people coming home for Christmas vacation on the great passenger trains of the 1930s and 40s. I love it because I too stood between cars when I was coming home from college and breathed the wintry air between Boston and New York. "We drew in deep breaths of it as we walked back from dinner through the cold vestibules, unutterably aware of our identity with this country for one strange hour, before we melted indistinguishably into it again." There is the taking in (air, dinner), the merger with the larger being (this country), the separateness from it and the melting into it again.

In those words, "indistinguishably" and "unutterably," you can hear the distinctive note of withholding. You could almost call Fitzgerald the Master of the Negative Prefix, particularly when he refuses to tell you something, that is, to give from his mouth. Listen to this astonishing statement of withholding from a narrator. A narrator is, after all, supposed to be telling us the novel:

> Through all he said, even through his appalling sentimentality, I was reminded of something—an elusive rhythm, a fragment of lost words, that I had heard somewhere a long time ago. For a moment a phrase tried to take shape in my mouth and my lips parted like a dumb man's, as though there was more struggling upon them than a wisp of startled air. But they made no sound, and what I had almost remembered was uncommunicable forever.

And for the same majestic theme of wonder and loss, listen to this, to me one of the finest bravura paragraphs in all American literature:

> Most of the big shore places were closed now and there were hardly any lights except the shadowy, moving glow of a ferryboat across the Sound. And as the moon rose higher the inessential houses began to melt away until gradually I became aware of the old island here that flowered once for Dutch sailors' eyes—a fresh, green breast of the new world. Its vanished trees, the trees that had made way for Gatsby's house, had once pandered in whispers to the last and greatest of all human dreams; for a transitory enchanted moment man must have held his breath in the presence of this continent, compelled into an aesthetic contemplation he neither understood nor desired, face to face for the last time in history with something commensurate to his capacity for wonder.

As I read of that fresh, promising breast, I cannot help but remember the torn, empty breast two chapters before of wretched, slain Myrtle Wilson. Notice how Scott Fitzgerald the writer continues the concerns of Scott Fitzerald the man; how the great themes of his writing—expectation and promise, loss and movements to control loss—show the same style as his attitudes toward Zelda or Princeton or Hollywood. His managing others, his alcoholism, his hobby of military history, his use of negative prefixes, or even his famous saying ("The very rich are different from you and me")—all coact in his style of giving and receiving from an infinity magically conceived in the global, oral terms of the first giving. Truly he was looking for a diamond as big as the Ritz.

My literary term "style," however, does not quite do justice to my claim to have understood Fitzgerald holistically as an "all" and a "one" dialectically interplaying. The classical word for such an idea of a person is "character" (etymologically the same as "style," both having to do with carving letters). The classical psychoanalytic definition is Otto Fenichel's: "the habitual mode of bringing into harmony the tasks presented by internal demands and by the external world." In the language of ego psychology and multiple function, character is "the ego's habitual modes of adjustment to the external world, the id, and the superego, and the characteristic types of combining these modes with one another, constitute character" (1945, p. 467). Fenichel's word "habitual" takes us beyond the momentary balancings of ego or id (as described, for example, by Robert Waelder's principle of "multiple function") into something that over a long period of time remains the same (Lat. *idem,* the root of

Identity

Indeed, in recent years, the word "character" has yielded to "identity," particularly as used by Erik Erikson and his followers: "the confirmation of the individual's sense of selfhood by his membership in the community" (Mazlish, 1975, p. 85). Such a definition turns inward, toward the individual's own feeling of wholeness, but also outward toward the way both individual and community confirm each other. From this version of identity, a "sense of identity," really, has come a great deal of admirable work in psychohistory and psychoanalytic sociology, and even folk psychology, as in "This week I'm having an identity crisis."

I want, however, to add to Erikson's "identity" a literary critic's precision. I want to define identity by an operation or procedure for examining the style in which particular individuals function. In one sense, I am refining the key term of Fenichel's classic definition, "habitual." In another, however, I am drawing into this concept of the I the most exact of the modern theories of identity, that of Heinz Lichtenstein as developed in his book *The Dilemma of Human Identity* (1977). I want to define identity as having three simultaneous meanings, as (1) an agency, (2) a consequence, (3) a representation.

An agency. The "I" represented by "an identity" is the I that is the subject of sentences like "I see," "I remember," or "I repress." This "I" tends to disappear in abstract discussions with nouns like "vision," "memory," or "repression," one reason that abstracting away from the person in philosophy sometimes leads to confusion. If "vision" makes a person vanish, imagine what "intertextuality" or "intersubjectivity" do.

Identity, in this first sense, is the agent initiating the actions that systematically create identity. One needs therefore to think of identity as a *system* (probably a system of information-processing feedback). Identity is not only the active, agentic principle of such a system but also the passive self that that system creates as it interacts with the world. Hence, identity is also

A consequence. Identity is what is being created as the individual brings an already existing identity (identity in the first sense) to new experiences. Identity in this second sense is the "I" that results because "I see," "I remember," or "I repress."

Identity as what is created by living is necessarily correlative to identity in the first sense of agency. Hence identity is, if not paradoxical, at least circular. We shall need to resort to feedback or something like it when we wish a fuller model. The "we wish" and "model" remind me, however, of the third term: identity as

A representation. Identity is a way of putting into words the dialectic of sameness and difference that is a human life. As I did with Fitzgerald, a person looking on from "outside" can formulate for all the infinite choices by which someone manifests himself, a unifying style by looking at what is familiar and what is novel in each new action. I am constantly doing new things, yet I bring to each new thing my characteristic way of doing. I understand that sameness in what someone else does by seeing it persist though change. Conversely, I understand change by seeing it against what has not changed.

The poets have long recognized that unifying dialectic between sameness and difference. Emily Dickinson, for example, began one of her poems,

> Each Life Converges to some Centre—
> Expressed—or still—

The insight is not only a poetic one, however. The philosopher Stephen Toulmin gives Newton, Darwin, and Freud as examples when he remarks how the very greatest scientists are often

> dominated and guided by a simple enduring 'vision.' Quite early in their careers, these scientists formulate for themselves, and set down in

writing, a tentative system of radically novel concepts and hypotheses, which can be seen at work throughout all their subsequent investigations, directing their curiosities and influencing the pattern of their analyses, like some kind of a cognitive 'field' (1978, p. 335).

Similarly, the aesthetician Anton Ehrenzweig notes "how a great artist's lifework possesses an inner cohesion like the single movements of a symphony; they are seemingly different and yet elaborating the same inspiring idea" (1965, pp. 76-77). "A man's work," Camus wrote in the preface to his essays, "is nothing but this slow trek to rediscover, through the detours of art, those two or three great and simple images in whose presence his heart first opened." Or, as I once heard Bernard Malamud, the novelist, remark in conversation, "Each novelist writes one novel all his life." In the same way, the theories constructed by such major theorists of personality as Freud, Jung, Reich, or Rank reflect the theorist's own personality (Stolorow and Atwood, 1979).

Interestingly, at least one brain scientist suggests that this persisting unity is something intrinsic to the human brain itself. "The brain," writes J. Z. Young, "has many distinct parts but there is increasing evidence that they are interrelated to make one functioning whole, which gives a unique and characteristic direction to the pattern of life of that one individual" (1978, p. 265).

One way of wording that characteristic direction or pattern—the one Heinz Lichtenstein suggests—is to formulate a human identity as a theme with variations. That is, if we imagine a human life as a dialectic between sameness and difference, we can think of the sameness, the continuity of personal style, as a theme; we can think of the changes as variations on that theme. I can understand another person as living out changes and variations on a persistent core just as a musician might play out an infinity of variations on a single melody, as a mathematician might generate a myriad of functions from a single variable, or as a linguist might transform one kernel sentence into hundreds of different utterances.

I can use the term "identity theme" for the continuing core of personality that I see a person bringing to every new experience, their theme or style or, to borrow a French term, cachet spécifique. I would arrive at someone's identity theme as I would a personal style, by abstracting it from its many, many various expressions. Then I can use the term "identity" for the history of that theme and the history of its variations over a lifetime.

In other words, "identity" in this third sense means the history of a person looked at as a theme and variations. Identity is a "representation" in the sense that a history requires a historian.

Lichtenstein, from whom I am adapting this concept of identity, thought in terms of a "primary identity" in the individual. Not unreasonably. We are born into the world with a certain hereditary endowment. That heredity manifests itself in a rather general style of "temperament" or "initial organizing configuration." As every parent knows, babies differ. Some are "easy." Others are "difficult" or "slow to warm up" or "persistent" or "distractable" (Thomas, Chess, and Birch, 1968, 1970; Burks and Rubenstein, 1979). Obviously, such traits are so general as to admit of a great range of behavior, some of which will suit the mother (or mothering person) and some not. Accordingly she will favor some and not others, and the infant will sense itself according to the way she reflects the baby back to itself. Out of the "fit" of mother and baby, close or jarring, easy or abrasive, abrupt or gradual, the child's personality will develop. According to Lichtenstein, "The specific unconscious need of the mother . . . actualizes out of these infinite potentialities one way of being in the child, namely being the child for this particular mother, responding to her unique and individual needs." This way of being Lichtenstein calls a "primary identity," "a zero point which must precede all other mental developments" (1964, pp. 53, 54, 1977, pp. 215 and 218–19).

Lichtenstein intends by "primary identity" a style of being which is a structure *in* the person, like the ego of traditional psychoanalysis. Created out of heredity and the earliest relationship between a baby and its first caretaker, such an identity is in, even is, that person. Formed before speech, it is a preverbal thing that can never be put precisely into words, can never be "known" in that sense. Just as we can never know the mind of another person, so we can never know this primary identity which is the essence of that mind, although we can approximate it by phrasings like the "style" I phrased for Scott Fitzgerald.

It seems to me, however, that people no more agree on "true" or "right" readings of identities than of poems. A statement of identity is a representation of some person but it also represents the represener's identity. If Fitzgerald interpreted Hollywood as a powerful, withholding mother, that says as much about Fitzgerald as about Hollywood. In the same way, when I read Fitzgerald in a series of polarities, that says as much about the way I see things as about Fitzgerald.

By the very act of interpreting someone, a represener of identity does something which thereby becomes part of the represener's style or identity. "Identity" thus has the same ambiguity as "history." It claims to say how things actually were, but it is necessarily someone's account of how things actually were.

Identity as representation leads to two possibilities. How do I represent the wholeness of you? How do I represent the wholeness of me? Identity can be perceived by the person in question, as when I think about me, or identity can be perceived by another from "outside," as when I think about you. The distinction is important because, even with empathy, we will never feel *exactly* the pleasure another mind feels, we will never know the knowledge we share in the same way, never love as that other person loves.

This distinction between the "inside" and the "outside" interpreter is also important because in it a theme-and-variations concept of identity poses and preserves the classical psychoanalytic polarity: conscious and unconscious. That is, to someone formulating an identity from outside, like Freud observing the young man or me interpreting Fitzgerald, a given piece of behavior is neither unconscious nor conscious. It is simply behavior. To someone experiencing identity from inside, however, like Freud's young man, behavior, and hence identity, are necessarily partly unconscious. (See the Appendix, pp. 334–36.)

Identity as representation is my view, however, not Lichtenstein's, and it may not be Freud's either. Freud himself seems to have believed in a unity *in* the personality. On November 6, 1907, Freud was speaking in his large waiting room, presenting a case history to colleagues and questioners assembled as the Vienna Psychoanalytic Society. One question he answered almost as though he were anticipating Lichtenstein's theme-and-variations version of primary identity. "In general, the human being cannot tolerate contrasting ideas and feelings in juxtaposition; it is this striving for unification that we call character" (Nunberg, 1962, I, 236).

The patient who occasioned Freud's remark has been known for many years by a horror movie epithet taken from the symptom that brought him to psychoanalysis:

The Rat Man

He is one of the five major case histories and the only one for which we are so lucky as to have Freud's original notes on the case. To Freud the patient was a changing, interacting twenty-nine year old man with a bewildering variety of problems, but, since we know him only as words in a verbal space we create between Freud and me and you, we can represent him as a text as much as any of Scott Fitzgerald's fictional heroes. I can reread him, in that sense, through this threefold concept of identity, but particularly identity as a theme and variations and its history. Perhaps it is appropriate, then, to give "The Rat Man" a name that is more like a name Fitzgerald might have given him. Fortunately, from Freud's notes, we now know his real name, Paul Lorenz.*

* Freud first reported the case on October 30 and November 6, 1907, to the Vienna Psychoanalytic Society whose *Minutes* for those dates transcribe his earliest thinking (Nunberg, H. [1962], I, 226–237). Freud published his fuller account in 1909, and he returned to the case in *Inhibitions, Symptoms and Anxiety* (1926d), to develop his new ideas of defense and

Paul Lorenz came to Freud because of a strange set of compulsions that seemed completely not I—alien—to him. While on maneuvers during his summer service as a reserve officer, he had lost his glasses during a halt. On that same halt, an older officer, a captain fond of cruelty and much in favor of corporal punishment, had described a Chinese torture in which rats were confined in a pot held against the victim's buttocks and forced to burrow their way up the rectum. As Lorenz described this torture, he seemed to Freud horrified both at the torture and at his own secret interest and pleasure in it. At the time he heard the story he had been seized with alien thoughts, that the torture was being carried out on the woman he loved and on his father.

He wired ahead for new glasses, but when a fellow-officer delivered the package to him he found he could not repay the postage because he was baffled by a series of "commands" that he pay different people, traveling to different towns to do so. Finally, completely paralyzed by the problem, he sought advice from a friend in Vienna. The friend suggested he consult a physician—Freud. Lorenz and Freud had their first interview on Tuesday, October 1, 1907.

The "commands" were his presenting symptom. They were not, he felt, his own inner moral principles, and thus they represented what he called "a dissociation of personality," some alien force. He felt he could resolve the dilemmas they created only by turning to someone else. His friend, as an outside authority, could counter these commands from outside (as he had done previously when Paul felt commanded to take his law examinations before he was ready). In his first interview with Freud, Lorenz told how he had turned (when he was much younger) to a male friend for moral forgiveness when he felt particularly guilty of criminal impulses. In this craving for absolution from outsiders, he showed his need to appease and yet deceive a superego still sought in external figures.

Lorenz sought other forms of outer authority. For example, he had to consult his mother about entering treatment. All that kept him from suicide was his fear of causing his mother pain, particularly in view of the early death of his sister. Certainly it fits the rest of Lorenz's personality that he was trying to become a lawyer and that the particular part of his studies that these obsessional commands disrupted was criminal law.

Although Lorenz craved external laws, he also wanted to be released from them. He recalled two occasions when he became sexually excited (and masturbated) on hearing commandments broken. One was when a postilion

signal anxiety. My own discussion of Paul Lorenz is adapted from Holland (1975b). See that essay for page references to Freud's account for the quotations, further documentation, and my indebtedness to other studies of this patient by Mark Kanzer (1952), Elizabeth Zetzel (1966), Leonard Shengold (1971), Michael Sherwood (1969), and Jacques Lacan (1953).

broke a city ordinance. The other time, he was reading how Goethe overcame his mistress's prohibition against kissing.

Indeed, Lorenz became able to masturbate at all only after his father's death. He would work on his law examinations until late at night (thereby pleasing his then-dead father). He would even leave the door open so that his father might reappear and see him hard at work. Then he would take out his penis and look at it in the mirror—hardly an action calculated to win paternal approval. Years before, on the occasion of his first sexual intercourse, the thought had flashed through his mind, "One might murder one's father for this." Similarly, he had felt that, if his father died, he could marry his lady.

Hence, not only did Lorenz feel conflicting demands from "outside," he also suffered from mixed feelings of love and hate toward the significant persons in his life. He reported these mostly about his father for, at this stage in psychoanalysis, Freud did not explore the early relation of mother and child as deeply as an analyst would today.

That early relationship, one would say today, necessarily couples love to dependency, frustration, and anger. It therefore poses one of the basic tasks of infancy: learning to live with feelings of love and hate toward the same person—like Lorenz's feelings toward his father. Today, one would guess that the roots of his ambivalence toward his father lay in his relation with his mother.

Freud, however, wrote of his patient's ambivalence in all kinds of other relationships. He noted, for example, how Lorenz attended all the funerals in his family, even of distant relatives. He was constantly killing people off in his imagination so he could show sympathy for their relatives. For example, he wished that his lady might lie ill in bed forever. On a solitary walk, he moved a rock out of the path of her carriage lest it hurt her, but then he put it back lest he seem foolish.

Freud interpreted, both in his theoretical remarks on the case and in his comments to Lorenz, these doings and undoings as the acting out of ambivalence. More specifically, he thought that in Lorenz's development the sadistic components of love had been exceptionally developed (probably by his father). Lorenz had therefore developed an unconscious hatred of his father which he then repressed. This unconscious hatred had given rise to an especially strong love as a disguise—and that love had constantly to be doubted (because of the hate underneath).

This pattern, said Freud, applied not only to his father and to Paul's strong identification with his father but also to Gisela, the lady he loved (who was also his cousin). Thinking of her, he sharply separated love from copulation, which he perceived as a hostile act. Thus he could fantasy, while he was with another, non-Platonic girlfriend, a dressmaker, "a rat for my cousin." He was punishing her but he was also imagining his sex with the dressmaker as a loving preliminary to sex with Gisela.

In the manner of 1907, Freud interpreted all these conflicting impulses as showing that Lorenz had disintegrated into three personalities. One was unconscious, made up of the passionate, evil impulses he had suppressed at an early age. A second was conscious—the law student. Then a third was conscious or preconscious, involved in the superstitious and ascetic rituals he had developed to counter his repressed wishes.

Given such a splitting, Lorenz overestimated the effects of his feelings on the world because he was unconscious of their internal, mental function. His love and hate seemed magically powerful because they overpowered *him* with these obsessional thoughts.

From the age of seven, he told Freud, Lorenz had felt that his parents knew his thoughts and that his sexual or aggressive impulses would be followed by disastrous consequences. Thus, he became a coward out of the fear of the violence of his own rage.

Lorenz's ambivalence, however, did not contrast love and hate only. He also expressed his mixed feelings in the more primitive emotions of simple pleasure and disgust—notably about rats. In telling the story of the rat torture, for example, he showed a mixture of horror and enjoyment. Rats themselves made him think of disease, notably sexual disease (syphilis). Hence they also had erotic values (as with the dressmaker).

In other words, as one would expect with a personality so bound up in commands and compulsions from outside, Lorenz was preoccupied with excrement. A child's excretions are not only the subject of parental commands; they are also the first objects to combine pleasure and disgust. Lorenz represented his excrement as his money—coins—or as his father's gambling debts (*Spielratte*) that had to be paid out, hence like *Raten* (installments) or *Ratten* (rats). Sometimes his concern with money revealed its bodily origins directly as when he dreamed that Freud's daughter had patches of dung instead of eyes. That is, he dreamed of marrying Freud's daughter, not for her charms, her *beaux yeux,* but for her money. In a still more blatant fantasy, he thought of himself lying on his back, copulating with Freud's daughter by means of the stool hanging from his anus. Lorenz took pleasure in sniffing and smelling, another derivative of the erotic value he put on excretion and its products.

At the same time, to excrete is to put out something that may be a living part of one's own body or may be dead matter. Two episodes Lorenz recalled bear on this aspect of anality.

When he was three or four years old, his father beat him for having done something naughty. The boy flew into a rage, but, since he knew no swear words with which to attack his father, he called him the names of all the common (dead) objects he could think of: "You lamp! You towel! You plate!"

Related to this episode was what Lorenz called the greatest fright of his life. He got from his mother a stuffed bird from a hat to play with. As he was running along with the bird in his hands, its wings moved. Terrified that it had come back to life, he threw it down.

These two strongly remembered episodes admit a pattern: a frenzy in forcing out of himself something dead and bad; then terror at the prospect that it could come to life and return. It was this pattern that Lorenz was acting out in another childhood episode he remembered, the time he played a cruel trick on his younger brother. Hoping to hurt his brother very much, he promised him he would see something if he looked up the barrel of a pop-gun. Then Paul pulled the trigger. In effect, he was forcing on his brother the thing he himself most feared: the disastrous recoil of his own wishes on himself. He made himself the active one, however, mastering the feared situation instead of fearing it.

Excreting was a highly charged modality for Lorenz. So was looking. Throughout his childhood, he wanted to look at naked girls but, he said, he feared something awful would happen if he thought about such things. For example, his father might die. Nevertheless, he enjoyed peeping at his sister's body until his mother put a stop to it. He had exhibited himself to his mother and to his governess while he seemed to be asleep. Earlier another governess (Fraulein Peter) had let him crawl up under her skirt and finger her genitals. Ever after, he was left with a tormenting desire to look at the female body, especially smooth surfaces like thighs. In later life, he fell in love with his lady's body, which his sister had described to him. During the analysis, he brought out a number of fantasies of looking at women's genitals, but associated with rats, insects, feces, and other sources of disgust.

In other words, Lorenz's lookings had acquired multiple functions in his mind. A looking could serve as a source of pleasure if it was also a source of reassurance, that is, when looking excluded the orifices of the female body. Looking also took the place of touching for him, and it is worth remembering that the whole crazy series of symptoms that drove him to seek a doctor's help began with a pair of dropped eyeglasses.

Freud's suggestion that looking had taken the place of touching for his patient matches another theme: a regression from risky acting to safer thinking. Thus, Lorenz impulsively attacked his servant girl and just as impulsively left off. Freud suggested the real purpose of this acting out was to evoke the inner prohibition. In general, Lorenz's compulsions to look instead of touch and his substitution of thoughts for overt actions, like his obedience to "external" commands, reversed outside and inside. Activities in the outer world he converted to forces in his mind, and he gave his thoughts existence in external reality.

This is a reversal in spatial direction, so to speak. Equally important in Lorenz's psychic economy were reversals in temporal sequence. For example, at the age of twelve, Paul had had a crush on a little girl. The idea came to him that she would be kind to him if he were to suffer some misfortune, specifically, his father's death. Here again Freud could see a reversed logic. She loves me. If I love her, my father will be angry at me, and I will want to kill him. If, however, he were already dead, then it would be all right. He would not be angry were I to love her.

At one point in Lorenz's long romance with his cousin Gisela, she was called away to nurse her seriously ill grandmother. He suddenly had a "command" to cut his own throat, and he was even going to fetch the razor, when he received another "command": "You must first go and kill the old woman." Freud interpreted these two "commands" as, first, Lorenz's hostile wish to go and kill the old woman who had deprived him of his love; second, a command to kill himself as punishment for this hostile wish. But, Freud pointed out, these wishes came in the *reversed order* so typical for this patient.

The same kind of complex reversing process gave rise to his presenting symptom, the contradictory commands about paying back the postage for his new pince-nez. The idea (or wish) had flashed into his mind: "As sure as my father and the lady can have children, I'll pay him back the money." To punish himself then, for this double insult, he had to promise himself to do an impossible deed, namely, to pay back the money to the wrong person. Otherwise the rat-torture would be carried out on his father (now eight years dead!).

This sanction was itself a reversal. To the image of rats creeping into the anus he associated babies coming out (or the intestinal worms from which he had suffered as a child). In this presenting symptom, as in his whole illness, Freud pointed out, "What appears to be the *consequence* of the illness is in reality the *cause* or *motive* of falling ill." That is, by falling ill, he avoided the task of reconciling his love for the lady with his father's pattern of marrying a rich woman—and indeed his father's more general role as the inhibitor of his sexuality.

This general pattern of reversal underlay his relations with men in many contexts. For example, once he got the idea that his lady was showing a preference for his brother. To quell his jealousy, he asked his brother to wrestle with him. Not until he himself had been defeated (and thus punished for his hostile wish) did he feel pacified. It was as though he had always to deal with hostility toward males before he felt free to turn to a woman.

What he described as the first great blow of his life took place when he was fourteen or fifteen. It involved a nineteen year old student who was a prototype of the male friend on whose external authority he relied—as he did Freud's. This student made much of him until he succeeded in being appointed his tutor. Then he began treating him like an idiot. Paul realized that the student had simply used him to gain admission to the Lorenz household to court one of his sisters.

This, his first recollection on the couch, led him to memories of his governess Fraulein Peter's genitals (and her male name was not without significance). In other words, as Freud comments, it was (again!) as though Lorenz had to bring out his hostile feelings toward males as sexual beings and external authorities before he could trust his male therapist enough to go into sexual material dealing with a woman.

Thus, in the presenting conflict about paying postage, he had displaced his duty to repay the young *woman* in the post office onto a male lieutenant. Further confusion arose because he transferred his wish to go see two girls who had looked on him with favor onto the two lieutenants. Again, he had had to deal with males before turning to females. Indeed, his whole confusion about women and money while he was in military service was much colored by his identification with his father's experiences while in the army.

Lorenz dealt with male inhibitors before female gratifiers. This pattern suggests that Lorenz's (anal) reversals of space and time relationships came before, and hence served as, the psychological strategy this son brought to his (oedipal) rivalry with his father for his mother. He came out of that oedipal struggle still more firmly committed to a pattern of reversal. In any case, the pattern appeared constantly in his adult re-creations of oedipal situations. For example, he had a fantasy that, if his lady were to marry somebody else, he would himself rise to higher rank in that man's department until one day he could grant his lady's entreaty and rescue her husband from the consequences of a dishonesty (like his father's?) that he had foreseen all along. Another example: his sister petted him and kissed him like a lover to the point where he felt he had to assure his brother-in-law, "If Julie has a baby in nine months' time, you needn't think I am its father; I am innocent!"

In general, of course, he found father-figures everywhere around him. Freud himself became one, specifically, a father trying to marry his daughter off to the patient. While telling the story of the rat torture, he addressed Freud as "Captain." The cruel captain had, by his very cruelty, become another father-figure. Indeed, in his response to the story of the rat torture, Lorenz thought of his father as alive, as he did in many of his obsessional ideas, although in fact his father had died eight years previously.

While Lorenz created fathers in the outer world, he also identified himself (in his inner world) with his own father. For example, he equated his own unpaid post office debt to his father with his father's gambling debt while in the army. What caused his neurosis was his conflict as to whether to marry his love or marry into the rich family of his mother (as his father had done). As Freud succinctly put it, he could not choose between his father and his sexual object.

His cousin Gisela was a relative, too old for him, perhaps sterile, and certainly in poor health—in general, a doubtful candidate for marriage. In this more or less unavailable woman, Lorenz had perhaps re-created his sister Katherine. She in turn may have played for Lorenz in childhood the role of the mother in the family triangle. Then his love for her would have been tempered by the opposite feeling: that when she was gone, what was left—his relationship with his father—was better. As Lacan points out in his reading of the case, Lorenz re-created in his present life and his inner world the family constellation or *mythe* of his father (1953; Evans, 1979).

He felt both love and hate for both his father and "the woman" in this constellation, be she mother, Katherine, or Gisela. His resentment of his lady therefore combined with his attachment to his father, and conversely his hatred of his father joined to his love for his lady. He could not choose between two such alternatives, Freud noted, since it was this very uncertainty that protected him from injuring either his father or the lady. "Our present patient had developed a peculiar talent for avoiding a knowledge of any facts which would have helped him in deciding his conflict," notably the facts about the operation on his lady's ovaries. "He had to be forced into remembering what he had forgotten and into finding out what he had overlooked," Freud wrote.

In other words, he used denials of his perceptions, memories, and knowledge in order to control what was inside and what was outside—to "place" his emotions outside himself. "He was at once superstitious and not superstitious." "He believed in premonitions and prophetic dreams," creating their effects by "peripheral vision and reading, forgetting, and, above all, errors of memory." Then he would project those shadowy, repressed connections into the outer world of reality evoking his superstitious awe. Finally, after analysis cleared up these obsessions and superstitions, he would smile at his own credulity.

By these rituals, he said, he was able to ward off *both* of the bad ideas that came to him about the rat torture, namely, that it would be done to *both* his father and his cousin. Similarly, he was able to suppress the episode of the captain who had told him where he really should pay the postage, to the young lady at the post office who had been attracted to him. By such means he had been able to think of his father as alive years after his actual death.

Closely related to these denials of obvious facts and perceptions was the patient's ability to keep things split. He could always keep up several attachments to women, to work, or to ideas simultaneously. That way, he never had to choose one and thus express his hatred of the other. As he imagined the rat torture, he split it: there were two rats in the pot. One bored into the victim and one did not.

That was the real issue: the denials, forgettings, and splits all served to control what went in and what went out. His greatest fear was that he would not be able to keep control, that something would burst in against his will. The rat torture, although it meant many things, meant this one above all others. It implied rats boring their way into his anus, his father's, or his lady's. In all these settings, "rat" could imply a penis (*heiraten,* to marry). The rats also seemed to be associated with the idea of coming out (like the popgun hitting his brother), particularly babies (or worms) coming out of the anus (confirming a childish fantasy that men as well as women can have babies, through the anus).

These were fantasies of things coming into or out of the body. Lorenz had similar fantasies about language. He feared that things could enter into his phrases and turn them into their opposite. For example, he dreamed that Freud's mother died and that he sent Freud a card with "p.c.," *pour condoler,* on it, but, as he wrote, something changed p.c. into "p.f.," *pour feliciter.* He used the conjunction *aber* ("but" or "though") as a verbal formula for repudiating "commands," but then he got the idea that the mute *e* of the second syllable was "not a sufficient protection against intrusions." Accordingly, he began accenting the word, *abER,* thus making it, Freud noted, almost *Abwehr,* "defense," a word he had learned in therapy.

He had another magic word, *Glejisamen.* After various complicated explanations, he concluded it came from combining his lady's name, Gisela, with *Samen* (semen) with no gaps in between. He had to say this magic word quickly so that nothing could slip into it, and he added the phrase "without rats." Even this was not enough, however, and to prevent its being reversed into its opposite, he contracted the whole word into just *Wie.*

In short, Lorenz distorted words by taking things out in order to prevent bad things creeping in. Taking out made what was left more secure. Coming in violently and catastrophically reversed the sense of what was being said.

This pattern applied generally to what went into and out of Lorenz's mouth. He began to heap the grossest abuse on Freud and his family, reporting it in a state of terror lest Freud beat him as his violent father had. It was only by getting it out this way that he could believe he had felt hostility toward his father. He had various related fantasies of defecating into the mouth of a cousin of his, or the mouths of Freud's children, or of Freud doing this to his mother. He associated these fantasies to his father's use of excremental swear words, but I think what is equally clear is the difference in his feelings between what is going in and what is going out. One threatens, the other improves.

He imagined Freud's daughter performing fellatio on a deputy judge (really himself). He was horrified at the idea of the fellatio, because for him the mouth had strong connotations of biting. As a child, he had been apt to bite people when he was in a rage. He associated rats with himself as a biting child, the rat he once saw on his father's grave (eating him? he wondered), and with the operation for the removal of his lady's ovaries. Syphilis gnawing and eating reminded him of rats—and he had feared that his cousin and his father were syphilitic. He fantasied that he saw Freud's mother naked and that the lower part of her body and especially her genitals had been entirely eaten up by Freud and the children.

Embodied in rats, venereal disease, sexual perversions, and coprophagy, taking in through the mouth became in Lorenz's fantasies as grotesque and repulsive as other forms of taking in. Thus, his feelings as an adult testify to a deep ambivalence toward his mother's feeding him. Theory in 1909 had little or nothing to say about early ambivalence toward a mother, but today it would explain his feelings about things coming into his mouth and the rest of his body. As an adult, he had handed over all his money to his mother (putting it "outside" himself), so he would not have to take from her anything that originated with her. He got from his mother, he said, everything bad in his nature; what was bad in him was what she put into him.

Nowhere does Rat Man's inside-outside pattern appear more clearly than in his imagining his diseased emotions as a lump of blood in his head. He had the fantasy of making a funnel-shaped hole in his head to let what was diseased in his brain come out. In doing so he had forgotten his father's description of the Nuremberg funnel, an instrument of torture for pouring water *into* a victim. As a child, he thought his parents knew his thoughts, supposing he had spoken them out loud without having heard himself do it. He had let them out without control.

One can see from unfolding one session's variations on Lorenz's identity how events like talking and listening could have a double meaning for him, coming in and going out, but also preventing and testing the entrance of things from outside. Then this adaptation, alternating between barring and permitting entrances into his psyche, would mesh with the general ambivalence Freud pointed to, heightening Lorenz's obsessive oscillations. Similarly, one can see how his father and the army served him as external controls, therefore as points for identification with the control he sought; yet, since they were literally controlling, they could also be threatening intruders.

I. *Getting things out*
    1-b must reject food
    3-b if father falls out . . .
    4-b wants to challenge officer
    6-b compulsion to talk
    9-a protectively moving
      rock out of road

improves what is left behind.
1-b dieting, exercise
3-b L. wants to help his father

II. *Things coming in*

    1-a food given by Freud
    2-b command to climb
      mountain
    4-a orders
    7-a compulsion to listen and
      understand
    8-b compulsions to kill
      himself

catastrophically reverse what they
    enter

2-a jump off mountain

4-a beaten for not obeying
7-b repeatings that sound different

[Preventing things coming in]
    6-a compulsion to count
      between lightning and
      thunder
    7-b compulsion to put cap on
      his lady
[Testing things coming in]
    7-a compulsion to listen
      and understand
    9-b hostilely moving rock
      into road

III. *I*
    [Identification with father]

must *control* these reversing
    movements

    5-a His father would be upset
    (at L.'s failure to
    manage in army)
    5-b His father both pleased
      and affronted superiors.

2-b fell out, marching up
    mountain
3-a was confined to barracks
4-a not obeying orders
8-a vow not to commit suicide

The Structure of the Rat Man's Association, December 28, 1907

All these pairings involve a variety of polarities that, in turn, work out variations on the key terms of Lorenz's identity theme. By writing the several motifs of his analytic hour under the important words, one can trace the sequence of his free associations as a restless, cycling movement back and forth among the themes of his identity—as in the outline which lists, under his identity themes, the successive motifs of his associations for one analytic session (numbered sequentially, a and b indicating opposites within one motif).

Such a tracing of motifs by means of a person's identity theme lets me give coherence to a stream of thoughts that would otherwise seem quite arbitrary. One can see Lorenz's characteristic neurotic cycle, for example, in 4-a: orders are perceived as a threatening penetration, so he disobeys them, and lapses into his typical passivity, which can only be relieved if he can arrive at an outward movement. So he challenges the harsh officer (4-b).

In general, then, one can see the details of what Lorenz was telling Freud in relation to the whole of Lorenz and the whole man in relation to those details. This dialectic is one purpose of a theme-and-variations concept of identity.

To control the reversals in the self caused by things going out and coming in—that would be one possible statement of an identity theme which would interrelate the many details we know about Paul Lorenz. Similarly, *by giving myself, I show I am part of a world that magically gives me infinite supplies of talent and grace; but by not giving I show I can stand alone, even at the risk of being broken*—that would be a way of linking features of Scott Fitzgerald's writing like negative prefixes, incapable narrators, or magical but withholding women to features of his life like a fondness for booze or boxing.

Such themes are both like and unlike the type of unifying reconstruction Freud spoke of in describing a crucial scene from another patient's infancy:

> how, after a certain phase of the treatment, everything seemed to converge upon it, and how later, in the synthesis, the most variable and remarkable results radiated out from it; how not only the large problems but the smallest peculiarities in the history of the case were cleared up by this single assumption (1918b, 17:52).

Freud always thought the reconstruction of specific "historical" truths an essential part of psychoanalytic treatment. He meant, not an isolated interpretation, but a "construction" that would unify large chunks of the patient's experience. In the words of Michael Sherwood's study of psychoanalytic explanation, "What is needed is not simply a filling in of missing information, but rather an explanatory reorganization of the data into some meaningful whole" (1969, p. 170). If you look at the behavior of a person as unified around a central organizing principle, you can reorganize the data out of a merely chronological sequence into a hierarchy of greater and less generalization.

The two modes of thinking, reconstruction and holistic analysis, thus complement each other. As early as 1896 Freud recognized the unity implicit in his patients: "Giving an account of the resolution of a single symptom would in fact amount to the task of relating an entire case history" (3:197). Freud's most frequent way of abstracting analytic material into a unity (not only with patients but also in works like *Totem and Taboo* and *Moses and*

Monotheism) was to discover one or a few crucial events *in time* that laid down a prototype for later events. I am suggesting a complementary mode of abstraction: from many events at many times toward a single theme that makes all events, both early and late, characteristic, thus allowing us to see the change from early to late thematically, as the continuation—and changing—of themes.

Such themes will show in large patterns and in small details. Sherwood suggests that psychoanalytic explanation is based on a "psychoanalytic narrative," that is, "a general, over-all account of the patient's life history and 'life style,' the peculiar modes and patterns of behavior which mark that history," "a narrative about an individual patient within which isolated pieces of his behavior come to be understood, fitted together and organized into a comprehensible whole" (1969, p. 110). Such an explanation seems grounded in a model of mind as ongoing history or fiction—narrative, anyway.

The model of mind I have used in these studies of Paul Lorenz and Scott Fitzgerald is very close to that: mind considered as an aesthetic object like a literary work or a piece of music, and therefore open to an analysis of themes and patterns through the assumption of organic unity which has proved useful since Aristotle. The aesthetics of an I. In Aristotle as in our own phrase, "organic unity," the deepest level of the analogy links work of art to mind to the *zoon,* the unified and holistic animal that has evolved beneath them both.

I realize that my emphasis may seem to run counter to the "deconstructionist" movement now so influential in modern literary criticism. Deconstruction proceeds by looking for the ways a literary text fails or undermines the assumptions on which it is based. Deconstruction looks for—and proves—disunity.

I do not, however, see this procedure as flatly contradicting the regular method, looking for unity. After all, to look for disunity, one must presume a unity against which to see the "dis-." Similarly, applying a theme and variations strategy, one is constantly aware of thrusts away from the unity being sought or imposed. One could think of any given variation on an identity theme as either the construction of that theme or its deconstruction. A vaiation is, after all, both.

In short, to see either unity or disunity one must seek—*and one will find*—its opposite. The two methods, holistic and deconstructive, seem to me complementary rather than contradictory. In that sense, identity theory is deconstructive as well as holistic.

Identity theory extends the holistic analysis that psychoanalysis has used from the very first to a field larger than the single dream, lapse of memory, symptom, or psychoanalytic session—to a whole I. Personal identity in this theory has at least three senses: an agency, a consequence, and a representation. As an agency, "I" is the subject of Fitzgerald's "I drink," "I am a poor boy," "I am broken," or Lorenz's "I lost my glasses." The second, the consequence, is the I who results from drinking, lacking wealth, feeling broken, or losing one's glasses *and* the I who results from saying "I drink," "I am a poor boy," "I feel broken," or "I lost my glasses on a military halt." And finally, identity is *my* way of representing Fitzgerald's or Lorenz's I (or my own) as a theme and variations.

By this theme-and-variations strategy, you can relate something as precise as a writer's choice of prefixes to his alcoholism, his attitudes toward money, his political beliefs, his pervasive sense of loss, his relation to his wife, or his continually promising and not quite delivering. You can relate an obsessional neurotic's bizarre rituals and compulsions to his made-up words, his love affair with a cousin, or his wishing—and failing—to be a criminal lawyer. A concept of identity as a theme and variations lets us organize myriads of details—in principle, all—of behavior into coherence.

Such a concept leads to an aesthetic model of mind. Unlike some models in which one "answer" rules out another, this aesthetic structure admits different interpretations. Indeed, it requires them, for in claiming that Scott Fitzgerald saw the world through his identity theme, the theory must also claim that I see the world—and Scott Fitzgerald in it—through mine. My interpretations of Paul Lorenz or Scott Fitzgerald make up a part of my history; they must be variations on my identity theme.

Identity, then, is paradoxical because the identity of each of us comes from an act of understanding that itself depends on identity. This concept of identity puts not only psychoanalysis into a shared symbolic dialogue, but every other human intellectual activity—for they are all functions of someone's identity. This loosening of the old moorings to an "objective" reality is the real revolution Freud began.

To be sure, some interpretations of Fitzgerald or Lorenz will bring together the details of their personalities with more completeness and directness than others. Some interpretations will therefore be more sharable by other interpreters who require completeness and directness. Yet there is a wide range of interpretations that are acceptable and that other interpreters can share.

Hence this kind of analysis does not offer a "truth" of the kind that the natural sciences promise, but a truth of the kind that has developed naturally in the human sciences. We construe an event collectively. We arrive at a sharing of interpretations. In the world of psychiatry, that may imply no more than clinical conferences. In the world of ideas and values, however, interpretations through identity ask for the traditional "marketplace of ideas" and all the politics and ethics of intellectual freedom.

3 | Three Identities and an Identity Principle

By looking at Paul Lorenz and Scott Fitzgerald through a concept of identity, we have been able to see the small details of their daily lives as part of a total life-style. We humans are constantly doing something new, but doing it in the same style or manner in which we have done everything before it. We can think through that human mingling of sameness and change by means of a verbal theme and variations. We can think of the sameness as a style or identity theme. We can think of the newness as variations on, and away from, that theme.

Each of us constantly meets new realities, to which we bring a preexisting identity (the history of that theme and its variations—"history" being understood always as someone's tracing of same). Then, in a dialogue of self and other, we shape responses which are new in substance but familiar in style. Identity cumulates.

The question one naturally asks, then, is, How constant is that personal style? To what extent does a person's "identity theme" change? To what extent does it become more of the same?

The classic case in the development of identity theory is also the first, a patient of Heinz Lichtenstein's,

A Prostitute

Anna S. was twenty-three when she decided she could no longer tolerate the anxiety, depression, loneliness, and despair that, she felt, had driven her into an impossible life situation. She sought psychoanalysis with Lichtenstein to extricate herself from a self-destructive cycle of alcoholism, unsuccessful homosexual affairs, suicidal impulses, and prostitution (Lichtenstein 1961, pp. 209–30, 1977, pp. 79–99).

She would fall passionately in love with another woman. So long as she felt sure of her partner's love, she would live with her quite contentedly, as she said, like husband and wife, she being the wife. Eventually, she would become intensely possessive of her lover and begin to torment her with jealousy. Fearing she would be deserted, she would panic, become depressed, and start drinking. Finally, as she became more and more despairing and lonely, she would begin to prostitute herself, often ending with a "flight" into a brothel. Once there, she said, she would regain some degree of inner composure and start the cycle all over again.

She had very special attitudes toward her prostitution. She felt strongly that she was not "really" a prostitute, that her "real self" was not involved. She was very threatened by the idea of being loved as a woman by a man, particularly in sexual intercourse. "More exactly," Lichtenstein reports,

> prostitution was for Anna a defense against the experience of shame that overwhelmed her when a man tried to flirt with her, court her, or wanted to make love to her because he liked her. To escape this deeply disturbing sense of shame she went to extreme lengths to make the relationships with men as businesslike and matter of fact as possible. She had a set of rules that a man who wanted to have intercourse with her should follow. He should not use any names of endearment. She liked it best if the man came out quite straightforwardly with his desire to have sexual intercourse with her. He should neither pretend to be affectionate, nor should he be vulgar or brutal. If a man offered her a specified amount of money in exchange for her services, this made her much more comfortable.

In general, not only the money but thinking of something else while she was having sex, or rushing out as soon as the experience was over to perform some other task—these were ways she proved to the man and to herself that she "*really* did not participate in it."

By contrast, the person she regarded as her "real self" was proud to have educated herself by her reading (including ethical and religious works as well as the books on psychology which led her to seek psychoanalysis). Family circumstances, she felt, had deprived her of any chance for a formal education, but she nevertheless loved poetry, painting, concerts, and ballet performances (she had once wanted to be a dancer). Although she never denied "the facts," she thought of her prostitution as a social role imposed for some external reason and quite alien to the artistic, intellectual person who was trying to grow culturally and whom she regarded as her "real self." She hoped that treatment would resolve the contradiction and enable her to be what she "really was." It did.

Anna and Lichtenstein found a paradigm for her problem in her early relations with her mother, whom she passionately wooed. Above all, she wanted to be what her mother wanted her to be and to replace all the others in her mother's glamorous if chaotic, theatrical world. She plotted constantly against her stepfather, intensifying her mother's own fights with the man. Finally, after he left her mother, Anna falsified her age (fourteen) and worked "like a robot," selling Fuller brushes or laboring in factories, to have her mother to herself. In effect, she played husband to her mother's wife. Nevertheless, her mother began a love affair with a man, and Anna felt completely betrayed and defeated. She ran away and worked as a dancer in a gay bar, where she eventually began the disastrous and self-destructive cycles for which she sought Dr. Lichtenstein's help.

In his account, Lichtenstein shows how a therapist can use an identity theme to interrelate the different branches of the patient's life, even though the patient herself thought of them as quite separate. Lichtenstein suggests that Anna's identity theme could be "transcribed"—and by the metaphor he highlights the importance of words for the purpose—as "being another's essence." That is, Anna tried to become a sort of distilled extract of what she took to be permanent and unchangeable in another human being. In particular, because of the separations and chaos of Anna's childhood, "essence" had a great deal to do with food, drink, and other forms of motherly nurture.

Unfortunately, Anna's mother was the kind of woman of whom one might say, she is nothing without a man. For her, the "essence" or "life-giving food" was a man, and as a female child Anna could not possibly succeed in giving her mother what she wanted and needed. Not for lack of hoping and trying, however. As a girl, Anna wished for large feet and no breasts, to be big and strong, to be a dancer, that is, an ensemble of body members. But finally, no such effort to be a manlike member for her mother could take the place of her mother's actual men. Further, the mother wanted her daughter to be a decorative part of her own self, an addition without individuality, but not her "essential" part.

Thus, later, Anna never felt she was as "life-giving" or "essential" to her lesbian lovers as she needed to be to fulfill the terms of her identity theme. In effect, Anna was saying to her homosexual lovers, I can add to you what you need, but the lesbian women were usually saying, I have everything already. Thus, she could never feel close enough in the homosexual setting. As Lichtenstein says, "The fulfillment of her symbiotic identity theme was possible only in relationship to a man, because only a man could convey to her the experience of being his very 'essence.' "

The trouble for Anna with being in love with a man, however, was that by becoming his essence, she feared she would lose her own existence. As a life-giving essence, she imagined she would be devoured and so destroyed.

By becoming a prostitute, she reached a manageable compromise. She could fuse with a man, yet keep a margin of separateness. She could permit the man to treat her as an extension of himself, negating her separateness and proving his own masculinity. In that sense, she became his life-giving essence, but she was able to keep her "real self" safe. The business ritual made her a mere purchasable object, but this very isolation set limits to the complete loss of self she would otherwise have suffered in the sexual act.

Lichtenstein does not say much about the therapy as such, since he is more concerned in his essay with presenting a theory of identity. Nevertheless, the therapy was successful. Anna did give up the sorrows and disorders of her previous life to become an English teacher.

Anna used therapy to change the variations she was playing out on her identity theme, but she did not change the theme itself—and, so Lichtenstein would argue, *could* not. A person's identity theme (he would say) acquires the strength of a compulsion or drive, and to change it, one would have to die.

For example, during her troubled life from fifteen to twenty-three, Anna enjoyed what might be called Mad Lover fantasies, sometimes writing them down as prose poems. Her Mad Lover comes to make love to her, but, by doing so, he destroys her mind and body. This carrying of her identity theme to its ultimate, she fantasied as an ecstatic happiness. (With real men, it had threatened her with overwhelming shame.) As one might expect, Anna used imagery of food and drink in her prose poems to convey the idea of being both inseparable and the "essence" of her lover.

> Is that you beloved, is that you returning to Drown in my madness, to baptize me with the Sweetness of our foolishness? . . . Bless you, and drink with me my blood to quench our starved thirstiness.—*Farewell, loneliness* of Sanity, for madness has come to save my Soul . . . Embrace me oh madness, let my nakedness and nudity quench thy thirst for madness with love of a longing heart.

To be loved this way is to be eaten, drunk—wholly, madly, and ecstatically merged into the loved one. By contrast, to be separate is to be sane and desperately alone.

> Don't leave me, for with you I am not alone. Keep me safe in your oblivion, safe from the haunting night with its thousands eyes [sic] upon my naked soul—for the love I have for you, I need you, for when you leave I find my Self in a reality upon this God's hell on earth, to breathe only the contemptuousness of man's Sanity. Come back, come back, my Sweet love, don't turn me out, let me bathe my Soul in your torment, bleed my body of its blood for a Smooth Vintage of men's liquer. Let me drink to our holy madness, to our love of Solitude, Oh madness, I love you, come back to keep me free from Sanity.

After therapy, Anna had for the first time a love affair with a man. This is an excerpt from a letter she wrote about her new feelings:

> Never before have I felt peace of mind with anyone, warmth and feeling of wanting to do. I feel so much part of him that when he tells me

something that was unpleasant to him, no matter what . . . I hate the thing or person for it. I feel it displeased him and that makes it terrible. If he is very tired, fatigue takes hold of me, and I seem to share his feeling and usually end up relieving him of it. Does real loving make one feel a part of another? When he makes love to me I really feel that I'm way down deep inside of him, that his arms are my arms, etc. When he laughs, and he does not often, but he really does, I am filled with sheer glee. When he is sad I long to whitewash all that has caused him his miseries and I feel compassion so deep that I usually have indigestion. . . . I seem not only to suffer these days with my own grieves but his too if only it [sic] could lessen his, it would be worth it, but it does not.

She goes on to renounce the idea of women working ("How can I like work when all it ever did was make me feel like a boy?").

As a feminist, obviously I deplore such a renunciation or the merger of her own personality into her lover's. It is not for me to judge, however. What is desirable for Anna must finally be left to Anna. It was she who sought therapy and she who felt happier as a result. The point here is not the right or wrong of prostitution, lesbianism, or women working. The point is that the concept of an identity theme makes it possible to think about the sameness and difference in Anna as a result of her therapy. As for ethics, one can infer no more from this concept of identity than from the ancient Greek maxim: Find out who you are—then be that person.

After analysis, Anna began to live a radically new life, but she lived it in the same *style* as before. She was still "being the essence of another" when she was "way down deep inside" her lover, laughing or sad or angry as he was, with her "indigestion" a colicky echo of her earlier ecstatic eating and drinking. Yet now she could love. She could enjoy her life with a sense of freedom that she missed when she was lurching through her cycles of drink, despair, and departure. In this new life she continued to embody the identity theme which was, is, and (so Lichtenstein would claim) will always be the organizing principle of her being.

The case of Anna S. gives us the testimony of a psychoanalyst that even psychoanalysis did not change his patient's identity theme. Lichtenstein was able, to be sure, to help Anna to change her variations on that theme in a fundamental, pervading way. She was able to stop her painful, self-defeating, conflicted cycles and find other transformations equally in tune with her underlying theme but more satisfying. Psychoanalysis changed her behavior, but not her style. A psychoanalysis, according to Lichtenstein, changes the variations (perhaps in a completely pervasive way), but not the theme they are variations upon. Psychoanalysis can change the places you walk to but not the style of your stride.

Is what Lichtenstein says true? Are we all so determined? Or is he speaking only of people as troubled as Anna or the Rat Man? What about personal creativity and innovation without a therapist? Do they change the theme itself or only the variations and transformations of the theme? Suppose Scott Fitzgerald had been able to free himself enough to try for the novelistic heights. He might have been able to stop documenting the Jazz Age and move on to the nature of history (as in *War and Peace*) or guilt (as in *Crime and Punishment*). According to Lichtenstein's experience, however, he would still have used his negative prefixes, his incapable narrators, his balancing "a beautiful word with a barbed one"—in short, his *cachet spécifique*.

But isn't what we mean by creativity precisely the ability to change one's style? We would do well to judge the persistence of an identity theme by a writer, indeed, one of the most creative people of our century,

G. B. Shaw

He made radical changes in his life, both literary and political, and he was sufficiently, if carefully, frank about his life so that one can explore his style from infancy to the end of his extraordinarily long life.*

As another psychoanalytic student of Shaw, Daniel Dervin, describes it, his was "one of the most elusive, most unbelievably expansive, contradictory, and achieved lives of recent times," yet he finds "organic unity." He finds Shaw's character, as I do, "a unified personality with a center out of which it acted and created . . . [and] brought to life the variety of works we call Shavian" (pp. 333, 207).

My phrase for the Shavian-ness of that center is: trying either *to find or to be a purposeful and fulfilling opposite*. As you may have noticed with

* My account here of Shaw's identity is adapted from Holland (1978). I have relied most heavily on Stanley Weintraub, ed., *Shaw: An Autobiography Selected from his Writings*, 2 vols. (New York: Weybright and Talley, 1969–70), but also on Shaw's own *Sixteen Self Sketches* (London: Constable, 1949) and, of course, Dan H. Laurence, ed., *Collected Letters*, vol. I, 1874–1897 (New York: Dodd, Mead, 1965) and vol. II, 1898–1910 (New York: Dodd, Mead, 1972). In addition I refer to Hesketh Pearson, *Bernard Shaw, His Life and Personality* (London: Methuen, 1961).

Three psychoanalytic studies of Shaw are: Daniel Dervin, *Bernard Shaw: A Psychological Study* (Lewisburg, Pa.: Bucknell Univ. Press, 1975), David J. Gordon, *Literary Art and the Unconscious* (Baton Rouge: Louisiana State Univ. Press, 1976), and Arnold Silver, *Bernard Shaw: The Darker Side* (Stanford: Stanford Univ. Press, 1982). At the time I originally formulated this reading of Shaw, I had not read any of them, although I have since learned from all.

A particularly intriguing study of Shaw is Richard Ohmann's *Shaw: The Style and the Man* (Middletown, Conn.: Wesleyan Univ. Press, 1962). Ohmann reaches, on linguistic grounds, many of the psychological conclusions I shall advance.

I am grateful to Professor Norman Rosenblood of McMaster University and the Shaw Festival (Niagara-on-the-Lake, Ontario) for the opportunity of developing these ideas in the Shaw Seminars of 1975.

Fitzgerald and Lorenz, when trying to get at some person's identity theme, I put that theme in as few words as possible, even though I know that any phrasing, by its very verbality, will be inadequate, and perhaps a concise one more than most. Nevertheless, without a commitment to some such phrasing, there is no way to test or change one's reading.

Further, it is part of my own identity to need to unify a life as elegantly as possible. I want a theme that will relate, key word by key word, to the details of the life. *To find or to be a purposeful and fulfilling opposite*—that phrasing brings together for me a series of terms, each of which I can use to encompass a cluster of Shaw's traits.

To find or to be: sometimes Shaw sought an outer force to put his trust in—it could be anything from Joe Stalin to osteopathy—and sometimes he became that purposeful force himself as when he tried to persuade people by his writing and speaking. By *purposeful* I mean a mentally directed—willed—opposite: the way Shaw always tried to impose his own will on the raw, bodily material of life. I mean the contrary of what Shaw attacked as the lies and unrealities of the bourgeoisie or the average theatergoer of his day. In *fulfilling* I include not only mental fulfillment but also Shaw's deep concern with physical well-being, quite literally how he and others would be filled with food and drink and warmth—and, of course, ideas. By *opposite* I intend any other person or force, really, lovers as well as enemies, but always seen through Shaw's eye for change and reversals. Again, he might be the opposite himself, or he might seek an opposite in some outer force.

Given a myth or "identity theme" like this, I can say how Shaw made the great, fertilizing ideas of his day (and, indeed, our own) functions of his personality. For example, he rejected the evolutionary principle of natural selection because it was (he said) a "fatalism" leading only to chance and randomness. He insisted instead on the Lamarckian idea that acquired characteristics can be inherited (which had no more scientific backing then than now) and on what he came to call Creative Evolution. Biology, to suit Shaw, had to have a purpose and direction, the improvement of the human species. Similarly he regarded Marxist communism not as the inevitability of "economic determinism" but rather as something to be arrived at Fabianly, constitutionally—in short, by purposeful choice. Freud he rejected out of hand as a "morbidity." "I did not believe," wrote Shaw, "that an author so utterly devoid of delicacy as Sigmund Freud could not only come into human existence, but become as famous and even instructive by his defect as a blind man might by writing essays on painting."

The pattern I see is that Shaw rejects "blind" determinisms in favor of a fulfilling purpose. Thus, he spoke of "the horror of [Darwinism's] banishment of mind from the universe." He substituted Creative Evolution, which Shaw often imaged as feminine, a muse-matriarch who would lead us to greater knowledge, understanding, and power over ourselves and our circumstances. Shaw was so opposed to determinisms that he scarcely even accepted death as reality. He did not deal with death in his plays until he answered William Archer's challenge to do so with *The Doctor's Dilemma* in 1906; even in that play, death has surely lost its sting.

To find or to be a purposeful and fulfilling opposite: if this identity theme truly enables us to say the consistency in what Shaw did and thought, then we should be able to see a rationale not only behind Shaw's intellectual style but also the strangest aspect of the man, his sex life, notably his much-vexed virginity, much vexed by biographers, anyway. "I lived a continent virgin," he tells us, "but an incorrigible philanderer, until I was 29, running away when the handkerchief was thrown to me; for I wanted to love, but not to be appropriated and lose my boundless . . . liberty." Then, at the age of forty-three he entered on a marriage marked, so he reports, neither by sexual intercourse nor infidelity. Shaw's only period of sexual activity, then, according to Shaw, was the fourteen years from twenty-nine to forty-three. In that time, he tells us, "there was always some lady in the case; and I tried all the experiments and learned what was to be learnt from them." (I find Shaw's phrasing quite clinical; Hesketh Pearson notes "a strain of fastidiousness in him.")

Shaw, says Pearson, told Cecil Chesterton that he found the sexual act "monstrous and indecent," and he "could not understand how any self-respecting man and woman could face each other in the daylight after spending the night together." In the opening play of *Back to Methuselah*, Shaw had Eve finish the first act with an expression of repugnance at the serpent's revealing the secret of sexual activity, and (according to Pearson) Shaw explained her expression to St. John Ervine as her reaction to God's incredible "combination of the reproductive with the excretory organs, and consequently of love with shame." When Shaw himself designed men and women, in the final play of the pentalogy, he had them not excrete at all, come from eggs rather than childbirth, and leave sex to the young and unthinking.

In this fastidiousness, I think, Shaw is expressing a fear of being enclosed or trapped by his lover. He is saying, "I will keep that sexual opposite truly an opposite—separate, away from me—unless I can give myself to it or her as part of my purpose, unless I can be a fulfiller, too." Thus Shaw did not prize sexuality as an end in its physical self. "I liked sexual intercourse," he wrote Frank Harris,

> because of its amazing power of producing a celestial flood of emotion and exaltation of existence which, however momentary, gave me a sample of what may one day be the normal state of being for mankind in

intellectual ecstasy. I always gave the wildest expression to this in a torrent of words, partly because I felt it due to the woman to know what I felt in her arms, and partly because I wanted her to share it.

As for physical, not mental ejaculation, he was almost contemptuous, complaining of his first mistress's "silly triumph with which she takes, with the air of a conqueror, that which I have torn out of my own entrails for her." His language treats ejaculation as a defeat or a mutilation of his body, the sort of thing lack of mental purpose leads to.

Shaw explicitly placed the importance of sexuality, of everything really, in its enabling him to enter into a larger, controlling force: "It is only when I am being used that I can feel my own existence, enjoy my own life. All my love affairs end tragically because the woman *can't* use me. . . . Everything real in life is based on *need*." As he said in the preface to *Man and Superman*,

> This is the true joy in life, the being used for a purpose recognized by yourself as a mighty one; the being thoroughly worn out before you are thrown on the scrap heap; the being a force of Nature instead of a feverish selfish little clod of ailments. . . . And also the only real tragedy in life is the being used by personally minded men for purposes which you recognize to be base.

I hear in that eloquent statement of the joy of being used the other side of Shaw's attitude toward sex, "I wanted to love, but not to be appropriated and lose my boundless . . . liberty." Two sides of the same coin. The danger is being incorporated into some larger, needing, hungry being. The defense is purpose, a guarantee of one's own mental existence. Together they seem an unchanging inner core against which I can read every phase of Shaw's life from the most public to the most personal.

Because Shaw could talk so freely about himself and his childhood, he lets us imagine how such a personal core might start. He tells us that he saw in his family's snobbish pretensions (which they had not a fraction of the money they needed to keep up) the same kind of anticlimax that he liked in his own writing. He traced it to his father's inability to resist capping a serious lecture to his son with a final, deflating joke. Yet George Carr Shaw represented in life a more painful kind of anticlimax: a devout teetotaler, he was at the same time a confirmed drunkard who could not even enjoy his own drinking because of his insistence that he be a teetotaler. "It had to be either a family tragedy or a family joke," Shaw wrote. "If you cannot get rid of the family skeleton, you may as well make it dance." Shaw's father was weakened in still another way, by the presence of the voice teacher G. J. Vandaleur Lee, who took up residence in the house. From him, Shaw says he learned "the scepticism as to academic authority which still persists in me."

Erik Erikson has written a brief study of Shaw in which he treats Shaw's relation to his father as crucial. I think it certainly was, but I also think that the shape of that relationship—the way Shaw perceived these two men in his family—was set even earlier, in Shaw's relation to his mother. Or non-relation, really, since she very largely left him to servants, who fed and otherwise treated him poorly.

From her, I think Shaw learned that he could not rely on ineffectual, anticlimactic others—opposites. He himself had to create himself. Late in life he said in a playful way that his mother was "the worst in the world," "the worst mother conceivable . . . within the limits of the fact that she was incapable of unkindness." "When her death set me thinking curiously about our relations, I realized that I knew very little about her." Other of Shaw's remarks suggest that his mother's indifference passed beyond mere "domestic anarchy" and into real aggression:

> Everybody had disappointed her, or betrayed her, or tyrannized over her . . . but as she never revenged, she also never forgave. . . . If at last you drove her to break with you, the breach was permanent: you did not get her back again. . . . From my mother I learned that the wrath on which the sun goes down is negligible compared to the clear vision and criticism that is neither created by anger nor ended with it.
>
> Under all the circumstances it says a great deal for my mother's humanity that she did not hate her children. She did not hate anybody, nor love anybody.

Lucinda Gurley Shaw must have been Shaw's first great disappointment, the prototype for his later sense of his father as an anticlimax and his persistent efforts in the face of such indifference to create his own nurturing world.

Another trait in Shaw leads me to think that the style of his early relation with his mother persisted throughout his adulthood. All of us first meet life in terms of body activities like eating, handling, standing, walking, talking, and seeing. It seems to me that Shaw's dominant body mode was the very first way we take in the world, especially as it is represented in the persons of our mothers: eating. Years later, he would have Jack Tanner proclaim in *Man and Superman:* "There is no love sincerer than the love of food," and suggest to the lover Tavy, "Your head is in the lioness' mouth: you are half swallowed already," only to find that he (Tanner) himself is "the bee, the spider, the marked down victim, the destined prey" for Ann the "boa constrictor." This, however, his Don Juan says, is what ought to happen: "Life seized me and threw me into [the lady's] arms as a sailor throws a scrap of fish into the mouth of a seabird." Again, that fantasy of being swallowed, contained, or enclosed.

Shaw was a lifelong teetotaler, a nonsmoker, and a vegetarian. He was a man much concerned with his mouth, but less with taking in (like the usual baby or adult), more with keeping things out of it. For example, he defined meat-eating as "eating the scorched corpses of animals—cannibalism with its heroic dish omitted." This was a man who never shaved and who, in the privacy of his home, every night before he went to bed, heard only by his mother or his wife or those who cared for him, sang. Opera, folksong, *lieder*—he used anything at all for his cantatory constitutional. This was a man who first made headway in the world as a compulsive orator of truly astonishing power. At the end, his cook Alice Laden reports (in her salutary collection of vegetarian recipes), he would dawdle over breakfast for two and a half hours and lunch for another two and a half. He was constantly nibbling on mango, chutney, marzipan, and thickly iced cakes. All of this suggests to me a man whose life-style—from beginning to end—might well be a response to an absent mother and an empty mouth.

Focusing down to just Shaw's mouth uses identity like the earliest psycho-analytic characterology, looking backward into infantile body modes. I can also use the concept of identity, however, to trace Shaw's development upward and outward from that baby, who seems never to have been an *infans*, unspeaking and helplessly dependent, to the hardworking but unsuccessful novelist, the overpowering Fabian speaker, the sparkling music and drama critic, and finally the magnificently quirky dramatist. Through all those changes, I can phrase a persistent style—an identity theme.

Shaw's childhood may have had peculiar deprivations, but from them Shaw must have built some extraordinary strengths. As I read him, he responded to hunger and perhaps a fear about things coming into his mouth by deciding to make things go out of his mouth. His father's early letters describe him as another noisemaker in that family of noisemakers. Instead of being the usual dependent child, he became a do-it-yourselfer. He would himself create the nurturing mother and stable father his family did not provide. His mother's "almost complete neglect," he wrote, "had the advantage that I could idolize her to the utmost pitch of my imagination and had no sordid or disillusioning contacts with her." It seems to me, too, that this necessity of creating and even being his own mother, father, sustenance, and world is the source of Shaw's boundless imagination and idealism. This is the bodily root for a mind that could imagine other people, places, and even universes.

The child, however, must also have felt loss and anger at the absence of those nurturing persons. As Shaw himself wrote, "The fact that nobody cared for me particularly gave me a frightful self-sufficiency, or rather a power of starving on imaginary feasts, that . . . leaves me to this hour a treacherous brute in matters of pure affection." Why "frightful"? Why "treacherous"? Perhaps because of the fearful knowledge that what his parents were was not what they purported to be, that *whatever* is, is not as it ought to be (including, perhaps, Shaw himself). Such a belief would provide an emotional base both for his ambition (to be something other) and his intellectual fury at all cant, humbug, illusion—or looked at another way, all his own futile wishes that things *would* be as they purport to be, that his mother would be a mother, his father a father, and the singing teacher only a singing teacher. Out of the early disillusionment perhaps, came that strange combination of idealism and realism that reveals Shaw as a disappointed romantic.

I am getting ahead of my story. Think back to the neglected child and to the identity you might form from a sense that the world was not as it ought to be. Try to feel the child's sense of loss and his resolution to do or be that world himself, a fierce sense of opposition which took the bodily form of putting things out of his mouth instead of taking them in. All this could have been the first body version of the distinctively Shavian style of the later life. Sensing it, we can unshrink Shaw. We can unfold that inferred identity theme as Shaw transforms himself into the adult genius.

"I must have been born able to read," Shaw remembered, "or else I acquired the power along with my first set of teeth." "I have no more recollection of my first book than of my first meal." He recalled a novel that greatly influenced him as a child: "The hero was a very romantic hero, trying to live bravely, chivalrously and powerfully by dint of mere romance—fed imagination, without courage, without means, without knowledge, without skill, without anything real except his bodily appetites." From his reading, Shaw imagined a fictional world that would compensate for his dissatisfaction with his family reality, a world in which he was all-powerful and victorious, supreme in war and irresistible in love, completely alone without friends or relations, a foundling superman. "In the world of reality," writes Hesketh Pearson, "he was excessively sensitive, diffident, and shy, quickly reduced to tears and wretchedly timid." But not in fiction, and his preference for fiction over fact persisted all his life. "You may read [an almanac like] the Annual Register from end to end," he told Pearson, "and be no wiser. But read *Pilgrims Progress* and *Gulliver's Travels* and you will know as much human history as you need, if not more." He could have said, as someone else might, *Madame Bovary* or *War and Peace* or even the Bible, but that would not be Shaw. Shaw picks two works about solitary, adventuring, and largely autonomous heroes.

The same do-it-yourself spirit governed his education. By rejecting the Church, the classics, arithmetic, the values of his family and class, and even death (so ridiculed in the galloping funerals his family practiced), he set himself free to create himself. "I hated school, and learnt there nothing of what it professed to teach." In the same way, he taught himself the piano, rejecting the conventional texts and exercises. "All the work of educating, disciplining and forming myself, which should have been done for me as a child I had to do for myself as an adult." Not least of that work, in a characteristic phrasing, was "purging us thoroughly of the ignorant and vicious superstitions which were thrust down our throats in our helpless childhood."

The young Shaw was a thoroughly disagreeable young man by all accounts, especially his own, precisely because of this fierce spirit of opposition for the sake of independence. "Never spare the feelings of touchy people," he told Pearson. "Hit them bang on the nose, and let them hit back. Then they can't quarrel with you." (As though that were not a quarrel!) Surely a remarkable audacity in someone as inwardly timid as Shaw. Yet he did not show the timidity—just the opposite in his search for opposites. "I had . . . an unpleasant trick of contradicting everyone from whom I thought I could learn anything in order to draw him out and enable me to pick his brains."

Yet this fierce opposition so as to feed on his elders, so displeasing in the brash young Irishman newly arrived in London, was to become one of the great English prose styles. "It is always necessary," he wrote in *Everybody's Political What's What,* "to overstate a case startlingly to make people sit up and listen to it, and to frighten them into acting on it." Or as Rodin slyly said, "Mr. Shaw does not speak French well, but he expresses himself with such violence that he imposes himself." It was not mere "paradox," said Shaw in the preface to *Man and Superman.* Rather, "I take hold of a stick by the right instead of the wrong end." The better to beat us with. It was this violent casting of himself as the opponent that gave him the tone for his outrageously perverse criticism of music and drama, even in such minute details as his idea that we should say not "my catching the influenza" but "the influenza catching me."

Shaw's need to find an opposite made his discovery of Marx no merely intellectual event, but, in his own words, a "conversion." He became, he said, a "speaker with a gospel." He "sermonized." This man who based his own motives in his physical needs found a theory that said the whole world ran by need. Shaw now could say that economics played the same role in his characters as anatomy in the figures of Michelangelo.

Marx promised the fulfillment of still another deep wish of Shaw's, the need to feel that whatever is, is not as it purports to be. In particular, said Shaw, "Marx convinced me that what the [Socialist] movement needed was . . . an unveiling of the official facts of Capitalist civilization." "I had no . . . difficulty . . . understanding that private property produces a government of 'damned thieves,' who cannot help themselves, and must, willy nilly, live by robbing the poor."

At the same time, the theory being a theory and therefore bigger than any one person, it could serve Shaw as the idealized, all-powerful, all-giving parent he never had. Further, because it was a theory that embraced not only contemporary politics and economics but all of human history, it offered Shaw the sense of purpose he so deeply needed. Even more, it was a theory of opposition, set out in the dialectic of thesis, antithesis, and synthesis. Hence it could provide a structure for any play he wanted to write or even any one sentence. Some well-made cliché would provide the thesis, Shaw would turn it inside out into an amusing antithesis, and finally he would resolve the conflict into a not quite so revolutionary finale—the synthesis.

Yet since Marxism was a determinism, Shaw had to oppose it. "My mind does not work in Hegelian grooves," he insisted, and he revised orthodox Marxism away from its revolutionary stance into its milder, Fabian, constitutional, and less inevitable form. Thus Shaw limited Marx's determinism, insisting in his later years that experience had required Joseph Stalin himself to become a Fabian!

Shaw's Marxist conversion led him in turn to Sidney Webb and a great friendship, perhaps because he felt it so precisely filled his need for an opposite. "Each of us was the other's complement," Shaw told Pearson.

> He knew everything that I didn't know; and I knew everything he didn't know, which was precious little. He was competent: I was incompetent. He was English: I was Irish. He was politically and administratively experienced: I was a novice. He was extraordinarily able and respectable: I was a futile Bohemian. He was at all points the very collaborator I needed; and I just grabbed him.

"From that time I was not merely a futile Shaw but a committee of Webb and Shaw."

Webb, Marx, and the Fabians all contributed in turn to Shaw's astonishing career as a political orator from 1879 to 1898. At first he was, in his own words, "an arrant coward, nervous and self-conscious to a heartbreaking degree," but once he had made his maiden speech he became irrepressible. "I spoke in the streets, in the parks, at demonstrations, anywhere and everywhere possible. In short, I infested public meetings like an officer afflicted with cowardice, who takes every opportunity of going under fire to get over it and learn his business." The energy he poured into this battle suggests how precisely it matched his inner need to become the purposeful opposite, "to make people sit up and listen to [the case], and to frighten them into acting on it." While he was the purposeful opposite to his audiences, he had his own purposeful opposite in Webb: "I was often in the center of the stage whilst he was invisible in the prompter's box."

Looked at as a child, Shaw was gratifying his deepest needs in their most primitive mode—he was putting something out of his mouth. Looked at as an adult, Shaw was shaping a part of his later dramatic triumph, the overwhelming, operatic style of the Shavian hero. He was to become the only playwright in English to achieve the Corneillian and Racinian *tirades* of French drama, and he learned how to do it by talking to provincial Sunday Societies and the crowds of Hyde Park.

As the great playwright at sixty-five looked back to the young writer at work on his first novel, he described that

> deeper strangeness which has made me all my life a sojourner on this planet rather than a native of it. Whether it be that I was born mad or a little too sane, my kingdom was not of this world: I was at home only in the realm of my imagination, and at my ease only with the mighty dead. Therefore I had to become an actor, and create for myself a fantastic personality fit and apt for dealing with men, and adaptable to the various parts I had to play as author, journalist, orator, politician, committee man, man of the world, and so forth.

> At the time of which I am writing, however (1879), I had not yet learnt to act, nor come to understand that my natural character was impossible on the great stage of London. When I had to come out of the realm of imagination into that of actuality I was still uncomfortable.

At some time during the eighties, however, "My imposture was at last accomplished, and I daily pulled the threads of the puppet who represented me in the public press. . . . Applause . . . greeted it."

That passage seems to me extraordinarily rich in the identity of both the young and old Shaw or, indeed, all the Shaws. I can hear in it the child retreating from the indifference of his actual world into the idealized realm of the imagination, "not of this world," where he could be king or messiah. In the phrase, "I was at . . . ease only with the mighty dead," I sense that the great unresolved relation for this man is that between parent and child; I think of a playwright who would dramatize that relation almost to the exclusion of all others. I hear, too, the frank lack of emotion in a man who is at home only with fantasies, puppets, disguises, and applause. I can understand in it Shaw's discomfort with others who have not had to transform themselves as he has, his profound distrust of people-as-they-are, hence his dislike of pure democracy, and his feeling that human nature itself had to be changed before people could govern themselves on this planet. In that need to tranform oneself, I find the solution to Shaw's odd admiration for abstract Creative Evolution and the ugly realities of self-styled supermen like Stalin, Hitler, and Mussolini.

Above all, I hear in the dramatic metaphors of this passage the man who finally found that the theater was the natural expression for his own personal myth, his identity. He had to become an actor. He had to make himself into a puppet in order to be controlled and fulfilled by others, but he also had to become that purposeful, fulfilling opposite himself and control the puppet and the actor. In short, he had to become a playwright.

Yet, being Shaw, he would define his new art into its opposite. Drama, he said, is "an art which is nothing more than the most vivid and real of all ways of story-telling." Hence his novelistic stage directions. His own vocation for the theater, he said, "was to give to tragedy itself the tactics of comedy." Hence, when he came to write plays, Shaw virtually created a form of drama to express his own identity: the vocal, perverse, emotionless extravaganza whose dominant theme is the rejection of parents by children or children by parents which we call "Shavian."

Like all of us, Shaw did to others what he did to himself. He made others into puppets to act his plays, spending long hours coaching his actors down to the last details of their performances. Then, in a larger sense, he decided that he and all of us were ourselves puppets in the hands of the Life Force. "The true job of life [is] being used for a purpose." Hence he gave us, his audiences, his kind of joy by making us into his puppets, too. "What I say to-day, everybody will say to-morrow, though they will not remember who put it into their heads. Indeed, they will be right; for *I* never remember who puts the things into *my* head: it is the Zeitgeist."

Thus Shaw was living out a kind of proportion in which his actors and his audiences played the puppets to his puppetmaster; but he in turn was the puppet to the Zeitgeist, socialism, Creative Evolution, life force, or whatever. He found a purposeful opposite in those larger forces. Then, in the theater, he cast himself as a purposeful and fulfilling opposite to us.

In effect, Shaw all his life was trying to free and not free himself from an overwhelming but emotionless parent. He both submitted to and became that figure, and in doing so, he achieved his own unique style of playwriting. He turned the conventional plots and wisdom of his day inside out, giving his characters arias of paradox and inversion. By his prefaces, he imposed his mind on the physical events of the drama, turning his plays into social pamphlets. He revealed painful realities—and denied them as well. Where other dramatists submerged their personalities in their characters', he exhibited himself throughout his plays, as if he had to insist, "I am still here." Indeed, he lived ninety-four years, as if to insist again and again, "I am still here." And we still listen to him. For all his dated themes and quirky plots, we are still giving him that life-giving attention, that immortality, his mother denied him.

Shaw was one of the most creative individuals our century has known. If anyone is capable of complete and radical self-transformation, surely he—with his energetic, self-creating style—was. He *did* greatly transform himself, politically, literarily, and sexually. His life is marked by radical conversions like his discoveries of Marxism and Sidney Webb and drama. He reached out to the world for people and ideas that he could convert to his own uses in his forceful, antagonistic way, and these "clicked." Yet from the conversions themselves I can phrase a Shavian style just as much as in, say, his schooling or his childhood. From infancy to death I can trace a Shaw-ness.

Through all the radical changes I can see a Shavian identity theme evolve new variations. Similarly, Anna S. radically transformed her life through psychoanalysis, yet I can trace a continuing personal style from before her therapy to after. Consider, however, a still more dramatic "therapy"—brainwashing. Consider the case of

Dr. Charles Vincent

the pseudonym of one of the victims studied by Robert J. Lifton in his engrossing researches into Chinese "thought reform" (1961, pp. 31–52, 109–19, and 234). Vincent, says Lifton, was a short, muscular, dark-complexioned Frenchman in his early fifties. He had practiced medicine for twenty years in China before being arrested after the Communists won the civil war in 1949. Lifton met him in Hong Kong after he had "confessed" and been released.

There, he described his life before his arrest. He had preferred to keep his distance from his children, and he said his wife was a " 'a very nice woman' because 'she never gave me any trouble and always respected my freedom.' " His career was of utmost importance to him. "To be a doctor—I liked it by instinct." After a troubled adolescence, he "embarked on the study of medicine, with a passion for his subject which almost totally consumed his intellect and his emotions. He worked night and day, . . . devoted all his spare time to extra work in clinics, and he graduated at the top of his class at the age of twenty-six."

After this brilliant career in medical school, however, he turned his back on Europe and sought work in China. "He was excited by the challenge of the difficulties, and by the absence of hospitals, physicians, and even rudimentary sanitary conditions. This opportunity for lonely accomplishment and exaggerated autonomy was probably the strongest attraction for him," concludes Lifton, and Dr. Vincent himself said:

> In my training I always liked to do things for myself, to do what is necessary. For a doctor to be master of himself is what the patient needs. . . . I took to China my microscope, all of my books and equipment, and a small microtome so I could do everything for myself and be completely independent.

Once in China, he worked with other doctors only at the beginning: " 'The competition started so I left.' " Outside his practice, he avoided personal relationships: " 'If I have a friend I have to invite him, and I don't like to be a slave to convenience.' " He developed solitary occupations like writing, painting, and hunting, and after World War II, he moved himself and his practice into the country (always placing his clinics near hunting areas):

> I lost myself completely living this kind of life. In the early morning and in the evening I would fish and hunt. I would work all day, sometimes travelling three hours to get to a patient, sometimes sleeping at his home. . . . There was no other doctor, and I was giving life to plenty of patients. . . . It was a necessity to see life in contact with poor people and with nature in order to have emotions—emotions which I can translate into writing and painting. . . . There was no man as happy as I.

Lifton does not use Lichtenstein's term "identity theme" to describe Vincent, but he does speak of "three convictions which he had been seeking to prove to himself almost from the day of his birth: *I need no one. No one can have my insides. I transcend other mortals.*" As Lifton sees him, Charles Vincent had to be "always on guard against his own inner urges in the opposite direction: his tendencies to seek intimacy, work cooperatively, and rely upon other people. These social and cooperative urges were, ironically enough, his negative identity"—a term from Erikson.

To arrive at a single identity theme, I can combine Dr. Vincent's positive and negative tendencies by thinking in polarities: needing or not needing; being above or below others; giving or not giving (but being given) insides. I can shape these polarities into one theme: *to need is to be below and to give up one's insides.* Two major variations on this theme would constitute the positive and negative poles for Dr. Vincent. If *I* need, then *I* am below others, giving up my body to them. Dr. Vincent's avoidance of this feared (but unconsciously deeply desired) outcome, led to what Lifton calls his "exaggerated sense of individual mastery." Conversely, if *they* need me, then *they* are below me, giving up their bodies to me. This variation suggests Dr. Vincent's career as a lonely doctor, working in isolated areas where no one else could compete with him, "giving life to plenty of patients." Both variations include what Dr. Lifton found "most remarkable," "his need to experience—and to manipulate—all thought, feelings, and actions through the medium of his own body."

Notice, by the way, how this description of a man through a theme and variations or polarities contrasts to conventional psychiatric categories: "prominent schizoid and paranoid character trends." Lifton tries these and concludes that they do not adequately express Dr. Vincent's successful adaptation as a "mystical healer," "lonely adventurer," "an isolated seeker of high aesthetic values," "a magical manipulator who could master his environment only through maintaining his distance from other people." From my point of view, the early and late characterologies, diagnostics as contrasted to identity (see pp. 160–64), differ in the degree to which I can use them to interrelate Dr. Vincent's choices in the various parts of his life, particularly as he describes them in his own (chosen) words. By means of an identity theme like *to need is to be below and to give up one's insides,* I can understand the way he used fishing or hunting or indeed the doctor–patient relationship itself to act out a pattern: the patient (or prey?) gives his body to Dr. Vincent, and the doctor gives something "higher," art or medicine or knowhow.

He played out a darker variation in an incident that preceded his going to medical school. At the age of nineteen, he fell in love with a fourteen-year-old girl. " 'She must fall in love with me,' " he decided, but he never even spoke of his feelings to her. "Instead, he studied an anatomy book to find out where on his body he could shoot himself without causing permanent damage, [sent the girl a one-sentence note,] took his father's pistol, and put a bullet through his shoulder. In telling me this," Lifton notes, "he showed me his scar" ("he" being the brainwashed Vincent).

> I realized I was foolish, but I had to go through my experience . . . I was sure that in this way she would have to have love for me. . . . I never had a thought to touch the girl—to let her know I was interested in her. But only through myself, you see, I did it. I am the master of myself, and do what I want to myself.

Lifton interprets his act as expressing "the conflict between his asocial style of remaining the 'master' of his own 'insides,' " and a sudden feeling of needing intimacy and love from another person, a conflict which his vocational decision to become a doctor then enabled him to master. Medicine provided a "solution to his identity crisis."

Before the episode with the girl, he had systematically isolated himself in school. " 'I was not interested in people around me, you understand—just looking only my way—just wanting to be out because I thought that way I could be more independent—to put a distance between persons who might still influence my goings on." "Vincent," says Lifton, "(with a certain pride) remembers school authorities complaining to his father: 'Your son has been here for four years and we don't even know him.' "

Even earlier, Charles tended to cut himself off from the people around him, notably his father. Lifton quotes him:

> My father looked at me as a wild child. . . . He was telling me all the time I didn't have any relationship with him. . . . We were in the same house but not in fusion. . . . He didn't succeed to have my inside.

"Charles," continues Lifton, "sought always to escape the confinement of his house: 'I didn't like to sleep in a bed. I wanted to sleep in a tree.' He remembers his father, on one occasion, chaining him to the house, but to no avail: 'I succeeded in escaping and I was happy.' "

In short, Lifton gives us a picture of a man with an unusually rigid adaptation to reality. I can phrase variations on his identity theme through his childhood, schooling, adolescent love, married life, parenthood, vocation, and avocations, but the variations get narrower and narrower. They do not branch the way Shaw's did, into different relationships, many-sided political activity, and novel literary creations. Rather, Dr. Vincent's variations on his theme seem to get more and more extreme, like a plant with one constantly lengthening stem, his medical career, and a few leaves clustered at the top. Yet, under brainwashing even he changed.

After his arrest, Vincent was placed in an 8×12 cell with eight other prisoners. The first night, he was interrogated in another small room for ten successive hours until 6:00 A.M. At the end of this first session he was chained hand and foot for his uncooperativeness and returned to his cell-mates. All day they spent in a "struggle" with him, continuously telling him to confess his guilt. He received little help from them despite his chains, for he was "too reactionary." He ate as a dog does. They had to open his trousers and clean him up after he went to the toilet, a tin can. By the end of the second day, Vincent was concerned only with getting some relief. " 'You start to think, how to get rid of these chains. *You must get rid of the chains.*' " At that night's interrogation, he made a "wild confession"—which was rejected. By the third night he had begun "building a confession." Nevertheless, the routine of all-night interrogation followed by all-day "struggle" continued uninterrupted for eight more days and nights. Finally he ceased all resistance:

> You are annihilated . . . exhausted . . . you can't control yourself, or remember what you said two minutes before. You feel that all is lost. . . . From that moment, the judge is the real master of you. You accept anything he says. When he asks how many 'intelligences' you gave to that person, you must put out a number in order to satisfy him. If he

says, 'Only those?,' you say, 'No, there are more.' . . . You do whatever they want. You don't pay any more attention to your life or to your
handcuffed arms.

Thus he completely surrendered himself, losing control. This fiercely autonomous man was putting out what others wanted.

Vincent began to construct an elaborate confession, but it was not until
two months later that the chains were removed (and, even then, they would
be reapplied for periods of two to three days if he showed "resistance"). At
the same time, he entered actively into his cell's organized reeducation
procedures of discussion and study, ten to sixteen hours a day of applying the
"people's point of view" to every detail of cell routine, past life, or world
events. After a year of this, the interrogations resumed, in order to build his
confession further. Then he went through fourteen months of full-time
"reeducation." After three and a half years, he signed his completed confession and was expelled from China to Hong Kong, where Lifton met him five
days after his release.

Lifton got the impression that by the end of his imprisonment Vincent had
integrated "his new identity configuration." He had brought the Communist
version of "the people" into his mysticism. He had begun "helping" his
cellmates in the role of "the teaching physician." "For he was a man no less
vulnerable to human influence than others; behind his lifelong avoidance of
people was both a fear of and a desire for such influence."

> When Dr. Vincent was imprisoned . . . everything was suddenly over-
> turned: the manipulator was now being manipulated, the healer was
> considered "ill" and in need of "treatment," the aesthetic wanderer
> was thrown into a crowded dingy cell, the isolate was forced to lay
> himself bare before strangers. . . . Under these circumstances, his
> personal myth of absolute independence and superhuman self-mastery
> was exploded. He had no choice but to become emotionally engaged in
> a human society, perhaps for the first time in his life. This reversal of
> such a basic identity pattern was a mark of thought reform's power. . . .

From Lifton's point of view, the external forces of brainwashing had
changed Vincent's identity. As Dr. Lifton points out, however, thought
reform was able to build on something already there in Vincent. The
reversal "was achieved only through the reformers' success in bringing out
Vincent's long-buried strivings toward human involvement, strivings which
he had until then successfully denied." Lifton describes these strivings as his
"negative identity."

In my vocabulary, his "identity theme" remained unchanged, but to cope
with thought reform he had had to work out a radically new variation on it.

To need is to be below and to give up one's insides. The thought reformers forced Vincent to pay the price of being the lowest and most self-exposed prisoner in the cell. Once the price was paid and, however painful, tolerated, he could accept the need to yield himself. What before had been conscious anathema but unconscious desire, now became not only possible to consciousness but compulsively sought. What before he had sought now became anathema.

Later in his ordeal, he was able to adapt by re-creating his old way of being above and getting out the insides of others, because his final role in prison was that of teaching physician. Yet he could even then need others in a new way.

When Lifton first met him in Hong Kong, he thought Vincent after release "was closer to psychosis . . . than he had been during the worst assaults of imprisonment," because he now found himself without the controls and support of the thought reformers that made the new variation on his identity possible while he could not practice the older adaptation at all.

When I am doing something I feel someone is looking at me—because from external manifestation he is anxious to look at what is going on inside of me. We were trained this way in our re-education.

I had dinner last night at the home of Mr. Su [a wealthy, retired Hong Kong Chinese merchant]. I had the feeling that Mr. Su was a pro-Communist. I had this manifestation. Everytime he spoke, I wanted to say, "Yes." I thought he was a . . . judge in contact with the Communists and can report everything. . . .

But this morning I wrote a letter to my wife, and . . . I denied completely my crimes. I know my wife—I know her well—she can't do anything to me, so I wrote, "How cruel they were to make a criminal out of someone like me"—and yet last night I admitted guilt. Why? Because there was a judge there. . . .

Today at lunch with the Jesuit Fathers, I know them well—I denied everything because they are my friends. *When I feel safe I am on one side. When I have the feeling I am not safe, right away I jump on the other side.*

He hovered between these two sides (or variations) only briefly, however.

"He was ill-equipped for close relationships." "He quickly sensed that hope lay . . . in a reversion to what he was best equipped to be—the mystical healer." As his recurring phrase, "I know [someone]," suggests, he reversed from the man who let others have what was inside his mind and body back to the man who possessed (knew) others' insides.

According to Lifton, he himself thought he had most significantly changed by becoming willing to "open myself to others." As for their interviews, "This is the first time a foreigner knows my character. I believe this comes through re-education—because we were instructed to know our internal selves. . . . I have never talked so frankly."

"Through thought reform," says Lifton, "he had learned to surrender his 'insides,' and had therefore been able to reveal more of himself to me than he had to anyone before." Having learned to open himself, Lifton continues, "first in prison, and then with me in Hong Kong, he was bent upon unlearning his lesson." As Vincent himself said, "I have left part of myself in Hong Kong." He began to crystallize again into the unneeding and therefore closed, transcending man he had been before. " 'You,' " he told Lifton, " 'cannot know—you cannot understand . . . about the compulsion they use. . . . I know everything about [it]. . . . It is the difference between a man who studies anatomy in a book and a man who studies anatomy on the body.' " " 'I can see the situation through my experience, a personal experience—physical and spiritual.' "

> Here [concludes Lifton] are echoes of the youth who put a bullet through his own shoulder to express his love for a young girl: the experience must be his or it is no experience at all. This basic core of character had survived parental criticism, strict Catholic schools, medical study, twenty years of life in China, and even thought reform itself.

If I read "identity theme" for "core of character," I hear in Lifton's words precisely Lichtenstein's theory of the persistence of a primary identity.

In Charles Vincent, we can find and formulate a sameness or continuity or invariance that persisted through as crushing a force as a society can impose and the ostensible change of personality that resulted from it. His captors turned him inside out like a glove: right became left, but the glove was still a glove. The unfortunate Dr. Vincent is someone to be remembered in all discussions of "nature vs. nurture" or the "impact" of culture on personality.

The sad exemplum of Dr. Vincent suggests that we humans hold onto identity even to the limits of physical and mental endurance. So does Anna S.'s case history. Even psychoanalysis did not change her identity theme. So does Shaw's more fortunate and creative life story. Seeing this persistence, Lichtenstein formulated what he called

The Identity Principle

By "principle" in this context, I understand psychoanalysts (from Freud on) to mean a basic trend that regulates mental functioning. Freud first

described motivation this way: the human organism seeks to avoid unpleasure. After *The Interpretation of Dreams* (1900a), Freud called this first
principle the pleasure principle, but he still intended its negative meaning.
We avoid unpleasure, notably the diffuse sense of objectless fear called
anxiety.

Such a regulatory principle is not enough, however, for us to survive. Any
organism must find ways of avoiding unpleasure or achieving satisfaction in
the real world. Hence Freud also posited a "reality principle." The addition
of the reality principle, however, implies no deposing of the pleasure principle but only a safeguarding of it. A momentary pleasure, uncertain in its
results, is given up, but only in order to gain along the new path an assured
pleasure at a later time (1911b, 12:213–26, see also 1915c, 14:134–36).

In this picture, the child begins life with the pleasure principle and an id
and an ego yet undivided, both given over to wishing or hallucinating
gratification. Therefore, the child begins living by the logic of dreams,
daydreams, hallucinations, and symptoms. Gradually an ego oriented to
reality develops and with it capacities for delay, judgment, attention, action
in the world, and, above all, thinking as "essentially an experimental kind of
acting." In general, by relating to reality, the ego arrives at secondary-
process or problem-solving thought.

With these two principles, Freud thought (as of 1911) that he had arrived
at a comprehensive theory of motivation. He went on to classify human
activities according to the proportion they had of these two kinds of thought
or these two orientations to reality: fantasying, sex, religion, science, education, art, and dreams. In effect (and as discussed in the Appendix), Robert
Waelder's principle of multiple function brought this first concept of motivation into the later, structural view of the psyche. Heinz Hartmann's autonomous ego enshrined the reality principle in a separate corner of the mind.

It soon became clear, however, that this two-level concept of motivation
was not enough. Under a variety of circumstances, people deliberately
sought unpleasure, and all these situations seemed to have something to do
with repetition. People suffering from traumas dream the original shock
over and over. Children repeat in play painful experiences from reality (the
doctor game). Patients in analysis transfer onto the analyst earlier failures
with parents and other loved people. Moreover, practicing analysts found
that merely interpreting a symptom to a patient did not end it. The analysand had to "work it through," repeating the pathological behavior for many
interpretations. "Here I go again."

Freud concluded that there was a compulsion to repeat, a basic conservatism in the instincts (or, we could say, the ego). The individual tries an old
solution to the competing demands from inner and outer reality before

trying to find a new solution. Anna goes through many painful cycles before she turns to therapy.

Freud went further, however. He thought the compulsion to repeat was part of a generalized tendency in all living things to return to an earlier state, ultimately the earlier, inorganic state of death. That was the reason he posited a principle opposed to the pleasure principle, seeking not just an equilibrium, but zero excitation—a death instinct (1920g, 18:3–64). Few later analysts in England or America have found much evidence or usefulness for such an instinct (although there is the notable exception of Melanie Klein and her school). Many French analysts also accept the idea of a death instinct.

I find the idea very general, difficult to make precise, consorting oddly with the exactitude I am used to in Freud's psychoanalytic interpretations. I find I can better use the "identity principle" Lichtenstein has proposed as a substitute for the death instinct. Lichtenstein suggests that "the capacity to maintain or hold on to an identity is a fundamental characteristic of all living organisms, one to which we refer when we think of 'self-preservation' and 'self-reproduction.' Animals and children deprived of identity maintenance simply die. Hence it is more than an ego function, more even than a drive. Like the death instinct, it overrides the pleasure principle.

"Thus," Lichtenstein concludes, "identity establishment and maintenance can be considered basic biological principles—principles defining the concept of living matter itself" (1961, pp. 246–47, 1977, p. 114). Such an identity principle would be stronger than desire or the drive for pleasure. Everything the individual does evolves variations on identity. Work ("useful" labor or "useless" art) and love ("nonprocreative sexuality") are both powerful ways we sustain identity—hence their importance in the psychoanalytic scheme of things. In this context, "repetitive doing"—the very phenomenon Freud sought to explain by the death instinct—serves the biological function of safeguarding the sameness within change which is identity (1961, p. 235; 1977, p. 103).

Thus, we arrive at a very large theory of motivation. It is double. That is, our lives proceed like sentences from beginnings to endings. Partly that forward movement answers to the momentary logic of the words. If I use a "the," a noun will soon follow. Yet an overall thought also guides the forward movement so that each choice of word is governed by the words preceding but also by the centering theme of my idea, as in, say, *The Great Gatsby*. Gatsby's monumental parties lead, event by event, to his meeting Daisy again. Each episode causes the next, but the whole answers to Fitzgerald's special vision of the world as promising and failing, "the colossal vitality of his illusion."

We can think of each event in our lives as one in a sequence of events, each "causing" the next and each describable in the language of ego psychology and multiple function (see p. 340–48). On each event a constantly changing reality impinges, but also a personal identity. Any given event takes its shape from preceding events, present reality, and identity. An account of an event like Dr. Vincent's "conversion" that talks only about the "force" or "impact" of society or about preceding causes leaves out an essential dimension, the identity which will give that conversion its highly specific form.

Accepting, along with hundreds of millions of others, a new China will be for *this* man an individual commitment to confessing guilt. As Lifton's book shows, Dr. Vincent's conversion will not assume the same form as anyone else's, however, even if all those hundreds of millions were subjected to the same coercion.

If Lichtenstein's "identity principle" is true, the need to maintain identity is fundamental and permeates each paragraph of a Fitzgerald, each session of Anna S.'s or Paul Lorenz's analysis, and each quip of a Shaw. Further, we seek to maintain that identity and *do so,* even against such strategies for fundamental change as psychoanalysis or brainwashing.

Even the act of ending one's life, since it is a chosen act, affirms one's identity. Summarizing some studies by others of literary suicides, I was able to show that an individual chooses death when he or she can no longer sustain a life that is bearable in terms of that individual's personal style. The mode of death, moreover, often continues the same style (or identity theme) the rest of the life did (1977).

Similarly, a study of people taking LSD shows that the effects of personality persist and shape the total experience more than the drug itself does (Zinberg, 1974, p. 32; Barr et al., 1972, pp. 158, 164–65). The same applies to other psychoactive drugs, according to an experimenter at the National Insitutes of Health: "Even if one were only attempting to control the minds of a homogeneous group of psychiatric patients with a drug with which one had had considerable experience, the desired effect would not be produced in all patients, and one would not be able to plan specifically that any particular effect would be produced in a particular patient" (Calder, 1970, p. 76).

Drugs, I think, are the ultimate in physical determination of the mind, yet even with drugs we respond individually. We keep a measure of idiosyncrasy, living a mixture of freedom and determinism. Society acts on us. Other individuals do. Language and culture both limit and enable us. Physical events and substances control us. Yet through it all we show traces of a personal style. Identity theory gives us a way of describing that mingling of freedom and constraint. By means of identity we can talk about individual differences in response even to brainwashing or drugs and still be rigorous and precise enough to meet at least some of the demands of a science.

According to Lichtenstein, we live by a principle of identity: we seek to maintain identity at all costs and through every experience. Even so, we need not assume as much as Lichtenstein does. We need not assume that there is some identity "in" a person that cannot be changed and that controls and limits behavior. We need only assume that we can formulate an identity theme. We *can* read a constancy in someone's chosen actions whether or not such a constancy is "there" in some abstract, impersonal sense.

We can think of identity simply as a way of inquiring into human actions. What in this action fits the pattern of earlier actions? Sometimes that inquiry will be successful, as I feel these readings of Fitzgerald, Lorenz, Anna, Shaw, and Vincent are. I can find a theme running through what I know of each of their lives. To that extent, I have confirmation of my identity inquiry. I have neither need nor warrant, however, to assume that I have "correctly" read their identity themes in some "objective" sense.

For example, another psychoanalytic student of Shaw, Daniel Dervin, traces a number of psychoanalytic entities in Shaw's life: the wish for union with a mother, a flight from reality into fantasies of omnipotence, a prodigious and prolific activity of creation, narcissism, and romantic fantasies of an exalted family. Dervin brings these together as three recurring character types, "rooted in Shaw's development and nearest his creative center." These three are: "the Diabolonian son, the symbiotically accessible mother, and later on the accomplished artist as creative father." "From these sources not only did the vital genius evolve, but Shaw's conception of the role of artist as well" (p. 301 *n.* 1). In his own way, Dervin has described a Shavian identity.

Now what are we to do with these differences between Dervin and Holland? One response would be to say Holland is right and Dervin wrong (not, I hope, the contrary). Such a verdict proceeds from the assumption that there is an identity theme *in* Shaw and the business of the identity theorist is to find it and report it correctly.

This one-right-one-wrong, zero-sum response is not a very clever use of the objectivist model, although an altogether too common one among reviewers of nonfiction. A more sophisticated use of the model would seek some compromise or combination or resultant of Dervin's and Holland's readings, and it would add still others, for example, David J. Gordon's reading of Shaw as combining martyrs and conquerors (see p. 56n above). By combining more and more such readings, one should come finally to the correct, objective answer.

Unfortunately, humanistic knowledge seems never to arrive at that utopian destination. Humanists rarely come to consensus, and then only in the most general, even vague terms—nothing like the formidably precise analyses from which Dervin, Gordon, and Holland proceed.

A more sophisticated response to divergent readings of identity themes would recognize that identity is a paradoxical concept. It would be quite inconsistent of me to claim "objectivity" about Shaw since any interpretation I make of him must be a function of my own identity. The words and episodes I choose to discuss will be functions of my identity. My interpretations make up a part of the history of me. They must be variations on my identity theme, as Dervin's and Gordon's are of theirs.

My view of Shaw has changed over the three decades I have been teaching his plays and thinking about him. If my own view in 1984 differs from my own view in 1954, I ought to expect Daniel Dervin's and David Gordon's views to differ from mine. The question is not, Which of us is right and which wrong?, but, What can we learn from one another about Shaw? Also, What can we learn about ourselves and why we see Shaw in our several ways?

Stating an identity theme for Shaw or Anna or Lorenz is not throwing a dart, hitting the target, and walking away from it. It is a continuing discussion. Naturally there is agreement and disagreement, but one does not expect final answers. Rather one hopes for an improvement in the clarity and precision of the discussion.

The similarity between Dervin's reading of Shaw and mine comes about because we are both looking at the same person in the same way. Had we different methods, we would read the same event differently.

To the extent that they are alike, then, our readings show a like commitment to psychoanalytic ideas and the principle that one can and should seek a unity in a person's life. Such consensus as human beings have about events comes not only from the events but also from a prior consensus about the way to read them.

Conversely, some differences between Dervin's reading of Shaw and mine stem from differences in the psychoanalytic concepts we apply to finding a unity in Shaw. He uses clinical and diagnostic categories, often in the technical language of psychoanalysis. Mine are ad hoc efforts to express identity in language like Shaw's own. Those differences in method reflect choices in method that are (in part at least) functions of our different identities.

Now, if two people chose to think about Bernard Shaw in exactly the same way, their two interpretations might resemble each other more closely than mine and Dervin's. But only resemble. They would not be exactly the same, and the differences, far from invalidating one reading or the other, are precisely what identity theory seeks to account for.

If we take the concept of identity seriously, then, we begin to go from simply agreeing or disagreeing to seeing why we think the way we do. We begin to understand how all knowledge is personal knowledge, bound up in the process of knowing. Even what we know scientifically, we know through methods. No matter how widely shared they are, we adopt these methods personally. They become part of our identities. These identities are themselves but forms of knowledge, ways we interpret others and ourselves.

We come again to the paradox of identity and to the new understanding that psychoanalysis proposes of our own understandings. Hence, Lichtenstein's identity principle leads to

A Sixth Metapsychological Point of View

In one of his last essays, Freud spoke of "the Witch Metapsychology" (1937c, 23:225). Earlier and less dramatically, he explained that he meant by metapsychology the kinds of statements a psychological (psychoanalytic) explanation had to include to be complete (1915e, 14:181). In setting them out, I can do no better than quote the fine summaries by David Rapaport and Merton M. Gill (1959; see also Rapaport, 1960b). They give five metapsychological points of view, this being the first:

> The dynamic point of view demands that the psychoanalytic explanation of any psychological phenomenon include propositions concerning the psychological forces involved in the phenomenon.

That is, a psychoanalytic explanation should include an assumption that there are psychological forces (like "drives"), that they have direction and magnitude like forces in physics, and that they add and subtract in both simple ways and complex overdeterminations (as in multiple functioning).

The second metapsychological point of view is similar. A psychoanalytic explanation should "include propositions concerning the psychological energy involved in the phenomenon." The assumption is that there are mental energies like physical ones and that they obey principles of conservation, entropy, and transformation, like the energies of physics.

Both these points of view derive from Freud's Helmholtzian commitment to create a psychology with principles like those of physics and chemistry (1915e, 14:117). More and more, however, today's psychoanalysts see psychoanalysis as a science that rests on interpretation, not physiochemical forces. Hence Freud's Helmholtzian ideal has come increasingly to be revised toward twentieth-century science, and the economic point of view, with its unmeasurable psychic energies, wanes.

The third metapsychological principle takes us to second-phase psychoanalysis (as described on pp. 331–33): A psychoanalytic explanation must "include propositions concerning the abiding psychological configurations (structures) involved. . . . " That is, a psychoanalytic explanation must include reference to the long-lasting configurations of id, ego, and superego among which short-term mental processes take place.

Fourth is the "genetic point of view," requiring statements about "psychological origin and development. Central to psychoanalysis through every phase, the genetic or "developmental" point of view rests on such basic assumptions as the explanation of present behavior by past history, the notion of biological stages of human development all of us pass through, the idea that earlier actions, even though superseded, remain potentially active, and the fundamental assumption of psychologial determinism: "At each point of psychological history the totality of potentially active earlier forms codetermines all subsequent psychological phenomena," as Rapaport and Gill phrase it.

The fifth, adaptive point of view evolved largely after Freud's death, although Freud did say that the tension between ego and external world was one "of the three great polarities that dominate mental life" (1915e, 14:140). This metapsychological principle demands an account of "relation to the environment." Here again, the assumptions are fundamental: that we are constantly adapting, that we must do so to survive, that we change in response to our physical and social environment, but also that our environment adapts to us.

I believe that the concept of identity developed in this and the preceding chapter leads to a sixth metapsychological point of view. Call it the personal—

> The personal point of view demands that the psychoanalytic explanation of any psychological phenomenon include propositions concerning the continuing identity of the person involved.

I am saying that, since any given psychological phenomenon involves the interaction of self and reality, the fifth metapsychological point of view entails a sixth. It is just as essential to talk about what the individual personality does in a given psychological transaction as to talk about the effect of reality.

Were we discussing the effect of World War I on Shaw, it would be important to take into account not only World War I but Shaw's personality. That seems obvious enough. What is less obvious, perhaps, is that we also need to take into account the personality of another "person involved," the one analyzing the effect of World War I on Shaw.

This personal point of view rests on a basic assumption parallel to the assumptions of the other metapsychological points of view: A holistic, theme-and-variations analysis of a person's chosen actions *can* succeed. For any one of a number of reasons, of course, it may not, but in order to analyze "any psychological phenomenon" from the personal point of view, I need to begin by assuming that a holistic analysis *can* work. Then, according to the feedback I get from the event and from other, parallel interpretations, I can say my assumption did—or did not—succeed in fact, and I can learn from the ways it failed.

One could, of course, assume more than one theme and variations, let's say, one theme for Shaw's literary and political career and another for his sex life. One would lose parsimony and I do not see what one would gain, but in principle one could analyze a life by positing two, three, or a dozen themes with variations on them. Alternatively one could treat these as subthemes and propose a master theme to unify them. The sixth metapsychological principle asks only that one address the continuity of Shaw's personality in time and the continuity as Shaw shifts from, say, novels to plays, from shyness to oratory, or from mother to wife.

The examples of Dr. Vincent's brainwashing, Anna S.'s psychoanalysis, and Bernard Shaw's political and literary creativity suggest further that an identity theme persists despite radical changes in the variations the individual plays upon it. Here again, we can make this assumption in more and less demanding ways. We can assume that there is an identity theme *in* the individual that persists no matter how radical the changes. We can be less demanding and assume simply that one *can formulate* an identity theme that applies to all past living and may apply through all subsequent living no matter how radical the changes.

Thinking of identity themes in the realm of constructs seems to me logically consistent with what must surely be a corollary to this sixth metapsychological point of view, namely: Interpretations (of identity, for example) can themselves be understood as functions of the identity of the interpreter. This proposition, as we shall see in the next chapter, enables us to talk psychoanalytically about the ways we perceive and know the world.

In the meantime, identity has given us a way to grasp the mystery of selving that Gerard Manley Hopkins describes in the poem that serves as epigraph to this book—

> Each mortal thing does one thing and the same:
> Deals out that being indoors each one dwells;
> Selves—goes itself; *myself* it speaks and spells;
> Crying *Whát I dó is me: for that I came.*

Hopkins, like Lichtenstein, speaks of an identity "indoors," in, each mortal thing. It is an eloquent and consoling measure of our century to hear how a twentieth-century poet, Elizabeth Jennings, describes personal identity as personal knowledge. The poem is called just that, "Identity."

> When I decide I shall assemble you

Or, more precisely, when I decide which thoughts
Of mine about you fit most easily together,
Then I can learn what I have loved, what lets
Light through the mind. The residue
Of what you may be goes. . . .

That you love what is truthful to your will
Is all that ever can be answered for
And, what is more,
Is all we make each other when we love.

Part II | A Psychology of I

4 | Symbols

Freud dreamt about spinach, Shaw wrote about spiders and lionesses, and Iiro talked about ducks and shoes. Symbols all. Objects all. Shoes and spiders and spinach are the stuff of reality but also functions within the symbolic worlds that Iiro and Shaw and Freud inhabited. As fish know the world as sea, we humans swim in symbols that we both live in and wonder about. They are us and we are them, yet we make and unmake them. How?

If I trace shoes in the all-too-convenient "Index of Symbols" that the final volume of the *Standard Edition* of Freud's works provides, I will read: "*Shoes* and *slippers* are female genitals" (1916–17, 15:158). "A spider in dreams is a symbol of the mother, but of the *phallic* mother, of whom we are afraid; so that the fear of spiders expresses dread of mother-incest and horror of the female genitals" (1933a, 22:24). Can Iiro's duck be considered the same as the vulture that nibbled at Prometheus's liver ("a penis—a meaning which is not strange to it in other connections, as we know from legends, dreams, linguistic usage and plastic representations in ancient times" [1932a, 22:189])? Or is that duck the phoenix ("which probably bore the significance of a penis revived after its collapse" [1932a, 22:190–1])? If so, then it too must symbolize a penis. Lions, on the two occasions Freud treated them as symbols, stood for big men or fathers (1900a, 5:462, 1918b, 17:39, 112). Presumably, then, Shaw's lioness is a mother.

Decoding symbols this way can become a bit bizarre. For example, when I used to walk down to the corner store to get my *New York Times,* I would pass lampposts (phalluses), cats (pubic hair), trees (phalluses), trash cans and cartons (uteruses), overcoats (genitals—ambiguous gender), hats (male genitals), and two churches (female genitals). Why wasn't that walk more interesting then? Why didn't I feel aroused when I passed the elaborate locks on the back door of the drugstore (female genitals)? Why didn't I feel anxiety when I passed the tailor's shop (castration)?

I have to ask (as indeed Freud imagined me asking), "Do I really live in the thick of sexual symbols?" "Are all the objects around me, all the clothes I put on, all the things I pick up, all of them sexual symbols and nothing else?" (1916-17, 15:158.) Freud answered his question only to the extent of demonstrating these and other symbolic equations from a great variety of sources, fairy tales, myths, jokes, slang, and folklore of all kinds. He could present a great deal of evidence, and he did.

Further, these symbolic equations can make a lot of sense. We know Shaw was much preoccupied with his mother. He was likely to translate any female animal into his concern. It seems equally likely that Iiro would translate his feelings of inadequacy about his hands and feet into a feeling that he was inadequate as a male child with a penis: hence his first association to a duck and later associations to eels and a sword.

I don't think these symbols are "wrong" so much as insufficiently spelled out. Because of their one-to-one quality—duck equals penis—they are substitution theories: the duck replaces the penis. It makes more sense to me to think of the symbol as a dual unit, involving both symbol and symbolized. The duck may represent a penis, but it *is* a duck (Noy, 1973). In general, one-to-one symbolic substitutions do not allow room for any complexity of the dream, joke, novel, symptom, or squiggle, the symbolic structure itself, or its relation to its human symbolizer (Rodrigué, 1956).

It is all right for a duck to have webbed toes. Might not that be the reason Iiro imaged himself as a duck? Merely to say shoe=vagina would leave out the complex feelings Iiro must have had toward shoes, because he had to wear orthopedic shoes. Could he hide his webbed toes in ordinary shoes? Could he have imagined that if he gave up his masculinity for femininity (became a shoe instead of a duck) his hands and feet would be cured? Similarly, in Shaw's phrase to the lover, "Your head is in the lioness' mouth," the lioness, be she mother or not, is primarily an eater. Freud's table d'hôte dinner might well symbolize a debt—Freud was certainly preoccupied with moral and monetary debts—but it could also represent gratification or nurture.

Ernest Jones set out the classical theory of psychoanalytic symbolism in 1916. In the first-phase manner (see p. 331), he proceeded by assuming an opposition between conscious and unconscious that led to other sharp boundaries.

First, he distinguished psychoanalytic symbolism from all other kinds. "True" symbols always represent repressed unconscious themes, as opposed to the flags, traffic lights, or trade marks we call symbols in the ordinary sense.

Second, he said, true symbols always have a constant meaning. He was following Freud:

> In this way [interpreting symbols] we obtain constant translations for a number of dream-elements—just as popular 'dream-books' provide them for *everything* that appears in dreams. You will not have forgotten, of course, that when we use our *associative* technique constant replacements of dream-elements never come to light (1916–17, 15:150).

Thus Jones and Freud find these symbolic equations quite opposite to free association, the usual evidence of psychic connection in psychoanalysis.

Third, said Jones, all symbols express themes about the bodily self, immediate blood relatives, or the phenomena of birth, love, and death. People often translate that crudely: "Freudian" symbols are "sexual."

Fourth, symbols translate thoughts that were previously in existence in another form but repressed. Hence, interpreting symbols always points us toward the past and usually the very archaic past of childhood fantasies and beliefs. Jones calls them "the most primitive ideas and interests imaginable."

In interpreting symbols Jones observes, as Freud had before him, that symbols often follow linguistic connections through etymology or slang. Similarly, symbols have parallels in myth, legend, folklore, fiction, and poetry, although (as Freud pointed out) not all these cultural symbols appear in dreams nor do all dream symbols appear in cultural settings. Clearly, then, one can compare "Freudian symbols" to a language (as in the various dictionaries of dream symbols), and Freud did—

> the dreamer has a symbolic mode of expression at his disposal which he does not know in waking life and does not recognize. This is as extraordinary as if you were to discover that your housemaid understood Sanskrit, though you know that she was born in a Bohemian village and never learnt it (15:165).

Before Freud recognized unconscious symbolism, he had spoken of unconscious activity only in terms of mental actions: the constant effort of repression, the conversion of feelings into body symptoms, the dream "work."

> Now, however, it is a question of more than this, of unconscious pieces of knowledge, of connections of thought, of comparisons between different objects which result in its being possible for one of them to be regularly put in place of the other. These comparisons are not freshly made on each occasion; they lie ready to hand and are complete, once and for all (15:165).

Like a language. Or like the ready-made sentences or arithmetical calculations that a dreamer recalls into his dream.

To explain this quasi language, only part of which dreams use, Freud and Jones resorted to a theory of the Swedish philologist Hans Sperber, that the sounds of speech originally served to call the speaker's mate. Then these same sounds, rhythmically uttered as our Neanderthal ancestors hunted and gathered, came also to denote acts of work. Hence we have many verbal roots (about spearing, say, plowing, or planting seeds) that denote work but that can be used as sexual symbols.

Farfetched as this theory sounds, some contemporary analysts have found a core of truth in it. If I think "Jane," I not only bring my mate to mind, I also remind myself of her absence or, even if she were in my study with me, the irreducible difference between Jane and the me who says "Jane." All language—all naming, anyway—by substituting the word for the thing, establishes both a presence and an absence. One could say, therefore, that in all naming "desire speaks," that is, the naming announces both the desire and the absence of what is desired. Following Jacques Lacan, many French analysts of the last decade have drawn just this analogy between unconscious processes and language.

With Freud and Jones, however, it seems to me that their analogy of dream symbols to language takes them out of the isolation of the psycho-analytic dream symbol that Jones first posited. As Charles Rycroft says, "When Balzac likened clumsy men making love to gorillas playing violins, or when Queen Elizabeth I said 'If I had been born crested not cloven, your Lordships would not treat me so,' they must both have been fully aware of the implications of what they were saying and used images which do in fact frequently appear in dreams in contexts which permit their interpretation as sexual symbols" (1979, p. 75).

In other words, dream symbols are not confined to dreams; we use them in our everyday metaphors, as in Freud's own evidence for his symbolic inter-pretations. Those who use the interpretation of symbols heavily in literary criticism tend to use them as a fixed, fully demonstrated system. (I wrote that way myself for perhaps a dozen years.)

If, however, you turn back to the sections of *The Interpretation of Dreams* where Freud first broaches the psychoanalytic idea of symbolism and follow closely the dates of his various interpolations (provided in the *Standard Edition*), you will find a good deal of hesitation and qualification expressed. Thus there is another way of thinking, derivable from Freud himself, that treats symbols in a far more flexible way.

Freud's whole idea of symbolism came into being after the main ideas of *The Interpretation of Dreams,* as an adjunct to "typical" dreams, the dreams that many people share of examinations, nakedness, and so on. Symbols were not whole dreams but particular images that many people share. In particular, symbols tended to appear as a substitute for free associations as if the dreamer took them over ready-made (like grammatical and arithmetic constructions in dreams).

Always, however, Freud insisted, even as he added the reading of symbols to *The Interpretation of Dreams,* that it was a supplement to the primary method of psychoanalysis, free association (5:359–60). Sometimes even a symbol has to be interpreted "in its proper meaning and not symbolically" (5:352). Symbols can have several meanings, and "as with Chinese script" one arrives at the "correct" interpretation from the context rather than through a dream-book decoding. Further, many of the original meanings given for symbols represent "the reckless interpretations of Stekel," who had the lamentable habit of making up his evidence (Jones, 1955, 2:134–37).

Freud puts aside all hesitations and decodes like the veriest dream-book, however, in his fullest and most vigorous statement of the theory of symbolism, Lecture X of the first series of *Introductory Lectures* (1916–17). Although these lectures precede a number of Freud's major discoveries, they are widely used as an introduction to psychoanalysis for students. Hence psychoanalytic symbols bulk large in most American undergraduates' idea of psychoanalysis (particularly psychoanalysis as applied to literature and the arts).

After 1916 the whole trend of psychoanalytic thinking about symbols opens up a less one-to-one, less doctrinaire theory. In particular, Melanie Klein (1930) and later Kleinians like Hanna Segal (1957) wrote important essays expanding the early psychoanalytic view of symbolism. Where Jones had maintained that "symbolism . . . constitutes a barrier to progress," Klein (working from a case history) claimed that symbolism made tolerable, structural, and creative identifications possible. Hence symbolism, by joining conscious and unconscious mental processes, made unconscious processes accessible and available for creativity or therapy. Klein thought that symbol-formation went along with growth within or without therapy. Segal used Klein's approach to explore the whole self-symbol-symbolized relationship.

This exploration took hold among all three of the English psychoanalytic schools. Notably, Marion Milner carried Klein's idea of identification farther, to fusion (1957a). Symbolism, she pointed out, involves a fusion of symbol and symbolized and symbolizer. (In the symbolizer's mind, the shoe *is* a vagina.) In play and artistic creativity, symbols take on a life of their own: the logic of the drawing or the toy dictates the outcome, instead of the will of the creator. Whatever the content, then, the *mode* of symbolic fusion recaptures the original fusion in infancy of mouth and breast or infant and mother. We temporarily give up the discriminating "objective" ego and undergo in favor of the symbol-other a temporary loss of self (that Ernst Kris described in the language of ego-psychology as "regression in the service of the ego"—1952). Thus art provides the adult a framed space, bounded time, and pliable medium with which one can at will, again and again, re-create part of the everyday experience of infancy (Milner, 1952, see also 1957b, 1969).

In a famous study of 1963, Werner and Kaplan related the child's learning of language to general psychoanalytic patterns. They too stressed the role of inner dynamics in symbolization as opposed to external similarities between the symbol and its object (very like the linguist Saussure's insistence on the "arbitrariness" of the relation between signifier and signified). In early childhood, symbols gain their significance in an interpersonal context, as part of the relationship of mother and child. Only later do purely linguistic considerations take over.

The sociologists Weinstein and Platt developed a cultural aspect to the psychoanalytic theory of symbols (1973, pp. 69-89). Symbols represent ways that all structures of a personality, even the id, become socialized. The id is a purely wishing agency, yet to wish one must have symbols to wish in, and those symbols will have a social origin. The argument applies with even more force to ego and superego. In the same vein, George Klein had put forward the view that unconscious fantasies (triggered by anxiety, threats to self-esteem, and the like) include directives of approach and avoidance. Unconscious fantasies induce symbols which in turn become the basis for behavior (1970, pp. 397–404).

In France, Lacan carried the whole idea of symbolism much farther and wider into "the symbolic," the symbolic order, the law that underlies—is really—our culture. Clearly, however, this is a much larger concept of symbolism than Freud's or that of most non-French analysts. (A lucid and lapidary account of Lacan's view can be found in Laplanche and Pontalis's dictionary [1968, 1973], s.v. Symbolic [sb.])

Less abstractly theoretical but intensely commonsensical (in the best British tradition) are the writings of Charles Rycroft on symbolism, particularly symbolism in dreams. For example, he points out that Jones's "ideas of the self and the immediate blood relatives or of the phenomena of birth, love and death" need not be thought "the most primitive ideas and interests imaginable." His own phrase, "imagery related to biological destiny," suggests rather that dreams and psychoanalytic symbols deal with the most fundamental and perennial concerns of humankind (1979).

Rycroft interprets a number of familiar symbols, although he says that it is pointless to list standard meanings for, say, dogs or horses in dreams. Rather, we should ask, What imagery does this particular dreamer have available for constructing his dreams? and, What determines the aptness of that imagery to express these particular ideas? In other words, Rycroft restores dream symbols to their proper context, the statement of a dreamer in his personal and cultural setting (1979).

For Rycroft, dreams are simply the way the imagination functions during sleep, and there is no particular reason to assume that symbolism is a device by which dreamers deceive themselves. Rather, dreams are continuous with other forms of imaginative thought. To be sure, the statements made by dreams tend to be of a kind that the dreamer is reluctant to understand, and this phenomenon amply justifies Freud's division of the human into conscious and unconscious parts (1974, 1975).

His is a considerable enlarging of the classical Freud–Jones view of symbolism. Even so, Freud himself gives hints of this larger view. He accepts Aristotle's view that a dream is thinking that persists into sleep. Although it is true that some waking thought differs sharply from dream thinking, metaphorical, imaginative thought does not. It provides a continuity between our dreaming selves and the most intelligent acts of our waking selves.

Freud himself suggests a very large idea of dreams in the famous last sentences of *The Interpretation of Dreams:* "By picturing our wishes as fulfilled, dreams are after all leading us into the future. But this future, which the dreamer pictures as the present, has been moulded by his indestructible wish into a perfect likeness of the past." Freud here refers to his basic definition of a wish as an impulse to bring back a perception linked to the situation of an earlier satisfaction. Dreams are wish fulfillments. Hence dreams and dream symbolism do always point us to a future, but one totally defined by the past wish.

When Freud wrote about creative writers and daydreamers, he developed this more open model:

> The relation of a phantasy to time is in general very important. We may say that it hovers, as it were, between three . . . moments of time which our ideation involves. Mental work is linked to some current impression, some provoking occasion in the present which has been able to arouse one of the subject's major wishes. From there it harks back to a memory of an earlier experience (usually an infantile one) in which this wish was fulfilled; and it now creates a situation relating to the future which represents a fulfilment of the wish. . . . Thus past, present and future are strung together, as it were, on the thread of the wish that runs through them (1908e, 9:147–48).

Freud here is setting out in a very compressed form a model of mental activity he derived from the study of dreams which we can apply to conscious fantasying and imaginative activity in general. It has three phases that we could picture by a sort of large square-root sign.

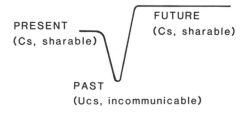

We have a conscious thought or perception. It sinks down, as it were, into "the unconscious," where it attracts to itself unconscious fantasies, repressed or from early childhood. We then transform that thought or perception (loaded now with some version of those fantasies) into conscious, sharable ideas.

Freud gives an analogy from business:

> A daytime thought may very well play the part of *entrepreneur* for a dream; but the *entrepreneur,* who, as people say, has the idea and the initiative to carry it out, can do nothing without capital; he needs a *capitalist* who can afford the outlay, and the capitalist who provides the psychical outlay for the dream is invariably and indisputably, whatever may be the thoughts of the previous day, *a wish from the unconscious* (1900a, 5:561).

As settings change, different phases of this process weigh more and less in the whole. Presumably, in imaginative planning or daydreaming of the future, the future aspect will be stronger than in dreams. In problem-solving or reality-oriented thinking, the effect of childhood or unconscious wishes will be less visible. Different dreamings will draw more and less on what in the present we consciously know.

In bringing out the similarities between daydreaming, night dreaming, and imaginative, metaphorical thinking, Freud establishes a spectrum of related modes of thought instead of a sharp boundary (as Jones seemed to posit). What Freud has set out is a paradigm for what the preverbal, unconscious past does whenever we think. The process of symbolization takes place in *all* our thought.

Nor need we assume that symbolic thinking always points backward in time. As Paul Ricoeur says,

> Are not dreams a compromise fluctuating between these two functions [regression and progression], according as the neurotic aspect inclines dreams toward repetition and archaism, or as they themselves are on the way to a therapeutic action exercised by the self upon itself? Inversely, are there any great symbols created by art or literature that are not rooted in the archaism of the conflicts and dramas of our individual or collective childhood? The most innovative figures that the artist, writer, or thinker can produce call forth ancient energies originally invested in archaic figures; but in activating these figures . . . the creator reveals man's most open and fundamental possibilities and erects them into new symbols of the suffering of self-consciousness (1970, p. 322).

Indeed Freud himself in those last sentences of *The Interpretation of Dreams* shows how "dreams are after all leading us into the future," albeit a future which is "a perfect likeness of the past."

Jacques Lacan has expanded the early Freud–Jones concept of symbolism another way, into *le nom du père,* a rich phrase that leads outward equally to the "name," the "noun," and the "no" of the father. In the name or noun of the "father," Lacan intends, not your father or any particular father in a literal sense, but a more metaphorical father, a "function" who embodies the whole symbolic order we inherit from our forebears as we are born into culture, notably language. In this as in other concepts, Lacan, as Murray Schwartz puts it, is drawing on first-phase psychoanalysis for metaphors (fathers, phalluses), with which to express the third phase of psychoanalysis, the psychology of the self (see pp. 331–33), one reason for the notorious difficulty of his writing. Obviously, in a literal sense, mothers embody the symbolic order, and maybe more so.

That order constitutes a storehouse or a treasury from which we draw our symbolic vocabulary. It is like a "promptuary," a type of book in the sixteenth century that stored quotations and other structured verbal information from which one could copy to construct one's own book (like a modern clipping file).

A symbol or "sign" in Lacan's sense (which here goes well beyond Freud's sense of "symbol") includes a signifier, the sound of a word or the written representation of the sound, and the "signified," its meaning, understood with all we mean by meaning in the word "meaningful."

According to some linguists, notably Jakobson, this symbolic order is structured by a series of negatives: a symbol is what it is because it is not this, that, or the other. "Duck" does not have a long vowel, is not inanimate, not human, and so on, following certain linguistic pairings, some peculiar to English, others characteristic of all languages, that mark "duck" off from "shoe." (Twenty such pairings would suffice to distinguish all the words in English—the reason we can play Twenty Questions.) Hence the symbolic order is defined by the not or "no" of the father, the negatives of language and culture, but also the prohibitions, the Thou-shalt-nots, that Freud allocated to the father as disciplinarian. Again, "father" is metaphorical here. In the nonmetaphorical world, both fathers and mothers say no. Yet how very French is Lacan's view—to link authority and language and call them the central qualities of the human experience.

According to Lacan, as each of us grows toward the adult world, we acquire our own version of *le nom du père.* For example, in Lacan's interpretation of the Rat Man, he formulates "the neurotic's individual myth," "the original constellation that presided over the birth of the subject, over his destiny, and . . . his prehistory, specifically the fundamental family relationships which structured his parents' union." For the Rat Man, this myth was: "the conflict *rich woman/poor woman.*" Lacan says that all the confusion about whether Lorenz was to pay one lieutenant or the other or the woman at the post office constitutes "a scenario . . . a schema which, complementary at some points and supplementary in others, parallel in one way and inverted in another, is the equivalent of the original situation." In other words, Lacan uses something like an identity theme for the Rat Man, but he limits it to "the neurotic" and to the particular symptoms that brought Paul Lorenz to Freud (Lacan, 1953, pp. 410, 415, 413, 415; Evans, 1979).

It seems to me that he thereby both overstates and understates the case. He understates it in that he limits his formula to the neurotic part of Lorenz, as if we could separate Paul Lorenz into healthy and sick parts, like a bin of apples. Lacan does not seek a myth that would cover *all* of Lorenz's life, a style that permeates all of his particular symbolic network. He overstates the case in that he sees Lorenz's life determined by his father's debt and marriage in a manner almost astrological.

Possibly I am being American in response to Lacan's intense Frenchness, but I think even someone as upset as Paul Lorenz has more autonomy than such a "scenario" suggests. It seems to me that each of us enters the symbolic order in our own way. We will use its symbols, its chains of signifiers and signifieds, for our own purposes, although (as Lacan correctly insists) this symbolic order exists before we arrive on the scene and after we are gone. Like a dictionary, it is open to all equally and equally binding on all. Yet, like a dictionary, we each use it differently. We may use the symbolic order very effectively or very badly, but it is we who do so by our own choices, not our parents' choices and not some pre-existing code.

If I look up "spider" in the "Index of Symbols" in the *Standard Edition* of Freud, I find, "the fear of spiders expresses dread of mother-incest and horror of the female genitals" (1933a, 22:24). Thus I can see the appropriateness of the metaphor in this passage about courtship: "it is assumed that the woman must wait, motionless, until she is wooed. Nay, she often does wait motionless. That is how the spider waits for the fly. But the spider spins her web. And if the fly . . . shows a strength that promises to extricate him, how swiftly does she abandon her pretence of passiveness, and openly fling coil after coil about him until he is secured forever."

The author is Shaw, writing in the preface to *Man and Superman.* Yet, in the play itself, when his hero realizes just exactly that, that he is being entrapped, he says, "Then—*I* am the bee, the spider, the marked down victim, the destined prey." He uses the symbol in a very Shavian way, opposite to its usual meaning. The spider is not the predator, but the prey, although in the same context of a woman's body swallowing a man's.

In using the symbol first with its usual coding and then with the opposite, Shaw demonstrates that we have considerable power over the cultural and symbolic order we inherit. We do not simply acquire a code to which we can only add variations. We can turn the code inside out. Shaw can have one of his heroes call the heroine a "boa constrictor" even though a snake is supposedly a penis. Therefore we need a more subtle way of thinking out our relations to our cultural aquarium. Just knowing how the muscles of our legs work does not tell us how we use our legs to get where we want to be. Identity gives us a way to inquire into this larger sense of symbolism as a dialectic between past and future, regression and progression, conscious and unconscious, signifier and signified, self and other.

Freud's dream of the table d'hôte we can read as some function of his identity. When Shaw wrote in opposites, we can say that he did so as some function of his identity. What is that function? We can best explore it in a more circumscribed situation than the lives of such great symbolizers as Shaw or Freud. We can turn to two readers reading.

Sam and Sandra

were two students of literature who were reading short stories for me as part of a study of literary response (and whom I have described before [1975a]. I do not know a better tailored sample of the ways we adapt the symbols the world provides us to our individual needs.) Among the stories they read was Faulkner's "A Rose for Emily." The narrator, speaking for the towns-people, describes two of the main characters this way:

> We had long thought of them as a tableau, Miss Emily a slender figure in white in the background, her father a spraddled silhouette in the foreground, his back to her and clutching a horsewhip, the two of them framed by the back-flung front door.

The passage is straightforward enough, and it has some "Freudian" symbols like the phallic horsewhip or the vaginal door and uterine house. As Sam and Sandra talked about the passage, however, I could see they had transformed it (by some such process as that diagrammed on p. 91) through their own unconscious desires.

Good-natured, easygoing, dapper Sam singled the tableau out as virtually the first thing he wanted to talk about in the story: "The father was very domineering. One of the most striking [sic] images in the book is that of the townsfolk looking through the door as her father stands there with a horse-whip in his hands, feet spread apart and between or through him you see a picture of Emily standing in the background, and that pretty much sums up exactly the kind of relationship they had.'' Sam was stressing the father's dominance and, in doing so, was positioning the townspeople so that they could see Emily between her father's legs. Emily became a mere appendage of her father, the very appendage that made him masculine.

Yet this picture was part of what Sam found highly romantic about Emily. "The frailty and femininity that that evokes!" he sighed. "Just that one frail, 'slender figure in white,' . . ." Yet, almost at the same moment he was imagining this helpless Emily, he could say, "The word 'tableau' is important. While they [the townspeople] may be envious and while they may be angry at the way that these people act, they yet need it, it seems, they in a way like to have it, much as one is terrified at the power of a god and yet needing him so much, and, you know, sidling up to him and paying homage to him and in the same way I think Emily comes to function as this god symbol." A curious turnabout from frailty and femininity to a "him" of godlike power.

Sandra liked this story intensely, had read it several times, and had even, in her freshman year, written a term paper on it. Yet she recalled the tableau very hesitantly: "They said they always had this picture of him standing, you know, sitting in the door with a whip in his hand." As for Emily,

> I see her as very young and dressed in white and standing up—I guess she's supposed to be standing up—behind her father, who would probably be looking *very* cross, say, if someone had come to call on her. No doubt, she would have a certain amount— Possibly fearful, but probably more regretful because she's being, they even say, robbed of something at that point . . . There would be a great amount of strain on her face because of her inability to do anything except just watch.

In other words, in their different readings of the story, their resymbolizings of it, Sam and Sandra actively shape it into a function of their identities. Even when they see and say much the same thing, they give it a personal touch. Sandra's phrasing, "with a whip in his hand," for example, seems less forceful or brutal to me than Sam's "with a horsewhip in his hands."

In interpreting their readings, I have the benefit of knowing their responses to Rorschach, TAT, and COPE tests, and I also know their readings of ten other short stories as well as a great many incidental remarks that enable me to read their identities as themes and variations.

Sam, as I read his personality, hovered between being masculine and feminine, active and passive, strong and weak. He wanted to be helpless so as to come close to and identify with supplies of love and admiration that would confirm him as strongly and safely male. Conversely, he would flee a male power that seemed too threatening. Thus, when he re-created the tableau for himself he composed a perspective in which, by identifying with the townspeople, he saw a frail, feminine Emily positioned under or between her domineering father's legs. At the same time, he thought both Grierson and Emily the possessors of godlike powers that the townsfolk needed to sidle up to. I think Sam is seeing the tableau through a preferred defense, that is, dealing with a source of threatening male power by identifying with it. He gratified this childlike wish to have power given to him by picturing the townspeople sidling up to the lordly Griersons. At the same time, however, he asserted his own safe separateness by putting the door between the viewers and Grierson's horsewhip.

In reading the tableau, Sam stressed the distinction between male and female. He searched out power, particularly male power. "The father was very domineering." The image was "striking." "One is terrified at the power of a god and yet needing him so much and . . . sidling up to him."

I saw Sam's need to confirm physical masculinity in what he said about Miss Emily's father at other points in the interview. "She lived under her father. Her father made the decisions. Her father kept things up. Her father was the leader, the member of the town council [not in Faulkner's text] . . . a very strong male figure in her life, and she was totally dominated by it [sic]." As if Grierson were not strong enough already, Sam elected him to the town council (Faulkner had not). He made him a dominating "it" and a "member," keeping things up. Emily is "under" him, and Sam makes her an emblem of "frailty and femininity." At other points in the interview he called her "the darling lady."

As I interpret Sandra from personality tests and from her remarks about stories and other things, she sought to avoid depriving situations and to find sources of nurture and strength with which she could exchange and fuse. In doing so, she used seeing or not seeing as her primary sensory mode (as opposed to Sam who used closeness and distance). Where Sam spoke of the tableau as an "image," Sandra said, "They said they always had this picture. . . ." She tried to bring Mr. Grierson down to manageable force by changing him from standing to sitting and "looking *very* cross," surely a dainty way of referring to a father who Faulkner says is "clutching a horsewhip." Emily would be "standing up," hence somewhat strong, rather than "fearful," but "she's being . . . robbed of something." Seeing is the mode of her distress and Sandra's: "There would be a great amount of strain on her face because of her inability to do anything except just watch." That would be the worst thing for someone with Sandra's character structure: to have to watch oneself being robbed of a source of strength or care.

Clearly, I think, Sam and Sandra are working more actively with the story than any notion of a fixed meaning or a symbolic code or a "right" reading leaves room for. For example, Faulkner refers in this story to a Colonel Sartoris—"he who fathered the edict that no Negro woman should appear on the streets without an apron." *Le nom du père* with a vengeance. When I asked Sam about it, he said:

> I hate, I hate to say. I like it. It's terrible. It's the worst thing. I mean, it's not terrible for me to like it. It's terrible that that kind of thing ever once existed. It's inhuman. It treats the Negro as animal. The Negro is *not* animal. But I can't help but be charmed by the naivete, by the total lack of concern that such a position of power places one in.

Later he admitted to a more sadistic pleasure: "I react with a kind of a smile that says, 'Oh, those were the good old days' type of thing, when I read that with the apron on the street." Interestingly, other readers of the story said similar things, ways (I think) of trying to mute the ugly cruelty. Nevertheless, that whipping or the edict or his wishes to be (in favorite phrases of his) "on the top," "in that kind of position," "such a position of power," all let Sam get a taste of the pleasures of masculine dominance in its crueler forms.

Sandra took a different tack. She reduced the edict. "I smiled a little bit, sardonically, I'm sure, because it's a great little touch of ironic humor. I think Faulkner meant it that way, and I think [of] the voice in the story as meaning it that way. Proclaiming it. 'He who fathered the edict.' Using these heroic terms to describe such a petty and obvious extension of bigotry." Having built up the narrator in other remarks as a wise and supportive figure, she said, "I smiled almost at the way he [the narrator] said it because it was such a perfect undercutting of the heroic Colonel Sartoris." (I think "undercutting" someone who "fathered" represents her weakening him specifically as a man.) "If this is—as he singles this out—his most important piece of legislature [*sic*], that's pretty good!" and Sandra laughed outright. Again she had reduced a threatening source of power and strength (the "heroic" Sartoris) to a safe size.

Sandra was an intensely visual person. I thought of her as constantly looking into an unknown world for a flow of strength or nurture that would equalize older and younger, stronger and weaker, or male and female. If she found such a source she wanted to see it more closely, touch it, even merge with it. If she found instead some extreme, a weakness or an overpowering, she wanted not to see it. If I were to word that theme in a single phrase, it would be: *to see and approach more and more closely a source of power and nurture, but not to see its loss.*

Sam tended either to flee into an isolated, boyish masculinity or to seek out mutual admiration leading to his passively identifying with a stronger male or asexual figure. If I were to state a theme for him, it would be *to take in or to get out so as to be male.* That is, he wanted to get out of dangers to his maleness and to take into his body love and admiration.

In many ways, he was like Sandra. Both were much concerned with power, particularly masculine power, and they tended to deal with their fears of being overpowered by physical or visual avoidance. If I were using an earlier psychoanalytic language, a characterology based on fantasy and defense (see pp. 160–64), I would say they were both phallic types with a preferred defense of denial. Indeed their remarks on the story are full of old-fashioned phallic symbols. Yet they responded very differently, so much so that even a very good characterology (like fantasy and defense) does not account for the difference in their readings. Using these identity themes, however, we can articulate different aspects of their responses as functions of their identity.

Consider the way they each read the character Bugs in Hemingway's story "The Battler." One night a young man, bumming around the country, wanders up to a campfire near the railroad tracks. The fire belongs to Ad, a punchdrunk ex-champion fighter, and Bugs, a black hobo, who takes care of Ad on their ramblings, as a squire might take care of a knight. As Bugs is making ham and eggs, Ad becomes increasingly and irrationally angry at the young man, to the point where Bugs, to protect him, has to knock Ad out with a blackjack he keeps for just this situation. While the fighter is out, Bugs gives the young man a sandwich and urges him on his way before the fighter wakes up.

Confronted with this character who cooks eggs but coshes his friend, Sandra concentrated on his giving food. "He's probably the easiest character to like in the story," she said. "Big and gentle and helpful." "He's all gentleness. Even when he's hitting his friend over the head, he's being [as] gentle as he could possibly be." "One of those generous people that it's hard not to like." "You have the feeling that he could handle a whole roomful of people and give each enough attention, make each feel pretty special."

Sam, however, focused on the blackjacking and a tiny detail, that Bugs, to revive the fighter, "pulled his ears gently." Sam said, "Bugs came across as kind of the nightmare element . . . kind of the devil of the nightmare and the excruciating type of oriental torture where [in a Chinese accent] 'Oh, you very nice. I'm now going to rip your ears apart. . . .' " "A kind of Fu Manchu person, kind of polite mingling with merciless from whom you never know what to expect." "This kind of exquisite, terribly polite type of torture which is to me more frightening than brutality." "Where you're kind of helpless before the politeness of the enemy and yet there's something behind the politeness that you can't deal with until it comes to the front, till you see it, and you've got to react only to his front, which is politeness."

In just these remarks I can hear Sam and Sandra positioning themselves and Bugs along two of the great axes of human experience. Sandra is setting him outside herself—"He"—but she is also taking aspects of Bugs into herself: "You have the feeling," meaning I, you, all of us. Similarly, in Sam's "Bugs came across as . . .," I sense he is distancing Bugs by looking only at "his front" but also becoming Bugs by imitating a Chinese accent. Both Sam and Sandra are setting themselves vis-à-vis Bugs on the axis between self and other.

Sandra speaks of her liking Bugs "in the story," in its immediacy and sequence. In thinking of Bugs as "one of those generous people," however, she sets him in a more enduring framework of her beliefs and experiences. Sam, too, dealt with the immediate Bugs, the ear puller, but also put him in a more timeless setting, "this kind of . . . polite type of torture," referring to fictions and movies about orientals. He, like Sandra, was placing Bugs between the immediate and the enduring.

These two continua, between inside and outside, between the timely and the timeless, provide angles for looking at the ways Sam and Sandra differently yet similarly symbolized Bugs. One can, I think, convert these axes of time and space, however, into more psychological modes of exploring Sam's and Sandra's different relations to Bugs.

DEFTing

First, Sam and Sandra brought to the Hemingway story certain expectations: about short stories, about Hemingway, about me, for whom they were reading this story, and about the kinds of thrills and satisfactions the story might yield. We all bring expectations to bear, most obviously from our cultural codes. Less obviously, we will seek—and find—in a literary work the kind of thing we as individuals characteristically wish and fear the most. Sam and Sandra's expectations about stories and Hemingway seem to have been more or less the same. Their expectations about another person, though, about Bugs, differed sharply. Sandra looked for something in terms of a source of nurture and power—and found it. Sam looked for something that would relate to his own masculinity—and he found that.

To be somewhat more precise, I can see them each approaching this new piece of the world, the story, expecting they could deal with it as they customarily dealt with other pieces of the world and other stories. To respond positively to something, a short story, for example, we need to be able to re-create from it our characteristic strategies for coping with reality, for achieving the pleasures we want from the world and defeating the dangers we fear.

Here Sandra hoped for a source of nurture or power and found it in Bugs, the cooker of eggs. Her characteristic pleasure was to draw close to such a source, provided it was not too strong, and she was able to do that with this story. She measured Bugs and found him "gentle," "helpful," "hospitable," and "generous." She found him neither weak (as some critics have) nor overpowering as Sam did, but a balanced strength. "If anybody's really in command, it's Bugs, the one that can hit him on the back of the head and wake him up. He's really in control," but nevertheless, "[as] gentle as he could possibly be." In effect, she was able to find in Bugs her characteristic mode of defense or adaptation: matching and balancing a source of nurture and power to her own strength.

Once she had matched her defenses, she could infuse the story with a pleasurable fantasy. She could imagine a sort of headwaiter Bugs who could "handle a whole roomful of people and . . . make each feel pretty special," an emblem of "true hospitality . . . that few people really have." "A lot of people can bring you over and throw a lot of food at you. [But Bugs's hospitality is] very different from just entertaining people, and it carries over, I think, to all kinds of different relationships." In effect, having matched her expectations in the character, having re-created her defenses through him, she was able to project a fantasy of hospitality into Bugs.

Sam had a rather different experience. He came to the story expecting that Bugs would have something to do with his, Sam's, masculinity. Sam perceived that something as a threat. Sam thus ignored Bugs the provider of food and concentrated on Bugs the blackjacker, whom he found a torturer, "merciless," "frightening," and before whom he felt "helpless." (In other contexts, masculinity meant for Sam being active, erect, and on top of things.) Having perceived this threat, Sam tried to deal with it by his characteristic defenses. He got himself out by distancing Bugs into someone unreal, a "nightmare element," "the devil of the nightmare," not an American black, but a faraway and fictional "Fu Manchu." He seems to have needed more defense, however, and he began to take Bugs into himself by introducing the social front. (Incidentally, one of Sam's own ways of getting people to admire him was through manners and dress.) "Politeness," he said. "You've got to react only to his front which is politeness," but "there's something behind the politeness that you can't deal with. . . ." I hear Sam's defenses saying, "Take in part of Bugs and get yourself away from the rest that you can't manage," but his defense didn't quite work. He was left feeling, as he said, "You never know what to expect." Finally, he took into himself both Fu Manchu and a victim and (complete with Chinese accent) imagined himself tearing the victim's ears off.

By contrast, Sandra had matched her defenses and adaptations. She had gotten Bugs to be just the right amount of power and nurture. Then she could enlarge on the wishes or fantasy she brought to the story as a whole. "After the feeling of loneliness . . . that coming up to a light is sort of a feeling of, well, promise, perhaps, relief. But it's a strange feeling, too, because there's always the element of whatever is unknown, is— You know, what kind of person is it? Is it somebody who's going to be happy to offer you some warmth with maybe some food? Or is it somebody . . . who would have turned on him right away?" Happily for Sandra, it was someone with food: "After you'd had the earlier feeling of loneliness, physical hurt, he [the young man] began to build up a sense of hunger. And it was really, *really* well described, like how he was *watching* him cook something so good, and just the way everything was described as he put together the sandwich and just how good everything tasted!" Sandra had found the source of balanced power and nurture she sought, and she was gratifying her wishes about that source.

Expectations being met (or not), defenses being matched (or not), fantasy being pleasurably enjoyed (or painfully avoided), a reader can bring a fourth principle into play. Sandra could "make sense" of the story. She used the defenses she had matched from the work to transform the fantasy she had projected into it toward some esthetic, ethical, intellectual, or social coherence.

Sandra said of the story as a whole: "Something like this in its very most isolated sense probably calls on any time that you've ever been . . . bullied or picked on when . . . the other person ran away or was out of range . . . for some reason, that, say the person was an authority. . . . Any time when *you* were put down and didn't have a chance to stand up and fight back on your own terms either verbally or physically." At an intellectual level, now, Sandra re-created her identity just as any of us makes a unity of a literary text, compares it to other works, associates to it, brings knowledge or expertise to bear, evaluates it, places it in a tradition, decodes it—in short, commits one or all of our characteristic strategies for tranforming crude daydreams into something respectable and meaningful.

Sam was more explicitly intellectual: the story "shows [the young man] Nick moving away from home and moving out into the big, wide world." "It shows what Nick has to accomplish, the symbolism of staying on the railroad track with the swamp to both sides and the railroad track, clear and well-paved, which made easy walking. . . . Nick has to stay on it to reach the goal. . . . In the story he digresses and picks up a bit of education of sorts." Even in abstract statements of theme, I can hear in their wordings these readers' identities. Sam speaks of a young male's moves toward and away from threats. Sandra contrasts being overpowered with an equal exchange of strengths.

A classic psychological study at the height of the Cold War showed how a group of ordinary men in Boston formed their opinions of Russia. "In each man," the authors wrote, "we find an effort to make the world congruent with or supportive of his way of life—within the limits imposed by the requirements of minimizing surprise, for contact with reality must remain the *pied à terre*" (Smith, Bruner and White, 1956). Each man symbolized Russia so that it would fit the economy of his particular personality. In effect, we are seeing Sam and Sandra do the same with these short stories (and there is less need to make stories fit reality than Russia). Sam and Sandra have resymbolized Faulkner's and Hemingway's stories so as to re-create their own identities.

In much recent European writing about texts (I am thinking of the philosopher Jacques Derrida and the semiotician Umberto Eco), it is customary to speak of the text as the active one in the combination of text and person, as though Russia alone shaped those Bostonians' opinions of Russia. This story, for example, might be said to "valorize," by the darkness of the scene, the strangeness of Ad and Bugs, and the danger of Ad, a general sense of education through "otherness." Yet one could equally say the story "subverts" this otherness through various hints that Nick's pose of toughness is simply a boyish version of Ad's fierceness.

I find this a jazzy set of metaphors with which to shorthand the way persons create texts and texts create persons. As for me, however, and this is very much a part of my identity, I feel uncomfortable with figures of speech that mask a human activity. I want to know what the people in any given transaction are doing. Hence, where others, seeing persons and texts mutually creating each other, talk about the text, I prefer to speak about the person. I also think, in all candor, that a model that makes the person active allows us to understand reading and listening and speaking more fully than a model that makes the text active. Hence I insist on the evidence of Sam and Sandra.

Sam and Sandra show how we can use these four aspects of their identities to explore the space between them and Hemingway's story: their characteristic expectations, defenses, fantasies, and transformations. If we shuffle those terms a bit we can get a convenient acronym: defense, expectation, fantasy, transformation, d—e—f—t, DEFT. DEFT is a way of exploring what people do in Winnicott's "potential space" or in the philosophers' "intersubjectivity." We can ask how Sam and Sandra DEFTed Hemingway's story.

Further, this DEFTing corresponds to two continua inherent in all human experience, the situating of an event between self and other and between the now and the beyond-now. One can think of Sam's "expectation" as a way of asking, How does Sam fit what he is reading into the immediate before-and-after sequences of his experience, his now? Conversely, "transformation" enables me to ask, How is Sam fitting this story into themes that are meaningful beyond the immediate here and now or before and after? With "expectation" and "transformation," then, we are asking about the relation between Sam's experience within a time sequence and his efforts to transcend time. In the same way, "fantasy" and "defense" come into relation along the axis between self and other. "Fantasy" asks, What does Sandra project out into the world? "Defense" asks, What does Sandra admit in from the world? DEFT gives us a way of setting "intersubjectivity" and "potential space" themselves in time and space.

In a famous essay Lionel Trilling showed that Freud had made poetry indigenous to the human mind. "The devices of art—the most extreme devices of poetry, for example—are not particular to the mind of the artist but are characteristic of mind itself" (1950, p. 177). We could, I am suggesting by this theory of DEFTing, turn Trilling's insight around. The activities of mind are themselves artistic. The diagram on page 91, which began as a way of describing daydreaming, night dreaming, or creativity, really describes *all* human thinking. We are all engaged all the time in that process of regression from the present into the past and projection into the future, expectation, defense, fantasy, transformation, and expectation again.

When Jones and Freud limited symbols to "the" unconscious, they presupposed a conscious mind free of symbolism that could see right through the symbolic disguise. As Ricoeur, Barthes, Todorov, and other French thinkers have pointed out, this is to assume a "cognition degree zero," a mode of thought free of symbolism, from which one interprets symbols. Freud's larger view and the later analysts' suggest the opposite: that symbolism is both conscious and unconscious, at all times a part of our relation to the world around us. Sam and Sandra demonstrate that, at least for the symbolic environment of short stories.

Symbolism, both personal and cultural, is the means by which we establish relations to an other. That is, in symbolizing, we fuse symbol and symbolized and thus selves and other, just as Sam and Sandra each in their own ways became Bugs precisely in order to recognize the otherness of Bugs, the essential Bugs-ness which was not Sam-ness and not Sandra-ness. Symbols are relations, and relations are symbolic. Through symbols and symbolization we can create a dialectic between inner and outer, an interplay of union and disunion.

In the act of symbolizing (the act of DEFTing, I would say, that being a more detailed term), we undo boundaries in order to discover them and in discovering boundaries we create them again. In imagining Bugs as a threat, Sam found a fantasy that worked for him, an image of an oriental torturer, and this idea set off a new set of already known possibilities and associations (to, perhaps, Ming the Merciless of the *Flash Gordon* comic strips, "mingling with merciless"). In a way, the symbol had, on its own, answered back to Sam's discovering.

Living itself consists in this continued growth of a sense of duality, the me-ness of me and the other-ness of the other. Yet this two-ness itself grows out of recurring states of one-ness. To be two, we need to have felt at one with another, or at the very least, that that was a possibility.

We need to have felt one-ness in order to make the world a part of ourselves—one with us. We sift the heterogeneous world of symbolic experience around us, editing it, so as to create an inner world, more homogeneous, more congenial (*con,* according to, the *genius,* spirit), a world we can live in and act on. We sift the world of symbolic experiences so as to add to ourselves realities that are congenial, and in the act of sifting, our *genius,* our identity, is itself both challenged by, changed by and able to accept the new. Thus DEFTing can model the very act of human growth or adaptation.

The psychoanalyst Joseph Smith puts the idea elegantly:

> Every naming, every instance of differentiating an aspect of the world, also names and differentiates the namer. For the most part the latter knowledge is tacitly organized while conscious attention remains focused on the objects of need, interest, or danger out there in the world. The fact that rupture of a prior unity has occurred is but dimly felt. The fact that a world and a self are being mutually constituted only occasionally flashes forth—as when, in recognizing water, Helen Keller recognized, became in some new way, Helen Keller (1978, p. xxvii).

Just as fish-ness consists partly of living in water, so a part of our humanness consists of our living in a world of symbols. The sea goes into the making of fish, yet fish also make the sea what it is. So we are created by the culture and codes around us, yet we create what we are created by. The four terms of DEFTing allow us to explore (through our own symbols) the symbols in which we swim and the way in which we create those symbols.

In effect, DEFTing suggests that we live in a psychological version of our basic adaptation as mammals. The body temperature of a fish simply equals the temperature of its water. We, however, have evolved beyond the cold-blooded animals. We create inside our bodies, in our blood, the warm, nourishing sea the fish finds outside. Physiologically, we create an inner environment. Psychologically, we create an inner environment of symbols. Then we live in a delicate tension between our inner and outer worlds of symbols.

We are active human beings precisely because there is a difference between the heterogeneous, constantly changing outer world and the more homogeneous, more constant world within. In acting we accept that difference, for example, the separateness and absence registered by language, but we try to DEFT it away. We try to make absence presence. We necessarily fail, and that is just as well, for without that absence or difference we would cease to act. We live in a feedback or deconstruction which requires difference for us to (try but not quite manage to) render difference into sameness.

Feedback, we shall see in the next chapters, is an important idea for understanding our relation to symbols. The furnace warms the living room, but it is also true that the living room turns off the furnace. To talk about either of these relations alone leaves out part of the transaction, for neither of these statements takes into account the thermostat or the person who set it to suit one particular taste. In the same way, culture creates us and we create culture, but neither of these statements alone captures the dynamic relation between the two.

We create a common human and cultural environment of symbols inside ourselves, but we also create inside ourselves our special variation of that world, just as physiologically we create an inner sea in which our lungs and heart can do their work. Our inner seas are generically human, but varied to be specifically our own. To understand how that can be, we need to explore the way we bring symbols from outside into ourselves. We need to perceive perception.

5 | Perception

"It's a duck's foot," said Iiro to the first "squiggle" Winnicott drew. "This came as a complete surprise to me," wrote Winnicott, "and it was clear immediately that he wished to communicate with me on the subject of his disability," that is, his own webbed fingers and toes. And Iiro went on to use the duck he had perceived to symbolize not only his webbed fingers, but himself as a boy who could swim but could not play horns and flutes.

Consider a four-word dream, one of the shortest Freud reports, although that did not prevent him from mentioning it three times (1900a, 4:232, 1913h, 13:194, 1916–17, 15:94). "One morning at the height of summer, while I was staying at a mountain resort in the Tyrol, I woke up knowing I had had a dream that *the Pope was dead.*"

He could not explain the dream, except that he could remember reading a short time before in a newspaper that the Pope was slightly indisposed. During the forenoon, however, Freud's wife Marthe asked him, "Did you hear the dreadful noise the bells made early this morning?" Freud replied that he had not—and that, he realized, was the explanation of his dream. "It had been a reaction on the part of my need for sleep to the noise with which the pious Tyrolese had been trying to wake me. I had taken my revenge on them by drawing the inference which formed the content of the dream, and I had then continued my sleep without paying any more attention to the noise." Evidently he had heard the bells (since he dreamt about them), but his dream that Pius X was dead had enabled him to sleep contentedly on. His need controlled his perception. Indeed, according to Freud's own theories, dreams are the guardians of sleep. If they are successful, they always serve to ward off stimuli that might wake the dreamer up.

Iiro's perception would seem to prove the old adage, "People see what they want to see." Freud's sleeping through the bells adds, "People hear what they want to hear." Such adages have become more than folk psychology, though, because twentieth-century psychologists have proved over and over again that perceptions follow motivation.

Freud, however, had inherited an earlier idea of perception. In his theories, Freud used a nineteenth-century concept that one analyst has nicknamed "immaculate perception" (Schimek, 1975). That is, Freud defined eye and ear into a system *Pcpt.* (perception), a part of the ego. The system *Pcpt.* delivers a faithful copy of the world to another system *Cs.* (consciousness), which might then *and only then* distort the original perception in response to unconscious pressures. "All perceptions which are received from without (sense-perceptions) and from within—what we call sensations and feelings—are *Cs.* from the start," Freud wrote (1923b, 19:19).

When he was writing clinically, however, he recognized that perception is not such a cut-and-dried affair. He discussed, for example, the way that dreams could control perceptions, as in his own dream that the Pope was dead.

Transference, too, hinges on the patient's altered perceptions. Patients attach new editions of old impulses to their analysts, using the physician to represent some earlier person, often a loved or feared parent. For example, one balding analyst told me of a patient who kept speaking of his thin red hair as Samson's long brown tresses. Indeed, by having the patient lie on a couch with the analyst out of sight, psychoanalytic technique deliberately encourages the subversion of the patient's manifest idea of the analyst by latent needs and feelings. The analyst can then use the patient's changed seeing and hearing as a point from which to discover the deeper, less conscious feelings coloring and toning his perceptions.

Freud had known about transference ever since 1882 and his colleague Breuer's horrified discovery that patient Anna O. had fallen in love with him. Freud, however, did not extend the concept to perceptions. Characteristically, I think, he needed the feeling of being firmly grounded in reality. Perhaps that is why, in most of his theoretical statements (as opposed to his clinical ones), he insisted that our eyes and ears faithfully copy the real world into our minds. But not in all.

> The projection outwards of internal perceptions is a primitive mechanism, to which, for instance, our sense perceptions are subject, and which therefore *normally* plays a very large part in *determining the form taken by our external world.* Under conditions whose nature has not yet been sufficiently established, internal perceptions of emotional and thought processes can be projected outwards in the same way as perceptions; they are thus employed for *building up the external world* . . . (1912–13, 13:64).

Freud, Murray Schwartz wrote me by way of comment, "clearly recognizes the active, constructive function of projection in creating the external world, which he usually calls 'reality,' but unfortunately, he also ends the last quoted sentence with the words, ' . . . though they should *by rights* remain part of the *internal* world.' " Freud, continued Schwartz, "is judging ('should') or denying his own insight rather than building on it. Nevertheless the insight remains.''

Similarly, in a remarkable passage in his late, "testamentary" essay, "Analysis Terminable and Interminable," Freud arrived at a powerful psychoanalytic idea about perception:

> The psychical apparatus is intolerant of unpleasure; it has to fend it off at all costs, and if the perception of reality entails unpleasure, that perception—that is, the truth—must be sacrificed.

> The mechanisms of defence serve the purpose of keeping off dangers. It cannot be disputed that they are successful in this; and it is doubtful whether the ego could do without them altogether during its development. But it is also certain that they may become dangers themselves. It sometimes turns out that the ego has paid too high a price for the services they render it.

> These mechanisms are not relinquished after they have assisted the ego during the difficult years of its development. . . . They become regular modes of reaction of his [the individual's] character, which are repeated throughout his life whenever a situation occurs that is similar to the original one. . . . The adult's ego, with its increased strength, continues to defend itself against dangers which no longer exist in reality; *indeed, it finds itself compelled to seek out those situations in reality which can serve as an approximate substitute for the original danger, so as to be able to justify, in relation to them, its maintaining its habitual modes of reaction* (1937c, pp. 237–238, italics mine).

That last sentence seems to me to coincide with the DEFTings we have seen in the perceptions of Dr. Vincent and the rest. To cope with the world, we need to see the world as the kind of thing we can cope with. As a doctor in China, Vincent sought in medicine a defense of mastery against a dependency that the adult Vincent no longer needed to fear, some childhood relationship from far away and long ago. Similarly, Sam and Sandra shaped Faulkner's story through their characteristic defenses to avoid dangers when stories cannot pose any real danger.

In general, our defenses are part of our character. Our defenses are also therefore part of our perceptual and cognitive style, even though the real dangers that gave rise to those defenses are buried in our childhoods. To keep our defenses functional and our character intact, Freud is saying, we seek substitutes for the original dangers that gave rise to the defenses. That seems to me an astonishingly true description of some of our most painful self-defeating tendencies as human beings.

It also seems to me that Freud is describing a theory of perception that one can easily develop into the one I shall urge in this chapter. Identity (characteristic defenses) governs perception. In doing so, he strikingly anticipates modern

Perceptual Psychology

Specifically he anticipates the "new look in perceptual theory" that emerged in the 1950s. When I looked at the scientific literature on perception, I found that one major group of psychologists has arrived in our century at virtual unanimity around the idea that people perceive *constructively*. There is considerable disagreement about the particulars of that transaction, but within that school all agree that we see as much with the brain as with the eye. That is, we bring concepts to bear on the inputs to our eyes and ears so they do not simply copy aspects of the real world onto our brains.

Think of the way we hear a language we do not know. The words seem to run together into an indistinguishable stream of syllables. When we listen to a language we do know, however, even if at a crowded cocktail party, we hear it as distinct and separate words. Perhaps the party is so noisy we cannot hear everything, perhaps not even coherent statements. Nevertheless we hear in words, not just sounds. We hear by means of constructs we already had (Bergson, 1896, p. 136).

Another example: if I am in a train station and, out of the corner of my eye, I see the train next to my train start up, I have a momentary and startling feeling that my own train is going backwards. I am interpreting what I see and hear through one of the basic guesses people supply to the perception of motion: the surroundings are at rest and the object surrounded is what is moving—my train instead of the other train that forms the background to my sight. I then correct my reading when my central vision shows that my train is not moving (Wallach, 1959, pp. 310–14).

Although they are very specialized perceptions, the study of so-called optical illusions provides the most telling examples of constructive perceptual theory. Transparent cubes seem to turn inside out spontaneously. Flights of stairs flip from right side up to upside down. A picture of a vase snaps into two profiles facing each other, then snaps back again. After staring at a red spot we look away at a gray wall and see a green spot. Flashing lightbulbs on the movie marquee seem to form moving arrows. Arrowheads at the ends of equal lines make one seem longer.

"When perceptual illusions were introduced as a topic of study in the 19th century," says one experimenter, Paul Kolers, "the prevailing attitude toward them was that they were . . . minor imperfections or errors in the working of man's perceptual apparatus." Hence they were called illusions, but, "The notion of error . . . implied that there is some 'real world' faithfully reported by the senses. Few contemporary investigators take this view. Instead of thinking of illusions as errors in perceiving they regard them as genuine perceptions that do not stand up when their implications are tested" (1964, p. 316).

"It is as though," says Richard Gregory, another perceptual psychologist, "the brain entertains alternative hypotheses of what objects the eye's image may be presenting. When sensory data are inadequate . . . the brain never 'makes up its mind' " (1968, p. 241). Instead, the cubes seem to flip back and forth, colors appear and disappear, vases and profiles alternate. But it is not the objects which change—they are fixed, after all—it is the brain which restlessly tosses back and forth between inconsistent hypotheses about those objects.

You can test the brain's role if you can find the "Rubin figure" (often reproduced in psychology books), a line drawing that you can see as either a vase or two profiles, and your perception will ordinarily flip back and forth between those two interpretations. You can "beat" the illusion, however. Imagine two people pressing their noses up against a vase, and you will "see" just that. Because your brain has supplied a hypothesis that admits both, you can (most people can, anyway) see the figure as *both* a vase *and* two profiles.

The brain's hypotheses interact with sensory data in at least two directions, from outside to inside and from top to bottom. That is, we perceive when data from an object pass through our sense organs to our brains. We perceive from outside in. Yet we also perceive as we bring schemata from our brains to bear on those data. In that sense, we perceive from inside out.

At the same time, we have to fit those data into the various levels at which our minds operate. Occasionally, we operate at the level of pure sensation or with continuities, flows, or invariants; in the familiar metaphor, we perceive at a "low" level. One might look up close at a television screen, for example, to see the colored dots. Most of the time, however, our minds operate our processing of sensory data at a "high" level of completed objects or even complicated abstractions or impersonal ideals. We don't see tv as dots but as "can of beer" or "patrol car." Psychologists speak of perception "from the top down" or "hypothesis driven" perception in contrast to perceptions which are "stimulus driven," which go from bottom to top.

In constructivist theory, the brain is perceiving at any given moment from outside in and inside out and from bottom up and from top down—much as we DEFT along axes between self and other and between the stream of experience and more enduring themes. Then, can we interrelate these directions of inside-outside and bottom-top? I think we can, using one of the great technological discoveries of the twentieth century,

Feedback

Gregory Bateson suggests (as many others have) that we can model this high-low, inside-outside interaction cybernetically, that is, through feedback systems. In general, "feedback" means a transaction in which someone or something tests some aspect of its environment and modifies itself as a result of what it finds. Bateson gives as his example, chopping down a tree. "Each stroke of the axe is modified or corrected, according to the shape of the cut face of the tree left by the previous stroke." We operate within a whole feedback loop, tree-eyes-brain-muscles-axe-stroke-tree (1972, pp. 317–18).

Herbert Simon, they say, is the only psychologist to win a Nobel Prize (by disguising himself as an economist). Simon uses feedback as his basic axiom: "Given a desired state of affairs, and an existing state of affairs, the task of an adaptive organism is to find the difference between these two states and then to find the correlating process that will erase the difference." With such a model, human living becomes information processing on the inside and on the outside a search through comparisons—"large combinatorial spaces" (1969, pp. 112 and 54).

Think of driving. If I see the highway ahead of me turn right, I turn the steering wheel of my car right. I do so in just such a way that I can continue to see the car's right front fender keep the same distance from the right side of the road that it has been. If I see the right fender get too close to the shoulder, I turn the steering wheel left. Inside my head I am processing information about the present and future position of the car's right front wheel, of the edge of the road, and of the steering wheel. In general, my *behavior* with the wheel controls my *perception* of the distance between the right of the car and the edge of the highway.

You could diagram such a feedback loop this way:

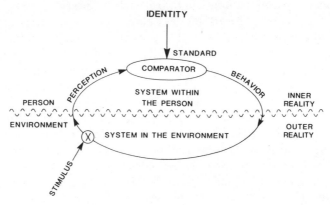

The loop has to have three things. First, a behavorial end that acts on the input—my hands that turn the steering wheel. Second, a comparator, like my eye and brain feeling out the distance between the right wheel and the shoulder. That comparison, my seeing, becomes the perceptual end that the behavioral end controls. Third, and this is the crucial item that is often left out, some standard or reference signal that is "above" and not controlled by that loop—like my need to keep three feet from the edge of the road. This is the "schema" I bring to bear when I drive. This is what determines whether the position of the car "feels right" to me.

Brain physiologists confirm this model and the importance of the standards *even if they are "teleological."*

> Objective study of living organisms shows clearly that they *do* indeed have targets and take actions that ensure survival.

> We now find that every organism contains systems that literally embody set points or reference standards. The control mechanisms operate to ensure that action is directed to maintaining these standards . . . (Young, 1978, p. 17).

The feedback picture also allows for various purposeful or random stimuli that disturb the equilibrium established by the loop of driver, car, and road. A traffic sign says "Right lane ends"—that would be a purposeful stimulus. More randomly, the road might take a turn or the wind blow across the road or a pothole twist the front wheels. The stimuli would be the same for everybody, but the responses will be unique (in speed of reaction, for example, or degree or shape of turn). These stimuli from outside the loop change what goes into the comparison, and I have to reset the car. I steer so that I get the right wheel back to a distance from the right edge of the road that feels right to me. *Behavior is the control of perception* (Powers, 1973a, see also 1973b, 1978).

Interestingly, that is exactly the way Freud defines a wish in the last, metapsychological chapter of *The Interpretation of Dreams*, as controlling perception. A wish seeks to re-create the perception of a satisfaction (1900a, 5:565–66). According to the "pleasure principle," all our waking behavior serves to gratify a wish—as opposed to our dreams, where we merely hallucinate our pleasures. Either way, however, a wish equals a wish for a certain perception. For Freud, just as for the computer scientist, behavior controls perception.

This feedback model, for all that it sounds electronic and high tech, is thus profoundly psychoanalytic. All his life, Freud used homeostasis, the organism's acting to bring itself back to a "normal" equilibrium, as a model for psychological processes, and homeostasis is simply a feedback through enzymes and hormones and other biochemical processes. Indeed Freud's 1895 *Project for a Scientific Psychology,* his first big psychological effort, provides drawings of cross-correcting processes that look very much like feedback diagrams, although, of course, feedback was not yet available to model his ideas.

Jonathan Miller points out that the scientific and engineering discoveries of any given age are not only useful in their own right but valuable for the models they provide us for other processes. The fountains of the Renaissance served as models for the circulation of the blood, as today we use radar and automatic gun-turrets to model the movements of our limbs (1978, pp. 284 and 4–7). There is nothing odd, then, in our using feedback as a framework for the insights of psychoanalysis. Frankly, I think psychoanalysis would have made faster and greater scientific progress had metaphors of electrical amplification and feedback been available to Freud instead of the hydraulic models to which he had to resort.

Further, a feedback loop combining stimulus and response, the individual and the shared, serves as a useful metaphor in other kinds of psychology besides psychoanalysis. In particular, it lets us articulate the long line of research in the psychology of perception, cognition, and memory demonstrating that we see and hear and know and remember *actively.*

Many, many experiments in perception have led these psychologists to the conclusion that all human beings perceive by checking an event against internal constructs, perhaps memory traces determined partly by previously sensed objects, partly by the personality of the perceiver (Noton and Stark, 1971, p. 219). One perceives not only familiar phenomena such as verticality but optical illusions, skewed rooms, and all the perceptual psychologist's bag of tricks by generating and testing hypotheses about the reality before one (Witkin, 1959; Ittelson and Kilpatrick, 1951). So with propaganda and mass communication: the media are not guns that shoot magic bullets of content into their audience. Rather, senders put out signs, and receivers choose among them, making such use of them as they can and will (Schramm, 1973). Even by the age of nine months, infants have begun to think in this way, by forming hypotheses with which to assimilate the world around them (Kagan, 1972).

Things don't just impinge on us. We impose schemata on things to assimilate them to our minds. We reach out to see, hear, know, or remember, using our innate capacities to see, hear, know, or remember. Hence this feedback picture of a self using inborn ("hardwired") capabilities to feed back into an internal equilibrium corresponds quite usefully to what the cognitive psychologists tell us. Presumably inside out and outside in and bottom up and top down all work together in intricate feedback loops at different levels.

Similarly, Jean Piaget's studies of children's intellectual and moral development led him to posit a short-term loop in which we take an external object through an internal schema (assimilation) and a long-term loop in which we slowly adjust that schema to meet the requirements of the object (accommodation). The first schemata are innate, but from them proceeds a cyclic interaction through all the stages of childhood into adult intelligence, morality, and the rest (1970). Chomsky goes farther, holding that for language at least and probably for other parts of our perceptual apparatus, our cognitive structures are inherited and their development preprogrammed, like our limbs or body organs (1975).

Whether we hold with Piaget or Chomsky or both, then, some of our perceptual schemata are innate—biologically defined. For example, we can smell only those molecules that the receptor cells in our noses are shaped to receive. The very shape of the cells acts as a perceptual schema. Images held motionless on the retina, not subjected to the three scanning motions of the eye, break up and disappear (Pritchard, 1961). Speech also disintegrates without the normal auditory input from one's own voice (Klein, 1970, p. 352). I do not feel my socks unless I think about them. Evidently, to feel, speak, or see, we have to be able to *do* something so as to bring a schema to bear and so create a sensory-motor feedback loop (Held, 1965). That, at least, is part of our biology.

Another part of our perceptual schemata is cultural. You and I, for example, live in a world of right angles, while Zambians do not. We see a certain picture made up of straight lines as a perspective of a box. They see it as simply a flat design (Deregowski, 1968). Colin Turnbull reports that his BaMbuti guide, who lived in a forest where the greatest distance he could see was a couple of hundred feet, could not recognize buffalo grazing some miles away as buffalo. He called them insects and even tried to identify the species of insect. On driving closer and finding that they were in fact buffalo, he concluded that he had been deluded by witchcraft. In effect, he was demonstrating that even so basic a visual schema as the correlation of size with distance rests on cultural experience (1961; see also Munroe and Munroe, 1975, Segall et al., 1966, or Lloyd, 1972).

Finally, some part of our perceptual schemata is individual. Herman Witkin found that the perception of verticality expresses the personality of the perceiver, so much so that one can even infer clinical characteristics (1959). Similarly, the eye movements with which people scan objects and pictures vary widely. George Klein was able to relate the eye movements with which people scanned pictures to the flexibility or constrictedness of control in their total personalities (1970, p. 185). "Every person," conclude Noton and Stark, "has a characteristic way of looking at an object that is familiar to him" (1971, p. 218).

In short, experimental psychologists have come to three conclusions about perception. First, we see and hear actively; we construe the world. Second, we mingle culture, personality, and physiology when we actively perceive. Third, the act of construction through which we perceive involves something like many nested feedback loops that link self and not-self and work up and down a hierarchy from sensory details to global aspects of personality, physiology, and culture.

To be able to say this much amounts to quite a bit. Alas, however, this account lacks one crucial element, our perception of language.

If you say to me, "Please pass the salt" or "Kiss me" or "What time is it?" and I respond by passing you the salt cellar, kissing you, or telling you what time it is, no theorist can say definitively what has gone on in my mind. Likewise no one can say what went through my mind so that I could say even the silliest sort of linguistic example, like "The bat is in the bin."

A half-century of research, say three major writers in the field, Fodor, Bever, and Garrett, "suggests that what subjects remember about a text is a complicated function of the literal text and their beliefs and values" (1974, p. 273). Except for some such general principle, however, we have no idea of the precise mechanisms by which we grasp meanings or make connections in language. "Almost every aspect of sentence recognition," note these psycholinguists, "remains unsettled despite the experimental attention the problem has recently received."

Nevertheless, there is some agreement, I believe, that we understand a sentence like "The bat is in the bin" by guessing what sounds and words are coming next and comparing what we then hear with our guess. In more technical language, a constructivist model for the way we understand speech would include a system in which we generate patterns inside ourselves to check against what we are hearing or seeing. "Patterns are generated internally in the analyzer according to a flexible or adaptable sequence of instructions until a best match with the input signal is obtained" (Halle and Stevens, 1964, p. 604). We keep trying patterns until we get a satisfying match with what our eyes or ears are taking in. We evidently have some sort of inner program for generating patterns according to a sequence that we can vary according to the context or the matches we do or don't get.

In other words, information-processing feedback. We understand (at least partly) by "an active internal synthesis of comparison signals" (idem). In interpreting sentences, we guess ahead, and we guess at the whole. We hear the same way you read a line in this book. Your eye skims over the various strokes and serifs of the letters and jumps from word to word forming a rough idea of what you are going to get which you do not correct unless I write something unexpekted.

When we speak, we "coarticulate" consonants and vowels into bursts of sound. When we listen, we have to decode those bursts back into individual speech sounds. Furthermore, the same piece of sound carries information about two or more successive phonetic segments. For example, when we say "bat," we don't make three separate sounds, b-a-t. We say one syllable. If an engineer displays that syllable visually on an oscilloscope, at any given moment the wave may be carrying information about *b* or *a* or *t* or all of them. Measured physically, the *b* in *bat* is different from the *b* in *boot*. Yet we hear them both as *b*. We are able, somehow, to decode syllabic bursts of sound back into individual speech units (Liberman, 1973).

The basic unit of listening is the whole syllable. We perceive individual consonant and vowel sounds only *after* perceiving the whole syllable. At the same time, however, it is the individual speech sounds that yield meaning ("bat" and not "boot"). In effect, when we listen to speech, we put into operation a basic psychological principle that applies to all perception.

We tend to organize our perception of the world in terms of the highest level of organization. We see a house, not a heap of shingles and bricks. We see a truck rather than an assemblage of tires, bumper, flatbed, and so on. More exactly, we *hypothesize* at the highest level of organization, and we check that hypothesis against smaller details (Bever, 1973).

In this constructivist view, hypotheses from the higher levels of the brain activate the small physical movements of the eye. The thing perceived is neither just a figment of the mind nor a revelation of a reality that exists apart from the perceiver. Rather, "Object and percept are part and parcel of the same thing." "The thing perceived is an inseparable part of the function of perceiving, which in turn includes all aspects of the total process of living"—so Ittelson and Kilpatrick (1951). "Vision is a dynamic process, using a series of scans, but these are not rigidly determined as in a television raster. They are varied according to the nature of the scene itself and the previous experience of the individual." "Seeing is not really representational but interpretive." "The brain picks out features of the pattern that combine with its internal hypotheses to provide programs of action" (Young, 1978, pp. 119, 123).

So far, in discussing perception of language and perception in general, I have been emphasizing the constructivist school, which holds that we perceive against schemata or constructs. In recent years another strong group of theorists has emerged around the work of J. J. Gibson. This "ecological" school believes in direct perception both of language and of things. A ball coming at you or a face beginning to smile or a policeman's whistle carries information, not in the sense of what a telephone operator gives but information as engineers use the term: the result of having excluded alternatives. In that sense, this page carries information even before anything is written on it because it is white, not black. A baseball has a certain speed and curve and not some other, hence information.

According to this "ecological" theory of perception, I perceive the page or the ball because I have systems in my brain and eyes for getting out the information, that is, telling white from black or determining the speed and direction of the baseball. As applied to "The bat is in the bin," you hear the *b* in "bat" or "bin" by distinguishing it from nonplosive voiced consonants like *v* and from non-voiced plosives like *p.* That is how you can hear both those *b*s as *b* although, if we were to put them through electronics to make their waveforms visible, they would appear quite different.

From this point of view, the one question, How do you understand a sentence? becomes two. What is the information a given sentence holds? *and* What systems do we have for processing it? (Gibson, 1977; Shaw and Bransford, 1977). The earlier form of the ecological approach, the "adaptive theory of perception," concentrated on the first of these questions. Information is simply "there" and need not be processed at all, only picked up. More recent "information processing" theories of perception concentrate on both of these issues, but more on the second. What are the systems we have for, as it were, reaching into the world of language or sensations and bringing out the information an organism like us finds useful?

Both versions of this "ecological" school set our perceptions of language and the world in a larger framework: How does this perception of information fit economically into what this organism does or needs at this moment? Not all information is useful at all times to all organisms. What a monkey can grasp may be of no use to a giraffe. We humans adapt our systems to process the information that is relevant to us (Verbrugge, 1977). When you hear me say, as a linguistic example, "The bat is in the bin," it is important that you hear the difference between an *i* as in *in* and an *o* as in *on,* but it doesn't matter, for linguistic purposes, whether the sentence is spoken fast or slow, loudly or softly, or by a woman's voice or a man's.

Within the constructivist or analysis-by-synthesis theory, we would treat our perceptions of language (or the world) as a feedback. You would recognize the *b* in *bin* by checking the plosiveness of the sound waves against your internal references for plosive sounds like *b* or *p* or *t,* and you would also check that *b* against your internal references for voiced consonants like *v* or *d.* You would hear the whole sentence, "The bat is in the bin," by checking it against your internal programs for fitting individual sounds together to form words and for fitting words together into sentences (Halle and Stevens, 1964).

Although the individual psychologists who hold these constructive or ecological or information-processing points of view tend to debate the nuances fiercely, it seems to me they share an important fundamental. As I read them, no one of the three suggests that it is simply a stimulus—either a word or a sound—that causes a given response. All three involve some sort of feedback or dialectic between reality and something relatively fixed inside us (an information processing system, a reference signal, or an ecological need). To that extent, all find the perception of language and of things a two-way street, although the ecological theory relies more heavily than I would on a subject-object distinction. Even within the ecological school, however, one can acknowledge:

> Knowing is itself the process which resides neither wholly within the subject . . . nor wholly within the world as a cause or stimulus; rather, as an ecological concept, it stands like the mythical Colossus of Rhodes, astride the physical and psychological domains, one foot planted firmly on either shore (Shaw and Bransford, 1977, p. 10).

The most fully developed theory of language perception, however, comes not from psychologists but from linguists and psycholinguists building on the thinking of Noam Chomsky. (An excellent introduction is Lyons's 1977 book.) Chomsky developed the idea of a grammar as a system of rules for generating the correct (and only the correct) sentences of a language, in the same sense that the rules of arithmetic will "generate" the correct and only the correct balance for a checkbook. To be sure, some person has to do the "generating," but the rules themselves are independent of that person. They are some complex mixture of linguistic universals common to all languages and the grammar of a particular language like English.

Given this idea of grammar as a system of rules that generate sentences, one can ask some of the very basic questions about "The bat is in the bin" with some hope of their being answered. How is it that I can produce as many new sentences as I please? How can I interpret an infinity of sentences I have never heard before? Indeed, children six years old or even younger can do that. How did they learn to do it so quickly? One cannot possibly answer such questions by a notion of language as behaviorist stimulus-response or a list of what everybody has already said in English or a dictionary of signs with fixed meanings, signifiers linked to signifieds in the theories of Saussure, for example.

According to Chomsky's "standard theory," every sentence in a natural language like English has a deep structure and a surface structure. The surface is what you actually hear as "The bat is in the bin." The deep structure may involve things like "noun phrase," "verb phrase," or "pre-positional phrase," which have no meaning ("semantic content") at all, no particular reference to a bat being in a bin.

Like Freud, Chomsky has continually revised and refined his theoretical structures around a largely unchanging core of data, sometimes in ways that go beyond his followers. He has kept, however, one basic assumption. Sentences can be declared well-formed or ill-formed *by linguistic criteria alone*. Thus, Chomsky himself does not claim that his grammar for "generating" sentences corresponds to anything that actually goes on in our heads, any more than the laws of arithmetic correspond to the way I know immediately, without any calculating, that 5 plus 2 is 7.

Psychologists, however, and psycholinguists (by definition) would like to get from a purely formal analysis to what our minds do in speaking, hearing, reading, or writing. The evidence suggests that Chomsky's abstract, almost mathematical analyses correspond somewhat, but only somewhat, to our thought processes. There are "divergences between grammars and recognizers." Also, researchers have not been able to show that what language learners, like children, learn is a transformational grammar (Fodor, Bever, and Garrett, 1974). Chomsky's linguistic criteria seem to correspond to some psychological reality, but no one has yet shown just exactly what.

The strongest antithesis arising from Chomsky's work drives in at precisely this point. The cumbersomely named "generative semanticists" say that Chomsky was wrong to assume that one could talk coherently about syntax without taking meaning and use into account (Lakoff, 1974). Generative semanticists therefore try to arrive at ways to "generate" not just sentences but contexts and meanings, too. In so doing, they confront head on the basic problem linguists face. Most linguists would like to be able to discuss the principles that govern language only in relation to language. They would like to box off all consideration of the real world and consider questions about language as though they could be answered entirely in terms of formal principles governing language. Yet is that possible?

I like apples.

The sentence says nothing about eating, but all of us know it doesn't mean the speaker maintains friendships with pippins and Macintoshes.

The policeman held up his hand and stopped the car.

Strong policeman? No. We supply a driver who saw the policeman and stepped on the brake (my examples are from Schank and Abelson, 1977, p. 9). In general, we have to use what we know of the world to interpret sentences.

Further, our knowledge of the real world enters into relations that seem purely linguistic. For example, the sentence, "The patrol cars were ordered to stop honking after 2:00 A.M." is ambiguous, supposedly on linguistic grounds alone. The surface sentence could come from two different underlying structures: "[Somebody] ordered the patrol cars to stop [somebody who was] honking after 2:00 A.M." "[Somebody] ordered the patrol cars to stop [the patrol cars who were] honking after 2:00 A.M."

However, "The elephants were ordered to stop honking after 2:00 A.M." is not ambiguous. There is a linguistic ambiguity. That is, the surface sentence about elephants could have come from two different underlying structures just like those for the patrol car sentence. But, since elephants cannot stop other beings from honking (a marginally useful bit of knowledge about the real world), I do not sense any ambiguity in the sentence about elephants. The ambiguity, then, is partly a matter of language and partly a matter of experience.

My lack of confusion involves another puzzle. The distinction between inanimate and animate beings is apparently a part of all grammars, a linguistic universal. In these two sentences, however, I accept the idea that inanimate patrol cars can give orders but animate elephants cannot.

Consider this pair of sentences:

1. Helen is Manny's widow.
2. Manny is Helen's widower.

As Robin Lakoff has pointed out, to understand the unacceptability of the second, you need to know that sex roles dominate our society's typing of women but not of men (1973). In short, "It is impossible to tell where linguistic knowledge leaves off and extralinguistic knowledge takes over" (Jackendoff, 1972, p. 19).

Within this general framework, I see a certain consensus among linguists and psycholinguists in 1984. True, no one knows just what it is we do when we recognize a sentence, and no one has discovered a psychological reality that corresponds to grammatical structures. Most students of the way we perceive language do agree, however, that we generate something—maybe a sentence, maybe a sentence plus what we know about its subject, maybe just part of a sentence or a set of phrase markers (like "noun phrase," "verb phrase"), perhaps nothing more than the rhythm of what a certain kind of sentence feels like—but we generate something sentencelike to understand someone else's sentence. That something can include principles either of language or of the world, and those principles support our top-down interpretation of language.

On that basis, it was possible for Frank Smith in 1971 to write a coherent, convincing account of what we do at the sentence level when we read, and for George Dillon to develop the same principles still further in 1978. We "predict" our way through a book. We project alternatives ahead of our eyes and then we eliminate alternatives until we arrive at a single interpretation. We eliminate some quickly, in advance as it were, because English (or any other natural language) repeats information. "The bat is in the bin."

After *in,* as soon as I have seen or heard *the* I can guess a noun is not far behind. Indeed, once I have seen *in* I can be fairly sure an article and a noun will follow. Hence, by the time I get to *bin* I have already had two clues that tell me to expect a noun and specifically a noun that *in* will fit—*bin* or *basket,* but not, say *binge* or *basketball.* This redundancy of natural languages allows us to eliminate most alternatives very quickly. Then, as our eyes pass over the page, they acquire just enough visual information to eliminate the remaining alternatives—to separate *bin* from *bun* or *ban.*

In other words, having read "in the," I project ahead some such hypothesis as "noun that a thing can be in." I get back from the text "bin," and that fits my hypothesis. The sentence makes sense. Had I gotten back "binge," grammatically possible but senseless in terms of my real-world knowledge, my brain would have flicked my eyes back to the capital that began so bizarre a sentence and started over, like jumping back through a German sentence after getting the verb at the end. Projecting a hypothesis ahead and then comparing the return one gets on the hypothesis with what was wanted is, of course, a feedback process. In this respect, our perception of language is like our perception of anything else.

In such a two-stage, feedback processing of language, the brain plays a far larger part than the eye—at least with fluent readers. The eye gulps in blocks of information, but to do so, the brain must tell the eye when it has absorbed all the information it can process in short-term memory.

Short-term memory can deal with between five and seven items at a time, but (interestingly) these may be letters, syllables, sounds, words, or ideas, depending on the fluency of the reader. The capacity of your short-term memory depends not on the total amount of information you are storing, but on the number of units into which your brain can group the information (Bever, 1973). A fluent reader carries five ideas, while a beginning reader carries five words or letters. Thus, to achieve useful speed in reading, we must be able to make brain and eye work together, using prior knowledge and skill, to shape processable units out of the whole conglomeration that our eyes perceive. Those units can be maps, structures, or cognitive schemata—according to the various schools of perceptual psychology—but they are what we see by.

Once our short-term memory has reached capacity with five or six units, the brain greatly reduces the eye's seeing (like turning down the brightness on a television set). It sends the eye into a jump (or, technically, saccade) to the next place on the page where the brain thinks it useful to process information (Smith, 1971, pp. 82, 104). Presumably, brain and ear work together in somewhat the same way when we hear language, with the important difference that we cannot actively "listen ahead" into the flow of speech as far as we can look ahead on the printed page.

According to Smith, the way we perceive a page—indeed, "the way in which we perceive the world depends on the manner in which we categorize the incoming information, not simply on the characteristics of the incoming information itself" (p. 74; Dillon, 1978). Conversely (says a group studying cognition), "Much more than the knowledge of words is required to understand a sentence: There must be general knowledge about the world as well." "To understand a sentence, we appear to combine general knowledge about the world with knowledge of the structure of language and the meaning of the parts of the sentence" (Norman et al., 1975, p. 5), for example, that elephants honk but do not understand or convey orders while patrol cars can be said to do both.

In general, then, understanding language involves a dual, active process, some sort of analysis-by-synthesis, so that, as Smith says, "Whatever meaning is, it must be defined with respect to a listener or reader" (p. 35). The psychologists—even this very hard-nosed experimental group—return us to the elusive I. In other words,

Perception, Symbolization, and Identity

all go together.

We can't be sure about the details of the way we understand language, but we can feel fairly sure about the broad outlines of the process. We perceive words, as we do the world, by an active process of analysis by synthesis. Perception involves both the low-level, nearly reflex actions of eye or ear and the highest processes of which the brain is capable. In the automatic actions of our senses, we use our physiology. In the higher processes of the brain, we use our cultural training. And somewhere in it all, we make a perception into a personal, individual experience.

Sam's and Sandra's perceptions of the Faulkner story worked the same way as their symbolizations. Sandra hesitated as to whether Emily's father was standing or sitting. (The word "spraddled" admits this ambiguity.) Sam placed Mr. Grierson in the door with Emily framed by his legs rather than the two of them framed by the "back-flung front door." In a class devoted to the exact reading of literary texts, a teacher might well want to settle whether Faulkner's "spraddled" meant sitting or standing and whether Emily and her father were framed by the door or the door-frame. Here, however, we can simply note that Sam's and Sandra's needs govern not only their symbolizings but their very perceptions. Sandra's hesitation between sitting and standing lets her make Emily's father a comfortable size. Sam's framing makes masculinity reassuringly dominant.

In the same way, Paul Lorenz, caught in a thunderstorm with his lady, felt compelled to count between the lightning and the thunder. That is, he perceived the time between thunder and lightning (not as I would, as a measure of the distance of the storm) but as a gap that could be dangerously penetrated. He had to prevent that. Similarly, he saw a stone in the road as a potential source of harm, therefore something to be moved out. Both of these perceptions work variations on his identity theme about controlling things coming in and going out.

Anna S. perceived her lover's behavior this way:

> When he tells me something that was unpleasant to him . . . I hate the thing or person for it. I feel it displeased him and that makes it terrible. If he is very tired, fatigue takes hold of me. . . . When he laughs . . . I am filled with sheer glee.

Again, at the very level of perception, Anna construes the effect of events on her lover to achieve the same state of mind herself and so "become another's essence."

Hence the defense, the D, in DEFT refers to a very large idea: strategies for deciding what can come into the individual's reality. "People see what they want to see." More exactly, *people see what they can cope with in order to cope with it*, just as Anna sees fusion or Lorenz dangerous penetrations. Freud anticipated this principle, we have seen, not only in his 1937 "testamentary" essay, but even from the very beginning, in the unpublished Project of 1895 and *The Interpretation of Dreams* (1900).

The defense (in DEFT) with which one can analyze a person's perceiving is thus intimately involved with that individual's style. So also is the fantasy. The individual builds on what he has taken in to project into the event a characteristic wish-fulfilling fantasy. The fantasy does not lie latent in the event, only the materials for it. People fantasy. Stories and events do not. By perceiving the lightning and thunder as a gap that he could fill, Paul Lorenz gratified both sides of his ambivalence: his wish to penetrate and see his lady hurt; his counterwish to protect her. Only by singling out her lover's feelings as the important part of his behavior could Anna S. acquire those feelings herself and so gratify her deep wishes to be at one with a caring, loving person as once she had wanted to fuse with her mother. Sam perceives Emily as frail and fragile in order to remove threats to his own manliness and conversely to imagine a strong masculinity on top of things. Sandra sees a Bugs who does not threaten, indeed who exemplifies hospitality. All these moves constitute a DF combination, negative and positive, defensive and gratifying, within a DEFT perception or symbolization.

In the same way, experimental psychologists show, for example, that the differences in a person's tendency toward active coping or passive submission will enter into the purely perceptual task of separating an item from its context (Witkin et al., 1954, p. 489). A brain physiologist, J. Z. Young, concludes: "What we see and hear is largely the result of our own programs of search" (1978, p. 69).

Getting an act of perception to fit one's characteristic defenses is quite delicate, for it involves considerable adjustment at the gateway between self and reality. The second phase—the projection of fantasy—is much more free precisely because the first has kept sources of anxiety to a manageable size. The third principle, transformation, has to do with the same general flow toward gratification as fantasy. We need to pack our intellectual baggage neatly, to keep on good terms with our cultural heritage and our intellectual paradigms, to bring events into tune with our personal view of the world—all to the degree that feels comfortable to us. Percepts that make sense do not evoke the anxieties that raw fantasies or wishes might. They help stabilize our coping. Hence political, ethical, and the most abstruse kinds of scientific or philosophical "making sense" all serve our personal needs. None are "objective," free of emotional investment.

Hence Sam reads the Hemingway story as being about a young male's education. Sandra reads it as a story about being overpowered. Anna S. (after her analysis) does not simply decide she wants to be at one with her mother. She generalizes. "Does real loving make one feel a part of another?" Or she develops a social theme: "Women should not have to work at a public job for money. . . . They should have a man to take care of that part, but they should . . . do all they can to make him happy."

Defense, fantasy, and transformation are ways each of us shapes an event to make it a tolerable mixture of what our ordinary psychic functioning can cope with and what feels strange or different. Hence, before any of those three came into play, there was a first and primary mode: expectation. Each of us approaches a new experience with a characteristic cluster of hopes, desires, fears, and needs. We trust that the new experience will let us act out this economy of expectancies to net us pleasure. Consciously, we expect satisfaction. Unconsciously, we expect to be able to DEFT the new experience in our particular way of DEFTing.

When we feel satisfied by an experience, as Sandra's perception of Bugs pleased her, that signal tells us we have succeeded in working through some system of matching defenses, projecting fantasies, and transforming into meaning characteristically. If we do not feel satisfied, if we respond to a perception with guilt or fear or pain, that signal of unpleasant affect tells us that so far our effort to fit the event into our psychic processes has failed. The event feels alien to us, like Lorenz's neurotic compulsions or Vincent's political coercions or Anna's sense that her real self was not involved.

Accordingly, we try to change that unpleasurable answer to our expectation. We do something about the event, or we do something about our relation to the event. We may even just blot it out—not perceive it—as

Freud managed not to hear the Tyrolean church bells or as Iiro was able to deny his inability to play the flute or do carpentry.

In any case, it is our *emotions* that monitor the moment by moment functioning of these four aspects of perception or symbolization. Whether or not our ego "can deal with" some feature of reality, we know only by the way we feel. The emotional signal we get depends in turn upon the whole circuit of expectation, defense, fantasy, and transformation.

Within that fourfold interaction, two aspects, transformation and expectation, relate to each other in a special way, around time. Meaningful minutes of experience build on instants of expectation. Each separate millisecond of eye scan which Iiro gave Winnicott's first squiggle was governed by his overall expectation (an unconscious E in a quite unconscious DEFT) that he could interpret this drawing as evidence that this new person would accept him as he was. The psychoanalytic theory of identity thus combines with the theory of perception that experimental psychologists have been developing.

The psychoanalyst looks at larger perceptions, more personal, more committed to entireties, but the shape of the psychoanalyst's theory has the same shape as the experimentalist's. What the experimentalists have shown in a great variety of contexts is: "Perception is never a sure thing, never an absolute revelation of 'what is.' Rather, what we see is a prediction—our own personal construction designed to give us the best possible bet for carrying out our purposes in action" (Ittelson and Kilpatrick, 1951, p. 179).

Thus, the particular studies of the perceptual psychologist and the larger theory of the psychoanalyst lead to a still more general philosophical position: a theory of knowledge (rather like that of Husserl). People are not blank sheets (Lockean *tabulae rasae*) on which the world writes its message, nor do we perceive the world through some kind of behaviorist conditioning. Rather, we confer meaning. You and I are freely emitting centers of meanings which others either share and so confirm or refuse to share and so deny (Poole, 1972). I remember the confirmations or disconfirmations and the feelings that went with them, and they form the basis for new expectations and new standards to govern the feedback loops of perception. Just as perceptual psychology describes the external confirmations of the meanings I confer, so psychoanalytic psychology describes the way they both express and create my identity.

Thus, when we perceive and when we symbolize, we are doing much the same sort of thing. To see a chaos of areas and colors as a bin, you and I need to be able to symbolize it as a bin. To symbolize it as a bin, we need to be able to see the lines and textures that make it up. The two processes are not contradictory, as Jones thought, perception faithfully copying the world and symbolization then distorting it. Neither does one come first. Rather, perception and symbolization work together. We see and we sign in one continuous process of feedback and dialectic. "The brain," writes physiologist Granit, "does what no computer can imitate: in growing and developing, it creates the world it needs" (1977, p. 128). The brain's ability to make experiences into coherent symbols (of Jones's kind or any other) enters into the very workings of eyes and ears. Hence, I can ask of Iiro's discovery of a duck in Winnicott's squiggle, How does this relate to the rest of what I know of Iiro? Combining the modern idea of identity with the modern idea of perception points toward an account of mind itself.

6 | A Model of Mind

In answer to my craving to know about mind, a philosopher, Jerrold Katz, once suggested to me that different theories of something as elusive as mind or matter are like different architectural drawings of a house. The perspective sketch of the house on its site will look very different from the floor plan which in turn will differ from the wiring and plumbing diagrams. Each of these blueprints has its different use for which the others may well be useless or invalid. One cannot use the wiring diagram to landscape nor find the electric outlets in the overall perspective sketch.

Blueprints are not simply right or wrong; they are each right or wrong within their particular context. It makes no sense to say a blueprint is right or wrong in some context for which it was not designed. We can ask, however, ,that the wiring diagram not indicate rooms which do not appear on the floor plan nor the overall perspective show a storey which does not appear in the lumber specifications. In other words, we can ask that a blueprint, whatever its context, not be inconsistent with some blueprint which is valid in its context.

In the same way, in physics, we can ask that macroexplanations of falling bodies and colliding billiard balls not conflict with the microexplanations in particle physics of electrons and muons. To be sure, the two kinds of explanations will look very different and will not transfer into each other's contexts. Nevertheless, they should not contradict each other.

So with mind. We can—and should—ask that psychoanalytic and psychological explanations of large-scale behavior not contradict models of the brain from molecular biology, but we need not ask that they take the same form (Weatherick, 1980). It is in that spirit that I want to propose a model of mind that will be consistent with psychoanalytic theory, with new physiological discoveries about the brain, and with new psychological theories about perception and language.

Psychoanalysis began (in a sense) with Freud's effort to make a nerve-brain model of the neurotic processes he was observing (1895), and recently Karl Pribram has updated Freud's model using holography (1969). Heinz Hartmann continued Freud's bias toward the natural sciences but included biology in one of his models; the other, according to Roy Schafer, proceeds from an analogy to government (1970). As long ago as 1959, Lawrence Kubie suggested using electronic models from communications engineering and computers for psychoanalytic theory and Emanuel Peterfreund has thoroughly developed such models for the therapeutic situation (1971).

For a model of mind in general, we can begin with the information-processing feedback loop that proved useful for thinking about symbolization and perception. Suppose you are expecting to read the letter *b*. You compare what you see to some internal idea of the features of *b:* consonant, lowercase, a unit round but with an ascender (hence not a *q* or a *g*) on the left (hence not a *d*). If the test checks out (provides satisfying feedback), you go on to the next letter. If the test does not, you bring another set of features up for comparison.

The loop has to have three features. One, a behavioral end acting on the input: my eyes scanning the print on the page. Two, some standard or reference signal that is outside and uncontrolled by the loop—like my ideas of what *b* and *q* and *d* are like. Three, a comparator like my brain, comparing the marks my eye sees to that standard.

Some psychology books treat feedback loops as though they had only two elements, an output and a comparator. That's wrong. There has to be that standard inside me but outside the loop sensing this *b*. Usually the way I know that standard is being met or not is by the way I feel. The car *feels* safely positioned—or it doesn't, and I feel anxious and reposition it so that I don't feel anxious.

Through that preestablished reference, I can link these loops into a hierarchy, by having one loop set the standard for another (as below). In the earlier example of steering a car, I can imagine a smaller or "lower" loop concerned simply with physically positioning the car where I want it to be. Suppose I have decided that the car should be one meter from the shoulder. If a gust of wind causes it to drift to half a meter from the shoulder, I turn the

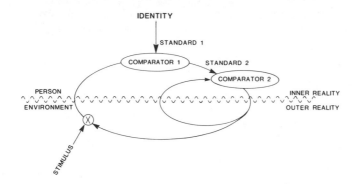

wheel left to get it back to one meter. That standard of one meter has to come from outside the loop positioning the car.

It could come from another, larger loop. If the smaller loop is "positioning the car," we might imagine that larger loop as something like "thinking about road shoulders." Suppose I come to a section of highway under repair. A sign says "No Shoulder." I see that driving off the right edge would entail dropping six inches into some loose gravel. Comparing my one meter standard for a smooth shoulder with this new riskier shoulder, my ideas of safety say I should now stay a meter and a half from the edge of the road. I change the standard for the smaller loop. I then *use* the lower loop to turn the steering wheel to position the car according to this new standard from the upper loop.

Suppose, however, that a child runs out from the left side into this construction work. Drawing on a still higher level of abstraction—an injured child is worse than a broken axle—I drive on the edge of the no-shoulder road or over it to avoid hitting the child. I have changed the standard for the "thinking about shoulders," which in turn changed the standard for the "position the car" loop.

Memory also enters in. My previous experience with road shoulders feeds back through memory to become one of the things I (a rather high-level I) take into account in setting my standard at one meter.

Notice that a two-loop feedback picture allows me to take into account cultural ideas within my overall style. It might be the custom in my part of the country to drive one meter from the side of the road. I, a conservative driver, customarily drive 1.5 meters from the shoulder. My son customarily drives 0.5 meters from the edge. Suppose, however, we lived in Quebec and the custom were 0.5 meters from the shoulder. A similarly conservative and not-so-conservative Quebecois father and son might drive at .75 and .25 meters, respectively, from the shoulder.

In 1948, Clyde Kluckhohn and Henry A. Murray issued one of the grand gnomic statements of modern psychology: "Everyone is in certain respects (a) like all other men, (b) like some other men and (c) like no other men." They were stating the puzzle of personality and culture, for example, my writing the *b* in *The bat is in the bin*. The marks I see on the page are the same marks that probably every other human being will see there, but not everyone will experience them the same way I do. A French writer's idea of *b* will not correspond to mine because his culture teaches a different way of writing *b*. Finally the *b* I write will be like no one else's *b*.

Will a two-level feedback picture allow me to interrelate the ways in which a given experience has some elements that are the same for all people, some that are true for certain groups (like cultures), and some that are unique to one person? Yes. This is just what William T. Powers suggests in order to generate a general model of mind.

A Linking of Loops

Powers is building on the achievement of Norbert Wiener, who worked out the mathematics of cybernetic systems and suggested as far back as 1943 that they could be used to describe living, adaptive organisms (Rosenblueth, Wiener, and Bigelow, 1943).

Powers states his basic thesis in the title of his book: *Behavior: The Control of Perception* (1973a). He intends a reversal of the usual stimulus-response view which would make perception the control of behavior. He goes on to model the mind as a whole by imagining a graded series of such feedback loops, a hierarchy, in which each loop corresponds to a certain level of perception and also provides the reference signal for the loop below it.

At the most basic level, Powers posits signals of muscular effort and signals of intensity, things like loudness, brightness, stiffness, or pungency. They are the most basic because one must perceive a certain minimal glimmering of light before one can see other visual qualities like color or an edge, a minimal faint hum before one can detect pitch, a certain minimal tactile pressure before flatness, and so on.

To develop the next step in the hierarchy, Powers seeks a set of control systems that is hierarchically above the first-order systems, but at the same time as close to the level of first-order systems as possible (p. 99). The inputs to the second-order control loops are combinations of such first-order intensities as pressure, light, sound, vibration, balance, or taste. Powers suggests thinking of the second order as controlling a sum (mathematically, a vector sum) of first-order intensities. He calls this sum a *sensation*, for example, of purple, chocolate, or G sharp.

In other words, our second-order controls organize first-order intensities into qualities loosely corresponding to the traditional five senses, although other groupings also occur. For example, when I hear the sound *sss*, I simply hear it. When I speak *sss*, however, I sense both sound and effort. Yet both times I "sense hissing." The sensation is nominally the same but actually involves different intensities, cutting across different "senses."

Powers comments on the " 'philosophical fact' that emerges from this theory." I taste "chocolate," but no physical entity corresponds to my taste—only a combination of sugars and oils. "Perceptual signals *depend on* physical events, but what they represent *does not necessarily have any physical significance*" (p. 113). In general, Powers concludes,

The brain may be full of many perceptual signals, but the relationships between those signals and the external reality on which they depend seems utterly arbitrary. At least we have no assurance that any given perception has significance outside of a human brain. . . . We may strongly suspect that there is a real universe out there, beginning a millimeter outside of our nervous systems, but *our perceptions are not that universe.* They *depend on it,* but the form of that dependence is determined in the brain, by the neural computers which create perceptual signals layer by layer by layer through transformations of one set of neural currents into another (p. 37)

In other words, Powers is describing at the perceptual level something very like the DEFTing we have seen at higher levels, the matching of expectations, defenses, and fantasies to form a top-down, bottom-up bridge from "in here" to "out there." He goes on to build a hierarchy that rises to the highest levels of mental functioning.

To think our way from a second to a third order, we need to imagine a system just above but as close as possible to the second-order system dealing with sensations. Powers suggests that we think of the third order as *configurations,* that is, an unchanging function of a set of sensations (second order) which are in turn sums of (first order) intensities.

For example, the retina's individual rods and cones generate first order signals of brightnesses. Still within the retina, computing networks of cells organize these signals of intensity into edges, areas, or gradients, that is, sensations (second order). Powers theorizes that the visual centers near the thalamus process these into configurations, the third order. He finds some confirmation in brain physiology for this arrangement of the three layers: Wilder Penfield's well-known experiments stimulating with electric probes the visual cortex of people undergoing brain surgery (1975, pp. 21–27, 55–56). The subject "sees" forms: a red star, a blue disk, a green ball, or a black wheel. Similarly, when Penfield stimulated the auditory cortex, his subjects heard ringing, humming, chirping, and other auditory configurations. One particularly important class of third-order perceptions, then, would be phonemes like the *b*s in "The bat is in the bin."

We may inherit some of these configurations. René Spitz showed that a three month old infant recognizes faces in one particular way: as forehead-eyes-nose. The baby will respond even to a Halloween mask having these features but not to a real human face in profile. It seems likely that forehead-eyes-nose is an inherited configuration for organizing experience, biologically a very useful one for a baby seeking to nurse and be nurtured by someone paying attention to him, as we say, "facing" him (pp. 86–96).

We adults have a similar ability. We can recognize faces from just a few features and even though they may change drastically. Since last I saw friends from college or graduate school, their faces may have wrinkled or their hair grayed, yet I recognize them. Indeed, I can recognize a cartoon of Winston Churchill or Hitler that shows no more than a globular head and a cigar or a mustache and a shock of black hair.

The opposite of this ability is the disease prosopagnosia: the victim can no longer recognize faces. "What is remarkable about the disorder is its specificity," remarks the psychologist Norman Geschwind. One can know people by name, and one can describe faces verbally, but one cannot put the image of the face together with the name. "The lesions that cause prosopagnosia are as stereotyped as the disorder itself." "The implication is that some neural network within the region is specialized for the rapid and reliable recognition of human faces" (1979, p. 189). Possibly Powers's third-order control systems are this sort of thing.

The idea of a third level dealing with configurations also gives us a way of thinking about the familiar but puzzling psychological phenomenon called "object constancy." We see a chair as a chair no matter what angle we see it from or even if we see it upside down. We see it as comprising horizontal seat and vertical back even though it may never, in the real, physical world, actually present those directions. In a feedback model, we do not have to think of the brain going through some very complicated "compensation" to make constants out of the varying ways our sensations present a chair to us. We need only assume that the reference signal for the chair configuration remains constant as the chair rotates and pivots with respect to us so that we always have a constant to compare our sense data to. In effect, for certain larger purposes, we tune out certain kinds of changes.

Then how do we perceive differences as we assume different positions with respect to the chair? Because we perceive distances and size and orientations as third-order configurations, says Powers. "What we express in serial language as 'the big chair cattycorner on the far side of the room' is probably perceived at third order all in parallel: big *and* chair *and* cattycorner *and* far *and* side *and* a room" (p. 126). These configurations may account for some of the familiar optical illusions: the staircase that turns upside down into a cornice or the vase that turns into two faces if you think of it that way.

A fourth level of control will account for our ability to see "motion pictures," the rapidly repeated images of television or movies. "When a human being is presented with two related configurations in sequence, within a short enough span of time, he perceives a new entity of experience not present in either configuration alone: *change*" (p. 130). Too fast a transition, and we see simultaneity, for example, the blur of the blades of an electric fan rotating faster than ten revolutions per second. Too slow a transition, and we do not perceive change at all as, for example, the minute hand of a clock, which moves at 1/3600 of a revolution per second. Between, we perceive change, like the turning of the second hand or a series of musical notes that seem to be a glissando or like the light bulbs on a theater marquee that make a moving arrow, although they are only stationary lights flashing on and off. We also control these transitions in any movement like raising an arm, creating a rising or falling tone of voice, or tracing out a path in space as when a child runs to catch a ball.

If the fourth level enables us to control movement, the fifth must enable us to choose one movement rather than another. That is, the fifth must involve the way we sense and control the *sequence* in which we sense lower-order perceptions. I decide how to move to get up out of my chair, go across the room, pick up the *Times,* read the headlines, and say "Damn!"

The saying of "Damn!" I find particularly interesting. It would be at this fifth level, *sequence,* says Powers, that we recognize words, and he goes on to design circuits of neurones that would do this job. At the third level, the recognition of phonemes like *ss,* only sixty or so circuits would be needed. The fourth level would involve common transitions from one phoneme to another, like *st* or the *ay* in *day.* The fifth level would provide circuits for recognizing sequences of phonemes, one circuit per phoneme in a word. Hence, he argues, in order to recognize 150,000 words, averaging six phonemes apiece, no more than 900,000 neurones would be required. Such a "lexicon" (to borrow a word from the linguist) could fit into a space of 150 cubic millimeters, about half the size of an almond. In this circuitry, as in the various speeds involved, nothing that Powers proposes is physically impossible for our brains.

Even so, this whole description of the brain as operating through five levels of feedback is speculative. Levels beyond the fifth are even more so. Powers suggests for the sixth level *relationships* among fifth- and lower-order entities: intensities, sensations, configurations, changes, and sequences. The relationships might be: and's, or's, cause-and-effect, if-then, space relations or relations in time, probabilities, or just plain association. At the sixth level, we organize and interpret our experience. We experiment with it. We understand how the six of hearts relates to the deck or why pushing a doorbell makes a sound.

For a seventh level, Powers suggests the *control of programs*: looking for one's glasses; playing chess; baking a cake; making love; holding a conversation. The seventh level builds on the ability to make and recognize relationships—the sixth level—but goes beyond it in setting up a series of tests and decisions leading to different procedures. I am trying to do the crossword puzzle. I need my pen. I go into the bedroom, lift up a jacket, grab the shirt under it, and poke into its pocket. These into's, under's, and on top of's are sixth-level relationships, but I have organized them into a complicated series of programs and subroutincs. These *strategies* or *programs* or *sequences of relationships plus control of sequences of relationships* illustrate what Powers proposes for a seventh level.

Powers raises the question of the role of language in this description of human rationality. There are two ways of thinking about language. In one, words are simply perceptions that evoke nonverbal perceptions—referents or "signifieds." I perceive the word *bat* and I think of a club you swing. Alternatively, I might think of the word *bat* as something that can be manipulated in a purely symbolic way without any reference to the bats of the real world (purely a "signifier"?). If the latter, we would have to assume a special level for recognizing and controlling verbal symbols as such, and Powers rejects this for several reasons, one of them parsimony. Either way, however, language fits into the model as the most powerful means we have for setting up and altering programs—although, as Powers notes, we also seem to have programs that are nonlinguistic, like tying one's shoes or touch typing.

For an eighth level, Powers posits a system for choosing among programs, setting up programs, or altering programs toward certain ends. He borrows the concept of "heuristic principles" from artificial intelligence: general ideas of how to win the game, sell the product, make it neat. *Principles* are facts confirmed by experience, such as strength in the center of the board is good to have, honesty is the best policy, or "I could show this psychologist up." Eighth order systems would operate in very complex situations that do not yield to exact procedures that can be set down ahead of time (like tying one's shoes—seventh level) or in situations with a lot of distracting detail where one needs to average out and select data. Eighth order systems are what computer programmers would call "executive programs." A psychoanalyst might think in terms of superego directives to ego.

Beyond the eighth level, Powers suggests a level that chooses one set of *principles* over another. He calls this level *system concepts*, a procedure for seeing some collection of moral, factual, or abstract principles as in fact a connected set. Such a loop would perceive things like the Unitcd States Army, the Democratic party, or "my family." With these entities all the physical things that embody them may change—everything that *was* the Democratic party during the Roosevelt years has disappeared—yet I recognize a thing I call the Democratic party above and beyond those sensory particulars.

This very high level would deal with the philosophical problem of "Locke's sock." A stocking may be darned and darned and darned until not the slightest bit of the original stocking remains, yet at no point (or at what point?) do we say this is no longer the original stocking. "System concepts such as Society or Culture are not to be found in the world represented by physical models of the universe; they are elements of psychological models of the universe . . . effective exactly to the degree the individuals learn to perceive them and choose goals with respect to them and develop means of maintaining their ninth-order perceptions in those goal states" (p. 173). Powers gives the concept of "the system" itself (that is, the system you can't beat) as such a ninth-level perception.

In psychoanalytic terms, I would say the boundary between Powers's imaginary eighth and ninth levels corresponds to the boundary between secondary-process, problem-solving thought and primary processes like dreaming or free association. In a classic study of opinions, the researchers concluded that an opinion was "a resultant or compromise between reality demands, social demands, and inner psychological demands. The three are inseparable" (Smith, Bruner, and White, 1956, p. 275). Their metaphor is "compromise" or "resultant" as "boundary" was mine. Powers's hierarchy of feedbacks offers us much more powerful metaphors for these complex psychological relations. Self *guides* cultural standards which *guide* bio-physical standards.

Oddly, it seems likely that our feelings, our intuitions, our half-conscious "gut reactions," primary-process thinking, in other words, directs our perceptions and movements, secondary processes, rather than the other way round. If we are working with reality, we use our lower-level processes of sensation and perception, and secondary-process thinking directly guides these reality-oriented processes. Primary-process thinking, however, connects to the feelings that tell us whether our secondary-process feedbacks through reality are working. If we are asleep, as Freud surmised, our primary processes can run free, unconstrained by the real world. When we wake, then our primary processes take control again. Hence primary processes *guide* secondary (see pp. 336–37).

Beyond the ninth level Powers bows out, offering only guesses. Perhaps *instincts* provide goals—and here, I think, Freud's notions of instinctive drives, combinations of love and aggression, might fit, for example, my own urgent need to understand that propels me through all this cerebration and lucubration. Alternatively, Powers suggests *memory,* surely an important element throughout the hierarchy since it allows for changing (or not changing) the personality embodied in all these reference levels. To do something differently or the same as before—at any level—one must have a memory of how it was done before. Memory is the way lower levels change upper ones.

For levels ten and beyond, says Powers, "Maybe our brothers from the East have something to tell us" (p. 174). I would suggest something less mystical, a theme-and-variations concept of identity. All lower-order processes, from notions like society and culture at the ninth level down to the mere sense of brightness or loudness at the first, serve to preserve the I, to make it feel "right." *I* need to know things. It is more than need. I hunger, I desire, I crave. I am an addict of ideas. Hence I feed on the authors I have been quoting (like Powers) and write the pages you have been reading, using lower-level systems, configurations or sensations, to do so.

I am in a continuing process of creating "I" through these various lower-order systems. Feelings tell me that at any given level my actions are yielding perceptions that suit the goals of my identity at that level. Memory at all these levels permits the accumulation of samenesses and differences in that "I" which you (or I) can read as themes.

One can imagine identity (in all three senses, agency, consequence, and representation) as the top level of the hierarchy. "All the programs of the brain constitute one single model or one single model or structured system," writes J. Z. Young, a brain physiologist. "The brain has many distinct parts but there is increasing evidence that they are interrelated to make one functioning whole, which gives a unique and characteristic direction to the pattern of life of that one individual" (1978, p. 265). I read him as legitimating the idea of a holistic identity governing a variety of programs, like Powers's hierarchy of feedbacks.

Having tried out Powers's richly imagined model of the brain, however, we now have to give it up—at least partly. A modern brain physiologist like Ragnar Granit agrees that feedback loops serve us well for a rough description of the self-correcting principle even in high-level processes, yet they can be no more than that. Our minds' circuits are nonlinear. Neurones do not simply switch on and off. These circuits work in incredibly complicated patterns in which one circuit excites or inhibits another in response to a comparison. While one cell in our retina responds to a color, the cell next to it suppresses its response in the interests of exactitude. Contexts enter into each on-off, and any one neurone may be the context for the next. These circuits, moreover, have a vast redundancy, nature's safety factor in the organ most important to our survival. All these circuits interact and are repeated so many times over that one cannot simply represent these three-dimensional structures by the two-dimensional diagrams of a computer scientist.

Perceptual psychologists of the ecological persuasion, for example, are showing that one needs to go beyond hierarchy. One needs to think in terms of heterarchies (in which control is passed back and forth from an upper loop to a lower loop) or even "coalitions" in which the system consists of part of the organism acting with its context in the environment. One must think of the "functional integrity" of the individual complementing an environment that also has "functional integrity" (Turvey, Shaw, and Mace, 1978)—dare I say wholeness, unity, identity?

Finally, though, I have to admit that we cannot use Powers' loops even repeated many times and ranked in a hierarchy to discover the workings of our eyes or ears or memories. Nevertheless the feedback model has its uses. For example, a certain area of the brain moves the eyes in response to an electrical stimulus. Moving the eyes is a motor action, notes a team of researchers, but the same action also reprocesses visual information. It is part of the sensory system. "The lesson is that no line can be drawn between a sensory side and a motor side in the organization of the brain" (Nauta, 1979, p. 106). In other words, Powers's general principle, that behavior—motor action—is the control of perception, is sound. Our brains do operate like feedback systems. We cannot use this broad generalization to map the cell-by-cell workings of our brain and senses, but it will serve as a framework within which to think about less detailed principles like psychological laws or psychoanalysis' idea of individuality.

Thus, Powers's loops fit the descriptions in some well-known psychological analyses of planning and thinking, for example the Test-Operate-Test-Exit (TOTE) sequence suggested by Miller, Galanter, and Pribram (1960). One checks the image of things against a plan—that is the test. One then operates to bring the two together. Test again, and if the result is satisfactory, stop. Newell and Simon's "heuristics" are very similar. You set a goal, judge the separation of the present situation from the goal, take a step, see whether the separation is reduced, judge the difference between the present and the goal, take a step, and so on (Simon, 1957, see also Bruner, Goodnow, and Austin, 1956). These are feedback procedures, as are most "information processing" moves of artificial intelligence.

Granit notes the "hierarchic stratification" of the various controls in the brain, and this is another central feature of Powers's model with which most brain scientists would agree. "Here," writes one authority, "one finds remarkable agreement among scholars of widely different backgrounds, disciplines, and eras . . . that purposive movements are built on a base of reflex processes." "Reflexes and voluntary movements are not opposites," he continues, discussing the brain's control of movement. He gives the example of a Russian study of the champion pistol shots in the Red Army. As they aimed, their pistols remained immobile, even if their legs or arms or shoulders moved. In effect, reflex mechanisms stabilized the position of the marksman's hand in space. He ends by thinking only of his goal: hitting the target. "The actual events that underlie the achievement of the goal are built up from a variety of reflex processes" (Evarts, 1979, pp. 170 and 179).

Further, those processes are relatively isolated one from another. As Herbert Simon has shown, evolution would favor organisms built on hierarchical principles, because disruption of parallel hierarchies would cause only partial loss (one finger among five, color blindness but not total blindness), whereas an undivided system would undergo total loss. Hierarchical systems thus have the important property of "near decomposability." That is, the connections within a subsystem are stronger than the connections between subsystems. Nature has separated the fast processes within a subsystem (seeing by an eye, say) from the slower processes linking subsystems (co-ordinating arm and eye in firing at a target). This partial isolation lets us think and use the systems as though they were separate. It corresponds to Powers's connecting his systems only by a reference signal.

When we speak or write, we *start* with an idea we want to express, and we then find ways to express it. In other words, we use grammar (whether we are thinking of a formal linguistic grammar or a psychological one) in the service of higher-level aims (Schank and Abelson, 1977, p. 7). Our grammar or "lexicon" functions as a separable circuit like the body's loops.

Granit, in his aptly titled book *The Purposive Brain* (1977), represents today's thinking, anchored in electrophysiological studies of the brain. The remarkable discoveries of recent years, he notes, allow scientists to list in detail "inhibitions and symptoms at synaptic loci," separate systems. Even so, scientists have to give those listings "teleological relevance" to make them more than merely lists (p. 175). The *scientist* has to take into account goals and purposes, and that is why behaviorism and the routine correlation of behaviors are bound to fail. We can understand the mechanics of voluntary motion by studying physical facts, but we can only understand the whole process if we set those mechanics in a hierarchy that involves "higher" mental levels. We need to be able to talk about goals. Hence we need to include in our physical model of the brain psychological concepts of purpose, will, or demand. Granit is performing an important service. He is placing alongside the "hard" research of brain physiology reasoning from such "soft" disciplines as psychology, psychoanalysis, or identity theory. We have to talk in terms of

Higher and Lower

systems.

If we accept this idea of a purposive hierarchy, a lower stratum in the hierarchy can never explain the *raison d'être* of the level above it. Rather, each level will require goals from higher levels to explain it—Powers's "reference signals" or "standards" from outside the several feedback loops.

By endorsing the principle of hierarchy and admitting considerations of purpose into physical accounts of the brain, a modern brain physiologist (like Granit) is continuing in today's thinking some of the classical experiments of Sir Charles Sherrington. Sherrington showed experimentally that reflex activities, such as a dog's scratching with his rear leg, persisted even though the cord to the brain had been cut so that there was no way the brain could participate in the act. This is not to say the act is not changed, however.

In his lectures of 1937–38, Sherrington explains that any individual organism's motor behavior has two components. One is reflex, and since it predominates in the lower, earlier levels of the evolutionary scale, it seems basal. The other is a superstructure, and it is not reflex. In the higher animals the roof-brain supplies this superstructure, whether the behavior be instinctive or rational. As one proceeds up the evolutionary scale, activities that were controlled at their site—the movement of a lobster's antenna, for example—become controlled in mammals in the brain. The roof-brain component increases the finesse, skill, adaptability, and specificity of the motor act. As we go higher on the evolutionary scale, this superstructure becomes more prominent, and it is most prominent in humans.

If the motor act is deprived of that roof-brain component (as in Sherrington's cutting the spinal cords of dogs), if it is reduced to its reflex foundation, the motor act becomes, in the highest animals and most of all in humans, imprecise, inconsequent, and without "skill." In lower mammals, evidently, the reflex has normally a larger share in the behavior and the reflex foundation is in itself more capable and complete, for the motor act suffers less on withdrawal of the higher, the nonreflex, component. Even as between dog and man, the dog can stand and walk and run competently after exclusion of the roof-brain. It can direct itself visually. But man not so. A dog, however, after its spinal cord has been cut, can no longer adapt its reflex acts to a special purpose, nor can they be given greater skill by training.

Evidently, sensory impulses get "long-circuited" to the roof-brain, which issues a "call" to reflexes to get them to cooperate. The call fits a reflex to this or that purpose of the moment which the animal's situation asks for. The dog not only walks, it walks to greet its master. "In a word the component from the roof-brain alters the character of the motor act from one of generality of purpose to one of narrowed and specific purpose fitting a specific occasion" (1963, pp. 182-83).

Sherrington's picture matches that of Powers. When Sherrington speaks of "long-circuiting" through the "roof-brain," his lower-level loops embody the dog's (or our) ability to walk or our ability (and perhaps the dog's) to recognize faces. These lower levels work within a hierarchy so that they serve higher needs of consciousness. Granit uses the term "cephalization" (which we could English as 'headening'). Von Bertalanffy speaks of three levels in the human. The spinal cord acts as a reflex apparatus. The ancient brain, the "palaencephalon," is "the organ of depth personality with its primeval instincts, emotions, and appetites." The cortex is the organ of the "day personality," that is, the conscious I (1952).

For all these theorists, mind is a gradual higher and lower. Aristotle decided that the lower limit of life defies demarcation. Sherrington concluded the same of mind: "There seems no clear lower limit to mind. . . . Ultimately mind so traced [downwards along the scale of being] seems to fade to no mind." "A well-versed observer of the one-celled animal world has said that were an amoeba as big as a dog we should all acknowledge its mind" (pp. 208, 209). Granit adopts the same position: "From the evolutionary standpoint of modern biology, consciousness is an emergent novelty, probably still existing in an increasingly rudimentary form as one descends in the phylum" (1977, p. 72).

Michael Polanyi, the biologist and philosopher of science, puts this gamut more formally by speaking in terms of boundary conditions. Think of a vacuum cleaner. It works under two distinct sets of principles. One set is the general laws of electricity and mechanics. The other is the special ideas that went into the design of this particular Hoover. Polanyi suggests that we think of the particular ideas that adapted the general laws to the cleaning of rugs as boundary conditions. One can think of any useful or purposeful restriction of nature the same way: the organs inside a body, for example, plants and animals, ultimately even we humans. There is no way the laws of electricity, chemistry, or mechanics can provide their own boundary conditions. A more particular or "higher" embodiment of those principles has to do that. Hence, one has to think of a continuum of control running from the highest to the lowest forms of life and even below that, to vacuum cleaners (1968, p. 1311).

Trying to simulate human understanding in computers, the psychologists Schank and Abelson found it necessary to posit a similar hierarchy, parallel but in terms of understanding rather than brain function. If a computer is to understand such ordinary human activities as going to a restaurant, "understandability is a function of the place of a piece of information in context. A script is understandable as a particular realization of a plan. A plan is sensible only if it leads to some desired goal. And, a goal is understandable if it is part of a larger theme" (1977, p. 132).

Thus, intelligence itself answers to a hierarchy, and at the top of the hierarchy is what they call themes: "A life theme is no more than a collection of goals that in some sense 'go together' and a set of behavior patterns appropriate to attaining those goals." In the hesitation Schank and Abelson embody in those quotation marks around "go together," I recognize the experimentalist's unfamiliarity with what is commonplace to me as a literary critic: the organization of ideas from details to a center by means of themes and themes of themes. They are finding in intelligence the holistic unity in variety that I find in personality as a whole.

Polanyi and Schank and Abelson provide us with a model as general as Powers's hierarchy of feedbacks and very like it. In effect, the structure of

the internal and external feedback connections for Powers's organism constitute boundary conditions for Polanyi's "forces of inanimate nature." Just
as Powers' single feedback network leads naturally to a hierarchy of networks, so Polanyi's higher levels provide boundary conditions for lower
levels until we get down to unformed physical and chemical laws. So also
Schank and Abelson's hierarchy provides successively more general contexts as one goes up the scale for events that are successively more specific as
one goes down the scale.

A variety of scientific perspectives, then, I find converging on one general
picture. The computer engineer (Powers), the brain physiologists (Granit,
Sherrington, Young), the philosopher of science (Polanyi), the simulators of
human intelligence (Schank and Abelson, Simon) all agree on two fundamental principles. First, one can symbolize mind at least partially as a
hierarchy of processes. They may be feedback loops, reflex arcs, TOTE
systems, or "scripts," but they all process information so as to correct
themselves against a goal beyond the loop. Second, therefore, in such a
model, higher processes provide reference levels, boundary conditions,
purposes, goals, criteria, or understandability for lower processes. Such a
hierarchy will span the "highest" functions of human individuality or intelligence down to one-celled animals or even inert matter. Even a cockroach
can have a style.

The model of mind I am suggesting is one more version of this ladder of
feedbacks. I see a hierarchy consisting of various forms of DEFT. There are
ways of looping wishes or fantasies out into the external world (fantasies)
and ways of controlling what shall be admitted from that external world into
the self (defenses). There are ways of looping low-level expectations in the
immediate flow of experience back into high-level transformations of experience into significance. Both at the highest level of that hierarchy and
permeating all the loops, I see a personal style. I can represent that style as a
theme-and-variations identity. It is the goal of goals, a unifying "life theme"
in Schank and Abelson's sense. It is

The Top

I am suggesting for identity a role like that often given by students of the
brain to consciousness: a giver of direction from the highest level, a unifier, a
centerer. Sherrington described it as "the unifying by the mind of its experience of the moment," "an integration." He gave as an example a familiar
"optical illusion": "What is being looked at as a set of steps suddenly
without warning becomes an overhanging cornice. But it is always the one or
the other wholly." The mind interprets its "now" into a situation with a
single meaning. Sherrington calls this constant unifying "the principle of

convergence." "That unifying of the experience of the moment is an aspect of the unity of the 'I.' "

Some forty years after Sherrington, a physiologist like Granit can draw on many more achievements in unraveling the networks that make up that I. For Granit the key terms are "purpose" and "creativeness." At the lowest level, we have the homeostatic balances of molecular details, further up, the holistic workings of the organs and limbs, still further up, behaviors, and finally, the processes we call mind. At every level, the creative purpose of a higher level shapes the working of lower levels. The body uses lower processes for its higher ends so that there is "a reorientation of purpose from level to level." "A warp of creative purposiveness is woven into the fabric of biological hierarchies with consciousness at its top level." One has to take that purposefulness into account, Granit insists, in one's explanations as a scientist, even if such explanations "never will end in the differential equations that the physicist uses for his world of interpretation" (1977, p. 85).

Long before Granit, in 1932, Edward Tolman had issued his well-known maxim, "Behavior reeks with purpose." Long before Tolman, William James was explaining, "why we ought to continue to talk in psychology as if consciousness has causal efficacy" (1890, p. 138). Consciousness brings efficiency to a noninstinctive brain by "bringing a more or less constant pressure to bear in favor of those of its performances which make for the most permanent interests of the brain's owner" (p. 140). "The study . . . of the distribution of consciousness shows it to be exactly such as we might expect in an organ added for the sake of steering a nervous system grown too complex to regulate itself" (p. 144). His metaphor, steering, looks forward to guidance systems that would be described mathematically half a century later by Wiener and applied to just this problem by Powers and the rest.

For example, one recent psychologist, Roger Sperry, speaks of the brain, by means of its own consciousness, monitoring its own activities. Consciousness does not, of course, check on the actions of individual cells. It detects overall qualities of different activity patterns. The brain does not "intervene," altering the laws that govern the generation or transmission of nerve impulses. Rather consciousness "supervenes," fitting the brain's activity within an envelope of larger configurations, as the drops of water swirl in an eddy in a stream (Calder, 1970, p. 260). Sperry sounds very like James.

"The cerebral activities of every [person] are a unity," writes another student of the brain, J. Z. Young (1978, p. 134). I am suggesting that we think of the unifier that supervenes or steers at the highest level as "consciousness" or "feelings," yes, but more precisely, as a theme-and-variations concept of identity. We have defined it as agency, consequence, but most importantly in this context as representation. In effect, identity allows us to "the" an "I."

The "interests" that James finds consciousness favoring may not be universal. Eating is a pleasure to most of us, but may not be to the dieter, the bulimic, or the anorexic. Not many people will "need to know" as hungrily as I do. A theme and variations concept of identity allows us to translate such general notions as consciousness or interests or pleasures into Shaw's interests, Freud's pleasures, Fitzgerald's purposes, Iiro's worries, or my own need to know things wholly and certainly.

Lichtenstein uses two different terms: primary identity and identity theme. Both refer to a theme that we infer, that runs through all we know of some mind's activities, and that we put into words. By "primary identity," he intends a style *in* the person. Created in the earliest relationship between the baby and its first caretaker, it is a way of being which is in, even is, that person. Formed before words, it is a preverbal thing that never can be put in words, "known" in that sense. Just as we can never know the mind of another person, so this primary identity, the essence of that mind, must remain mysterious.

By contrast, an identity theme (as I use the term) is my way of representing a human being to myself. To be sure, when my inference of Bernard Shaw's identity theme "fits" or makes sense (feels right by my criteria), I can say it must approximate his primary identity. I can never be sure of that, however, nor need I be.

"Identity theme" is a paradoxical concept since it puts the essential me-ness of me somewhere between me and you. On the other hand, as we have seen, this between-ness in our interpretation of another fits what we know of the ways humans see the world or put it into words and other symbols. We mingle ourselves with the "out there," creating and re-creating it as we bring to bear on the world our characteristic ways for perceiving it.

In a purely psychological sense, a theme-and-variations identity governing a hierarchy of DEFT networks will provide a model for the processes of perception and symbolization by which we continue both our one-ness and our two-ness with the world. At the same time, however, we need to remember that even simple perceptions are a function of a person's

Culture

as well as of a person. The identity *cum* feedback picture allows us to portray the relationships among identity, biology, and culture.

Recall Colin Turnbull's BaMbuti guide who had grown up in a jungle where he saw nothing beyond a couple of hundred feet. He saw buffalo at a distance of some miles and thought them insects. In effect, the guide demonstrated two things. First, culture can limit biology, removing some possibilities in even so basic a visual schema as the correlation of size and distance. Second, if so, culture must even more deeply and pervasively color the way we perceive family relations, politics, the meanings of words, beauty, funniness, or the feelings we have on hearing a story.

In our feedback metaphor, we can take the role of culture into account by compressing Powers's multitier hierarchy back into a two-tier diagram:

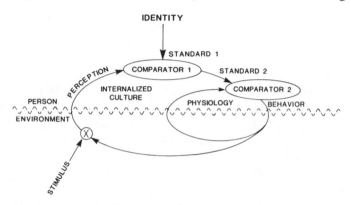

As before, the human being lives in the world by means of behavior that controls perception. That is the lower loop: a person acts on the physical world to change perceptions so as to feel better emotionally. An upper loop lets me visualize the way a "social factor" can limit or add to biology by setting the reference level for the lower loop. The upper loop uses the lower, just as the I uses the upper. The individual uses the culture he has internalized, which in turn uses physiology. Physiology both equips and limits culture, and culture both equips and limits the individual.

For example, my body is built for sitting. In that sense, my body makes something possible for me. I can't twist my waist enough to sit with my knees facing backwards, however. My body makes something impossible for me. In the same way culture makes things possible and impossible for me by means of physiology. I can spin my swivel chair around—my culture makes that a possibility for me—but by sitting in chairs I have atrophied the muscles for squatting that Africans and Asians find so useful.

In general, the culture we internalize changes what our physiology can do. Not vice versa, notice. As I internalize my culture it equips my body with a language. So provided, I can fashion the words you are reading. That language then sets limits to what I can physically hear or think or say—as our students keep demonstrating and even our most eloquent poets:

> . . . every attempt
> Is a wholly new start, and a different kind of failure
> Because one has only learnt to get the better of words
> For the thing one no longer has to say, or the way in which
> One is no longer disposed to say it.

Culture provides words for T. S. Eliot as for the most inarticulate of us. Physiology provides a tongue and vocal cords with which to speak, ears with which to hear, and (so Noam Chomsky might say) part of my brain wired for language. Culture also confines us to what Frederick Jameson has called the prisonhouse of language. We can say only what we already know how to say.

My body, like everyone else's body, is built for language. But I speak English and not Italian. That means I can't even hear the difference between "r" and "double-r" in Italian, and even though I speak some French I have trouble not hearing "nom," n-o-m, and "non," n-o-n, differently (which I have to avoid if I am to read Lacan). Further, my English is not quite the same as yours. I speak with a certain drawl and pitch. I write using sentence modifiers like "nevertheless" and "however" more than most people do. In linguistic jargon, I write and speak an idiolect *and* a dialect *and* a language. My identity sets the standards for the particular brand of language my culture provides me, English, which in turn tunes my body's speech equipment to certain sounds and not others.

Language, tools, cooking, family structure all provide standards for eyes, ears, tongues, and fingers. The ground of our lives is physical and biological, yet culture can limit our physiology, as it did with the pygmy guide.

The two-tier diagram provides a metaphor for him. Quite unconsciously, you or I would "set" our reference levels for judging distances. We would program ourselves with data about the angles, the hues, or the sizes and silence that indicate a buffalo is two miles away. We do so by means of cultural resources, but the pygmy's culture has never let him learn about a buffalo two miles away. In effect his social loop has never set this reference level for the biophysical loop, and a buffalo two miles away simply can't exist for him.

The culture we internalize both enlarges and limits biology. Finally the individual *uses* or *works with* his ability to see buffalo at a distance or, indeed, *works with* his inability (says they are bewitched). Language functions the same way, as a tool, as when we speak of the "linguistic resources" of different cultures (Hymes, 1973).

Identity as a hierarchy of feedbacks also allows us to model expression and communication in a world of private minds. I express myself according to my identity. To do so, I use cultural resources like language, chapter divisions, the apparatus of scholarly reference, or the system of university presses. Through them, I create a physical object: the book you are holding.

You, in turn, see my book. You perceive it physically, testing it against your schemata for seeing lines, curves, or serifs as letters and words. You measure my syntax and grammar and spelling against your knowledge of English, your vocabulary about minds or Shaw, and my book (I hope) passes these as well. You can then test my writing against your knowledge and experience of people, your belief or disbelief in feedback, say, or unity, and your idea of what constitutes evidence and truth.

I wrote by using a system—English—and you understand by using a system—English. But I write and you understand by using that same English on behalf of two different identities. Your private feelings and beliefs will guide and finally govern your perception of my English words, but it was the expression of my private feelings and beliefs through an English we both share that made communication possible in the first place. Your and my private feelings make communication personal, the English we share makes it transpersonal, and neither mode makes the other impossible.

This picture of reading and writing as two similar feedback loops acting on a single text provides a model for our situation in a culture. We share loops with our fellow-citizens, but each of us uses those shared loops for personal purposes.

This is a very different picture from the usual metaphors about "social pressure" or "political forces" or "economic squeeze" or "the impact of society." To be sure, societies enforce a consensus as to what is real, true, and valued. No doubt people often experience this enforcement as a "pressure." Even so, it is a confusing metaphor. Culture does not exert "pressure" or "force" or "impact" so much as it either gives us means or takes them away. It gives me a Toyota but denies me a Rolls Royce. It gave me English but withheld Homeric Greek. Society may make one or another choice very costly or painful, the loan company may even take my Toyota away, but society cannot exert a physical force the way chains or walls or drugs do.

What culture does do is give us resources. Within those resources, some things are possible for an individual to choose and others not. Some cultures deny some individuals some choices (being able to see buffalo at two miles), but that is as much as culture can physically "coerce."

So far as freedom is concerned, the individual is to culture as culture is to physiology in our two-loop picture. The most rigid of totalitarian regimes can do no more than take over the lower two loops, the way Orwell's *1984* society takes over language and history. No matter how coercive the society, it can only reach the private, individual choice through those lower processes. Even a slave is free in his thoughts.

In this feedback picture, as I use the language or the technology or the symbolisms of my culture, they act back on me, as a hammer both enables and limits a carpenter or as words let Eliot start anew but doom him to failure. The realities we use change us.

They change, even, the very structures of id, ego, and superego. From the first, Freud and later analysts understood that intrapsychic structures develop out of a person's adaptations to reality. The id manifests the body's biological drives psychologically. The superego internalizes our acceptance of our parents as parents and ourselves as children with all the limitations and delays that acceptance implies. The ego sophisticates the pleasure principle: we continue to seek pleasure (or the absence of pain) but with a canny eye for possible advantages by delay or compromise with the demands of reality or the laws of logic or cause and effect.

The ego also embodies, however, the individual's seemingly inborn ability to cope with an "average expectable environment." Hence the ego must have existed from birth, and psychoanalysts of the 1950s tended to think of functions of the id, ego, and superego as absolutes, like functions of heart, lungs, or liver. Most psychoanalytic theorists of that time assumed that id, ego, and superego, as structures, would be much the same for any human, independent of cultural or historical setting.

The later analysts were close to Freud's own thinking because at the time Freud created psychoanalysis reality meant an ordered universe of eternal natural laws which set boundaries within which humans had to work out their lives in a similarly ordered society. Freud himself believed in the reality of reality with especial intensity. If reality is as constant as human biology, then it doesn't matter whether psychic structures are inborn or adaptations to reality.

The turmoil of the 1960s turned that fixed reality upside down. We have seen technological and social change accelerate to the point where very little in our environment is "average" or "expectable." Today, when the very dimensions of space and time have stretched beyond all comprehension, reality may attack more than support one's sense of a meaningful and continuous self.

If so, then, as Heinz Lichtenstein points out in his analysis of the crises of the late sixties, the functions of id, ego, and superego may change (1973, 1977). The id and the pleasure principle may become ways of affirming one's own reality, and an ego whirling in a spiral of change may need to seek stability in mystical states of union. The superego may cease to be the incorporated voice of parents and culture, for they are lost in a distantly fading past, and instead become a way of claiming for oneself the authority the elders once had.

Societies exist because they permit a consensus as to what is real, a consensus that finally they have to coerce. A revolution marks the replacement of one consensus about reality by a new one, and the various revolutions of the 1960s (colonial, sexual, civil rights, drugs, musical) all did or tried to do just that. As these movements changed realities, the psyche that reality feeds back into also changed. In a very real sense, the ego and the superego of the 1970s and 1980s is different from the structures of the 1950s and early 1960s—at least in the patients American psychoanalysts see. The instability of "objective" reality (in the nineteenth century sense) lets us realize once again what reality "really" is—the sharing of experience with meaningful others through processes of shared feedback.

As Erikson said, there is no person without society. Theme-and-variation identities are social and political as well as individual. More precisely, theme-and-variation identities are the way people are social and political. Still more precisely, theme-and-variation identities are a way to describe the way people are social and political. As in the famous 1956 study of the Bostonians' views of Russia,

> A man's opinions inevitably bear his personal stamp. His capacities for abstract or practical thinking, for intense feeling, for forthright action set limits on his response to public issues, and indeed, on what he makes of any significant event that impinges on him. His intellectual and temperamental qualities, general features of his behavior stabilized in the complex interaction of constitution and personal history, give distinctive form to his opinions about Russia no less than they do to his copings with a psychologist's ink blots. . . . If the trivial ink blot evokes a valid sample of his personal style, so does a question about Russia. The tasks are more similar than might appear at first glance (Smith, Bruner, and White, p. 259).

What this book does is make terms like "capacities" and "qualities" more precise: a theme and variations concept of identity governing a hierarchy of personal, cultural, and physiological feedbacks. The individual sets the limits within which culture sets the limits within which he puts limits on the physical world so as to control his perceptions to yield satisfactions. This being feedback, physiology enables and limits culture, and culture enables and limits the individual. The individual manipulates culture and culture manipulates physiology.

Metaphors of social "forces" or "determinism" do not convey that curious mixture of limitation and freedom. I think it more accurate to say the individual *uses* what cultural resources are available to him which in turn *use* what physical and biological resources are available. I like John Dewey's term "transact." We transact cultural and physical realities, much the way we carry on affairs, both of the heart and the briefcase. When it comes to culture or language, we are lovers or dealers, artisans or even artists.

There is a way, then, that we can combine thinking about limitation, freedom, beauty and laughter and love, semantic codes and transformations, neurones and synapses and feedback, all these levels, by closely examining the lower levels, even in a two-loop simplification. Identity is the reference level governing the hierarchy which is mind. The lower loop has to do with the feedbacks through which we move and sense the physical world. The upper loop has to do with the cultural systems and codes we have internalized. Although they may feel to us as though they have a "force" or "impact," they do not coerce us like a wall. We should define them dialectically. Identity represents choice and freedom, whatever is a function of the person, and it is the thesis. The lower loops must be the antithesis: whatever can *not* be chosen.

What cannot be chosen in a cultural sense is what any normal member of the culture *could not find otherwise.* "Furiously sleep ideas green colorless" —there is no way I can find that sentence grammatical. At the movies, the sound track carries a woman's voice, and the camera looks over the left shoulder of a woman to a man's face, then cuts and looks over his right shoulder to the face of a speaking woman. There is *no* way I can read that as her *not* talking to him. The camera shows a basketful of what look like potatoes, then cuts to a close-up of a potato. There is no way I can read the second picture as other than an example of the potatoes in the first picture. Someone else, however, who knew no movies or no English would simply find these questions incomprehensible—out of their cultural loop (like the African natives who, on being shown a United Nations agricultural film with close-ups of potatoes in it, ruefully said, "But our potatoes aren't that *big*").

The second loop, in short, makes use of codes and syntaxes that admit no options—unless one steps out of the culture. If, however, normal moviegoing adults could differ—some people, for example, might see the woman as angry, others as alarmed, some might see the potatoes as pale, others as dark—then we are in a higher loop where identity governs cultural perceptions.

That kind of cultural or linguistic or semiotic code differs fundamentally from another kind, from the conventions we adopt, for example, as interpreters when we accept a shared idea of what is relevant, what will count as data, or what qualifies as confirmation. These are rules of a game that we adopt only from and toward other players who are doing the same kind of feedback as we. They are rules we get from our "interpretive community" (Fish, 1980).

A semiotic code, it seems to me, has to be defined as "No normal member of this culture could read this otherwise." Interpretive communities are more elastic. They provide us with something like ready-to-wear hypotheses to wear while going into the world, but they leave us choices between ready-to-wear and tailor-made and even between various styles and colors of ready-to-wear.

In other words, we should include in our feedback picture one of Chomsky's most useful concepts, degrees of grammaticality. The loops that govern eyes and ears are physiological, almost as limiting as physical laws. In our picture, they are the hard-wired connections from behavioral output to perceptual input. The loops that govern the way we see letters and words are cultural, not physical, but to be understood as "No normal member of this culture could see this otherwise." They too need to be understood as hard-wired connections. In our diagram, a code like that functions almost like the hard-wiring or environment of the feedback loop.

By contrast, the interpretive communities to which we hold temporary allegiances provide us with ready-made conventions, expectations, or gambits, for example, the whole idea of thinking of a person as a theme and variations. These are simply hypotheses—outputs—which we feed into the world by means of hard-wired connections and to which we get either positive or negative feedback. They would appear in our diagram as behavioral outputs from an individual, the content of the hard-wired semiotic codes rather than the wirings themselves. This kind of convention does not limit or enlarge us in the willy-nilly way that physical or (I would say) cultural codes do. They open up possibilities, to be sure, but we are quite free to choose otherwise.

We defined identity as agent, consequence, and representation. Our abbreviated feedback diagram gives us a picture of identity as agent. Identity as agent sets the reference level for our cultural resources which in turn sets the reference level for our physical abilities. Psychoanalysis and brain physiology are, to be sure, very different, but psychoanalysis can provide blueprints of mental processes that accord with the blueprints the neurologist draws. With this simplified picture, we have, in effect, arrived at a metaphor that fits different but consistent blueprints of mind, as Jerrold Katz prescribed. This is surely what Freud, when he was an ambitious young neurologist just beginning to study the mind, always wanted: a

Model and Definition

of mind.

The house of mind is built with small functional networks. As a first approximation, we can describe them as feedback loops, although "feedback" alone and even "information processing" are too simple for the complicated, nonlinear patterns of inhibition, excitation, mutual regulation, and redundancy with which our nerve and brain cells combine. DEFT provides another first approximation for sorting out the trends that run from inside to outside and from "low" to "high" functioning.

As those terms "low" and "high" presuppose, we can think of mind as a hierarchy of functional networks. Higher levels use lower levels to do their bidding, controlling them by reference signals, much as an artisan controls a lathe or an angler the line. Lower levels contribute the information that higher levels need to function, the tug on the fishing line or the sound of the bowl turning on the lathe. Thus there is an interaction all up and down the hierarchy. At every level, an upper level pipes down into a lower one some personal standard—identity.

One can inquire into and explain much of human behavior by assuming for the top of this hierarchy, identity: a final, pontifical, unifying I—like the relentless analyzer and knower who has hauled you through these theoretical chapters. That I creates itself as a consistent I by means of satisfactions and reassurances (for me, knowings) that fit the I's nature up to that moment.

Yet this I is also between observed and observer. It is a way for one human being to represent another. Your idea of your identity will not coincide with someone else's idea or mine. While at the lowest levels everyone will find in you much the same circuits of seeing and hearing and reading as in anyone else, at the identity-finding level, we are engaged in a human interaction that is as unpredictable, as "different" as any human relation.

In Kluckhohn and Murray's gnomic statement, each of us is partly like everybody else, partly like somebody else, and partly like nobody else (1948). The two-level feedback picture allows me to think about those relations, to think about an earlier example, writing the *b* in *bat*. The marks I see on the page are the same marks every other human being will see there, but not everyone will experience them the same way I do. In France, they teach a different way of writing *b*. Hence, a French person's perception of *b* will not correspond to mine. Finally no one else writes *b* with the same handwriting as I do. In general, the picture of an identity governing a hierarchy of information processing feedback loops allows me to understand how I am unique, cultural, and human all at once.

This picture of an identity governing feedbacks also allows us to define "mind": that which adapts less-than-mind toward identity. Less obliquely, *mind* (as opposed to body or matter) consists of the reference levels (in Powers's sense) or the teleological elements (in Granit's), the boundary conditions (Polanyi), the "life themes" (Schank and Abelson), or the purposes and goals (James and Sherrington) which guide lower functions toward higher aims. In the three elements of the feedback network (the first two being behavioral output as compared to perceptual input), mind must be the third: the comparison and reference level. Mind reveals itself, however, only as the goal supplied to a lower network by a higher one. In a simplified picture, the reference level for one loop—its mind—is simply the next higher loop.

Mind is therefore future-oriented, mind is more abstract, but what is more important, mind is relative to the level we are talking about. What is mind to the individual cell of the retina is less-than-mind to the process of seeing a face. What is mind for seeing a face is less-than-mind to the process of recognizing Winston Churchill.

In these various levels of mind, we can use a higher level to look down into the levels below, but we cannot use a lower level to look up into the levels above. The higher comprehends the workings of the lower and thus forms the meaning of the lower. Hence, as we ascend a hierarchy of boundaries, we reach to even higher levels of meaning. Our understanding of the whole hierarchic edifice keeps deepening as we move upward from stage to stage. We can generally descend to the components of a lower level by analyzing a higher level, but the opposite process involves an integration of the principles of the lower level, and this integration may be beyond our powers. In other words, we can always get knowledge of the lower processes in the brain, but we may not be able to have knowledge of the highest levels of mental functioning, those we customarily call mind and to which I would add identity.

This limitation on our knowledge offers a sort of answer to our century's strong philosophical critique of the very idea of "mind." Gilbert Ryle and, following him, Stuart Hampshire and many others have criticized our common usages of the term as, for example, a location: "He was out of his mind." "The first thing that comes to my mind . . ." Or as a manikin: "My mind refuses to accept the idea that . . ." "He has a healthy mind" (Ryle, 1949, Hampshire, 1962a, b).

They extend their attack to such ideas as motive or intention. If I decide to buy a bag of popcorn, why should I assume that there is some personlike mover of that action prior in time and somehow inside or behind the scenes that "intended" to buy popcorn? Thinking that way gets us into an infinite regress: I made up my mind to buy popcorn, I made up my mind to make up my mind to buy popcorn, I made up my mind to make up my mind to make up my mind to buy popcorn, and so on. If one action requires a preceding intellectual move, why not all?

The psychoanalyst Roy Schafer has extended the argument to much of psychoanalytic language: ego, id, superego, impulse, defense, libido, and even everyday words like love, guilt, aggression, or anxiety. All entangle, he says, actions with pre-actions and pre-pre-actions and pre-pre-pre-actions (1976). Even the word "I" becomes an elusive fiction from this point of view, a phantom of the opera loose in the mental works.

Yet the brain physiologists do not shy away from the infinite regress as the philosophers do. If the brain works by a hierarchy of functional networks, and if the lower networks require reference signals from the higher, then we *are* dealing with a regression. I can look down through any given level, but I may not be able to look up from a low level into a higher one, just as I may not be able to look through the words of a poem toward a meaning for it or a purpose or an intention.

"Mind" and "I" will be more than my mind when I am trying to think of "mind" or "I." They will be, in a philosopher's phrase, "systematically elusive." Yet it is possible to explore and to infer things about them.

Powers, using his electrochemical model of feedback networks, can infer how long before an action its intention must be, how long before the intention the higher levels that give it the necessary information have to be set, therefore at what frequency they must cycle. While we cannot say those "higher" levels are in fact "higher" or "within," we can say they are prior in time—and by how many microseconds. Herbert Simon, similarly, concludes that the speed within loops greatly exceeds the speed of the loops controlling them, guaranteeing the "near decomposability" of the various loops. Up to a point, it does seem as though we can interpret concepts like "purpose" or "goal" or phrases like "I intend" as referring to physical entities (1969, p. 106).

We can and should purge psychoanalytic language of fictions like "I" or "ego" if they conflict with other blueprints that have equal claims on our belief, such as the work of the brain physiologists. We should cling, though, to the blueprints that accord with radically different cross-sections of the house of mind like the brain physiologists' account of mind as a hierarchy. So far as "mind" is concerned, identity theory provides just such a summing of different blueprints within the general system of psychoanalysis. Mind is 1) the body's hierarchy of 2) feedback (or information-processing) networks whose reference levels are a function of 3) identity.

This identity at the top—and therefore permeating the system—is three-fold. It is an agency, the "subject" of the various loops that initiate our seeing or walking or talking or reading. It is also the consequence of those acts as they feed back into the being who initiated them, the I created by seeing and walking and talking and reading. That identity—that I—uses culture as culture uses physiology. Culture both limits and makes possible the aspirations of an I, as physiology both limits and makes possible culture, as language limits and makes possible the realization of the poet's vision. Finally, identity is a representation, necessarily partial or elusive, by one I or another of this whole. This last—this between-ness—is the mind modeling mind that permeates its own modeling yet cannot ever be represented in it.

Identity theory yields not only a model but a necessary paradox, an elusiveness intrinsic to a thinking, changing being, the I as it grows in time, the I with a history.

Part III | A History of I

7 | Development as Dialogue

The I is a way of relating. To be sure, we often think of a Dr. Vincent or a Sigmund Freud standing alone, as it were, against a photographer's white backdrop. Yet, really, they are always in a world of people and things—and time.

Part II dealt with the ways we form an I out of momentary acts of seeing and hearing and knowing and remembering, an individual and psychological I. Part III explores the ways we make an I and a life out of the biology and culture we inherit, a historical I, an I in years, an I in a world of other people.

The geneticist C. H. Waddington describes plants and animals as involved in three time scales. The smallest time scale measures in seconds and hours, the middle scale in years, and the largest in decades, centuries, even eras and eons. The largest is evolution. A horse comes from a long line of ancestors and gives rise to a long line of descendant horses, all of them implicit in this one horse's history. In the shortest time scale, a horse lives in gallops and heartbeats and the munching of oats, immediate transformations of chemical energies. On the medium scale, writes Waddington, when we see a horse pulling a cart past the window, "the picture must also include the minute fertilised egg, the embryo in its mother's womb, and the broken-down old nag it will eventually become" (1957, p. 6).

With seeing, hearing, speaking, remembering, and knowing, we have been thinking mostly in the short scale. These particular, momentary DEFTings, however, happen in a social, linguistic, and even evolutionary world that long outlasts any one of us. We also have the middle scale, our gestation, infancy, adult life, and aging in a long arc of uncertain beginning but all too definite end.

What Freud and later psychoanalysts added to these three scales was a method—free association—for tracing systematically the way traits established in early childhood can steer an adult life. Hence Freud was offering a way of relating the middle scale, a lifetime, to the shortest scale, our second by second living. Similarly Freud's insistence on grounding psychology in biology gave a way of relating the single life to the evolutionary scale. Psychoanalysis thus gave rise to—and inherited—systematic ways of thinking about human character but also created some radically new ways of

159

tracing the history of a self, an I in time, starting at birth or even before, new

Characterologies

We all recognize that humans go through a life cycle from womb to tomb. We pass through certain obvious stages, infancy, adolescence, young adulthood, maturity, middle age, old age, and death. Yet within that trajectory, a person smiles or walks in a certain "characteristic" way; falls in love only with certain kinds of people; works in a particular style; engages his society in some ways but not others. As children, we develop a style that one can trace through all the later biological and social stages. The problem of human "character" is to account for both that persistence and the changes in our lifelong parabola of recurring traits and patterns.

A characterology offers a system for understanding these persistences, usually by interrelating them. In its eighty-odd years of existence, psychoanalysis has used four characterologies. Each constitutes a way of grouping details of behavior into a total personality. Each seeks a unity in the personality but in different ways.

The first predates psychoanalysis and serves still: diagnostic categories. We can speak of a paranoid personality, an obsessional neurotic, or an autistic child, applying any of the scores of categories offered by the handbooks of psychiatry. The American Psychiatric Association's *Diagnostic and Statistical Manual of Mental Disorders,* for example (the 1968 edition), provides 168 possible diagnoses, and the DSM III offers even more. Such categories do not in themselves suggest how the paranoia or the obsession came about, but they do fit the medical model: diagnosis, treatment, prognosis. They lend themselves nicely to the prescribing of drugs, for example.

Psychoanalysis, however, quickly went beyond the categorizing of mental illness to engage the dynamic causes behind symptoms, and in doing so Freud made one of his discoveries that never fails to awe me. Not only do we go through stages like youth and old age in adult life, we go through a series of stages in childhood: oral, anal, urethral, phallic, oedipal. Children are much concerned with the processes and products and persons associated with key parts of the body: giving and getting through the mouth, the actions and results of defecation and urination, being "big," standing erect, walking, having genital sensations, loving and hating male and female parents, or wanting to be a grown-up, that is, a parent oneself.

Freud's analyses of adults showed these themes persisting all through life but transformed into adult activities: anal pedantry or miserliness, oral smoking, phallic flying, or oedipal jealousy. It was possible by listening to adults' free associations in analysis to trace roots for the grown-up's actions in the child's development. The method also brings traits together, quite strikingly, by means of a body model: the withholding of an "anal character" or the intrusiveness of a "phallic character" or the dependency of an "oral personality." The holistic evidence Freud and his early colleagues obtained from adults for these connections was quite overwhelming, and now experimenters have "objectively" confirmed these traits (Masling and Schwartz, 1979).

The stages are quite visible—once they are pointed out. Analysts or just simple nursemaids, as Freud said, were able to see them. Further, although different cultures may stress different phases differently, the sequence remains the same. No one suggests, for example, that children go through an oedipal phase before an oral one. Hence, the whole sequence of stages may represent a biological program we inherit.

A second characterology, then, classifies adults by the childhood stage that colors their adult life, the stage at which (we might say) considerable psychic energy became fixated: an "oral" personality, a "phallic" character. More psychoanalytic than psychiatric, such descriptions assume that normal development is progressive (or "epigenetic," developing according to some complex blueprint, not just "getting bigger"). Conversely, pathology is fixation or regression, getting stuck at one stage or retreating to it.

This method of understanding character became one of the five fundamental principles of psychoanalysis, those large "metapsychological" generalizations that a full clinical interpretation or theory should admit. The genetic point of view says that a psychoanalytic explanation of any phenomenon should "include propositions concerning its psychological origin and development" (Rapaport and Gill, 1959, p. 158; Rapaport, 1960b). The genetic point of view thus states Freud's determinism in a stern and vigorous way: "At each point of psychological history the totality of potentially active earlier forms co-determines all subsequent psychological phenomena." "All psychological phenomena," say Rapaport and Gill, "originate in innate givens which mature according to an epigenetic groundplan," that is, a step by step process of elaborating structures built into the organism.

Falling in love comes from earlier experiences of love, with mother, say, or father, which in turn involve other events in childhood that are enmeshed in these apparently biological oral, anal, phallic stages. Further, a child's need to be erect, to be big, to be capable, to be like mother or father, persists into adulthood. Hence the child's style will likely persist in the adult's life even if the content of that adult life becomes very different from the parents' life. "The earlier forms of a psychological phenomenon, though superseded by later forms, remain potentially active" (ibid).

On the evidence, I find this genetic hypothesis sound when stated generally this way. It does, however, point always toward childhood and toward biology, saying little about adult achievements. It has no way of showing how some traits, even if they look pathological, can be adaptive, particularly in an artistic context. It was an "id-characterology" or, as Erikson was to criticize it many years later, an "originology" (1958a, p. 18).

A third type of characterology would define personality more by the actions of the grown-up. It focuses on the adult's preferred defenses and adaptations. Many analysts, starting in the thirties, have suggested this approach. A recent example is George Vaillant's book describing the "Grant Study," which traced thirty-year histories of Harvard graduates of the class of 1939. Each individual's style (and prospects of success) the researchers define by the kind of defenses he uses. Samuel Lovelace, for example, Vaillant described as a "lonely, gentle, loyal liberal with an unhappy marriage and few social supports," a "man who used intellectualization as a dominant defense." Thus Vaillant combines his cramming before exams in college—useless but it gave him "reassurance"—with his statement that in the army he engaged in a "sociological study of my fellow soldier." His marriage was painful, but "abstractly, I feel the same fascination I did before marriage." "Through my wife's illness, I learned what a complicated thing the human personality can be." "You can even rationalize Adolf Hitler" (1977, p. 135).

Vaillant traces the life history of such an individual by the way one defense (or adaptation) evolves into or takes the place of another, more mature or more successful. Lovelace's isolation of his loving emotions led to loneliness, but another man, a college dean, by isolating his anger, became a highly successful mediator in the turbulent universities of the 1960s (pp. 132-35).

One could achieve a still closer description of the individual by combining characteristic defense with libidinal phase, the third characterology with the second. It is true, for example, that "oral" characters, concerned with taking into themselves, often use identification as a defense and adaptation. "Anal" characters, preoccupied with the backsides of things, often reverse or overcompensate their impulses. Such a combination would live up to Fenichel's classic definition of character: "The ego's habitual modes of adjustment to the external world, the id, and the superego, and the characteristic types of combining these modes with one another, constitute character." Character is "the habitual mode of bringing into harmony the tasks presented by internal demands and by the external world" (1945, p. 467).

This is an "ego-psychological" idea of character, and, by including the "external world," it ends the idea of character as wholly internal to the individual. Fenichel's definition sets character in relation both to other characters and to the physical world exterior to the self, building on Heinz Hartmann's classic *Ego Psychology and the Problem of Adaptation* (1939).

Hartmann uses "adaptation" in analogy to evolution or ecology, not in the reactionary sense that one should "adjust" to the way society is. Humans fit into the world of people and things around them the way butterflies or giraffes evolve so as to camouflage themselves and then live in environments where they are camouflaged. So people work their way into the social world around them, sometimes altering that world to make it suit, sometimes changing themselves, but always making the two "fit together" (*zusammenpassen*).

Hartmann was introducing a new metapsychological principle. As Rapaport and Gill state it, "The adaptive point of view demands that the psychoanalytic explanation of any psychological phenomenon include propositions concerning its relationship to the environment" (1959, p. 159).

Hartmann emphasized adaptation to the physical world. Erikson (in his masterwork, *Childhood and Society* [1950, 1963]) emphasized adaptation to the social environment. Thus it was natural for him to extend the original sequence of childhood phases (oral, anal, and so on) into the whole human life span. He added a midlife period of creative work and reproduction and the end of life with its accumulation of wisdom. Society meets all such stages with characteristic institutions. Mothers mother infants, parents train toddlers, the community allows adolescents a time to find themselves, and society acknowledges (sometimes) the wisdom of its elders. Each stage was therefore not just psychological but psychosocial. I read Erikson as both enlarging and particularizing the idea of adaptation as Hartmann had left it.

In effect, Erikson, Hartmann, and others (the English object relations theorists and Lacan) were all following through the opening Freud created in the first chapter of *Civilization and its Discontents* (1930). By suggesting that the infant's, the lunatic's, the lover's, or the mystic's ego might extend beyond itself to include some part of the external world, he radically opened psychoanalysis from a psychology of one individual bounded by his skin to a psychology of the individual in and including a social context.

Earlier, in *Group Psychology*, he had written: "The contrast between individual psychology and social or group psychology . . . loses a great deal of its sharpness when it is examined more closely." "In the individual's mental life someone else is invariably involved, as a model, as an object, as a helper, as an opponent; and so from the very first individual psychology . . . is at the same time social psychology as well" (1921c, 18:69). Freud could almost have been echoing Marx: "It is above all necessary to avoid . . . establishing 'society' as an abstraction over against the individual. The individual *is* the *social being*" (1844).

Lichtenstein's theme and variations concept of identity offers what seems to me a fourth and still more powerful way of relating the interpersonal and the intrapersonal in stating the unity of a personality. We can use a theme

and variations to put into words a consistency between, say, Scott Fitzgerald's way of falling in love and his use of *un-* and *in-* in his writing,
between his interpersonal and his personal traits. Just as the third characterology of defense, adaptation, and drive included and enlarged upon the
second characterology of drive alone, so this fourth mode includes and
enlarges upon the third.

In the first three characterologies (diagnostic, childhood phase, ego
strategies) the two that are psychoanalytic point to an historical I, an I in
time. Earlier psychological events cause later ones, and the adult is to the
child as effect is to cause. The fourth characterology, identity, makes it possible for me to open that determinism up. How much are we determined by
our history and our biology? Just what is the process of this determinism?
Does the evident continuity in my life-style leave a space for my creativity
and freedom?

Development as Hike

For the process by which an animal's biological qualities fit into its
environment, the geneticist C. H. Waddington introduced an intriguing
metaphor, the "epigenetic landscape." He drew a picture of development as
a surface like that of a sloping landscape with hills and valleys. He imagined
the organism with its biological properties as a large round boulder rolling
down these slopes. The boulder would go to the left or right as a certain hill
would force it to roll into this or that valley on either side. Having gone to the
left, the boulder would encounter the next hill on the left which would again
force a choice of left or right, and so on down the whole geological pattern.

The landscape represented the environment as the animal might or might
not fit into it. Rolling down a valley would represent a forced line of
development: to survive, the animal has to develop along these lines. Not
being able to roll up a hill would image an impossible line of development.
Settling into a hollow would represent a successful ecological balance between animal and environment, an ecological niche.

Erikson may have had a similar figure in mind when he used the word
"groundplan." For both Erikson and Waddington "epigenetic" implies a
schedule. Certain developments must take place at certain stages, just as a
certain hill in the landscape requires a boulder to roll to left or right. That
outcome determines the next hill to be encountered, which will in turn
require new outcomes.

Waddington's figure of something rolling down a geometric surface like a
ball going through a pinball machine accents the evolutionary and biological
time scale in which the individual plays a relatively passive role. If we
consider the individual life span rather than the evolution of the species, the

individual or his culture has much more say as to what hills he will encounter. To be sure, the early moves favor some futures over others, but the individual chooses those moves, or his culture (rather than his biology) prescribes them. To model this shorter time scale, we might think of someone playing through a golf course. Perhaps an even better figure would be that of an explorer hiking his way through what life must be to each of us, a new territory.

We begin our hike abruptly, landing like parachutists on an alien terrain of physical and social surroundings already formed. In the first stages of the trek we carry only the materials we started with, our heredity. After the very earliest stages, however, our trek begins to have a history. We come to the next hill having marched down a number of the valleys that represent experiences we have had. We have fed, slept, known contentment, and felt nurtured. These experiences have changed us and our feelings about the hike. As a result of those experiences and of our growing equipment of memories and skills, we will choose this way or that as we search out the paths around some new hill. If our parents send us to a nursery school, that choice forecloses some futures and favors others. We will learn differently thereafter, perhaps better, perhaps worse—that depends on the individual and the school. Nursery school will have provided new sights and sounds to add to this continuously developing combination of self and landscape which is our trek. Kindergarten, then first grade, new friends and games, crushes and quarrels, they all both require and permit new relations to the human and nonhuman realities around us. So with marriage and career, parenthood and grandparenthood. It is an ever-new self in this continuously developing trek that will choose at the next hill, and so on down the sloping landscape to the cliff of death, whose pull is relentless.

In general, all characterologies allow us to account for events that have taken place, often quite completely, but they do not give us a way to predict how Lorenz would react when Freud gave him food or recommended a novel or when he came upon a stone in his lady's road. One can look backwards and see how he became blocked, but it is harder, perhaps impossible, to look ahead and see how he might free himself. Both Waddington's landscape and Erikson's groundplan are retrodictive, not predictive.

Partly, we can imagine human development as each of us facing a biological and cultural environment forced on us, like death or my height or the economic and technological forces of our culture, which none of us seems to be able to change. Partly, however, we choose our environment from alternatives that are given us, as when I chose to be a college professor as that profession existed in America in the 1950s. Partly we choose even more freely from alternatives we make up ourselves, as when I write this paragraph. All these fates and choices in their varying degrees and kinds of freedom cumulate to become a history of my "I" which is the "I" that actively chooses the next word or passively enjoys a sunny December in Florida.

The landscape we hike through has certain large features that are the same for all of us. We are born, grow, ripen, and die. We pass through the oral, anal, and other childhood stages that Freud and the psychoanalysts discovered. Some features of the landscape are normal, but not everyone shares them. Some of us mate. Some of us find satisfying work. Some of us grow beards, and some shave them off.

Still other features of the landscape depend wholly on early choices, hence are largely individual. Having decided to be a college professor, I found myself marching up the ritual stages of assistant, associate, and full professor. Someone who had chosen advertising, acting, or acupuncture would never have hiked those particular hills and valleys. Having decided to be an unconventional college professor, I have always taught in unconventional departments, and that implied still other rises and falls in my professorial trek. Others are unconventional, too, but only I have written this particular book, and nobody else will feel the consequences down the trail as I will.

Freud and the first generation of psychoanalysts stressed the biological features of the landscape we I's are exploring. They are indeed the most fixed, and a landscape represents them well. Erikson, with his groundplan, stressed the social and communal aspects of development, making it the same biologically for all of us (infancy, generativity, old age) but a somewhat different epigenetic groundplan for each culture. In effect, an Indian baby walks toward adulthood over one terrain and a Canadian baby another. Again, the metaphor of a hike through a landscape represents a culturally "epigenetic" growth fairly well.

Erikson emphasized the social and communal aspects of the terrain. Part of Jacques Lacan's importance is that he demands we see that landscape as a cultural and verbal one. Lacan, despite his claims to the contrary, is writing in the tradition of the late Freud, Hartmann and Erikson, and the English object relations theorists. Lacan begins, as they do, with the relation of mother to infant. He thinks, as they do, that in the first six months of life the infant feels merged with the person who nurtures it. Then, during what Lacan calls the mirror stage, from six to eighteen months, the infant perceives that nurturing Other as simply an extension of itself. As the child is forced to recognize that the Other is not and cannot be a part of itself, it accepts *le non du père* or *le nom du père*, the cultural world of language which both represents its frustrated desire and provides the means to overcome it. Hence, where Hartmann spoke of "average expectable environment" and Erikson of society and community, Lacan speaks of language, but in the largest sense, as a network of signifiers and signifieds by which we can describe our culture. The child must enter that network and let that network enter him (1979, see also Muller and Richardson, 1982, Wollheim, 1979).

In a remarkable anthropological film called *Four Families,* which features the commentary of Margaret Mead, we can see culture flowing before our very eyes through the mother and the family into the baby (MacNeill, 1959). The film compares families in four different societies: Indian, French, Japanese, and Western Canadian. Each of the four families is rural and farms, and each has a one year old boy baby, but the differences in their physical and cultural worlds are immense.

The Canadian family is surrounded by noisy machines like the vacuum cleaner and the washer-dryer with their cold, hard surfaces of metal and porcelain. The other families are machineless, while the Indian family has scarcely a wall to its house. The Canadian family, by contrast, has to have a special transitional space between indoors and outdoors for taking off overcoats and snowsuits. The Indian family in its tropical hut has no boundary at all between indoors and outdoors. The Indian mother gives her baby's body religious markings, but it is the French father who makes the sign of the cross over the bread before the evening meal. The Japanese mother prays before the ancestors' shrine, but in the Canadian family the youngest child says grace. The Canadian baby goes to sleep in a room by himself, while the other three share the common living space of the family. The Indian father spends his evening in the village, the other three at home. The French and Canadian mothers bathe their babies vigorously, handling them dispassionately, almost like packages. The Indian mother bathes her baby caressingly, sensuously. The Japanese baby gets his bath when his grandmother takes him into the bathtub with her. All of these variations provide the baby with a sense of the way his world is and shall be.

This is how we learn what nurture is and love, what closeness means, how valuable religion is, what the relation is between indoors and out, between animate and inanimate nature, what is important—virtually every basic thing we know. The message is culture, but the medium is body, the bodies of all the family, but especially the mother's and the baby's. Culture sets limits, to be sure: one cannot live in a tropical hut in Alberta in March, nor can the Alberta family shed its need for achievement. Culture provides a style for living and mothering, and it would be rare, if not impossible, for a mother to change it deep down. Yet each baby knows that style of mothering only as each mother translates it to the baby through her own identity. Further, the mother is herself the result of a style of mothering achieved through culture as embodied in her mother.

One can see such a style not only in the baby's physical relationships, but also more abstractly, in its perception of the world, its sense of time, space, objects, its basic conceptions of the universe. As Jules Henry says:

> When one is imbued in this way—as if sun, water and time were filtered
> to one through the body of another person—it becomes difficult to
> change one's perceptions, for change would be a kind of death—a
> detachment from the person through whom the universe was absorbed.
> Thus consciousness itself is learned and acquired through another
> person. From the time we are born we are taught *how to be conscious.*
> Consciousness is a sociocultural phenomenon, and the consciousness
> of a Pilaga Indian baby is therefore very different from that of an
> American one (1972, p. 60).

Mother and the family surround the baby, permeating its very being. In the
same way society surrounds and permeates the family.

Unfortunately, our metaphors for this internalizing of culture, this making
it a part of each of our personalities, are not very cogent. As Henry points out,
"teach" and "learn" hardly convey the idea of contacting one's universe
through another person. If we say "nature and nurture combine" or if we
speak of "social factors," we sound as though culture was simply added or
multiplied into some preexisting personality. At other times we refer to our
"cultural heritage," as though it were a possession that could be bequeathed.
Still other metaphors introduce the idea of social "pressure" or "impact" or
"forces" as though we could model the process by images from freshman
physics.

Social values cannot become a part of the baby's world so simply or
directly. My own metaphors for the infant's developing into a social being—
culture flows, culture permeates and pervades, culture sets limits, culture is the
message—may be somewhat, but only somewhat, better. More telling would
be metaphors that imply a complex transformation in which culture determines a social style of biological mothering which each mother translates
through her own individual personality to a baby who combines it with its own
unique heredity.

Waddington's evolutionary landscape is suggestive but gives too fixed a
picture. The landscape does have certain fixed features (like the childhood
stages), but also we each have our own landscape, which (in the triad of
Kluckohn and Murray) may share features with everybody else's, somebody
else's, or nobody else's. The developmental landscape is simultaneously
deterministic and undeterministic, "objective" and "subjective," and universal, cultural, and individual. That's asking a lot of a landscape. How can
one imagine a terrain that has certain features for all humanity, others for
Americans, other features for college professors, and still others for just me?

I think the two levels of feedback developed in part II provide a better
metaphor. An identity *using* certain cultural codes which in turn *use* the

body will image what happens between the mothers and children of *Four Families*. The baby's needs draw out of his mother a culture that becomes part of the baby. In fulfilling the baby's needs, she endows the baby with cultural loops as her identity uses those loops. Thus the baby internalizes the culture but specifically its mother's version of that culture. It is like learning *The Star-Spangled Banner* by hearing only Charles Ives's version or Puccini's.

With such a feedback model in mind, consider Anni Bergman's description of an American baby boy and the effect of his mother's state of mind:

> Jason was a boy who could not outgrow the elated state accompanying the feeling that he could conquer the world. He was a motor-minded little boy who started to walk freely at the early age of nine months. His mother was a depressed woman with a rather poor image of herself. It was most important that her son be precocious, a narcissistic completion of herself. . . . Jason's mother, in awe of her fledgling, . . . seemed to impart to her son the idea that he could manage no matter what. She did not temper his age-appropriate feeling of omnipotence with her own ability to be a rational judge of danger. She allowed him total freedom, and Jason never seemed to learn to be a judge of danger himself. Recklessly he would throw himself into space. He was forever falling but, interestingly, he hardly ever cried. It as was if the sense of omnipotence and of his own invulnerability dwarfed his physical pain (Bergman, 1978, pp. 156–57).

Jason's mother's identity used not only Jason but the American fondness for throwing people and things into space as a way of fulfilling herself. Jason, possibly building on his own innate temperament, fulfilled her needs by his fearlessness. In effect, she set standards for cultural behavior which in turn set standards for bodily behavior. She and Jason were each using the other *and* the American style to create a network of positive feedbacks.

I think the double feedback picture is useful, but I also think Lacan and Lichtenstein are right when they suggest using language as a model for this individualizing of the general human fate to form an I. The interrelation of baby and mother is a cultural and verbal one. Jason's mother is, as it were, feeding back his behavior to him in the language of the American kitchen, bedroom, or television set. Further, a society that itself likes to hurl things into space may applaud both her and Jason for his bodily recklessness, giving them a reinforcing positive feedback. English society, less committed to change, speed, and the taking of risks, might make Jason and his mother uncomfortable with their lack of restraint.

Lacan accents the linguistic aspect of human development, and since we can only think about these questions of nature and nurture in language, I think we can improve the feedback model by recasting it in linguistic terms. Erikson spoke of the biological and social landscape or groundplan as posing "tasks" we all face. We might introduce into his metaphor a Sphinx that poses us riddles at crucial junctures. Questions and answers, moreover, embody a feedback process. Oedipus had to solve the Sphinx's riddle before he could enter the gates of Thebes. So with each of us. We each must solve the childhood riddles of how to postpone gratification or how to control impulses or how to turn passive experiences into active ones before we can go on to the next stage. We must choose a career before we can progress in it. We must acquire a child before we can become a parent.

We could say that development asks us questions. Some of these questions all humans face. Some occur only in certain cultures. Others are unique to one person. All of them, however, we hear first in the individual body language of one particular mother and one particular baby, then later in the style of one particular I.

The answers an I gives to one particular question, for example, how to reverse passive into active, will "determine" the way the individual hears the next question. One answer by an I "determines" (in the loose way that the two sides of a dialogue "determine" each other) the question from the environment in response, which in turn determines (in that same loose way) the next answer by the I. The answers we give affect the next questions, making some more likely and foreclosing others. We find our way through a conversation in much the same way that we take this path or that through a landscape.

The Canadian family in *Four Families* was speaking to its baby not only in English, but in a language of vacuum cleaners and washing machines. The infant Shaw made loud noises. Iiro drew ducks and shoes and table lamps. We in turn try to understand these transactions in our own languages. We can talk about all these different individual versions of what is generically the same through a language which is both a function of our individual identities and a resource that we hold in common. I think then we can best model

Development as Dialogue

since a dialogue embodies in a feedback relationship the human biology of speech, the cultural dimension of language, the personal style of conversation, as well as the totally unique event of some particular dialogue.

For example, we could look at Winnicott's interview with Iiro as a dialogue whose focus we could phrase as the boy's wish to be loved as he was, deformity unchanged. After that interview, Winnicott went on to talk to Iiro's mother (again through an interpreter "whose translation quickly became forgotten by both of us"). Confessing for the first time her feelings about Iiro, she said,

> I know that everyone has guilt feelings about sex. For me it has been different. All my life I have felt free sexually and in marriage sexual experience has been a fulfillment. Instead of feeling guilty about sex what I have always felt is that my condition of fingers and toes will be handed down to one of my children. In this way I would be punished. Since marriage, with each pregnancy I have become increasingly anxious about the baby that was to be born, anxious in terms of the inherited disability. I knew I must not have babies because of this disability. Each time when the baby is born and the baby is normal I feel immense relief. With Iiro, however, I had no relief because there he was with fingers and toes like mine and I had been punished. When I saw him I hated him. I completely repudiated him, and for a length of time (perhaps only twenty minutes or perhaps longer) I knew that I could never see him again. He had to be taken away from me. Then it came over me that I might get his fingers and toes mended by persistently using the orthopædic surgeon. I immediately decided to persist in getting Iiro's fingers and toes mended although this seemed impossible, and from that moment I found my love of him returning and I think I have loved him more than the others. From his point of view, therefore, it could be said that he gained something. Nevertheless I have been obsessed with this drive to use the orthopædic surgeon.

Winnicott recognized that what she was saying dovetailed with what Iiro had told him. "He may have gained something from this mother's special love of him, but he had to pay for it by being caught up in an obsessive drive which indeed the orthopædic surgeon had noticed, and the staff of the hospital . . ." (1971b, pp. 25–27).

The dialogue of Iiro's development began with his unfortunate heredity and his mother's guilt. She translated a common adult guilt about sex into a more literal fear of consequences. At his birth, when the feared punishment seemed actually to happen, she managed to love Iiro by resolving to mend his fingers and toes through surgery. "You must change in order for me not to feel guilty but to love you"—this was the message she sent Iiro from his birth, and he responded in the way that a baby does. It would overimplify to say that the message "pressured" him or "shaped" him; those metaphors are too crudely deterministic. I think of the dyad this way: Iiro became the baby who could receive the message his mother was sending. He fit.

Jules Henry describes that process as the baby's sending his mother*
messages of contentment by his eyes' following her, by smiling, relaxing in
her arms, gurgling or cooing. She in turn sends messages of her contentment: she cuddles him, gurgles and coos in baby talk, and follows him with
her eyes. Mother and baby both show they know they are each giving the
other something the other needs. Gradually, in the normal course of events,
"love" messages replace the "contentment" messages. "Between the baby's
inherent tendencies and the mother's requirements, a code is worked out
. . . with neither mother nor child knowing that anything is being learned or
taught." In effect, mother and baby learn to fit together (Hartmann's
zusammenpassen), first in the business of feeding and sleeping and caring,
later in their loving responsiveness to each other. The mother gives the baby
the love and care he needs. He gives her something of himself in return, and
in so doing learns to love (1972, 192–93).

The mother and infant have, of course, a paradoxical dialogue, since in
the nature of things, it must be without words: *infans* is Latin for
"unspeaking." Lichtenstein suggests, therefore, still a different figure of
speech: "The way the mother is touching, holding, warming the child, the
way in which some senses are stimulated, while others are not, forms a kind
of 'stimulus cast' of the mother's unconscious, just as a blind and deaf person
may, by the sense of touch, 'cast' the form and the personality of another
person in his mind." Lichtenstein's idea of a "cast" of the relationship of
baby and mother corresponds to the "mirroring experience" described by
Lacan, Greenacre, and many other psychoanalytic authors without committing us to a primarily visual learning. Rather such a "cast" would be in its
very body-ness the first "sexuality" in the classical psychoanalytic sense:
pleasure from specific organs, not necessarily related to genitals or pro-
creating. In this bodily relation, "while the mother satisfies the infant's
needs, in fact creates certain specific needs, which she delights in satisfying,
the infant is transformed into an organ or an instrument for the satisfaction
of the mother's unconscious needs" (1977, pp. 76-78). Iiro becomes caught
up in his mother's need to expiate her guilt through surgery, and Jason
compensates for his mother's sense of her own inadequacy. Somehow the
infant gains in the wordless preconscious dialogue between himself and his

* Henry here, like most writers in this field, uses "he" as the pronoun for the baby and
"mother" and "she" for the caregiver. I shall do the same, but only to avoid confusion and
periphrastics. I do not think the male baby a norm from which the female departs. Nor do I
mean to imply that female parenting is a norm, for I believe that anything I say about a
nurturing "she" could apply equally to a nurturing "he." I am writing of a psychological
mother, a caregiver who is responsible for the psychological birth of the infant into personhood.
This "primary love object," in the technical jargon, may be—usually is—the biological mother,
but can be any other caregiver. Indeed, this "mother" can be "father," and, as two-gender
parenting becomes more common, often will be.

mother an inkling of her unconscious patterns and of the person he is expected to be in order to "fit."

No one has observed the bodily, sexual relationship between mother and baby more closely than Daniel Stern. By videotaping the interactions of mother and baby in feeding and diapering and holding, he has been able to analyze such things as "gaze behavior" to the millisecond. (We humans live in a world where a fraction of a second more or less in a "Hi!" is all the difference between "Hey! she likes me!" and "What's eating her?") He describes one such relationship—this one not "the normal course of events."

"I first met Jenny," writes Stern, "when she was almost three months old. Her mother was an animated woman . . . intrusive, controlling, and over-stimulating by most standards. She seemed to want, need, and expect a high level of exciting, animated interaction. . . . Furthermore, the mother seemed to want the level she wanted when she wanted it." As a result, she was always pushing the level of Jenny's stimulation about as high as the baby would tolerate.

> The dance [another metaphor!] they had worked out by the time I met them went something like this. Whenever a moment of mutual gaze occurred, the mother went immediately into high-gear. . . . [That is, in response to Jenny's gaze, she would loudly and eagerly start talking and making faces to her.] Jenny invariably broke gaze rapidly. Her mother never interpreted this temporary face and gaze aversion as a cue to lower her level of behavior, nor would she let Jenny self-control the level by gaining distance. Instead, she would swing her head around following Jenny's to reestablish the full-face position. Once the mother achieved this, she would reinitiate the same level of stimulation with a new arrangement of facial and vocal combinations. Jenny again turned away, pushing her face further into the pillow to try to break all visual contact. Again, instead of holding back, the mother continued to chase Jenny. The pillow and side wing of the infant seat now prevented the mother from swinging around to the face-to-face position. So this time, she moved closer, in an apparent attempt to break through and estab-lish contact. She also escalated the level of her stimulation even more by adding touching and tickling to the unabated flow of vocal and facial behaviors. . . .
>
> With Jenny's head now pinned in the corner, the baby's next recourse was to perform a "pass-through." She rapidly swung her face from one side to the other right past her mother's face. When her face crossed the mother's face, in the face-to-face zone, Jenny closed her eyes to avoid any mutual visual contact and only reopened them after the head aversion was established on the other side. All of these be-

haviors on Jenny's part were performed with a sober face or at times a grimace.

The mother followed her to the new side, producing volleys of stimulation that again progressively pushed Jenny's head farther away until she performed another pass-through. After a series of these "failures," the mother would pick the infant up from the infant seat and hold her under the armpits, dangling in the face-to-face position. This maneuver usually succeeded in reorienting Jenny toward her, but as soon as she put Jenny back down, the same pattern reestablished itself. After several more repeats of these sequences the mother became visibly frustrated, angry, and confused and Jenny, quite upset.

At that point the mother would stop playing with Jenny and put her to bed. After some weeks of watching this, when Jenny seemed more and more withdrawn, Stern became concerned. Eventually, however, the mother became slightly less intrusive, and Jenny became much more able to handle her mothrer's craving for a response. She gave her mother more of the gurgling, happy feedback the mother needed, so that her mother could relax somewhat—although it was Jenny who did the major part in breaking the vicious circle.

What is telling from the point of view of forming an I, however, is Stern's description of the years after Jenny and her mother had fit: "At each new phase of development Jenny and her mother have had to replay this basic scenario of overshoot and resolution, but with different sets of behaviors and at higher levels of organization." Stern does not use a theme-and-variations concept of identity, but he is here describing exactly the process I visualize for an identity's coming into being. Out of their fitting, mother and baby establish a theme for their relationship—"this basic scenario of overshoot and resolution" is Stern's phrase for it. The baby then becomes the baby that fits into that theme. *I am the kind of child (or later, person) who always feels as though I am coping with too much.* Even Stern's metaphor of a "scenario" echoes mine of a dialogue (1977, pp. 110–114).

The dialogue between mother and baby answers to a theme and variations reading just as the behavior of a single person does. Holistic readings can prove useful for the dyad here as well as for the self.

Indeed, if sufficiently skilled at "It fits" inferences, one can even read the individual baby holistically, although the media are often semiverbal or nonverbal. Here, for example, is Margaret Mahler's account of the behavior of Bruce, aged twenty-five months:

> One morning, after having a bowel movement in his diaper, Bruce looked for his mother. When he could not find her, he picked up a book on trains, his favorite book; he pointed to a picture and talked about the

coal car which happened not to be in this particular picture. He knew the train had a coal car, even though it was not shown. Similarly, he had just looked for his mother but could not find her. Also, he had moved his bowels, which he felt in his diaper, but which he could not see. Subsequently he found another book and looked at the picture of a family. He pointed to and named the father and the boy, but he did not name the girl and mother who were also in the picture. Then he went to the toy mail box, pointed to the flap that had come off it, and then clearly enunciated: "doo-doo" (bowel movement). Subsequent to this he played with hollow blocks, putting a small one into a big one (quasi hiding it) and then putting them in order. Then he looked out the window, where he had often seen boys playing in the yard and said, "boy," even though nobody was in the play yard at this point. He called the observers' attention to all these parts that belong to a "syncretic whole," which at that moment, however, were missing or invisible. Thus, with his free associative sequence of words and actions, he disclosed his concern about missing part-objects or whole-objects, particularly the absent love object, his mother (1975, p. 131).

Mahler has "read" a theme, 'whole but with a part missing,' in Bruce's symbolic use of a variety of media: his bowel movement, a train in a book, a picture of a family, a toy mail box, blocks, the play yard. All of these provided Bruce a language with which to talk about the physical and emotional absence of his mother. Mahler then translated it into her own language.

Perhaps Mahler was aided by her prior knowledge of Bruce and Bruce's situation. Bruce always translated a lot of things into missing parts: "Bruce could not easily express his needs directly: he touched his mother while avoiding looking at her." Similarly, when his baby sister was born a few months earlier, he avoided the sight of his mother with the baby—as long as he could. Later, at thirty-three months, "Bruce liked to poke holes in the play dough, then cover them up, and say with great relief: 'Hole all gone.' "

Bruce's life involves one child's style interacting with events that many children share: the birth of a sister, fears about body losses, controlling his bowels, standing up, or walking. A central problem in understanding child development is to put the two different kinds of phenomena together, the unique and the shared. Sometimes we need to look at Bruce in isolation, as if he were in front of the photographer's blank backdrop. At other times we need to walk Bruce away from the backdrop and see him in the context of his mother, his family, and his society.

The classical if-then generalizations of psychoanalysis give us a way to talk about Bruce as being like many other children. The holistic analysis of individual themes and style gives us a way to talk about Bruce as a unique individual. How can we put them together? I have suggested three models. Waddington and Erikson's "epigenetic landscape" or "groundplan" image an individual marching through a widely shared terrain. A two-tier feedback network models an individual identity making use of shared cultural and biological tools to act on and receive feedback from reality. Finally the model I prefer, dialogue, portrays one individual addressing people and things by means of the shared resource of language, hearing their answers in his own idiolect, and responding—feeding back—in turn.

By listening to the growth of a child as a dialogue, we are in a new position to explore the way an I comes into being. Identity—the I—as this I has been developing the idea, is:

—an agency that initiates a feedback response from the world outside the self;

—the cumulating consequence of that feedback;

—the topmost and pervading reference in a hierarchy of feedbacks;

—the verbal representation of the above triad as a theme and variations. Given this idea of an I and language as a medium, we can model human development as a dialogue of question and answer. Physiology, family, and culture pose questions to babies, but what are the questions? That is *our* next question.

8 | The Birth of an I

Late in his career, Freud put forward two hypotheses that have given rise to an immense body of research, greatly lengthening our perspective on early infancy. First, in 1930, in the opening chapter of *Civilization and its Discontents,* he asserted that the baby only gradually separates a self from the nurturing world around it. That slow differentiation provided the basis for all situations in later life in which the boundaries between self and other blur or dissolve entirely: mysticism, love, imaginations, or (I would add) the whole process of DEFTing.

Second, he acknowledged the importance of a major developmental phase prior to the oedipus complex. So momentous was his realization that he compared it to Sir Arthur Evans's discovery of a Minoan-Mycenaean civilization that had flourished ten centuries before the classical Greece we, and Freud, studied in school (1931b, 21:226). The early months form the geological substratum—or the basic fault—on which all subsequent development, including the oedipus complex, builds. I want to "read" both the older theories and the new knowledge in the light of "the I."

In psychoanalytic thought in general since Freud, the early relation between the infant and his mother has come to overshadow the later triangle of child, mother, and rival, even though Freud himself emphasized the triangle and discovered the dyad only near the end of his life. Indeed the whole tenor of the development of psychoanalysis after Freud's death has found more and more importance in the first year of life. This emphasis on the pre-oedipal marks one major difference between "Freudian" theory (in the strict sense of what Freud stated) and "psychoanalytic" theory (referring to the ongoing science Freud founded). It provides yet another bridge between psychoanalysis and regular psychology.

In recent years, there has been a virtual explosion of interest in the psychology of babies, often based on completely different methods. Daniel Stern is one among many "baby watchers" who are trying to understand children by direct observation. He videotapes the eloquent ballet between mother and infant as she feeds or bathes him or simply responds to his cry or his gaze, as, for example, he filmed the struggle around stimulation between Jenny and her mother. One mother will dart the bottle in and out of her baby's lips. Another will slowly, lingeringly roll it round his mouth. Some other might doze as she gives the breast in a midnight feeding. Typically, a mother speaks to an infant in a slow, high voice that adult humans use in no other circumstances. She gazes at him as long as he is willing to look at her. It is he, not she, who turns away and so breaks off this communication through the eyes (1977). Jenny's mother, by contrast, forced her stimulation on the baby. Her intrusions defined their relationship, defined, in effect, Jenny.

The opposite of Stern, Jacques Lacan is a theorist who analyzes babies by reason rather than observation. For example, he has visualized the development of the I through a mirror phase (*le stade du miroir*). The baby perceives himself, in an actual mirror, as having a bodily unity which he feels inwardly is still lacking. The baby therefore identifies with this image. Unfortunately for the theory, babies do not behave this way with mirrors (Lewis and Brooks, 1975, p. 123). Rather than restrict human development to a particular experience of mirrors, however, I (like Winnicott) read Lacan's metaphor as referring to the mirroring that takes place between mother and baby. She reflects him back to himself, but through the wholeness she perceives or wishes to perceive in him. In either case, this first sense of self is a self through another, a self that is radically not the baby's actual, experienced self. Yet it is the basis for future growth. The I comes into being through otherness, Stern's conclusion, but reached in an entirely different way (1936).

Such new observations and theories from both psychoanalysis and psychology mean that we have more incisive ways of thinking about some of the traditional riddles of human nature. These particular riddles are especially pivotal because we have to think them through before we can reply to social and political questions on which millions of destinies hinge. Our social policies rest on our assumptions about the relative importance of heredity and environment or, in the neater phrase, nature vs. nurture.

Psychologists translate that contrast into the balancing of learning theories against nativist or rationalist theories. Do we learn to see or do we inherit that ability? Can a person who went through all the stages of childhood development deaf and then is granted hearing learn to hear as normal people do? Do we learn how to use language (as Piaget seems to maintain) or are we (as Noam Chomsky claims) biologically programmed with a certain linguistic capacity that defines and is defined by the universal features of all grammars? To the extent that we believe in learning theories, then we may believe efforts at political and social control will eventually succeed and seem natural. We may also believe that we can educate many more people and better than we presently do. If we believe in innate capacities, however, then any attempts to force or override them will seem tormenting and futile. There would be no point in making a special effort to educate the children of the "underclass," no point in a Head Start program. We should simply learn to live with a *lumpenproletariat.*

In psychoanalysis, the nature-nurture enigma finds an equivalent in the debate between those analysts who hold to a "classical" drive theory, defining instincts physiologically, and those who have adopted the "English object-relations theory." Is the developing human being propelled by biological instincts (*Triebe,* properly "drives") with fixed stages associated with body zones (oral, anal, and so on), or should we say the infant is born into a relationship and all development, pleasure, learning, and adaptation must be defined within that and later relationships?

I do not see any *necessary* contradiction here. Drives presuppose objects, and objects presuppose drives. The relations between a baby and its objects must change as the baby's drives evolve, and the drives must change in relation to the baby's changing objects. Indeed the ego-psychologist David Rapaport thought one of Freud's outstanding ideas was making the object of a drive a defining characteristic of the drive (1960a, p. 202; see also Loch, 1977, p. 210).

The task for psychoanalysis, it seems to me, is to find ways for these two approaches to enrich each other, not cancel each other out as mutually exclusive. In the same way, I see the exciting discoveries of those who observe or test children as contributing to psychoanalytic knowledge, not competing with it.

The Baby-Watchers

Today's experimental psychologists have considerably revised William James's oft-quoted image of the newborn baby's world as "one great blooming, buzzing confusion." Babies are capable of a lot more than we used to think.

To be sure, a newborn sees only 5 percent of what an adult sees, but that provides "functionally useful" vision. Stern says the newborn baby's eyes are focused at eight inches, forming a "perceptual bubble," adapted to the perception of his mother's face during feeding and little else. Other experimenters, however, seem to suggest that babies are born with more perceptual capacity, abilities to see distances or the position of objects in three dimensions. Often, apparently, these abilities are lost and later relearned in another form, as though they were first innate, then learned in a more adaptive way in response to experience and other forms of knowledge.

After four months or more, the baby begins to be able to accommodate his vision for near and far objects, probably as a result of improved acuity (Atkinson and Braddick, 1981). Vision probably develops according to "a preset, presumably genetically determined program" (Held, 1981). Indeed all of infant development probably takes place as part of the program by which the neurons in the body and brain grow their sheaths of myelin and begin to function as they do in adults (Freedman, 1981). From the very beginning, however, babies show they like to look at some things more than others, at curves and depths and many small events rather than a few large ones (Fantz et al., 1975).

The newborn's hearing is much more sophisticated than his vision. Films have shown infants as early as twenty minutes after birth spontaneously moving their bodies in time with speech (Condon, 1976; Condon and Ogstron, 1966). As one researcher remarks, if this observation proves true, it is surely one of the most significant discoveries of any modern science, because it suggests that we are *by nature* speaking animals and social beings. Infants do, in fact, have social exchanges from the very beginning. The days when a newborn first comes home from the hospital (in our culture) provide a period of intense negotiation during which mother and baby try to mesh their two schedules (Sander, 1969).

Babies can move their bodies in rhythm to speech at one day, and at one month they can distinguish a *p* from a *b* (Spieker, 1982). Moreover, a four month old baby apparently hears that difference not just as a random difference in the timing of the voice but as a difference *in linguistic category*. Again, the inference seems inescapable that *we are born knowing that language is made up of discrete units* (Eimas, 1975). From the moment we are born we are getting ready to speak.

Indeed, newborns either have or develop quickly a number of what I can only call intellectual categories. Babies recognize almost from the start whether something is familiar or not. Babies can also predict, and they are able to act in response to familiar events or, conversely, to expect events to occur in response to their own actions. All of this presupposes (to me) surprising capacities of association and memory (Papoušek and Papoušek, 1981). Babies seem to understand sameness, difference, cause, effect, and sequence from birth.

By the second month of life babies are able to recognize specific individuals *and behave differently toward them* (Lamb, 1981). From a psychoanalytic point of view, however, these persons are "part objects." Before two months, a baby's sight is drawn just to the greatest number or size of visible elements ("contour density"). According to the experimenters, a very young baby neither sees the object as a whole nor is sensitive to the arrangement of features. After all, vision at two months is 20/500 and at four months, 20/150. Also, because a baby has little stored information about pattern and form, no schemata for perception, he cannot at first see an object (or a person) as such, only as a sequence of features. Probably that is the first meaning of an "other" for us: a figure or pattern or, more exactly, the feeling of alternately scanning and focusing on a sequence of critical features (Salapatek, 1975).

An eight-to-ten week old baby will kick and continue kicking to keep a mobile spinning (Suomi, 1981). That is, the baby can perceive events as events and act in response to them. It "perceives contingency," in psychological jargon, and again that implies some sophistication of concepts.

One of the most important of the baby's early concepts was "faceness," the invariant configuration of eyes, nose, and mouth. At four months, the eyes are the most salient feature of a face and "faceness" is not yet established, but by five months, a baby could recognize distortions of the mouth or inversions of the nose. An infant evolves a "face configuration," and that means the baby can understand the facial communication patterns that adults use (Campos and Stenberg, 1981). A four month old can tell whether a person he sees speaking is the source of the voice he hears by detecting the relation in time between face movements and the voice. A four month old knows that a speaking face normally goes with a speaking voice (Spelke and Cortelyou, 1981).

Around this time babies make another major cognitive leap. Before twelve weeks, experimentalists find only "very spotty" evidence (despite all claims of adoring and delighted mothers) that a baby knows the difference between its mother and a stranger. Somewhere between twelve and twenty weeks, however, that ability clearly and decisively appears.

Smiling helps in this. Babies start smiling toward human voices by one month and toward faces at three months, choosing between faces by four months. In general, babies show a spurt of response to all social stimuli around four months and, most important, they begin to show *expectations* about persons (Olson, 1981).

All of this shows the development of a rudimentary "person concept" (Olson, 1981). Conversely, a disruption of this interaction with persons spells trouble, as, for example, with blind children who cannot elicit or return the loving gazes that ordinarily pass between parent and child. For these unfortunate children, the risk of autism (a complete breakdown of development and interaction) greatly increases—unless their parents are taught to recognize and use other signs of interaction (Freedman, 1981).

It is clear, then, that infants have from the very start far more sophisticated abilities to sense and think about the world than people just a few years ago believed. From the outset, they have some sort of inborn, nonverbal mechanism for knowing, that is, for representing in their minds the concepts they are developing and by which they organize their environment into a world that is full of differences and meanings. From the first hours after birth they are able to draw on concepts in order to perceive, and their perceptions sophisticate those concepts in turn. In short, they engage in the same kind of feedback as adults who are DEFTing.

For example, studies of how infants perceive physical things show concepts shaping perceptions. A baby up to five months old ceases to look for a rattle placed on a table or, in general, any object placed on another, larger object. The infant ceases to look for it. Why? In general, when a five-month old tries to find a vanished object, how the object disappeared is important. If it disappeared on a trajectory, the infant can follow the object and will look for it. If, however, someone throws a blanket over it, the object has, as it were, ended. It is "inside" and the infant has no concept for inside. Similarly, if one puts an object under a transparent cup, it ends. The rattle on the table is "inside" that way and it, too, simply ends. With a seven-month-old infant, if one places a small object on the palm of his hand, he will close his hand over the object and that puts the object out of sight. The infant will then act as if the object no longer existed; eventually he just drops it. "Inside" doesn't mean anything yet, even if it is inside the baby's own hand. In other words, a seven month old has a concept of trajectory but not yet of inside, and psychologists can watch the latter concept come into being (Bower, 1975). Before it does, a baby simply does not have the same kind of spatial sense we adults have.

A great many concepts have to come into being before we can say an infant has begun to establish human relationships. For example, a baby has to learn that others can be relied on or that it is itself capable of affecting its environment, indeed is in partial control of its experiences. A baby has to have some notion of its mother's continued existence despite her momentary absence for us to say that the baby is crying *in order to* bring her back. Then, once these concepts do come into being, a baby begins to have a more active and intentional role in its relations with other people (Lamb, 1981).

The experimental baby-watchers have made, then, at least one very important point. Emotional and cognitive development go together. Cognitive skills make emotional relations possible, and emotional relations motivate cognitive skills.

The crucial event in their mutual progress takes place usually by the third quarter of the first year of life: a baby begins to have a sense of the permanence of persons (Lamb, 1981). Once it does, it begins to have a sense of its own self. In psychoanalytic thinking, this is self-object differentiation, the basis for all relations with others and all sense of self. Piaget dated this watershed later, but it appears that the psychoanalysts' surmise was correct: the eighth or ninth month (Gouin Décarie, 1965).

To its parents, a baby's newfound sense of self and other shows as "stranger anxiety," fear or crying at the presence of adult strangers, male or female, but not, normally, of the mother. Interestingly, babies do not show stranger anxiety *to other infants*, evidence that their fears proceed from a genuine concept of who and what the others are. A twelve month old who is looking through magazines or newspapers with pictures of adults will sometimes point at them and say "baby," showing that he is judging size per se. He is not compensating as we would for the reduction of a person to the size of a page, but he is fitting the apparent size of these persons into a one year old's concept of person (Lewis and Brooks-Gunn, 1982).

Indeed by the end of the first year, you could say a baby has something like a full-fledged theory of mind. The one year old, for example, understands that people have identity over time despite changes in location or behavior ("Daddy at work," "Mommy mad"). The baby knows that you have to influence people by asking for things or telling them. ("Watch me.") Hence the baby knows that people are self-moving. People identify one another (for example, by correctly using pronouns). People sense things within a limited perceptual field. Outside that field, things are not perceived. ("Did you see me jump in?") People have intentions ("I want") and moods ("Daddy loves me," "Mommy is sad"). People postpone or restrain or retain or repeat behaviors. ("Daddy will come home." "I can go home" —and *can* says the baby knows about what psychologists label "action potentials.") People share rules about what is appropriate and who can do what, when, and how. ("Norman is a good boy." "That's Daddy's hat.") In general, the one year old understands that people communicate messages through words and gestures. These are related to context, although not always unambiguously. Indeed, you have to infer the internal states of others. ("Are you mad, Daddy?") All in all, the one year old has a fairly sophisticated theory of persons, although, obviously, he could not express it in abstractions like the ones in this paragraph (Bretherton et al., 1981). You could even say that he knows about as much about people as the psychologist knows about one of the rats in his mazes.

Most important, the one year old is beginning to detect genders and by two years will have made gender identity a part of his own self-identity. A basic principle in the child's development of self is "I will act like others who are like me," the principle of "attraction of like" (the opposite of magnets). The motivational system of the child thus rests at least partly on the ability to distinguish types of people and to decide to be like them. Thus the infant constructs sex-roles from the biological and cultural differences around him: hair length, type of clothes, different first names, work patterns, and so on. These cues provide information for differentiating oneself from others. Then the principle of "attraction of like" comes into play, and the child moves toward conformity in sex-role behavior. Each new behavior the child adopts provides a further basis for establishing what is like and what is unlike. Hence sex-role behavior tends to feed back onto itself, leading the child further and further into one gender or the other (Lewis, 1981).

Not only does a baby have a theory of the human and of gender by the end of the first year, he has begun to evolve his own personal style (Yarrow, 1982). From the beginning babies are active, information-processing organisms, engaged in feedback with their environment. They try to reach objects and get responses from them, preferring novelty and change to a static environment. Hence reaching out to people or to objects tends to be self-reinforcing. This positive feedback leads to a "generalized expectancy model," a belief that one *can* affect one's environment (notably through "contingent mother-infant interaction," in the jargon). This trust provides the basis for a personal style, that is, continuing some behaviors or, if you will, a way of DEFTing that the baby finds successful. It seems likely that even newborns have some rudimentary sense of self, developed out of the consistency and regularity of and the feedback from the baby's own actions. For example, each time a baby closes its eyes, the world becomes black. A self does that. In the same way, a self feels pain. A self makes the pain stop. Mother reflects back what I—a self—do (Lewis and Brooks-Gunn, 1982).

Also, by the end of the first year, infants have probably developed a sense of the styles of the people around them (their "behavioral propensities," in the jargon). Erikson's notion of basic trust, for example, presupposes that the baby can distinguish between the various people around him and predict their different responses to him. Infants develop different relations with their mothers than with their fathers. They also generalize from their experiences with parents to new people, trying out the social modes they know from their parents on newcomers. That generalizing means that a one-year old has developed a style discernible to the observing psychologist (Lamb, 1981), and *that,* from the point of view of this book, is an identity.

In all this vigorous experimenting, John Bowlby is an important influence with his concept of attachment, which he defines as an affectional tie from one person to another, binding them together in space and time. Bowlby was trying to situate the early mother-child relation in an updated psychoanalytic instinct theory, as grounded as Freud could have wished in biology and ethology. From observing primitive peoples and ground-living apes, Bowlby suggested that the baby's attachment to the mother served to protect the infant from predators and other dangers, balancing closeness to the mother with the child's necessary adventurousness.

Bowlby traced four stages in a modern baby's attachment. Until three months, a baby uses his behavioral repertoire, sucking, grasping, looking, smiling, and so on, to bring any person in his environment nearer to him, in general, to relate socially to any human around him. From three to six months, a baby clearly discriminates between his mother and other persons, wanting her near but not wanting the rest the same way. From six or seven months on, a baby becomes more active and takes more initiative in relating to people. Bowlby says the baby has become "goal-directed," changing its strategies according to the reactions of the other persons. This is the period when, according to Bowlby, a baby is truly "attached" and, in regular psychoanalytic theory, true object-relations begin—a baby relates to others as others and feels its self as a self. Finally, in a fourth period, beginning about three, the baby begins to be able to infer things about his mother's goals, and the give and take of mother and child becomes much more intense (1951, 1958, and 1969).

Bowlby's phases correspond in several ways to stages in babies' play described by two later researchers, Belsky and Most (1982). At first a baby plays in a completely undifferentiated way, manipulating and mouthing objects more or less at random. You could phrase this stage as, "The object is what I do." Then an infant begins to tailor its own procedures to fit the object, fingering and mouthing and looking at it according to what fits a mobile or a rattle or a box. "What is this? And what can it do?" Eventually, children begin to draw conceptual relationships between objects, and they start to use their own previous experience with mobile or rattle. They assert control of the relationship between the object and themselves. "What can I do with this object?" At about a year, the child gets beyond the physical limitations of the object—or the self. He begins to be able to do pretend play, to use a seashell as a cup or to mimic driving a car. "What can I make this subject or object into?"

In effect, the baby-watchers are demonstrating some of the basic assumptions of psychoanalysis. Their work asks for a psychoanalytic response.

One, a child develops in a progress (which is probably genetically programmed) from earlier and more primitive abilities to later and more complex skills. Such a program fits the psychoanalytic notion of developmental phases or stages. It is not consistent with the romantic idea of childhood that we began life in some unrepressed, utopian state of mind that later succumbed to repression and other civilizing ills. Rather, the newborn, as compared to the child of three, is not so much free as limited. The loss of infancy is growth.

Two, we did not, like Topsy, just grow. There is a logic to child development. We do not lurch abruptly from one stage to another, unrelated stage. Rather, an earlier stage transforms into the next in ways that we can understand commonsensically. A child develops in a continuous, sensible way.

Three, from the moment of birth (and perhaps before), a child is engaged in a feedback or dialectic with his environment, particularly the persons who surround him. They act on him, his response affects their subsequent actions, and that response to him enters in turn into his next action.

Four, in this feedback, what a baby feels emotionally and what a baby knows cognitively intertwine. One cannot separate a baby's affective development from his developing perceptual and cognitive skills. Each aids or interferes with the other.

No doubt we could glean other psychoanalytic fundamentals from this, to me, extraordinarily exciting line of psychological research, but we also need to recognize that the psychoanalysts and the observers and experimenters are coming at childhood in rather different ways. One could trace all of the above principles in Freud's account of childhood, not, to be sure, always fully explored. Freud's (and later psychoanalysts') accounts come almost entirely from observing this particular adult or that particular child, a clinician's concern. The baby-watchers, by contrast, concern themselves with categories, a certain kind of stimulus, a certain kind of gazing, a certain kind of play.

One experimenter, Michael Lewis, has addressed this difference by distinguishing two aspects of the self. One is categorical, the self I intend when I say, "I am male" or "I am big" or "I am writing a book." The other is existential, a more basic self, the "I" who inhabits all those sentences, whom I have known from the first moments of my existence as the self who opens my eyes or feels pain. Clearly, the existential self comes into being before the other, yet the existential self, starting at a very early age, is constantly discovering and defining itself as being like or unlike this or that category (Lewis and Brooks-Gunn, 1982). Categorical and existential selves exist in a dialectic relationship.

Characteristically, I would translate Lewis's dialectic into observables. The categories are what the observers and experimenters provide, and indeed what I provide myself when I look at myself "objectively," "out there," as an object, an other. I would translate the existential self into what an observer would see as the individual self, a unique being with a unique history which one senses as a personal style. Just as, when I write, I use categories, nouns and verbs, but choose and combine them in my individual way, so the baby uses categories, significant persons and stimuli, but chooses and combines them in an increasingly individual way. One could model a baby like a sentence, as drawing on socially and biologically given categories but using them with a certain personal style. That model brings us back, in effect, to earlier ones: identity governing a hierarchy of feedbacks or an identity hearing the questions all humans share but hearing them and answering in a personal idiom.

We can put the new knowledge about early infancy together with identity theory and feedback to explore the ways heredity and environment, nature and nurture, learning and faculties, or instinctual drives and object relations interact to form an I. We can use identity theory to imagine a moment by moment dialogue that will model the way we learn to see, hear, know, or remember reality. We begin with a paradox, namely,

The Preverbal Dialogue

Until now, I have been describing the baby's developmental dialogue as calls from his community and family. These relations of the baby to the people and things that environ him are "there," in the sense that you can even videotape them and see how they call to him. Less obviously "there," but a balance of evidence from experimental studies confirms them, are the zones and drives that Freud and other early psychoanalysts, notably Karl Abraham, posited (Fisher and Greenberg, 1977, pp. 131–37 and 163–66). These sound the calls from his own body.

Early psychoanalytic theory said that, as the baby grows, different areas of his body become the focus of psychological concern and excitability of the nerves. For the first year of life, the inside and outside of the mouth become the focal zone, with eyes and skin taking on a related importance. Later the key zone will be the anus, and later still the genitals.

As each of these zones becomes focal, it provides a mode of behavior, taking in through the mouth, for example, or expelling from the anus. The zone also provides a focus for the significant people in the baby's environment, leading (in Erikson's phrase) to "decisive encounters." In the dialogue I am proposing as a model, these body zones provide a major part of the language in which the family and the community speak to a baby and a major part of the vocabulary he builds to respond.

In the earliest period of infancy, the baby lives through its mouth. He relates to the world by incorporation in its most literal sense, taking it into his body. Mostly he sucks in milk, but he also takes in sights through his eyes and feelings of warmth and cuddling through his skin. We can understand this taking in as one side of a developmental dialogue. Family and society are saying to the baby, This is how we give. Some societies offer plenty, others famine. Some cultures swaddle, others encourage movement of arms and legs. In my own childhood a rigid schedule of feeding was the norm. In my children's childhood, we fed on demand. In the largest sense, however, all cultures, in giving, pose the same question: How will you receive what we give? And a baby answers in "personally and culturally significant ways" (again, Erikson's phrase), and so grows. The I comes into being through otherness—a profoundly paradoxical twist to our ideas of human nature, a decentering.

Lacan uses the word "alienation" for this state of affairs, giving it a negative tone, but one could equally well state it positively through a word like "community," as, say, Erikson does: the I can only come into being through a community of I's. The essential idea, however, is the same: self comes into being through another person's experience of that self. The mother gives back to the baby her version of the smiles and gurgles and cries the baby has given to her. Further, she perceives the baby more integratedly than the baby can perceive itself. Hence the other reflects a more integrated, a superior, so to speak, self back to the originating I, which takes it in and uses it to model a possible future I and to elicit other reflectings and hence further growth of the I. Generally this feedback is good, but it can be destructive. Jenny's mother was telling Jenny, you are not responsive enough for me, and Jenny gave back in her mother's scheme of things precisely what her mother reflected, a nonresponsive baby, and this bad feedback threatened her very sanity.

Within this dialogue of giving and receiving, early psychoanalysts distinguished an earlier and a later mode. In the first (say) four weeks of life the baby mostly receives passively, sending out massive signals of total body pleasure or pain as a response. Gradually, however, he begins to take a more active role in shaping his environment. He not only sucks but clamps his gums onto the nipple. His brain learns to single out the human face from the stream of sights that passes before his unskilled eyes. His fingers clasp particular objects. He begins to take as well as to receive. Soon, with this new activity (as opposed to passivity) comes the pain of teething and the pleasure of biting. He feels angry because his mouth, hitherto the focus of pleasure, has become the focus of pain. Associating the change with mother, he bites her and perhaps she in response retaliates for being bitten, the first of many situations "in which the intensity of the impulse leads to its own defeat" (Erikson, 1963, p. 79). In effect, the baby's body and family are asking him, How will you take?, in a double sense. How will you actively take instead of passively being given to?, but also, How will you "take it?"

The mutuality of mother and baby can and almost always does sustain them through this confrontation and reversal. To the extent it does, Erikson theorizes, the baby builds the first layer of a basic sense of trust that will provide the base for a sense of hope and confidence throughout life. To the extent the mutuality of mother and infant does not overcome the baby's frustration, the baby develops a sense of doom, failure, and loss. In extreme cases, the baby can become psychotic, but most of us simply develop a trust that outweighs the sense of distrust. Always, however, we have both, as Iiro combined a sense that he was loved with a feeling he was loved on condition he get caught up in his mother's obsession to correct his fingers and toes.

My account of babyhood thus far follows Karl Abraham's early and Erik Erikson's later descriptions of "orality," based primarily on Freud's positing of drives associated with particular zones. This early idea of orality rested mostly on adult character structures explored in the therapy of adults. Another way of exploring the first, wordless year of life would be to look back at the zero year old from the perspective of a one year old and account for some of the things he has become able to do.

He can be "alone together" (in Winnicott's phrase) with his mother, he playing by himself, she doing something of her own, yet each aware of the other. He can love a blanket or teddy bear and use it as a source of solace. He can let another take care of him while his mother goes out, knowing that it is another and accepting the stand-in. He can walk or crawl into another room out of his mother's sight and stay there, returning when he wishes.

To do just these simple things, a baby has had to achieve ever more and more sophisticated answers to a constantly growing array of questions, answers far beyond those he was born with. To be "alone together" asks that the child accept the separateness of his mother and himself. Now he can "be held" in a symbolic as well as a literal way. To love a teddy or a blanket as "security cloth," he has learned to adapt pieces of the world outside himself to his own needs, another relation to otherness. To accept a babysitter, he has learned to distinguish different persons in the stream of people who attend to his needs, to accept them as persons, and to trust that the one person who matters most to him will return even if he accepts a temporary substitute. Simply to crawl into another room involves a willingness to be separate from that primary caregiver and a trusting belief that the union can be reestablished at will, either by physical crawling or by crying out. It implies also an ability to wait the necessary time to be reunited, to "tolerate delay."

Infants are unspeaking, and in imagining what goes on in the mind of a child who can't say, one must infer. I have been using two inferences widely accepted by psychoanalytic observers of very young children. The first is that the newborn baby does not recognize *otherness as otherness*. I do not mean to rule out some degree of sophistication in the newborn about what he sees and hears. The baby may be able in a purely perceptual way to grasp the position of an object in space or relate the occurrence of a certain voice to a certain face, but he does not see these things as discontinuous with himself—as "other." Everything is referred to inner comfort or discomfort. When he does begin to know otherness (around the eighth month of life), he senses it as a rude awakening from a world previously felt as lovingly, embracingly centered on himself, intensely and quickly responsive to his wishes.

The second inference is that at some time during the first year or year and a half the child accepts that otherness. Not permanently, not irrevocably—but he becomes able to make the distinction between self and other, to hold it, or to give it up, more or less at will. The psychoanalyst speaks of the baby's achieving "object constancy" but means by that term something different from the psychologist who also uses it.

Most psychologists mean by "object constancy" your ability to perceive, say, a postage stamp as such. You see it from many different distances or points of view, at different angles and under different lighting. You may never see it as a rectangle of a certain size and color, yet you "know" it is a pink oblong and, moreover, the same pink oblong, although its image on your retina keeps changing. You have the ability to make a concept of the object and hold that constant even though your perceptions of the object vary widely. Certainly this is essential to what Mahler and other psychoanalysts call "object constancy," but it is not all of it.

Piaget speaks of "object constancy" as the ability to keep track of a ball when it rolls behind the sofa, to know where it is and to imagine it, even though it is out of sight. This, too, is part of what a child needs in order to achieve psychoanalytic "object constancy," but only part.

For the psychoanalyst, "object" means an emotional object like a mother or a teddy bear. Selma Fraiberg, in an inspired guess, formulated the difference between psychoanalytic object constancy and Piaget's by watching her dog, Brandy. Brandy learned early to recognize the can of dog food when it appeared: "recognition memory." Babies quickly do the same with breast or bottle. Brandy also learned to recall the can of dog food when he was hungry and it had not appeared. He would stand in front of the refrigerator and scratch and plead. This Fraiberg called "evocation memory": recalling the object when it is wanted but absent. But Brandy never gave a sign of imagining the can of dog food simply at will (1969).

That is the human thing. That is the imagining that babies achieve. Having this ability, a baby can imagine his mother apart from his love of (or anger at) her. He can begin to feel her as really a part of himself—internalized. Simultaneously, he can begin to think of her as wholly separate from himself, a whole other being, not just a source of satisfactions. Further, he has shown that he can turn passive into active, memory prompted by need into memory he himself initiates.

A mother is likely to see this rather abstract achievement as the baby's calm at her absence. Erikson's term for it is "basic trust," "the basic faith in existence," the sense "not only that one has learned to rely on the sameness and continuity of the outer providers, but also that one may trust oneself and the capacity of one's own organs to cope with urges; and that one is able to consider oneself trustworthy enough so that the providers will not need to be on guard lest they be nipped" (1963, pp. 248, 252).

As Erikson makes clear, the baby's growing sense of constancy and trust embraces not only the outer world, but the inner. Object constancy implies self constancy. That is, feeling that another is trustworthy makes it possible, indeed requires, that one know that the other is in fact other. This knowledge, this "self-object differentiation," is probably the key achievement of the first stage of development because it marks the child's entry into the specifically human world of symbols.

To imagine itself, its own body, or to imagine another person—these abilities mean that the infant has to use a symbol. Symbolization grows in an atmosphere of trustful sharing of contemplated objects. For a baby, symbols and the ability to symbolize are what he and his mother have shared. Conversely, if the infant's relationship with his mother is seriously disturbed, symbolization will very likely miscarry as well (Werner and Kaplan, 1963, pp. 73, 79, 83).

We can only infer a baby's state of mind, but theory suggests that the child can put relatively neutral objects into symbols before being able to symbolize itself or its mother. A rattle or a block bears very little of the mingling of frustration and desire that the baby brings to that all-powerful other who satisfies his needs. Sometimes she satisfies quickly and rightly. Sometimes she cannot figure out what it is he wants, and then he can feel overwhelmed by need. He can dissolve into paroxysms of angry frustration. Inevitably, then, toward the caregiver, the baby feels that mingling of love and hate for which Freud coined the term "ambivalence." For the baby (as for an adult) ambivalence must make it difficult to single out an other as a defined concept.

The very nature of infancy poses the baby the question, "How will you deal with your ambivalence?" Classical theory, beginning with Freud, holds that the baby copes by imagining his caregiver in two parts, a bad part outside him and a good part inside him. One of the tasks of the first year is to put those parts back together into a whole person. If a baby can imagine his mother as a single person, he has brought his ambivalence within manageable bounds. He has found a neutral space free of his own passionate love and hate in which she can simply be or in which they can be "alone together."

To bring his love and hate within bounds implies that over a period of time he has learned to wait to be fed, to have the room made warm, or to have the light turned off, without being overwhelmed by need. He has learned, in the psychoanalysts' phrase, to tolerate delay, because he has been able, from time to time, to have the experience of endurable and successful waiting. He has had what Winnicott called "good enough" mothering. He has been hungry and has had to wait to be fed, but *was* fed before he was over-whelmed by desire. His body was warmed—not before he could know it needed to be, but before he had been swamped by the agony of waiting. The light was turned off, not before it had begun to bother him, but after he had become tetchy and irritated without being able to communicate why.

Key to this toleration of delay is hope and trust in another being. René Spitz concluded from his studies of babies separated from their parents during World War II that there must be one primary person toward whom the infant can form a relation, no matter how many others assist in his care (1965). Recently, in the interests of freeing women from the tyranny of *Kinder, Küche, Kirche,* some researchers have challenged Spitz's conclusion that the baby needs some one person to relate to. One researcher, for example, finds "nothing to suggest that mothering cannot be shared by several people." Chodorow and others point out, however, that the psycho-analytic point of view does not advocate exclusive mothering, only that there be one person with whom the child can form an affective bond (1978, pp. 74–75 and references there cited). Out of that bond comes the child's ability to wait, to symbolize, to tolerate delay, to achieve object constancy, and all the rest.

These abilities we have inferred by looking back from the one-year-old to the zero-year-old. Another source of evidence, obviously, would be to watch actual babies. Two important psychoanalytic groups have done so: René Spitz's, starting in the 1930s, and Margaret Mahler's, beginning in the 1950s. The psychoanalytic baby-watchers divide this first major stage of the I's becoming, that is, the baby's first year or two or three, into six phases, with one important division taking place around the fourth or fifth month. The division into stages before then has to rest largely on inference from the analysis of adult and child psychotics with disorders stemming from that early period. After four or five months, however, one can learn much more by directly watching babies.

There is, of course, plenty to watch in the first few weeks, but it is difficult to interpret, as every caregiver knows who has tried to relieve a newborn's massive but unnamable distress. In our society, the baby and mother come home from the hospital a few days after birth. The hospital has often separated mother and baby so that it is only when they get home after some days' delay that they begin the intense process of fitting their rhythms together. These negotiations take place in the language of feeding. The baby demands food peremptorily in response to overwhelming need. The mother responds in adult time, perhaps nudging the baby toward a three- or four-hour schedule (Sander, 1969).

A problem for this negotiation is the undifferentiated quality of the infant's inner life—at least as we guess at it. He and his mother relate as needer and satisfier, and he feels that relation as all or nothing. He is either needing and crying or not needing and content. Researchers describe him as a purely biological organism, his responses as "reflex" or "thalamic." Spitz calls his sensing of the world "coenesthetic reception," in which all the senses overlap; he contrasts it to perception proper (1965, p. 134).

In that single-mindedness one percept stands out, the human face. From the earliest feedings, a baby has looked into his mother's eyes as part of his total gratification: the satisfaction of mouth, skin, stomach, and eye, her face marking the presence of his need gratifier. Around the fourth week of life, a baby begins to single out her face from its surroundings, seeking it with his gaze. This happens so early that it may even be biologically programmed (Spitz, 1965, pp. 81, 86).

In thus singling out a face, the baby is making a momentous reply, but what has the world around the infant asked, and how can we understand the unworded answer? In our society, perhaps in every society, the all or nothing needs of the baby have to be matched to the family and household around him, to brothers' and sisters' play, a father or mother's work, to all the family's concerns and wishes. Most important, the people around him want the baby to respond to them, to their need to evoke a human response in another. This need is scarcely a question that adults could phrase. It is more like a call of nature, a beckoning that has to be interpreted. I think we can say that gesturing to the baby means, Fit! Join! Become part of our human group.

What the baby hears or how he interprets it, I can imagine only by reading back from his response. By singling out a face, he says, in effect, I can "be toward" someone. I can come out of this world I have, in which I am totally self-absorbed and omnipotent, in which I *am* the world. I can "be toward" something or somebody—that face which is a sign for ecstatic contentment. If the baby has answered, I can be toward, then the first form of that call from mother, family, and community must have been, Be toward *me,* and the baby's being toward a face accepted that relationship. Conversely, as Selma Fraiberg has shown, blind children who cannot return gaze for gaze risk autism or psychosis, the catastrophic failure of that first mutuality, unless one can train their parents to recognize other signs of "being toward" (1977).

To answer, Yes, I can "be toward" implies another answer as well. It says a baby has mastered another fundamental ability, which underlies many others and which, in the context of his family's need that he join, is completely paradoxical. He shows that he can single out a physical object in space. He can *dis*join. He can give a person an edge. He can separate a presence in time, giving an event a beginning, middle, and end. This bounding is nothing definite or willed, just a "toward," but it is a beginning.

Around the third month of life, Spitz reports, a baby makes another response to that insistent call from his community. He smiles, not the haphazard gurgling sort of glee he may have shown before, but in response to a specific stimulus: any human face. Curiously, a baby responds to the combination of two eyes and a nose in motion, even if the "face" is a Halloween mask. A baby will not smile at a profile and, presented with a side view of a face, may even stare perplexedly at the ear as if to wonder where the other eye went. In other words, the child is not responding to his mother or any particular person. He is greeting a sign (or *gestalt*) of need gratification, and he will smile at any face, real or drawn, white or black, known or unknown. Spitz calls it a "pre-object." Nevertheless, this action, too, is momentous as a reply in the developmental dialogue. Not only can the baby single out this sign from the stream of sensations, he can smile at it.

In effect, by "smiling toward," a baby shows that he has discovered that he has a partner in the dyad of baby and adult. Further, he has actively used what Spitz calls his "snout," that is, the configuration of lips, chin, nose, and cheek. Up till now this snout had been primarily his way of taking in the world passively, either as satisfaction or as perception. He now has made this "snout" into something that puts out as well as takes in, expressing as well as absorbing. He has turned passivity into activity (Spitz, 1965, p. 107).

Until this time the baby had been a passive receiver of nurture. When he becomes able to smile at a human face, he has given a first answer to the communal call for him to join the human race, to turn from being wholly passive to being active (Spitz, 1965, pp. 52–85).

He thus shows, in psychoanalytic terms, a rudimentary ego. That is, he demonstrates the beginnings of two abilities that will someday underlie all his adaptations to reality. First, he can bound something. Second, he can reverse direction from passive to active, from coming in to going out. Mahler speaks of two intertwined developmental tracks of separation and individuation. Separation is the move toward distancing, differentiating, distinguishing. Individuation is the move toward personal autonomy: perception, seeing, hearing, remembering, knowing, or testing for oneself (Mahler et al., 1975, pp. 39–41).

The baby who is able to "smile toward" has passed through only two "pre-object" stages, however. Mahler sees four more stages in separation proper before the infant achieves true object constancy: first, differentiation, from 4–5 months to walking; second, practicing, from walking to 15–24 months; third, rapprochement, from 15–24 months to the middle of the second year (but with great variability); fourth, the consolidation of individuality and the beginnings of object constancy, a developmental period that in Mahler's experience does not begin before the third year and then continues all through life. Throughout, the community around an infant is asking him to join, not mindlessly or conformingly (although sometimes that way, too), but as an individual who thinks, feels, and acts on his own and in relation to others (ibid.)

A baby changes from indiscriminate smiling to a smile reserved for one special caregiver, mother. That smile signals a transition. It is the "first organizer" (in Spitz's term) and marks the transition passage from the "pre-object" stages toward Mahler's first stage in separation proper: differentiation. In the pre-object stages a baby molded and nestled into his mother's arms. Now we see him pushing away from his mother's body. She holds his arms and he uses the newfound strength in his legs to push against her stomach, almost standing, so that he gets a better look at her. "Stemming" the baby-watchers call it.

Erect this way, he can turn his head to scan his surroundings. The baby pulls at his mother's hair. He pokes into her ears or nose. He may put food into her mouth. He may become fascinated by a brooch or necklace or eyeglasses. Having discovered an other, he now explores and bounds her (Mahler et al., 1975, pp. 52–55).

This exploration peaks at six or seven months and then shades into what Mahler calls "checking back." A baby continues to learn about mother, her look, her feel, her texture, her sound, her smell, and her taste, but he begins to compare her with not-mother, to other sights, sounds, smells, and textures. In exploring eyeglasses, hair, or bracelet, he finds out what belongs and does not belong to mother's body. He sharpens the discrimination signaled by the special smile he gives mother and not not-mother (Mahler et al., 1975, pp. 55–58).

Spitz coined two terms for the kinds of perception going on. The earlier, in which the baby focuses inwardly on the state of his own well-being and perceives events globally as pleasing or displeasing, satisfying or frustrating, he called "coenesthetic." The word literally means that the different senses all act together as one sense, leading to a feeling of total pleasure or displeasure. The perceptions that develop in true separating he called "diacritic," literally separated judgments, in which the eye sees and the ear hears and a baby discriminates between sight and sound (1965, p. 44).

These heightened perceptions and distinctions lead to the familiar "stranger reaction" around the eighth month. Some babies are frightened of strangers. They cry and strain toward their mothers. Other babies explore. They check out a stranger's finger, clothing, pen, or necklace. They may even run their hand over her face or hair. Having made this "customs inspection" (as the baby-watchers call it), a baby relaxes into his mother's arms, and his face and eyes tell of the joy of reunion. In other words, a baby does not just turn away from the stranger; he turns away *toward someone* (Mahler et al., 1975, pp. 56–58).

This is the time when the baby begins to be able to play the familiar games of childhood. At three months, like Jenny subjected to her mother's relentless stimulation, a baby is relatively powerless. So is a five-month-old. As Louise Kaplan describes him, when he sees his mother disappear through a doorway, he can't do much about it, but, if he has come to feel confidence in the sound of her footsteps or a typewriter or water running, he does not panic.

One sign of that confidence is his ability to enjoy her games of peekaboo. She hides her face and when his worry reaches just enough of a tension, out she pops again. That was at five months or so. Around ten months, the baby can play his own peekaboo. How does mother react to *his* disappearance when he puts a blanket over his head or when he sticks his face down into his mattress? Then she hides *her* head and he looks worried until she reappears and he can crow with triumph just as she did. The game satisfies many needs. Perhaps that is why it is played all over the world (Kaplan, 1978, pp. 143–47).

The most famous game in the literature of baby-watching, the one that Freud watched his small grandchild Ernst playing, also satisfied the need to master parental disappearance. At one and a half, little Ernst would throw toys out of his bed, crying as he did so a long, drawn-out "o-o-o-o-o." Freud and the boy's mother agreed this was the German word *fort,* "gone." One day the child was playing with a spool with a string tied round it. From the floor, he threw the spool over the edge of his crib so that it disappeared and he said "o-o-o-o-o." But then Ernst used the string to pull the spool into his crib again and cried *da,* "there!" Freud's interpretation of this *fort-da* game (as it has come to be called) is much more tentative than those theorists who have erected virtual systems of metaphysics on it. Freud reads it as like peekaboo, a way of demonstrating that what disappears returns. It was a way of mirroring a situation he had suffered passively, his mother's going out, by one he actively created for himself. In other games, he played at making himself disappear from a mirror and his father disappear at "the front." In all these situations he was using objects (almost as an adult would use an artistic medium) to re-create an intensely personal situation involving his own relation with his mother (1920g, 18:14–16; see also Kaplan, 1978, pp. 151–52).

Once a baby learns to crawl, he can play catch-me. The baby scrambles off with his mother in hot pursuit, but she just barely can't catch him! He stays out of her reach until he tires and lets the menacing pursuer of babies catch him—to his great joy. Here again, the baby has made active what he experienced only passively, being caught up by his mother. He mirrors something she did, thereby turning into active play the perhaps frightening reality of her great power and his helplessness. Again, he proves in a cognitive sense that what disappears comes back (Kaplan, 1978, pp. 147–151).

Obviously, a baby cannot play catch-me until he can crawl. This game and the others depend on the particular infant's physical abilities and coordination, and at any given age, say ten months, these will vary widely. So too will the baby's temperament and his mother's. These games, like everything else the mother and child do together, are played in a vocabulary unique to each mother and child, although the developmental tasks they involve and the abilities they require are common to all children—and mothers. Their dialogue takes place in a universal physiological language, a cultural dialect, and a unique and individual style.

What happens in that conversation is that the child is evolving a variety of answers to the persistent call of his family and community to join them. His earliest response was to "be toward." As he begins more and more to separate the continuum that first surrounded him and to individuate himself, he can answer more complexly: can be apart-from-toward. Can be toward but can also wish to be "apart from." Can move from the one wish to the other. "Can be"—where once he was only passive and receptive, now he can choose and act. Not quite an I yet.

"Hatching" is Mahler's term for the infant's first pulling away from the orbit in which he and his mother formed a union of two people wholly focused on each other, a dyad. "Practising" is her term for the second stage, in which a baby uses physical separations to prepare for the far more important psychological separation that is to follow. Thus, a baby progresses from the pattern of checking back, playing or crawling close to his mother, to his first unaided steps away from her, taking off on one's own.

What sets this second stage apart from the first is the baby's increasing ability with his legs and arms as he progresses from crawling to unaided walking. During the first part of this transition, the baby sits up, crawls, paddles, creeps, rights himself, and sometimes clambers up to a standing position by holding onto the coffee table. In the second part, he stands unaided and begins free walking. Interestingly, according to Mahler's observations, the baby usually takes his first unaided steps *away* from his mother (not as in folklore and poetry, *toward* her—Mahler et al., 1975, pp. 65–76).

It is impossible to overstate the symbolic meaning of being upright. Each baby lives again the exhilaration our hominid ancestors must have felt when they stood up and looked far across the African savannas and realized that they alone surveyed all that land. Other creatures became beneath and lesser. Imagine the feeling of first being able to turn the muscles in your neck and back to deliberately locate what you want, to look down on obstacles and objects that once you had to eye on their own level, to take a grand survey of your environment.

Many of our words and metaphors reflect this pride in standing. "Survey" itself, for example, means to oversee or see over. Moral terms like "erect," "upright," or "upstanding" gain force from our childhood achievement of verticality, just as words like "grovel," "cower," "squat," "crawl," and "creep" take on moral connotations of an infant's powerlessness.

This second stage is a transition from a "fall" to a "rise." To a baby, standing and walking mean a vastly increased scope for all the skills he was born with but has yet to perfect: seeing distances and dimensions, turning his head, locating objects by sound, understanding relations of higher and lower, left and right, in front of, behind, above, beneath. To be sure, at this stage the baby will do all these things close to mother's knee, but he will do them. He can exult to himself, I am upright the way *they* are. He meets his mother now when *he* is erect, a new kind of face to face closeness in which he is much more of an equal partner. Moreover, his new powers allow him to come to mother, not just she to him. He thus strengthens his bond to her, at the same time that he makes it a matter of his own choice and will. Jason's sense of omnipotence was thus right for his age, although his depressed mother did not answer him with realistic responses to dangers. The more usual outcome is a negotiated balance between the omnipotence of the child and the caution of the adult (Mahler et al., 1975, pp. 70–75).

This new position of control and will implies a loss of something else, the snuggly, cuddly world of a few months before. To make the most of what his legs can now do, the child needs to take the security of that world with him as he walks. He needs to get it inside himself, as his own confidence and trust and perhaps in a more tangible form as well. Hence the importance of

Teddy Bears

In the first months of life, a baby finds in his fingers, thumbs, and fist a way of easing the discomforts his psyche feels. In his mouth, they simulate the comfort of the breast. By holding a hand to his cheek he can imitate the feel of breast against cheek and hand against clutching breast. From fingers, fist, and especially thumb, a baby moves on to dolls and other toys, without, however, giving up the sensuous comforts of his hand. He finds what the English have happily called "soft toys," the teddy bear, the floppy dog, or the lopeared bunny, or he can seize on, in the American phrase, a "security cloth."

The thumb was only one step away from the breast, a sign accompanying rather than a symbol standing for pleasure in the mouth. The teddy or the blanket, however, serves as a reminder of the feel and warmth and smell that accompanied mothering. It is a sign of a sign, so to speak. Two steps away from the actual gratification, the teddy or blanket is a true symbol, for it has an arbitrary connection to the mothering for which it stands: there is no reason inherent in *this* blanket why it can give the baby a feeling of security while some other blanket cannot. Yet, of course, there is, for this symbol is only partly created by the baby. Partly the teddy or blanket has a history as well as a good smell and a warm, worn feel that derive from that history. Partly it is, in Winnicott's term, "found" (and for me the word has the sudden, joyful feeling of "The lost is found!").

Hence the teddy bear is both a symbol and a sign and even, to some extent, the thing itself—mothering—embodied in a set of sensations as well as an object. Winnicott coined the term for this special entity: a "transitional object." It is transitional between sign and symbol. It is a created object standing for something else, hence a symbol. It is also a found object that either is or is a sign of the presence of that something else (mothering) and of the desires mothering satisfies. Also, to the extent that it is a sign or symbol of mothering, not mothering itself, it is a sign of the *absence* of mothering as well. The teddy bear embodies the transition between the presence and the absence of mother (Winnicott, 1971a, particularly chap. 1).

It can also be transitional between self and the world of not self, between inside and outside, between the child's inner memories of merger and the outer world, unmerged. Most of all, the teddy bear stands for oneness, the earlier relation when the baby and his world were perfect and, as Louise Kaplan phrases it, "differences between inside and outside and between me and not-me did not exist."

> As the baby presses the security blanket to his cheeks and nose it caresses him. It smells of the sweetness of a yes-saying mother and also of smells that belong to the baby. The blanket's molding softness is like the time when he and mother were one. The blanket exists "out there" in the inanimate world of rattles, bottles, pillows and mobiles. Yet it is alive with reminiscences of human dialogue. Furthermore, the baby can scratch, pinch, rub and slap his blanket around without a no or a don't or any possibility of real destruction. The blanket withstands the baby's passionate excitements and it never lets him down. It's always there when he longs for it (Kaplan, 1978, pp. 154–55).

The soft toy thus can stand for the mother in a mystical oneness between baby and mother, a creature who, in a way, never existed, yet was imagined and needs to be imagined again and again, now especially when the baby is venturing out on hands and knees or upright into new and wonderful spaces which are, nevertheless, challenging, hard, even dangerous and frightening. Sometimes there will be strain and frustration. Sometimes outer reality will be harshly unresponsive to inner desires. Then the baby—and even the adult—will try to bring back the illusion of a union that includes otherness. A security cloth, a soft toy, a hum, a stroking gesture, or a rocking motion can bring it back for the infant. A poem or a special memento can bring it back for the adult (Kaplan, 1978, p. 156. For the artistic implications of a baby's objects, see Milner, 1957b).

Looking back at the birth of an I, we can see the establishment of five intertwined themes or problems that make up the I which the child will bring to new situations (see the chart on pp. 244–45). First, the child must have learned to tolerate delay and hence must have begun a sense of time. Second, out of the ability to wait comes the ability to imagine and to symbolize what is being waited for. Third, by waiting the child also makes a sign that it has distinguished an external other separate from its own inner states. The baby has made its first moves toward control of the boundary between inside and outside. To recognize an outside is the first step in acting on it, while accepting an inside as such provides the basis for passivity (as Dr. Vincent had to do when brainwashed). Hence the baby has also taken a fourth step, distinguishing activity from passivity. Fifth, by imagining the other as other, the child necessarily learns there is a not-other, an I. He has opened the door to all the distinctively human things that follow from that I's knowing it is an I.

We begin to see the adult human's ability to DEFT take form, still in what Piaget would call the "sensorimotor stage." The baby acts out in literal, physical ways ideas that tax the metaphors and metaphysics of adults.

How will you separate and re-relate self and object?
By endowing the admittedly not-me with my inner wishes and fears—as I do this blanket (F).

How will you bound inside and outside?
As by holding this blanket, I hold onto what I have projected from inside, even by acknowledging it is now outside (D).

How will you symbolize?
By means of external, 'found' objects which themselves have and which I imbue with symbolic value (D).

How will you accept delay by yourself and by others?
By displacing my attention to symbolized and imaginatively endowed objects (like this blanket), to which time is irrelevant (T).

How will you tolerate loving and hating the same person?
By displacing my love and hate onto other, less vital objects, like this

blanket (D), and by trusting that my love and hate will no more destroy them than they destroy this blanket (E).

Even with a teddy bear, a baby does not learn these things irrevocably, of course. As an adult, how well do I tolerate delay in love or recognition? Am I able to see those I love as wholes, faults and all? Do I see myself uncolored by my own wishes or fears? Can I always keep a sharp boundary between what I think and what the rest of the world thinks? Does any of us?

It is probably with the baby as with the adult. The I wins these abilities at first for a brief moment or two, then for longer periods, as favorable experience accumulates, but never without the possibility of lapsing back toward an undifferentiated, unsymbolizing self. In the 1950s when these ideas were beginning to circulate, psychoanalysts tended to think of a crucial moment of "self-object differentiation." To be sure, there must be one moment when, for the first time, the baby imagines an other and a self, but it seems easier to think of this ability as also a relative thing, coming into being over a long relationship of dialogue between caregiver and care receiver.

We can tease out, then, five strands of achievement in that first year of becoming I, five experiences the child must have had in order to do things like crawl out of sight of its mother, call her or itself by name, or be "alone together" with her. The child must have tolerated delay, mastered ambivalence, distinguished self from other and activity from passivity, and symbolized those distinctions. No doubt there are other ways of thinking about the achievements of the first year, but these will serve to outline the origins of an I.

Also, they correspond (not entirely by coincidence) to four fundamental capabilities of an ego, as defined in second phase psychoanalysis, that is, ego psychology. An ego, to deal with the demands of inner and outer reality, uses four modes of displacement. The baby achieves object constancy when he has acquired corresponding abilities (Holland, 1973a).

The ego displaces	The baby begins to
in direction.	separate inside from outside.
in time.	tolerate delay.
in number.	distinguish self from other.
through similarity.	symbolize.

Most important, a baby makes these achievements in and through a special emotional climate. At first there was only pleasure and unpleasure. As the baby came to know the nurturing other, he split positive and negative into good inner and bad outer or into good and bad other(s). Full acceptance of an other, though, means acceptance of both the satisfactions and the frustrations she brings. A baby has to master the intense ambivalence its helpless situation engenders. Only then can an infant form an ego (with these basic abilities for starters) in and through a basic trust that satisfaction will come despite the anger and despite the fear of being overwhelmed with need. Once these five themes or issues are sounded in the developmental dialogue the baby is ready to proceed to the next stage.

Of course, one stage does not suddenly leave off and the next begin. Stages may be completed, may overlap, be separated or linked, and the problems posed by one may be heard in the language of another. Indeed, one of the important ways to account for the tremendous variety in human development and personality despite a relatively small number of stages, three or four or five, is precisely this possibility of almost infinite variability.

Differentiation, discrimination, distinction—development proceeds by a kind of parting or separation, Juliet's "sweet sorrow." "Individuation," writes Hans Loewald, "comes about by the losses of separation" (1978, p. 46). He is stating one meaning of what is often called Freud's tragic sense. To become an active little toddler, the baby gives up the ease and passivity of the cradle. To become a speaking baby, he gives up the undifferentiated gurgle and goo. To become a baby at all we gave up the blissful union of the womb.

Not entirely, however. We give them up but partially, hesitantly, and never irrecoverably. When we suffer a loss, we mourn. That is, we incorporate what is lost "out there" as part of the "in here" which is our continuing mental processes. We carry these earlier states with us, and we come back to them as we give ourselves moments of extreme passivity or ecstasy. We return like travelers to that most ancient, Mycenaean self that existed in a prehistory before other had become other.

9 | Zones and Modes

In the classical psychoanalytic picture, throughout the birth of an I, the mouth was the baby's main window on the world. Once the baby acquired new capacities for relationships with things and people, other body zones became important. In particular, much of his mental and nervous energy became focused on the process and product of squeezing wastes out of his body.

Freud believed that different zones of an infant's body became focal because of purely biological promptings. Modern object relations theorists believe that it is the people around the baby who focus his attention now on the mouth, later on the anus, still later on the genitals. I am inclined to think that that social call to the child fits a bodily determined matrix: the baby's body can answer only within certain limits, and hence only certain demands can be addressed to, say, the process of defecation. Conversely, the body process provides a way for the baby to model his parents' and society's demands. Thus Erikson sensibly calls this anal stage "letting go" and "holding on." He gives the case of a little girl trying to let go, yet hold on, to her mother, using her bowel movements as the medium in which to express her struggle. Bruce (p. 174 above) symbolized his mother's absence by the bowel movement he could feel separating from himself, but could not see. Similarly Little Hans (Freud's child case) analogized from his *lumf* to the birth of his sister. *Lumf* is also language.

Communications aside, Western societies take the emptying of the bowels seriously and circumscribe the process with rules. Other cultures have customs or climate that permit fewer strictures. All cultures, however, place some restrictions on defecation. Further, all cultures ask a new generation to abide by the laws of the existing society. The first laws the baby encounters have to do with feeding, and usually the next have to do with excreting. We might do well, then, to think of this "anal" stage more generally. I shall call it

The "Nomic" Stage

one concerned with rules, customs, and the usualness of things.

By the end of such a nomic stage, the child must have established a style of relating to the rules of others. By the end of the oral stage, the child has learned to symbolize his mother. Now his parents and his society are asking the child to take symbolization a step further. Think rules! By the end of the nomic stage, the child will have answered by forming his individual pattern for dealing with rules, obeying or disobeying, minimizing them, extending them to new subjects, making the rules of others his own internal rules, or formulating rules for himself or for others. To the extent that he can create rules for himself and follow them, he will have begun to find his own style of control, both self-control and the control of other people and things, although what he actually controls may seem very primitive in the eyes of adults.

To satisfy both the child's need for pleasure and admiration and the parent's need for order, child and parent need to come together in a mutual regulation. Social rules need to be brought into that potential space between parent and child where they can be both found "out there" in society and accepted and resymbolized "in here" in the child. Around these rules, earlier emotions of love and hate become more precise as attraction and disgust, both in an immediate physical relation to people and things and more abstractly, as the beginnings of values.

The child who has completed the oral phase has achieved a sense of self, perhaps even some sense of what his body can do and where his body leaves off. Now, as interest focuses on defecation, the question of what is part of his body and what is not assumes a new importance and complexity. That is, the stool comes from inside the body, yet the parent defines it as disgusting and to be thrown away. The sense of self must now acquire a social dimension. Cultural values, rather than the earlier boundaries of pleasure and displeasure or inside and outside, define what is or is not to be included in the bodily self that you want to be loved.

In the oral stage, self and other met in the process of feeding, holding, gazing, and other nurturings. The baby was given to and accordingly took in. In the nomic stage, self and other meet in a new way: around rules that are to be followed and taken in and made a part of oneself, as before food was taken in. These will be rules about eating, defecating, making noise, handling ashtrays, and a myriad of other body and household actions.

The parents are likely to speak these rules. Hence although we do not know (in 1985) how children learn to speak, we can be sure that some of the rules they learn in the nomic stage are those for language. Whether or not the capacity for language in a larger sense is innate, the child will learn a right way of saying what he wants to say to these parents in this society in this language. What in the oral stage was symbolization in a very general sense now becomes something more precise. The child simultaneously learns the grammar of a particular language and the rules in a particular culture for cleanliness and order.

Time was the teacher from whom the child learned that there was an other and hence a self, an outer source of nurture that followed its own time rather than the time of the child's inner needs or wishes. Simple delay in the oral stage now becomes a sense of cyclical recurrence in the process of excretion and in the daily round of a society whose rules the child's time must now fit. We ask the child to focus its sense of time into a sense of timing.

In the oral stage, the healthy child has learned to tolerate (at least some of the time) the mixture of love and resentment he feels toward the mother who, in the nature of things, must both gratify and frustrate him. In the nomic stage the same ambivalence focuses on the process and product of defecation. To love is to hold onto (as Erikson suggests), to gain the almost masturbatory pleasure of keeping back the column of feces, now perceived as a precious part of the newly sensed self (1963, p. 82). To let go is to lose it.

Throughout the oral stage, the baby made one psychological maneuver over and over. He turned a passive experience of nurture into an active ability. Similarly, throughout this nomic stage, the child uses one maneuver over and over. Symbols become rules. Language becomes grammar. Time becomes timing. The body's boundaries become social as well as physical. Love becomes keeping. Hate becomes disgust and throwing away. If, then, there is a learning beneath and beyond all these other achievements, we could call it transforming toward precision or, if you will, "precising." The child learns how to focus the large concerns of the oral stage into more precise versions.

Is it this that makes the nomic stage so markedly *visible?* Every parent knows "that stubborn stage at two," and almost every parent can tell an anecdote about a child's fondness for making a not-overly-welcome gift of the precious contents of its diapers. "Anal" traits are especially visible in adults. The first personality type Freud discovered (and that as early as 1908) was the "anal character" with its distinctive triadic style: "orderly, parsimonious, and obstinate" (9:168–75; see also 1913i, 12:313–26). Classic papers by Jones (1918) and Abraham (1921) became encyclopedic anthologies of all kinds of adult transformations of the process and product of emptying the bowels: miserliness, fussiness about time, collecting mania, pedantries, obscure little dirty habits, compulsive cleanliness, odd quirks about money, or preoccupations with certain sounds or smells. In literature, one finds in the writings of "anal" writers like Ben Jonson or Nikolai Gogol a concern with the same themes that Abraham and Jones and Freud found in their patients: rules, pedantry, miserliness, obstinacy, fussy precision, or explosive anger. The writers themselves show a strange restriction of the imagination. They can elaborate endlessly in some directions (odd habits, "humours," for example), but turn curiously vacuous in others (heroines).

Perhaps we see these traits so clearly because they are precisings. Erikson points to the importance of the baby's being able to sit "not only securely but, as it were, untiringly, a feat which permits the muscle system gradually to be used for finer discrimination" (1963, pp. 85–86). In this sense the nomic (or anal) stage would correspond to a transition in Piaget's account of the development of thought. The baby shifts from large actions directly on the environment characteristic of the first, "sensorimotor" stage to a more precise and distant work with physical symbols during the period of "concrete operations." We can also understand the nomic phase (like the oral) as one prototype of human development: it proceeds by differentiation and specialization. Conversely, human aging is represented by the opposite: dedifferentiation accompanied by loss of control over excretions. In the nomic stage, the child learns both to focus his concerns and to defocus them, both to make and to unmake precisings of earlier knowledge.

In general, then, we can think of the nomic stage as asking the child five basic questions, continuations of the five questions associated with the birth of an I (see the chart on pp. 244–45). How will you love and fear in this new bodily and social context? How will you symbolize? How wait? How will you be a self, both one person alone and one person with others? How will you separate outside from inside in this mode?

The answers can be quite various despite the narrow context. 'I will separate outside from inside as a loving gift.' 'I will separate outside from inside by pushing out a disgusting part of my body and keeping inside a totally pleasurable self.' 'For me to give up that pleasurable inside means giving up my very self' (that would be Dr. Vincent). One can imagine an infinity of paradigms, any of which will cumulate into a growing I.

Despite the variety, however, one can jump ahead in the landscape or dialogue to the end of the nomic stage. Looking backward, one can then surmise what must have happened for the nomic stage to have run its course.

The child must have learned to say, 'I will not,' curtailing his own pleasures to meet the demands of his family and society that he not do this or that. He must also have learned to say, 'I will not' to those very demands. He must have learned, out of that conflict (that "ambitendency" as Margaret Mahler would call it), to achieve an I that can say both 'I will' and 'I will not,' just as a still earlier I emerged from the emotional conflict of simultaneously loving and resenting mother. That emotional conflict becomes in the nomic stage the tension between holding on (one kind of loving) and letting go (one form of losing). That might be Erikson's way of putting it. Fenichel would see a special form of fear, the fear of the loss of love, balanced by a special form of love, possessiveness (1945, pp. 77, 276). Love and hate become polarized into the desire to keep and the disgusted wish to get rid of (corresponding to the earlier pattern, 'What I love is part of me, what I hate is out there').

Within this emotional climate, the child makes the rules of others his own. In yet another way, passive becomes active. Similarly the passive waiting of the oral stage becomes the active demand and the self-timing of the nomic stage. Both intellectually and emotionally, the child is being asked to learn what is me and what is not-me in the most immediate body sense. What are the parts of my body I must keep, and what are the parts I must force outside of me and get rid of? By the end of the nomic stage, in finding a personal repertoire of answers to these questions, the child will have added a new set of dimensions to its I.

Planning

Anal functions call for one kind of control. Urination involves a control similar in some ways but different in others. A child who has learned to control urine has learned to hold on and let go urethrally as well as anally. Urination, however, occurs more frequently than defecation. The product is watery, not weighty, lighter in color, less smelly. Arrangements for urination are likely to be less elaborate. Failures of control are less disastrous. In general, the urethral control seems thinner somehow, more abstract, less messy, less enforceable, than anal.

If we state the issues of the urethral stage in their largest terms, the child who has reached the end of the stage must be able to say, 'I can plan my urination so they will give me admiration, not shame.' The basic question the phase poses must be, then, Can you relate your impulses to your long-term wishes? Can you *plan?* The language in which the child answers is, as in the earlier nomic stage, sphincter control, but extended into control of all kinds.

I suggest thinking of this stage as "projective." To hold on or let go anally, the baby has to concentrate on the spatial back or the temporal past. In planning, the child projects himself forward in time and, often, in space. The child also projects fantasies. A boy projects his urine, but all children, dealing with urethral control, project their image for their parents' admiration or shaming.

Perhaps the abstractness of planning or projection is the reason that psychoanalysts have written less about a urethral phase and a "urethral character" than the more familiar oral, anal, and oedipal stages. Perhaps, too, the shift from rules about a visible, weighty, smelly product to the control of a watery liquid accounts for the association of urethral control with a sense of abstract consequences rather than a set of rules (Michaels, 1955; Fenichel, 1945, pp. 68–69, 232–34, 371, 492). The adult anal character is ridden by a constant conscience and an unrelenting set of rules. He is *com*pulsive. The adult urethral character is *im*pulsive. He does not think well in abstractions and has difficulty reasoning through to consequences. Clinically, a child's fixation at the urethral phase provides the basis for an adult's "antisocial personality." The character type corresponds to the all-too-familiar stereotype of the juvenile delinquent or the psychopath or sociopath: antisocial, truant, aggressive, impulsive, often in particularly violent or sadistic ways. Antisocial personalities show a marked indifference to ordinary social or moral values, do not learn from punishment, and often offer grandiose but obviously specious rationalizations for behavior (Freedman et al., 1972, pp. 210, 214, 368–70, 788). Often they are charmers and manipulators, indifferent to the consequences for either the charmer or the charmed.

Freud linked urethral erotism specifically to fire. Fire, he said, was "discovered" when some Paleolithic man found a naturally occurring blaze, say, from lightning and overcame the impulse to urinate on it and put it out. Surprisingly, statistical studies tend to justify Freud's rather odd idea. Setting fires (or pyromania) correlates positively with persistent bed-wetting in youth among delinquents—and among arsonists and volunteer firemen (1932a, 22:185–93, Michaels, 1955, pp. 30, 34–36, 67–68; see also Lewis and Yarnell, 1951). Some strange emotional paralogic may connect the water we excrete, fire that is put out by water, and the burning sensation of having to urinate. Several times, from 1908 on, Freud linked fire to urination (or bed-wetting) as infantile correlates of the more adult trait of ambition, saying simply that analytic experience had convinced him repeatedly of this connection. (Presumably his first analytic experience of the urethral was his own vivid memory of urinating in his parents' bedroom and his shame at his father's reprimand, "The boy will come to nothing"—1900a, 4:216). Other writers have suggested that the special shame of uncontrolled wetting provides a basis for ambition: if I achieve greatly, I do not need to be ashamed. (Any ambition, of course, rests on an ability—or perhaps an inability—to think of consequences.) Still others see urination as gratifying sadistic or self-assertive needs or, alternatively, as a passive giving oneself up and foregoing control (Fenichel, 1945, pp. 69, 233, 371–72).

The whole topic of a urethral phase in child development deserves further exploration. In the meantime, I can see parallels with nomic development. In the earlier, anal phase, the child is supposed to obey and have rules. In the later, urethral phase, the child is supposed to have plans and bow to farther-off consequences—abstractions, really. The earlier phase leads to compulsiveness, the later to impulsiveness. The earlier involves a sense of duty and guilt (Thou shalt not), the later of ambition (Thou shalt). The two phases dovetail—with one important difference.

All human babies suck more or less the same way, and all human babies defecate more or less the same way. Now, however, for the first time in the growth of an I, we come to a difference between boys and girls inscribed in their very bodies. For all but children with physical abnormalities, urination will differ in simple bodily terms for the girl and the boy. It may be that children learn first of the bodily difference between male and female through the different ways boys and girls or mothers and fathers urinate. This is the first time in our human development where the *body*—the genitals, really—make a gender difference a focal point.

It is in connection with urination therefore that the development of boys and girls first has to differentiate. Indeed, in one of his stranger readings back from psychoanalytic cases into history, Freud went so far as to suggest that woman had been made "guardian of the fire" in the domestic hearth because her anatomy made it impossible for her to yield to the impulse to put out the fire by urinating on it (1930a, 21:90).

Since the child's new ability to control and plan urination elicits admiration, its failure or its "being different" can elicit the opposite, shame. Thus shame can attach to the necessary differences between adult parent and child or between male and female and especially to *not* being able to manage as the grown-ups do. These contrasts between activity and passivity, masculine and feminine, grown-up and child become crucial issues for the next stage.

In traditional psychoanalytic language, we would call it the "phallic" stage. To get beyond this obsolete, "phallocentric" view of development which takes the male child with a penis as the norm and the female as a deviation, I would like to borrow a term from Erikson (1963, pp. 87–88) and call this

The "Intrusive" Stage

We are talking about the two- and three-year old, standing, toddling, walking out into the world and adventurously crashing about in it. Parents will recognize the stage as one of loud noises, physical banging on either parents or playmates, persistent talking, and a charming, if tiresome, curiosity. The child seems to be trying out different ways of getting into the world, both the world of grown-ups and the world of children. The child's body is talking the language of in-and-out and answering the question, How will you enter the world?

Wilhelm Reich described adults fixated at this stage as "self-confident, often arrogant, elastic, vigorous and often impressive." Athletic in body, their faces usually show "hard, sharp masculine features, but often also feminine, girl-like features." They are likely to make an "exaggerated display of self-confidence, dignity and superiority." (Think of Hemingway, Mussolini, or Napoleon.) Reich found the type most frequently among "athletes, aviators, soldiers and engineers," one of the most important traits being "aggressive courage." (Nowadays astronauts, as portrayed, for example, in *The Right Stuff,* provide striking examples.) They like "being on top," and they resent being subordinates "unless they can—as in the army or other hierarchic organizations—compensate for the necessity of subordination by exerting domination over others who find themselves on lower rungs of the ladder" (Reich, 1949, pp. 200–07). The type, however, is by no means confined to men. Erikson speaks of both men and women "being on the make," either by boyishly enjoying head-on attack, competition, conquest, winning the goal or (most often in girls) teasing, provoking, or otherwise "snaring" (1963, p. 90). A fluttery, "hysterical" type of woman, all ribbons and bows and seductive helplessness, shares the underlying trait: meeting the world with one's body, someone like David Copperfield's Dora or, in a lighter vein, Blondie of the comic strips. If the mask slips, the strength and manipulativeness underneath show through, as in the stories of Scarlett O'Hara or Becky Sharp.

Classical psychoanalysis called this stage "phallic" and attributed this intrusive style to the boy's discovery of pleasurable sensations in his penis and its mysterious power to rise and fall (our constant metaphors for achievement and power). Today, I would want to complicate the idea that a penis is the source of this "phallic" intrusive style, because it seems to me too simple and confined to only one sex.

Perhaps, as the child gets bigger, he senses new physical ways in which the elders want him to be in their world, ways that require penises. Perhaps simple growing leads to a desire to get into the world that heightens the importance of the penis. Perhaps, then, the "organ" whose mode this phase represents is the whole musculature (as Erikson hints).

One of the commonest answers children find in our culture to the question, How will you get into the world? is, I will get big. One of the most dramatic signs of something small becoming something big is the penis with its power of erection. The penis may thus be a key symbol for the child in the intrusive stage. May be. It will depend on what other resources the culture opens up to developing children, male or female. The little girl may feel the absence of a penis as a traumatic lack that must be compensated for, as in the classical psychoanalytic idea of "penis envy." Yet the wish for a penis does not seem today as biologically determined as it once did. The wish may be exaggerated or tempered or, indeed, nonexistent.

I think we need to begin by assuming that biology and culture work together to pose tasks (or questions) for the developing child. The answers the child finds will depend on who the child is or perhaps how. That is, the answers will depend on the personal style that the child has already achieved and the resources available to the child for answering the questions that culture and biology pose. One of those resources may be a penis or it may be a vagina. Having a vagina may be perceived as a lack, an advantage, or simply a difference.

Having or not having a penis, however, affects development much more decisively in the next phase, the oedipal. In our trek through the developmental dialogue, we are still negotiating the pre-oedipal phases, and we need to consider the relation of mother and child during all this questioning and activity. What I have been calling the "intrusive" stage, Margaret Mahler terms "rapprochement," the period from fourteen or fifteen months to two years or so (Mahler et al., 1975). That is, in her observations, the upright baby in "practising," crawls, climbs, stands, begins to walk, all at some optimal distance from his mother. The toddler now stretches out that distance, moving definitively away from her, asserting his own independence. At the same time, however, he finds this a dangerous project and returns to her side. *He* returns. In the earlier period, it was she who closed the distance between them. "Bye-bye" was the key word. Now it is "Hi!" as he goes to her.

Thus, during the "rapprochement crisis," the baby develops two conflicted tendencies ("ambitendency," Mahler calls this): "I am not weak and dependent. I can do all these things. I am superior to the child I was." At the same time, "Help me! I can't manage, and I am worthless because I can't." In other words, during this crisis the child goes to and fro, sometimes proclaiming a grandiose self, sometimes wailing about the exact opposite, a self mortified by feelings of dependency, helplessness, failure, humiliation, and fear.

Mahler specifies the crisis by four elements. First, the child wants to be big and therefore not to recognize help from outside. Second, however, the child also fears being passively "left behind." Third, "stranger reaction" (such as a resistance to babysitters) resurges, and people are likely to comment on the child's "shyness." Fourth, as in the earlier period, the child splits bad mother from good mother, identifying more strongly with the good, giving mother and trying to coerce what he wants out of the bad, resistant mother. All these strategies can appear later in life in borderline patients (just as the loss of boundaries in earliest infancy can appear later in psychotics).

What comes to the child's aid in this crisis is language and the ability to symbolize. If "Hi!" is important, so is "Cookie!" and even more, "Look, mommy!" and "No!" By "No" the child uses his mastery of the nomic stage. He actively takes over the "No" of his parents and uses it to coerce the behavior he wants from them, mirroring the way he perceives their "No's" to him. By the end of the rapprochement crisis, the child becomes able to name people (and also photographs) and, most interesting, to use "I" of himself. Through language and drawings the child can express his wishes, and he can use symbolic play with dolls or cars or toy animals to imagine mastery over his growing abilities. In general, the child moves from symbols shared with its family to symbols the child itself owns (Werner and Kaplan, 1963, p. 83).

Mahler reports that the ups and downs and variations among the children she was observing became quite large during rapprochement. The children ceased to be an example of a phase and became individually distinct and different from one child to the other (p. 102). We are seeing identity (in our sense) emerge in itself, not just as our referring later traits back to infancy.

Mahler also reports the emergence of gender identity. Boys become acutely aware of their penises. They learn about erections. Their own upright posture makes it easier for them to see their penises from different vantage points. Girls become aware of the contrast between their genitals and those of boys, often by their different ways of urinating.

The anxieties of the stage heighten this sensitivity to gender. The child fears, as it has before, the loss of love from those he relies on. Now, however, that fear is intensified by inner promptings of "Thou shalt" or "Thou shalt not" because the child has begun to internalize parental wishes and values. Further, the child is more aware of body feelings and pressures, especially those related to the bowels, urination, and gender differences, all matters about which adults are likely to be very edgy.

The child's physical ability to move out into the world, to stand up, to poke into things, to walk, and even to fall down, all together serve to create a firmer sense of self. I can *do* things. The "intrusive" stage contributes to identity as did the negativism of the "nomic" phase. Both 'I can do' and 'I can say No!' are ways of saying I. Now too—we are talking about the second year of life—the child's verbal abilities have grown. He can name things and call people. "I can *say*," even though he may not yet have a sufficiently stable sense of self to say "I."

All these abilities in turn rest on the basic sense of trust that the child must have achieved during the first year of life to be functioning later at all. Out of the confidence that waiting is not forever, that separation is not loss, and that needs and desires will be satisfied, the child can build an emotional trust in an essentially benevolent other.

Experimentalists have made a most important contribution by showing— indeed measuring—the carry-over of a style from that first, "oral" year of life to the second stage. Matas et al. have shown that the quality of attachment to the mother in the earliest stage continues to become the quality of competence and obedience in the second stage (1982). The competent two-year-old does not automatically comply but shows a certain amount of noncompliance. Gradually, however, a general pattern of cooperation takes over—as Erikson's remarks on basic trust would suggest. The data gathered by Stayton et al. did not fit the behaviorist models that say one has to bring an essentially asocial or antisocial infant to obedience and controls by schedules of reward and punishment (1982). Rather, a responsive, accommodating social environment leads naturally toward patterns of obedience in the context of an attachment bond (of the kind Bowlby describes), a trust in others.

Besides that emotional knowledge of otherness, the child needs to know otherness intellectually through cognitive skills of seeing, hearing, knowing, remembering, saying, or counting. Together, the emotional thrust and intellectual belief in "the other" provide the child a foundation on which to maintain a stable inner figure of the one he loves, even when she is absent. It is that ability—and it is not something we can always do even as adults—that marks the beginning of the stage defined by what Mahler called "object constancy." It is a stage that the child will be in for the rest of his life.

During the rapprochement crisis, the child suffered from conflicting aims. He wanted to assert himself as a separate other and thus to use his new motor skills and cognitive abilities to distance himself from his mother. At the same time he would use his newly learned negativism to coerce her into being an omnipotent extension of himself. And he also longed for their earlier state of oneness. He wanted to cling to her, physically and emotionally. Given this "ambitendency," he would show clinging and negativism in rapidly alternating sequence, but if development went well, by the end of the rapprochement period, he would have begun to find his own optimum distance along this line between absolute closeness and absolute parting. Having, for a time, split his mother into "good" (identified with himself) and "bad" (separate, absent), he would be able to bring her together again. He is approaching "object constancy" in the psychoanalytic sense, making her into one person whether she is good or bad, whether or not he is kindly disposed to her, whether or not she is satisfying his needs. He has to unify the good and bad, loved and hated aspects of this mothering person, in order to bring her (or, more exactly, his relation with her) permanently and as a whole into his own personality. That is his task in the fourth and last, but unending, phase, according to Mahler's description of the child's growth in terms of object relations.

In that fourth stage, the child internalizes the relationship he has by this time established to his mother, making it part of his personality. He brings her nurturing inside himself, where she will always be "there" to love and support his growing "self-identity" (in Mahler's term). Now, in this later version, the child becomes emotionally more self-sufficient. He builds a sense of security and confidence by incorporating in himself the original source of that confidence, the assurance that sustained him at the beginning of his life: his needing and his mother's satisfying those needs in due measure. He builds a whole and consistent self which can, therefore, perceive others as consistent and whole. The abilities of the earlier stages come together to begin an adult way of dealing with other human beings. Hence, from two years of age and on, peers may make some contribution to emotional and cognitive development in and of themselves (Eckerman et al., 1982). This is an important issue that, as far as I know, psychoanalytic researchers concentrating on mother and father have not raised.

Now, however, this new ability to think of people as wholes opens to the child what is perhaps the greatest challenge of all. Until this point, the child's tasks have fitted a two-person relationship between the child and a mother *or* a father. Getting, taking, holding on, letting go, shame, admiration, planning or intruding—all can take place within a dyad.

The next stage brings us from a dyad to a triangle: child and mother *and* father. The child has to answer how he will deal with the relationship *between* mother and father or, more generally, between child and two parent-figures. Moreover, the sexual part of the relationship becomes important. Society, family, and his own body begin asking the child, How will you make your way into that more complex relationship? How will you keep on seeing these people as wholes? How will you deal with your own love and jealousy and hate and desire? How will you deal with theirs?

10 | Gender and Oedipus

"Only one idea of general value has occurred to me [in my self-analysis]. I have found love of the mother and jealousy of the father in my own case too, and now believe it to be a general phenomenon of early childhood." Thus Freud, writing to his friend Fliess on October 15, 1897, announced the oedipus complex (1950a, pp. 226–27).

Strangely (or not so strangely), he thought of the oedipus complex as something originating entirely with the child's "love" and "jealousy" alone, as though the parents had nothing to do with it, as though they had no feelings of desire, resentment, jealousy, or simple fatigue. Strangely (or not so strangely), although most of his patients were women, Freud discovered the oedipus complex as male. A little boy wants to replace his father (kill him) and have his mother all to himself (marry her). Freud remained puzzled all his professional life about the little girl's version of the myth.

Nevertheless, Freud also thought that the complex was mythic and universal and decisive for all children, *fondateur* as the French analysts say, founding. Freud thought of the oedipus complex as intrinsic to the human condition, perhaps even inherited. "The Greek myth seizes on a compulsion which everyone recognizes because he has felt traces of it in himself" (1950a, p. 227, the "he" and "himself" being the German pronouns for "everyone").

Others, less resolute, alibied that children might feel that way in decadent Vienna but surely did not in more civilized—or more primitive—areas of the world. The redoubtable anthropologist Malinowski countered Freud's claims of the universality of the oedipus complex by pointing to Trobrianders, who did not know the facts of fatherhood. Hence, he said, they could not have an oedipus complex. Ernest Jones showed, however, that the mother's brother, who took the role of the father in the family, served as the focus for the child's oedipal projections. Hence the form of the complex could vary from culture to culture, but the complex itself was universal.

Recently, the anthropologist Anne Parsons has updated the old Freud-Malinowski controversy by studying South Italian families, where the son's attachment to the mother remains strong (1964). (Freud, by contrast, had written of the "destruction and . . . abolition of the complex" [1924d,

215

19:177]. "It is literally smashed to pieces by the shock of threatened castration" [1925j, 19:257].)

Parsons's study suggests that we can understand the combination of a universal complex with different cultural versions as a borderline between instinct and culture, "for the original question of whether the oedipus complex is universal or not . . . is no longer very meaningful in that particular form. The more important contemporary questions would . . . be: what is the possible range within which culture can utilize and elaborate the instinctually given human potentialities, and what are the psychologically given limits of this range?" (p. 383, for her history of Freud-Malinowski, see pp. 331–34).

The identity *cum* feedback model lets us imagine those limits as a set of universal questions, posed to all of us because we are part of the human species. Then the answers that different cultures permit and different individuals give vary considerably. A push comes from the child's own drive to grow up, yet the child is also answering a call from parents, society, and culture. All humans are asked to become women or men by their physiology and by the society they need. Yet what it means to be "womanly" or "manly" in a given culture can vary tremendously.

At first, Freud thought this fateful complex of ideas (at least for the boy) simply enacted in fantasy the Oedipus myth. The boy wants to get rid of his father and take his place with his mother, as Oedipus did. Under the fear of castration, however, the boy gives up his wish for his mother and resolves to be like his father. Indeed he brings his father's authoritative voice into his psyche as the superego, and in that sense the complex disappears. It is replaced by this new agency in the mind, the incorporated voice of parental (and through the parents, cultural) authority. Later Freud realized that there was a "negative" oedipus complex as well as this positive one: the boy longed to be loved by his father as his mother is, to be feminized (castrated) and take the mother's place. For any one boy, the positive and negative complexes interplay dialectically.

Since for girls, in Freud's version of development, castration has already occurred, it can no longer be feared and is resented instead. The girl becomes angry at her mother for not having provided her with the same highly valued part of the body the little boy has. Moreover, the mother, since she lacks this same instrument, herself seems valueless. The little girl resolves to acquire a penis and turns to her father, who seems able to give her one. Eventually she sublimates her desire for his penis into the wish to have a baby from him. Where for the boy, the castration complex broke up his oedipus complex and "resolved" it, for the girl, the castration complex begins her slower and later oedipal growth. She does not incorporate into her psyche the figures of father or mother, keeping them as real objects of her love and resentment. Hence she does not develop the same internal voice of the father, the superego, as the boy.

For both boy and girl, the oedipal stage marks a transition from a numerical two to a numerical three. (Curiously, two and three mark another famous Freudian distinction, between the comic—involving two persons—and the joke—three.) In the earlier stages, oral, nomic, and even intrusive, our object relations took place in a dyad: feeder and fed, ruler and ruled, penetrator and inhibitor. To be sure, the dyad could be mother-and-child or father-and-child, or a child might perceive both parents as the opposite side of the dyad, but dyad it was. Now the child has to deal with a triangle. Further, he has to deal with a mixture of love and hate (jealousy), not simply toward one other but toward two others, hence an eternal triangle in still another sense.

In the dyads up to oedipus, the girl and the boy have developed alike—or have they? Has the classical focus on the genital difference led us to overlook other, subtler differences between the sexes in the earliest phases of life? In recent years, researchers have suggested differences in brain structure, in hormones that affect the amount of aggression, or in responses to the "startle reaction," the little lurches of consciousness that babies show (something like the abrupt wakings we adults sometimes feel as we are dozing off). Boy babies respond to startles by having an erection and going off to sleep, girl babies by crying. How real these innate differences are or what difference they make in development remains very much open to further investigation and evidence. So far we have only hints.

Studies of people born with abnormal genitals have shown that it is not the genitals, nor even the chromosomes, that determine gender, but the way parents treat the child. Whatever gender the parents firmly believe in will become the child's gender, overriding either gonads or chromosomes. Further, this gender identity is firmly established by the age of two and a half or three years. To be sure, both boys and girls progress through an oral and a nomic stage in a passive relation to a mother, but otherwise boys and girls are born different and develop from birth on differently because parents treat boys and girls differently (Money and Ehrhardt, 1972, Stoller, 1968a, 1968b, 1972).

Nancy Chodorow has pointed to still another source of early gender difference. Today, in our society, parenting is left primarily to the mother or some other woman. Few men serve as the primary caregiver for an infant, and a movie like *Kramer vs. Kramer* dramatizes the panic many men of today feel at the prospect. In our society, the human who first mirrors the infant to itself is probably female, and she is mirroring and nurturing precisely because of her gender. It seems very likely, says Chodorow, that under these circumstances, she will feel differently toward a boy baby than toward a girl, leading to differences for the two genders in the very process of identity formation.

Just as anybody DEFTs novels or newspapers, one who takes care of an infant would DEFT the sex of the child. I, as usual, think the DEFTing of gender would be a function of the identity of the individual caregiver. That there would be a difference between male and female caregivers confronting male and female babies, however, seems to me most probable. Further, if the caregiver finds herself defined by her gender, I would expect the sex of the child to seem even more intensely a subject for expectation, fantasy, defense, or transformation. To be sure, we do not have much evidence about this, but the inference seems to me irresistible.

Chodorow makes another sensible suggestion: that mothers of daughters will tend to see daughters as less different from themselves than sons. They will see a baby girl as "just a baby" and not as much of an "other" as a "baby husband" or a "baby father" might seem. Hence, she suggests, a mother and a daughter will tend to keep a symbiotic, merged relationship longer than a mother and a son. Conversely, the son will separate sooner and with more recoil. Hence—and this is Chodorow's highly important inference—mothering by women tends to create women who will be mothers and men who will resist mothering impulses. Mothering reproduces itself, and the sex roles that society imposes today will seem natural tomorrow. Unless, of course, psychology can provide the insight into our ways that enables us to replace unconscious script with conscious choice (Chodorow, 1978, chaps. 5–7).

It may well be, then, that children have already been differentiated by sex when they come to the discovery of the differences in their genitals or their urinatings. Here again, I would like more evidence about our pre-oedipal development. Whatever happens in those earlier stages, however, all observers agree that from the time the baby stood up, walked, and was dressed for walking, society's call to the child to establish its sex became much more urgent and explicit, and so did the child's own inner need to become gendered.

Seen in this larger context, we can understand the oedipus complex as a continuation of our parents' (and their and our culture's) call to us to grow up into the society the parents already inhabit. For them and us at that point in our young lives, the most important divisions in that world are parent and child, male and female. Our bodies and our culture asked us, How will you fit yourself into those alternatives? Our bodies ask through our genitals and the genitals of other children or of our parents, as Freud first pointed out. Our culture asks us in a thousand other media. Will you dress as a boy or a girl? How will you walk? Will you play with dolls? Will you roughhouse? Dance? How long will you wear your hair?

The intrusive phase had asked the child, How will you get into the world? The genital phase then asked us the same question in more specific terms: How will you get into a world which consists of two genders, male and female, and two generations, parents and children? "Genital" here has to connote both "gendering" and "generationing," for in this phase the child has to situate itself with respect to both. It has to face the differences between boys and girls (however they might be defined by the culture surrounding us) and become one or the other. Similarly, it has to accept the fact that, at least for a long time, it will not itself be an adult, at least as instanced by our parents.

In the classical oedipal situation, described by Freud, a boy child begins the phase by answering, I will kill my father and mate with my mother and so become a male parent. A boy ends the phase by answering, I will become *like* my father and mate with someone *like* my mother in the distant future. That, however, as Freud pointed out, is only one solution for one gender. There are many others both "normal" and "abnormal" (terms whose meanings will differ widely from culture to culture).

It is not only the cultural oedipus complex that varies. Individual oedipus complexes diverge so much that generalizations, even at this early stage, the third and fourth years of life, become very difficult. Mahler's group, for example, found that by twenty-one months, it "was no longer possible to group the toddlers in accordance with the general criteria hitherto used" because they had become so differentiated as individuals. "Their individuation . . . [was] changing so rapidly that they were no longer mainly phase specific" (1975, pp. 101–02).

The difficulty of generalizing is particularly regrettable because of the pressing social and political need to understand more about

Little Girls

Today our society rewards with money and position a man's manufacturing children's blocks or advertising disposable diapers, but a woman's actually playing blocks with a child or actually changing a diaper gets little status and next to nothing in salary, if pay at all. The inequity is compounded by social patterns and laws restricting women to housework and childwork and excluding women from traditionally male activities. Feminists, in trying to remedy these and other injustices in women's lot, have bumped into early psychoanalytic theories that claim to reveal traits of little girls and adult women which justify these asymmetries. Any such claims and any such theories deserve the closest examination and, if they are found wanting, prompt revision.

Examination they have certainly had. A number of writers have ably summed the history of Freud's ideas and those of his early followers, both the ones who agreed with him about femininity and those who disagreed. At the same time these writers have chronicled the early feminist criticisms and the more recent, those dating from about 1968 (Chasseguet-Smirgel, 1976; Chodorow, 1978; Mead, 1974; Mitchell, 1974; Moore, 1976; Stoller, 1968b; Strouse, 1974).

Very briefly, however, before his 1925 essay, "Some Psychical Consequences of the Anatomical Distinction Between the Sexes," Freud thought that the development of boys and girls was symmetrical. As we have seen, he traced in detail the path of development in boys, generalizing from his adult male patients and, most importantly, from his analysis of himself. Freud frankly admitted that he had been unable to discover a similarly detailed pattern in the development of little girls and simply reasoned out an analogy.

By 1925, however, he had become dissatisfied with the "precise analogy" between the little boy and the little girl. New clinical observations led him to state a theory of female development in the 1925 paper, a paper he apparently hoped would settle what was becoming an irritating and divisive question within the psychoanalytic movement.

According to this paper, the girl begins, as the boy does, by loving her mother, treating her father as a distinctly secondary figure, but she makes the shocking discovery that the boy has a penis and she and her mother none. The girl blames her mother for not giving her this body part, thus finding her doubly deficient, and transfers her love to her father who has what she wants. Faced with realistic biological limitations, she transforms her desire for a penis into a desire to have a baby by her father. Not until puberty, however, does she realize that this is impossible, at which point she angrily rejects her clitoris (her substitute penis up to that point) and transfers her genital sensitivity to the vagina. In this development, she does not identify with the father (as the boy does) nor, really, with the mother, and hence does not acquire the same kind of superego the boy does. Hence we see, he claimed, certain "female" personality traits that males do not share.

Carol Gilligan states (1982) that women develop an ethic of care, relationship, and responsibility that is simply different from the male ethic of justice and treating everyone the same. Freud and modern theorists like Lawrence Kohlberg fail to see this ethic as a separate, different experience, and therefore treat it as a lack (the moral equivalent of the missing penis?).

As Roy Schafer has suggested (1974), if Freud meant that women lack the kind of abstract, inhuman moral values, the isms, that often permeate male-dominated politics and warfare, perhaps that is no bad thing *if* it is true that women do not have that kind of superego. If. Fisher and Greenberg, surveying the experimental literature, conclude, "There is a trend favoring Freud's hypothesis. But . . . it is hardly of such proportions as to support the rather dramatic distinction that Freud sought to make between the male and female superego" (1977, pp. 207–12, 220–21, 212).

Today, it seems obvious to us that any explanation of child development or of femininity should combine elements from physiology, culture, family relationships, and the individual personality. It would take a bold theorist indeed to claim that one of these explanations excludes the others, yet that is essentially what Freud did. A neurologist by training, a scientist seeking Helmholtzian principles for the mind that would be as rigorous as physical or chemical laws, a man whose commitment to truth and "reality" amounted to a passion, Freud translated what he observed in a Rat Man or a Little Hans into what seemed the most direct explanation.

For Freud, what must differentiate the boy's growing up from the girl's is their anatomy: their genitals (or perhaps their hormones, the existence of which Freud early guessed—1905d, 7:216n). In recent years, only the most conservative American and the most innovative French analysts, following Jacques Lacan, have tried to continue this early reliance on anatomy. Lacan, for example, whimsically metaphorizes the phallus as "a major yardstick for the categorisation of human beings." For Lacan, the oedipus complex consists of a dialectic: to be or not to be, to have or not to have, the phallus, understood both as a man's real penis and as the "signifier of desire," the symbol of symbolization.

As Murray Schwartz says, what makes Lacan so hard to understand is that he uses the words and concepts of early psychoanalysis to state the ideas of much later psychoanalysis. Hence part of the French "manner" of psycho-analysis is to use words that could apply to the genitals to describe object relations. The female, for example, is "an absence." The feminist Luce Irigaray suggests that because women's genitals have the form of two lips, "Woman 'touches herself' all the time." "She is already two—but indivisible into ones . . ." (1977, p. 24). Genitals serve as a metaphor for something she is claiming about the inwardness and doubleness of woman's whole self.

I do not want to let the modish puns of this way of writing obscure the profound truth it seeks to convey. The puns I see as an effort to alter our perceptions, to persuade us by confronting directly the means by which we see and believe. That is, we use symbols from the body to represent our adult world. This is one great wisdom we have gained from the free associations of psychoanalyses, and the language of today's "French Freud" foregrounds that truth. It is equally possible, of course, to use the language of relation-ships to describe a genital world. That would be the manner of Erikson: understanding "phallic" strivings as intrusions, "anal retention" as "holding on," or "erecting, constructing, and elaborating" as male tendencies and including, enclosing, and holding safely as female (1963, pp. 97-108). Both *façons de parler* illuminate the same profound connection between the body and personality. Both assert that anatomy is at least a good part of destiny. Incidentally, then, both reveal a parallel between the most recent French psychoanalysis and some American ideas of the 60s.

We need to understand that "woman" and "femininity" are themselves constructs, defined not by chromosomes, genitals, or customs—or defined by all of these, depending on how we construe her. Thus, when we analyze woman, woman analyzes us. Freud's ideas about women say something about Freud and about the society in which he lived and in which we, to some extent, still live. In this sense, Freud's ideas about feminine development have proved useful to feminists by giving an understanding of the present situation as a first step toward changing it.

One group of feminists, like Luce Irigaray and Juliet Mitchell, has advocated using Freud more or less "as is," as a neutral, scientific, value-free way to understand how girl babies become women in a patriarchal society. To be sure, they do not naively believe that Freud is free of bias or that they themselves are. Nevertheless, they find it useful (as I do) to stretch the unbreakable lifeline between fact and value. It helps to pretend, for the moment, to be value free in order to understand what needs the inequities of patriarchy serve and what ideas of maleness and femaleness it engenders. Freedom from prejudice (prejudgment) is an illusion, but it can be a useful one.

In our patriarchal society, many boys and girls think of female genitals as a lack—and so did Freud. For him, the discovery of that "fact" was decisive for both the little boy and the little girl. Frightened by the prospect of such a "castration," the little boy is propelled into his oedipus phase. His new knowledge makes into a real threat what was before only imaginary or meaningless.

The fear of castration takes its place in a succession of childhood fears. First, there was an oral fear of the loss of the breast and annihilation. Then came a fear of the loss of one's bowel movement in the nomic stage, and with it fears of the loss of approval or love, a narcissistic blow, so that the fear of the loss of a bowel movement could become a model, both physical and emotional, for the fear of the loss of a body part. Fearing such a loss, a little boy may give up the use of his penis as an instrument of his desire for his mother. Instead, he may resolve to "be like" (identify with) his father and to be a penis-wielding father later. He thus smashes to pieces his oedipus complex because he abandons the libidinal parts. His desires become desexualized and sublimated into the games and superboyish behavior of latency. The aggressive drives are turned outward, away from the father. The objects, the real persons of father and mother, become figures in his ego, the basis for the superego.

Where for a boy, the castration complex broke up his oedipus complex and "resolved" it, for a girl, the castration complex begins her slower, later oedipal growth. She does not incorporate into her psyche the figures of father or mother but keeps them as real objects of her love and resentment; hence she does not develop the same internal voice of the father, the superego, as the boy.

In this script, both boy and girl read the female genitals as a lack, and Freud wrote as though this were a necessity, a primal fantasy (*Urphantasie*) that must be part of every child's world view whether he or she actually experienced it or not. Near the end of his life Freud wrote that castration anxiety and penis envy were "bedrock," beyond which psychoanalytic treatment could not dig (1937c, 23:252). Freud even proposed that castration anxiety was inherited.

This concept of an *Urphantasie* represents a somewhat puzzling departure from his usual procedure. Schafer notes that it is the hallmark of psychoanalytic investigation, and particularly of Freud's thinking, to question further and further. Freud usually tries to establish the fullest understanding possible of the particularity of individual responses to specific circumstances, "especially when these reactions are intense, disturbing, profoundly formative, and enduringly influential." Yet at this point, where all children form their genders, Freud resorted to a "shock theory" based on a momentary realization of inherited fantasy (1974, pp. 474–75, cp. Lasch, 1974, for a somewhat different account).

It is also surprising that Freud did not raise the question of cultural variability. Indeed in *Totem and Taboo* he seems to say that castration and the oedipus complex provide the basis for religion, morals, art, and society in *all* cultures. Yet today we know that in some cultures, as Margaret Mead reports, "It is men who envy women their feminine capacities. It is men who spend their ceremonial lives pretending that it was they who had borne the children, that they can 'make men' " (1974, p. 118). Aborigines aside, Freud was well read in the classics and would have known the Isis-worship described by Apuleius in his *Metamorphoses*. That cult reverses our ideas of genital lack or absence. The penis is perceived as an unwelcome presence and the vagina as the ideal. The most devoted priests would castrate themselves to become more like the goddess. In a less extreme, symbolic version of the act, the priest would shave his head (a rite which survives as the tonsure worn in some Roman Catholic orders).

To be sure, in Freud's culture and our own, castration anxiety and penis envy are probably the norm. When he assumes that they are biological givens, however, he is succumbing to what Margaret Mead (generally a sympathetic reader of Freud) calls a "socially conditioned naiveté."

Freud thought of himself as a scientist, not as a poet or philosopher. He did not expect his texts to be treated as ends in themselves, never to be updated, like Shakespeare or Schopenhauer. Freud expected his writings to be the basis for further investigation that might very well lead to their revision. He himself energetically revised his earlier work when he thought it outdistanced. It is with that same tone that feminists like Nancy Chodorow have reworked Freud's thinking on female development by bringing in object-relations theory.

Freud thought that boys and girls developed essentially the same way until the penis became important in sensation and fantasy. Recent observers would agree that there are no differences in kind, but point to differences in degree. That is, the boy is hormonally more aggressive than the girl. The mother may respond to the girl as less of an other than the boy (Chodorow, 1978, chaps. 5–7). There are at least these, and there may be other gender-related differences. Nevertheless, Freud's basic view holds in the sense that until the discovery of the importance of the penis there are no psychologically important differences visible in the child's body. Differences between individual boys and girls are probably more substantial than the differences between the genders.

With the "discovery" of the penis Mahler observed changes in behavior for both boys and girls, and she makes the point that the "discovery" takes place about the same time that the child masters walking—seventeen or eighteen months. At that point boys and girls diverge. The boy becomes more aggressive, more disengaged from mother, and the girl becomes more engrossed with her (1975, pp. 101–06).

Today's observers agree that to both sexes the penis may symbolically represent a paradox. In a question-and-answer model, the penis (for either boy or girl) may represent an answer to two inconsistent questions. How can I achieve mother? (Father who has a penis did.) How can I distance myself from mother? (She does not have a penis.) Both sexes shared the problem of being a baby helplessly dependent on a mother who held the power of life and death. As a way to undo that trauma, the penis can thus become a symbol for power (Serebriany, 1976, Stoller, 1974).

Modern psychoanalysts would agree that the penis can represent several other important answers to questions. Through the penis, the child (of either sex) learns the difference between the sexes. The child may also learn about the mother's role in giving birth. The child may learn about girls' or women's genitals. The child may learn about either mother's or father's actions in conceiving a baby and therefore have to accept some fairly terrifying imaginings of parental sex (McDougall, 1964, Chasseguet-Smirgel, 1976). Also, there will be wide variations in what individual children do and do not learn from the existence and nonexistence of the penis.

In our society, at least, a girl may want a penis in order to triumph over the mother (in several possible ways): to become independent of her, to be like the father, or to have what she lacks. A girl cannot have a penis, though, and she may transfer to her whole body the narcissistic pride a boy can reserve for his special organ, or the fear, dissatisfaction, or fantastic imaginings (Chasseguet-Smirgel, 1976, p. 285). The girl may fantasy that the boy will lose his, or she may imagine various ways she could acquire a penis: by medicine, by surgery, by eating, by making up to her father, by being penetrated by one, or ultimately, by having a baby who would be a symbolic substitute.

Again, what a girl imagines and what life experiences she draws on will vary widely. These fantasies are, in any case, secondary to her primary ambivalence: the wish for and frustration with the mother. A little girl oscillates between her primary one-to-one relationship with her mother and the later heterosexual triangle in which she is her mother's rival for her father. She has what Freud called a "complete" oedipus complex. She has a "positive" one in which she loves the parent of the opposite sex and resents not being able to take the place of her parent of the same sex. She has a "negative" one in which she loves her same sex parent and wants to get rid of the intruder of the opposite sex. This more complex interpersonal structure may remain her preoccupation through latency and into puberty and adolescence, as she goes through various individual phases in which either the positive or the negative triangle weighs more heavily (Mahler, 1975, p. 106).

The little boy, by contrast, has available to him a penis with which to symbolize and undo his dependency on his mother. For him, as for the little girl, his attitude toward the penis is not primary but secondary, a way of coping with the earlier trauma of his life-and-death dependence on her. That was a wound to his narcissism, a source of fear and resentment, and the source of dangerous aggressive wishes. All this a boy may try to defeat by overvaluing the organ that he has and his mother lacks (Chodorow, 1978, pp. 107, 122). He may break loose from her, asserting his independence and separateness, thus weakening or even denying the interpersonal tie to his mother. To some extent his new oedipal love for his mother may continue the way he had to cling to her in his first years, and to that extent the new love becomes a source of danger. He may push away all the harder, turning more and more toward his father. To be loved by his father as his father loves his mother, however, he would have to lose his penis (as his mother apparently has). He may counterbalance, therefore, by forming a new, more distant kind of love for his mother. 'I am not her. I am not female, but I want the female.'

In general, a boy is likely to weaken the interpersonal ties that remain strong for a girl, and he tends to have only the "positive" oedipus complex.

That is, he tends not to seek a dependent relationship with his father like the earlier relationship with his mother (as the girl may). He is more likely to assert his pride, aggression, and anger toward the outer world, but he is also more likely to fear injury. He will probably try to become the idealized, powerful—and feared—father, identifying with the most "fatherly" aspects of father, trying to control himself and others (Horney, 1932). As with the little girl's interpersonal involvement, his detachment persists through latency, the period of relative calm after the oedipal tempest when, as Peter Blos says, there are no *new* instinctual demands and the old methods of solution hold up (May, 1980, Blos, 1968). His detachment may persist into the urgent drives of adolescence and perhaps beyond into a life-style which many in our society call "typically masculine."

The feminist criticism of Freud's first and second theories of female development has led to a realization of how various the experiences of little girls are. That realization in turn leads to recognizing that the situation of a little boy, which Freud treated as uniform, is equally various. We simply have not questioned it as much because little boys have not been curbed as little girls have.

Today we need to underline the importance of these variations. Throughout both their scenarios, each child's experience will differ. Each child will experience the first mother differently. For each, walking will be different. Each will differently know what a penis looks like, feels like, or does. Each will see father differently. Also, of course, each mother and father will be different. The variations are so great as to make all talk about "the" boy and "the" girl suspect if applied to "this boy" or "that girl." Rather, the genital stage poses universal physiological and cultural questions which children hear and answer in their own private styles (Fenichel, 1931).

Similarly, societies differ greatly, and what a mother and father do in modern America they may not in Nigeria or Korea. This whole scenario might change in an African society where several mothers bring up children by one father, so that there may be no primary attachment to one omnipotent mother. (Or is that not possible?) Little Hans's parents thought it all right to threaten him with castration. We no longer think so. Within a few years, modern American fathers may do more mothering than, say, I did.

How these social variations might affect character we have no way of knowing. If we did, it would be sensible to advocate this or that change. We don't, though. The best route to reform, therefore, is to understand more about the way children make the experiences of childhood into adult character—or identity.

Nevertheless, Freud's great "founding" stands. Margaret Mead phrases it as the discovery "that the Oedipus complex is a reality in all societies, since in all societies boys and girls go through a period in which their investment in their budding sexuality is both threatening to their elders and inappropriate for their stage of physical and mental maturity" (1974, p. 116). The consequences of this stage for our biology and our cultures is immense. Understanding how we are gendered and generationed offers a key to the best of social reforms, those that touch human nature itself.

Freud thought he could explain our gendering primarily as a result of our genitals. Early analysts sometimes wrote as though a person had a certain kind of genital and willy-nilly the person behind that genital, so to speak, or around it had to grow up a certain way. In the more than ninety years since Freud wrote, "I have found love of the mother and jealousy of the father in my own case too," we have come to realize that we also need personal and interpersonal explanations. There is a person inside a body and a culture outside that body. Rather than simply say, Anatomy is destiny, we need to ask, How do anatomy and culture coact to become an identity?

As Mahler's observations make clear, we grow up through phases that we share (apparently) with all other humans, yet we experience those phases in highly individual ways. By the twenty-first month, in Mahler's work, individual differences seemed to outweigh "phase specific" ups and downs, yet "developmental conflicts that are phase-specific, even though individually variable . . . occurred with amazing regularity from the second half of the second year on" (Mahler, 1975, pp. 102, 228). The trick is to see how those of Freud's generalizations that we still find valid and the individual's highly personal version of them go together. That is the usefulness of the model of a theme-and-variations identity governing a hierarchy of feedbacks.

For example, consider a patient of Heinz Kohut's who repeatedly dreamed she was urinating standing up and someone was standing behind her watching. In an earlier analysis, the analyst had interpreted these dreams as a wish to have a penis and urinate standing up like a boy. Kohut added that the dream might express her need to pull away from her relation with her bizarre and flighty mother and to turn toward her more responsive, down-to-earth father. The patient responded to the interpretation by remembering that her mother had cautioned her not to sit on toilet seats other than those at home lest she get dirty or diseased. The toilet seat figured in miniature her mother's generally suspicious attitude toward the world, and the patient's dream symbolized a wish not to be like her mother and see the world as dangerous and infected but to be like her father, to gain his support (as she had admiringly watched him in the bathroom) so that she could "sit down on the toilet." In other words, in her dream she used the commonplace wish of a little girl to urinate standing up to say, not 'I want to be a boy,' but 'I want to be a more joyful and alive person.' Paradoxically, because of her personal history and her individual feelings about toilet seats, a dream about urinating standing up could embody a wish to urinate sitting down (Kohut, 1977, pp. 220–22).

Once again, individuality turns out to govern—to use, really—physical, social, cultural, and family constants. To be sure, all humans face an oedipus complex, and all humans use it to build a gender identity. Generic explanations of maleness and femaleness, however, tell only part of the story. Each individual makes his or her own maleness or femaleness and may indeed create

Other Sexualities

that quite vary the ideas of gender maintained by the surrounding culture.

Freud wrote that other sexualities—"perversions" (although I intend that term in the special sense of page 231)—developed as events forced changes from "normal" sexuality. That is, regular maleness and femaleness came into being as boys coped with the fear of castration and girls with the "fact" that they had already been castrated. Any conflict, any excessive fear or stimulation or guilt, could interfere with the regular oedipal outcome. The boy or girl would fall back on earlier gratifications, through the mouth or anus or urethra, and become fixated there. (Hence the homosexual seeks oral, anal, or other pregenital intercourse.)

Freud thought fetishism the prototype of all these sexual variations, and in the course of analyzing a number of fetishists, he derived a pattern. A boy cannot face the knowledge—typically the sight—that his mother does not have a penis. He transfers the feelings he would have had toward a penis to something else: stockings, a shoe, panties, typically what the boy saw just before he saw the fateful lack. Freud's chief case had focused his desire on a certain shine (*Glanz*) on the nose, which was really a "glance" at the nose. Other fetishisms involve cutting women's hair or binding their feet (the Chinese custom).

The boy "disavows" the missing penis. He denies it is missing, yet in providing a substitute, he acknowledges it. He splits his ego, making one part respond to reality, the other to his wish. He thus loses touch with reality but only within a certain narrowly defined context. An "other" sexuality thus serves as an alternative to and defense against psychosis: putting it in an erotic capsule. A perversion is a *defense*. In my question and answer model, the phallic-intrusive and genital stages pose questions, and a perversion is simply an answer outside the customary male or female range.

For later psychoanalysis, however, neither regular nor alternative sexuality derives simply from fear of castration or the oedipus complex. Rather, sexuality draws on the relationships of all of infancy. Freud's basic hypothesis still stands, that the purpose of a perversion is to deny the difference between the sexes, but the missing penis fits into a long history of things missing. At first, it was the mother herself, leaving and making her hungry infant wait. Later it was the mother's breast (or bottle), understood now by the baby as something separate from mother herself. Later it was the baby's own stool, a part of himself that would be taken away. Finally, it is (for either boy or girl) the penis.

Long before arriving at the oedipus complex, some boys and girls must have established a pattern of looking in the external world for what they feel missing in their internal world. Indeed this must be a common pattern based on the feeding experience (McDougall, 1972). Associated with all these absences are fear and anger. When the absence is the penis, feared or seen as missing, the child may mobilize all that earlier fear and anger.

What primal fear or anger the child senses in himself, he also imagines in his parents. If I feel this angry and afraid, they must too. They must fear me and be about to retaliate on me for the way I hate them. In developing a perversion, according to Robert Stoller, the child splits the parents, putting all this destructive emotion into one and none in the other (1975). Thus either the mother or the father, depending on the particular sexual variation, will be idealized and the other debased. This way the child holds the parents apart, yet keeps them in relation to each other. The child reinterprets their sexual relation as between one frightening, angry person and a victim. The sexual variation yields another paradigm for turning sex into hostility.

Joyce McDougall sums up her theory by saying, "There is a condensed primal scene . . . in every perverse act." Traditionally, "primal scene" refers to a child's real or imagined sight of his parents in a sexual act, but McDougall carefully enlarges the term into "the child's total store of unconscious knowledge and personal mythology concerning the human sexual relation, particularly that of his parents" (1972, pp. 383, 372). As with knowledge of feminine genitals, a child may acknowledge the sexual relation between his parents but deny it by turning it into something else.

In creating such an alternative, a child usually imagines sex as charged with hostility, in which one party is the victim and one the victor. To some extent this is a distortion of reality, at least as other children know it. The child is coping with inner danger by using psychotic defense mechanisms, not changing inner reality but altering his perception of outer reality. Instead of simply repressing feelings or reversing pleasure into unpleasure or retreating to earlier kinds of gratification (repression, reaction formation, regression), the children we are talking about deny reality, split it, or project their inner states onto reality.

Just what factors might predispose some children to deny the difference between the sexes rather than fantasy about it, no one knows, but some do deny the missing penis or the sexual relation between their parents, some split those parents into one artificially good and one artifically bad, and some project their own massive feelings of fear and anger into their parents. All these maneuvers are answers to the questions of the genital stage, answers that will feed back and form part of a cumulating identity.

Psychotic defenses represent an element of madness. Most of us deny, split, or project our perceptions of reality some of the time, but if someone does so all of the time, he is indeed psychotic. The person devoted to some variant sexual script confines these perversions of reality to one sphere of life, the sexual, but does so compulsively. He or she "can do no other." In that sense, a perversion is a "miniature psychosis."

This "psychosis" is highly structured. Perversions amount to a script that has to be followed exactly. Any change in the recipe beyond sensitive limits spoils the fun. The sexually deviant individual is acting out a personal myth about sexuality and the genitals, and this myth has a universal, driving quality. As some homosexuals say, "I was homosexual before I knew I was homosexual." That is, before there was any sexual act, *this* sexual act felt like the right one.

Yet all of us have our sexual preferences, and most of us have the feeling about our sexuality that the way we do it is *the* way. Everybody would do it this way if they had the chance or the sense. Freud concluded that each individual combined traits with early influences to arrive at a specific sexual method of his own; each uses specific instincts, aims, and preconditions for love. "This produces what might be described as a stereotype plate (or several such), which is constantly repeated—constantly reprinted afresh—in the course of the person's life, so far as external circumstances and the nature of the love-objects accessible to him permit, which is certainly not entirely insusceptible to change in the face of recent experiences" (1912b, 12:99–100). There is a similarity, then, between the heterosexual male's falling in love with a woman like his mother, a male homosexual's need for "rough trade," and a voyeur's interest in peering through windows only in houses that look like homes of families.

Such scripts, duplicating the primal scene of a child's own watching, require a spectator. In most people's sexuality this may simply be the sense that this is the way sex ought to be, the voice of a parental supervisor, a superego of sex. As the stakes rise, as the sexual act becomes more imbued with anger, perhaps with fantasies about parents' sex or with ideas about the mother's missing penis, the need to be or have a spectator may become more insistent, precise, and literal. The spectator may represent some lost internal object. It may represent the perverse individual himself, projected onto another. It may represent the superego, a voice of conscience, society, or father. To give McDougall's statement fully, "There is a condensed primal scene involving three people in every perverse act" (1972, p. 372).

In a curious way, then, these literary metaphors for the perverse act, the "spectator," the "script," the "scenario," or the "myth," are scarcely metaphoric. The perversion shades off into the creation or enjoyment of pornography. Robert Stoller makes this connection and pinpoints the crucial element that leaves me unaroused by, say, transvestite pornography but stirred by *Playboy* centerfolds. There is aggression in perversions and, indeed, in all sexuality. Excitement comes from a favored pattern of risk, reversal, and triumph. My boredom tells me I do not feel the risks in transvestite pornography as risks, and my excitement says that the risks in the *Playboy* centerfold (nakedness, immobility) are truly risky for me.

As McDougall analyzes it, the perverse sexual activity serves to reverse roles. The child who was once the victim of anxiety at castration or the primal scene is now the agent of somebody else's anxiety, someone who may stand for the original threatener of castration. The once helpless child is now the controller and producer of excitement, either his own or his partner's. The onetime child is now the castrator or the fornicator or the rapist. In fact, many perverts are preoccupied with manipulating the other person's sexual response, making their partners suffer what they themselves once passively endured. Thus the perverse sexual play functions as a defense, warding off intense castration anxiety (1972, p. 378).

There is a truth here about all art, not just pornography (as Stoller points out). An artist like Scott Fitzgerald is driven to create and re-create the risk of being withheld from because that was the risk that mattered to him. Through his art he reverses and triumphs over it. In the same way, the types of art that I prefer allow me to imagine risks that are real risks for me, reverse them, and come out triumphant (1975, pp. 116–17, see also Holland, 1968a, chaps. 4, 7; Peckham, 1965). Within my range of preferences, I need a constant flow of works on the edge of what I already know so that I can reach new versions of the risks that are basic to my character—my identity. We come back again to the individual. In effect, art works as sex does, both to gratify drives directly and to ward off anxiety defensively. In this sense, a person's sexual preferences, either normal or perverse, are individual creations: works of art shared only by partners. Works of art are perversions shared by thousands. Perhaps.

Robert Stoller makes the sensible suggestion that "perversion" is not a diagnosis or an evaluation (despite its connotations) but a mechanism, like repression or sublimation. However we evaluate perversions as a society, we cannot use psychology to judge them, for "perversion" is simply a defense mechanism like repression or sublimation, in and of itself neither healthy nor unhealthy, moral or immoral. That is, in perversion, the erotic is charged with hostility, with the reversal of risk into triumph, and with the ability both to act out and to deny the material at the heart of the risk (typically, the sexual relations between the parents or the difference in male and female genitals). This is a process that finds its place in the creation of art and normal sexuality as well as perversion. It is a blank, providing in itself no basis for social judgment or action.

We create all our sexualities from a dialectic between the individual and the given. We have biological givens like the anatomical difference between the sexes or the difference in size between parents and children. We have social givens like the kinds of clothes we wear or a legislative decision to make only heterosexual sex legal. The individual *uses* these givens to situate himself within the matrix of male and female, parent and child.

Yet even these givens exist "between," "in relation to," as part of an identity. There really is no such thing as "the" boy or "the" girl or "the" pervert. Boys and girls and deviants are creations of I's. Sexual identity is one part of a total identity that uses and is limited by the human and cultural resources available to that identity.

We create our genders and our generations as we find personal answers to universal questions. At birth, the questions are strong and simple. By the time we have reached three or four years old, they have become various, and our power to give individual answers has grown. Once we have embarked upon the genital riddles, the combinations are so various and individual and our own creative power has so grown that we can generalize very little. That is why psychoanalytic accounts of development beyond the age of oedipus are so few. Like this chapter, they face the miracle of human variety, and those who would generalize about it would be wise to let themselves be awed into silence.

11 | Questions and Answers

When planning this book, I had hoped at this point to outline a full question and answer model of the development of an I. I had in mind a type of flowchart developed by T. G. R. Bower in his 1974 study of the development of children's understanding of spaces and physical objects.

In the first year of life children learn that when a rattle rolls under the couch it has not disappeared forever. If you look for it starting where it disappeared, you may find it. Similarly, if an object passes behind the headboard of a bed, you can imagine it traveling at constant speed behind the headboard and spot it again when it emerges. It is fun to watch a two year old who has just learned "inside" endlessly putting things into a box, closing the lid, and taking them out again. We even have toys specially designed for just this kind of play: nested cups or the series of Russian dolls each with a smaller doll inside.

As children, you and I learned about "under" and "behind" and "inside" by guessing—framing hypotheses—about paths and speeds, testing them, and framing still more hypotheses from the feedback of success or failure. It is even possible that we were born with some of these hypotheses already in place.

Bower found that he could organize the child's growing knowledge of spatial relations by putting these hypotheses into words and hence into logical relations. For example, a child begins by guessing, 'If it disappears from sight it is gone forever.' A young baby loses interest in a ball if it rolls out of view. Later, after some further development, *how* the previously seen ball disappears becomes important. If it goes *inside* something (for example, if you throw a blanket over it), the infant does not try to find it. Curiously, this can be true even if the object remains in plain sight, if it is in, say, a transparent cup or sits on a larger object like a table. If the ball rolls *behind* a chair leg, however, the baby knows to look there and does so. Bower renders this change in hypotheses by a kind of flowchart or "modified epigenetic landscape," which can cover a wide range of the child's knowledge, showing how hypotheses combine and complicate one another.

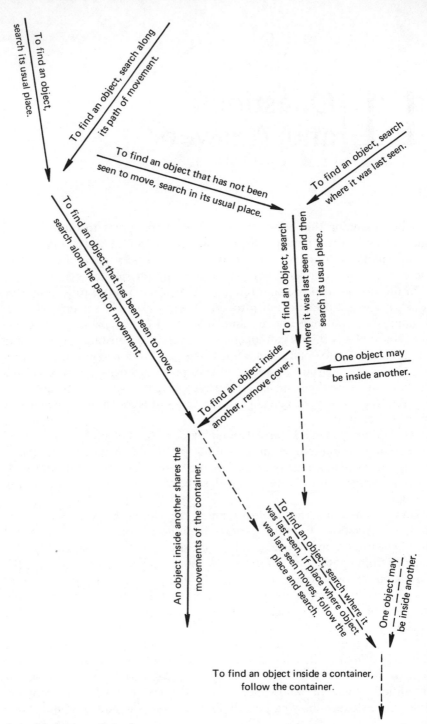

To find an object, search its usual place.

To find an object, search along its path of movement.

To find an object that has not been seen to move, search in its usual place.

To find an object, search where it was last seen.

To find an object that has been seen to move, search along the path of movement.

To find an object, search where it was last seen and then search its usual place.

To find an object inside another, remove cover.

One object may be inside another.

An object inside another shares the movements of the container.

To find an object, search where it was last seen. If place where object was last seen moves, follow the place and search.

One object may be inside another.

To find an object inside a container, follow the container.

A modified epigenetic landscape.
From *Development in Infancy* by W. H. Freeman and Company. Copyright © 1974.

Possibly because I am a literary critic, I tend to think of the flowchart as a series of questions and answers:

Ball: Okay, where am I?
Baby: I saw you before and not now. How did you disappear?
Ball: Inside something.
Baby: I don't know "inside." You're gone as far as I'm concerned.

Or—

Ball: I rolled behind a chair leg.
Baby: Are you along the path you rolled? That's where I'll look.
Ball: You found me, kid!

I had hoped to work out as detailed a dialogue or landscape for setting out the development of the path of identity through the oral, nomic, and other stages as Bower's diagram. As his work suggests, however, such a dialogue even for the straightforward problem of the child's developing an idea of object constancy becomes very intricate very quickly. Nevertheless, I believe I have sketched out, in the chart on pp. 244–45, some fundamental themes or questions such a dialogue would have to include. I think of this chart as summing up not only chapters 7–10 of *The I,* but the now well-established psychoanalytic account of development as set forth in many introductory texts (see, for example, Waelder, 1960; Hendrick, 1958; Buxbaum, 1959; or Smirnoff, 1968). There is, however, one glaring omission.

I have not tried to include the "psychology of the self" developed by Heinz Kohut (1971, 1977, and 1979, see also Ornstein 1974). Kohut proposes major modifications in the classical psychoanalytic picture of development. It is one-dimensional. The child proceeds along one track, passing through stages like a train going through stations. Kohut proposes a "bipolar self" with energy going in two directions: toward objects (as in the classical view), that is, persons or organs of the body, and toward "ego nuclei" within the self. The bipolar self thus goes through two sets of stages, the classical oral, anal, or phallic phases plus phases in the development of "narcissism."

Kohut defines narcissism not in the classical way, by the target (narcissism is libido directed toward the self), but by the quality of the instinctual charge: grandiose, unreal, or archaic. Narcissism in Kohut's sense (see Appendix, pp. 360–62) can be and is directed not only to the self but to objects as well. "Self-objects," he calls them, parts of the not-me "used in the service of the self and of the maintenance of its instinctual investment, or objects which are themselves experienced as part of the self" (1971, p. xiv).

The "self" in Kohut's theory is a cohesive, coherent, unified structure that the individual can invest with loving energy. The "self" is also a content of the mental apparatus, one's self-representation. In a way, then, Kohut's self is, like the ARC model of identity, simultaneously agent, consequence, and representation. For Kohut, however, "representation" means representation by the self, while in ARC, "representation" is representation by anybody. Nor does Kohut (so far as I know) use either theme-and-variations or feedback. He refers to the self-representation as the "self in a narrow sense" and the structural self (agency and consequence) as the "self in a broad sense."

Were one to try to add Kohut's doubling of the classical psychoanalytic picture of development to the identity-directing-feedback model, one would do so by allowing for double answers to a given developmental question and by adding the precursors of identification to the chart on pp. 244-45. The latter, in particular, seem like a useful addition to theory.

I have not, however, tried to include Kohut's contribution, despite the enthusiasm it has awakened in many American analysts (and despite its curious resemblance to some features of Lacan's *stade du miroir*). For one thing Kohut carefully confines his observables to the analytic situation. Only in the transference of a psychoanalysis can one detect the grandiosity, mirroring, or idealizing to which his theory refers. That observation in turn rests very heavily on the analyst's empathy, a far cry from the directly observable miserliness or dependency that mark classical anality or orality. As of now, Kohut's is a category theory, very diagnostic. I would like to see the Kohutians transform it into the holism that I think central to psychoanalytic thought. Most of all, I want to see how the theory fares in therapy over the next decade—that is the only test I know for a psychoanalytic theory, and the best.

Except for that omission, I think the chart and the following series of questions and answers present the classical psychoanalytic account of child development, a history that establishes a paralogic in the adult in which experiences that have no commonsense connection (like, say, eye and mouth or flying and gender) run together beneath the surface.

An Epigenetic Dialogue

During the first, "oral" stage, a baby is primarily an eater. The question his world asks him every day and several times a day is, How will things from outside you get inside? The world is asking the baby such things as, How will you incorporate? How will you take into your body? How will you get? (All terms from Erikson.) Of course these questions are not asked only or even primarily of the baby. They involve asking the mother, How will you give from your body to your child's? How will you make yourself available to your baby's sight, touch, hearing, and imagination? How will you fail your child? These are all questions for the unit of mother and child.

An even more profound question, then, dominant throughout the first three or four years of our lives, is, How will you (two) cease to be a unit? How will you (baby or mother) become a separate I? Or, as the chart says, How will you be a self?

As children, we coped with issues like, How will you get? or How will you separate? by acting the answers out bodily. Our environment responded to those answers with satisfactions or frustrations. We had, however, an underlying fear that toned the way we heard those demands and what we did in response. A child dreads hunger, dreads cold, dreads being left alone, dreads abandonment, but in earliest infancy, a child dreads most of all (says psychoanalytic theory) being overwhelmed. That is what analyses of adults suggest. A baby fears that suffering will not stop but will go on and on from suffering to more suffering to utter annihilation. How much his nurture energizes that fear tones the pleasures and unpleasures the baby feels at the questions he is posed and the answers he provides.

In the earliest phase of babyhood, we were primarily passive. We answered the demands on us mostly by waiting, giving signs of either patience or impatience. Mother was the active one, feeding and bathing us, taking care of our requirements, and leaving us so as to take care of her own and others' needs. As a baby, our task was to learn to tolerate her absence. We cried, we fretted, we gurgled, or we slept. Gradually, we learned to handle the delay by symbolizing our absent mother, and this, we have seen, represented an important state in our growing ability to know the world around us. Emotionally, our being able to imagine our absent mother (and our mother absent) provided the foundation for our ability to trust in her return, for our more general "basic trust."

Symbolizing a mother already represented some growth beyond our original total fusion with her. As we have seen in the research of Mahler's group, to symbolize her we had to have passed through a subphase of "mirroring identification." Bodily imitating a mother provided us with the felt body movements, intentions, feelings, sensations that formed a basis for imagining her.

We acquired these body movements colored by the love and resentment we felt toward a mother who both gratified and frustrated us. According to Freud, Melanie Klein, and many other observers, a baby deals with this intolerable mixture of love and hate by splitting the image of his mother into a good mother inside him and a bad mother "out there." Gradually, as we worked our way through the various subphases in which we separated ourselves from total fusion with a mother, we put these two split images together. We became able to feel both love and hate toward the one person without shattering our symbolic representation of her. We could hate without feeling that we were destroying, and we could love without feeling that we had to engulf her.

Earliest infancy was completely preverbal, just body states, yet I know of no way that an adult can think about the experience except by putting it into words. Hence I image our progress through the first, "oral" stage as answering a series of questions. We were acting out—feeling out—answers to questions like these: How will you separate from this dyad of mother and baby to become a distinct you? How will you replace your physical and psychological fusion to your mother with a symbolic union and boundary? How will you tolerate delay? How will you turn your massive responses of love and hate into a steadier trust? I can think of the answers to these "How's" as becoming a personal style, an identity (still invisible to any observer) but which we brought to our next stage.

In the first stage, we were primarily taking in from outside. That was our "modality." In the second we gave from inside out. We emitted cries, noises, actions, smells, body products. Of course we had been "expressing" in these ways from the beginning, but now they became a new focus for that dyadic relation between mother and child.

Further, what was large and global in the first, passive phase, we now began to make more precise in this second, active stage. In the earlier period, we feared utter annihilation. Now that dread became more precise: the loss of love, the failure of that sustaining otherness that made life and feeling possible.

These two moves, precising and making active answers out of questions that had been posed to a previously passive child, mark an infant's progress from every stage to the next stage of development. At this point in the dialogue, precising and making active marked our passage from the first, "oral" stage to the second, "nomic."

In the earlier stage, we had been receivers. Now we both received and gave. Newly precise muscles allowed us to control more and more of our bodily activities, especially evacuation. In the earlier stage, we began to rework the physical merging of mother and child into a symbolic boundary that could be created or undone. Then that doing and undoing took the form of defining what was self and what was not self. Body products posed the most perplexing issues. This stool, is it a living part of me or something dead, disgusting, to be thrown away? The sound I make—it leaves my mouth and is no longer part of me, yet am I to be held responsible for it? Transitional objects like soft blankets and teddy bears become part of the I, and yet the I knows they are also or primarily part of the "out there," the not-me.

In the earliest part of the earlier stage, we expressed love by keeping what we loved inside, either literally or (later) symbolically and imaginatively. What we resented or hated, we put outside, into the "out there" either literally or symbolically. Then we had the choice of holding on to the various things we were creating with our bodies or letting go, defining the me and the not-me by an active process—or letting them be defined as our body processes took over. The creation of trust in others in the first stage (and throughout life) acquired another dimension in this stage: the trust in self. Erikson introduces for this stage the term autonomy, self ruling, as opposed to being ruled by others or by happenstance.

The earlier development of symbols (and, of course, this too goes on all through life) acquired a new precision: symbolizing rules. Later we "had" our own rules and may even have tried to impose them on our parents. Symbolizing others, taking them in or putting them out imaginatively, acquired the meaning of accepting their rules or having one's own rules—with all the complex shadings of government that those alternatives provide. Some of these rules concerned symbols, now precised as speech. Some concerned what goes into and out of the body. Some concerned when. In the earlier stage our sense of time was a sense of delay, simply waiting and wanting. Next it became something more precise, a sense of *timing:* When is this or that appropriate? The earlier determination, "I will be me," acquired a special tone, "I will decide for myself." This is the stage of "No!" and "Not now!" At first we simply followed rules.

By active answers, we turned the earlier questions posed us by our parents and society into preciser modes. The achievement of a symbolic union and boundary that can be created and uncreated led into such questions as, Who decides? Who rules? Do I do as I wish? Do I live by their rules? Or by my own? Or can I make theirs mine and mine theirs? The chart's early question, How shall I let the outside inside? now acquired a second dimension, How shall I let the inside outside? and hence the question became, How shall I control that boundary between inside and outside? The early question, How will you become a distinct you? shaded into, What is me and what is not-me? What is animate and inanimate, living and dead? The earlier question, How will you tolerate delay? includes, When will you do it? Similarly, the earlier, How will I fuse love and hate into trust? becomes, How will I turn *their* rules, some of which I resent, into rules for myself that will be the basis for my own self-rule, self-confidence, and self-respect?

Less well known is the stage after the anal or nomic: the urethral. We can enlarge Freud's linking the control of urine to ambition by thinking in terms of a *projective* stage. What had been at first a reaching toward symbols, then a mastering of rules, now became an attempt at plans and abstractions, a projection into the future or the general. The child tried to generalize his experience into concepts and categories like animate and inanimate, big and small. The most important of these were, of course, parents and children and male and female.

To the nomic concern with establishing rules for himself the child added a projective concern: What shall I plan for myself? The sense of timing he had already acquired in connection with rules, he now applied to actions that were not governed by rules. When shall I be a parent? When shall I go out into the world?

That question of entry pervades the next, intrusive stage. What began as a boundary between inside and outside became a barrier to be penetrated in a burst of aggressive energy. Our first concern with symbols, transformed into rules and concepts, became a body language and the use of that language and speech to dominate, intrude, and explore.

Parents recognize the intrusive (or "phallic") stage as a child's bursting into noise, physical attack, constant talking, and endless curiosity—the Why? games. All were ways of pushing ourselves into the world through bodily activity.

Partly we explored our own bodies, curiosity fueled now by new sexual knowledge, for example, about the different ways boys and girls urinate. That difference became part of our sense of personal power or the lack of personal power, for throughout this period our ambitions and projections far outran our actual abilities, so we felt not only constant aspiration but also constant frustration. "Good enough" mothering in the first stage meant not letting delays become overwhelming lest we be overcome by the primal fear that suffering would only lead to more suffering and annihilation. Now "good enough" mothering meant tolerating and even enjoying our bursting activity, not creating a massive sense of frustration or the belief that "I won't ever be able to enter the world," or, "I will never be big."

As children we constantly confronted the limits of our bodies. We felt, "I can't stand these limits on me, yet I can't escape them either." What reminded us of those limits was the daunting difference between what we could do and what we imagined ourselves or our parents doing, or, perhaps, saw them doing, possibly in a sexual way. All the more intense, then, became our ambition: *I want to be big.*

The earlier fears that colored our experience, the fear of annihilation, the fear of loss of love, became transformed into the fear of losing a body part. Our interest in our own and others' bodies intensified in this period, partly because the body had become the key to being big, to entering the adult world. Any bodily deficiency could mean the end of your or my future as a member of that community of adults. It is in this context that a four year old boy or girl interprets the anatomical difference between the sexes. Do they see that difference as a difference or as a lack?

Physiology plays an obvious role here. A boy has a visible organ that gets bigger and smaller, playing out the drama that both boy and girl imagine of becoming big. A girl does not, and she may therefore see her difference as a lack. May. What she feels she has instead depends a great deal on her culture and her family. If they use femaleness as a reason for depriving women of avenues to various adult activities, then indeed a little girl is likely to feel that the difference between her and a boy is a plus for him and a zero or a minus for her. One can easily imagine cultures, however, in which a little girl would perceive her situation as different from a boy's without being inferior. One can visualize a society in which women are given equal rights with men in the workplace. One can visualize—indeed observe, as Margaret Mead did—societies in which pregnancy and birthing are women's great power, not a hospital procedure run by male doctors. One can observe societies which value mothering equally or beyond other kinds of work. One can imagine settings in which men do as much mothering as women. In such contexts a little girl may come to feel that what she has instead of a boy's penis is less visible, less touchable, but a power and a privilege, both mystery and mastery.

The intrusive stage, understood as both a phase in body development and the result of three years of parenting, asked us as children, How will you enter the world? And we answered, Through my body. I will be big.

How will you be big? Here there was a great deal of room for individual answering: big at thinking, big at spending, big and strong, big and cruel, or big at football. At the same time, biology and culture insisted that we find our ways to one of two specific ways of being big: "I will be a man." "I will be a woman." "I will have—be, really—a sex." "I will become a parent." In this context we reinterpreted earlier fears about our bodies as either preventing our taking a place in that matrix or foreclosing one place and forcing another.

"I will become a parent." That answer does not imply that the child will literally become a five-year old parent, although that may have been part of your or my imagining. We imagined ourselves in the situation of one or both of our parents. We included a child's confused idea of adult work in that imagining, and we included a child's even more confused idea of sex and the origin of the babies that define parents as parents.

In the oedipal period we had to learn an answer to the question, How will you situate yourself in a world divided into male and female, parents and children? The answer all existing societies want is, "I will have—be, really—one of the genders our society accepts." "I will be like one of my parents." We had to learn that we could not be both parents, only one. We could not have both genders.

We were supposed to identify with the parent of our own sex. That is, we were to take in as our own aspirations (at least for a start) the social values represented by that parent. At the same time, we had to learn that we could not be that parent or even be like that parent now. Our early experience and acceptance of delay became first a sense of excretory timing and planning, then a sense of time in the long, generational sense. Now it had to become something more, an acceptance of generational difference, a long, long wait indeed. The identification with one of our parents meant acceptance of some of his or her values, building them deeply and firmly into our own character for the duration of that long wait.

This oedipal stage required identification. It demanded anti-identification as well. In identifying with one parent, we accepted the other as the object of our love, and in so doing we said, "I want that parent, but I am not like that parent." A little boy says, "I want to grow up like my father. I want to have my mother or someone like her. I am not like her. I am not female." A little girl says, "I want to grow up like my mother. I want to have my father or someone like him." For her, however, the anti-identification blurs. She cannot look at her mother and say, I am not like that parent, for she is.

For a little boy, the anti-identification also blurs, but differently. He may say he is not like his mother, but in fact he had identified with her and internalized her values for the first and most formative years of his life. For him now to say, I am not like her, I will not be like her, requires a separation from aspects of himself. It is a distancing almost as drastic as that first, "oral" separation in which he began to become a separate person.

Similarly, a little girl's love for her father exists over an earlier love for her mother, a love that permeated the first and most formative years of her life. Nancy Chodorow, who has written most convincingly about these blurrings of the oedipal choice, points out that this may establish for a little girl a style of being which is more complexly interpersonal and for a little boy a "masculinity" based on distance and emotional silence. Either of these patterns might change were that first "mother" to be a male (Chodorow, 1978, pp. 130–41).

Indeed, I sense that the oedipal situation itself is changing, at least in the United States. In this question-and-answer model, the questions remain the same but the answers are less firm. In the culture of poverty or in the serial marriages now common in American society, family structures make it less and less possible to answer the question, "How will you be big?" by a strong identification either with one parent's gender or that parent's "manly" or "womanly" values. Without that strong identification with a future, a child has to make do with earlier modes of relationship, getting or taking or holding on or letting go or dominating instead of loving (or, for that matter, hating) in the full, adult sense.

In half a century of living I have seen two major changes in the psychological life of my country. One is the sexual revolution, combining sexual freedom with the loosening of marriage ties and the creation of one-parent or extended families. Whatever the virtues of the new sexual permissiveness and stimulation—and I think they are many—they make it more difficult for children to answer the oedipal question with a firm identification with one parent.

The other change is the (to me) striking rise in the "consumer society" or the "me generation," or what I would call in an older psychoanalytic jargon, "orality." The ability to receive, nurtured by long hours in front of the television set, is an important part of the new freedom and easiness in our society. It also instills a dependency and inactivity, however, which can persist into adulthood as an alternative to the foreclosed oedipal choice of a decisively adult personality.

Together these two trends mark, if not the end, the weakening of those traditional "puritan" virtues associated with the work ethic: the inhibition of desire and the postponement of gratification. Some manifestations of these "virtues," no doubt, we should be happy to see passing. Others, I fear, we will miss more and more. With our technology we depend more and more on one another, but our psyches become less and less dependable.

	ORAL	*NOMIC* (Anal)
Zones and Themes	Mouth - Skin - Eyes	Anus
	[I] can "be toward"— I can be . . .	"I will rule myself"
Emotions:		
How will you fear?	Fear of further trauma (=annihilation)	Fear of loss of love

How will you desire?	Love
	  (split) Trust (passively)
	Hate
		Possession (active)
		  Autonomy vs. shame =>
		Disgust

How will you symbolize?	Mirroring - Object
	constancy
	Passive===> active
	    Precising ===>
		Rules - others' (passive)
		  - one's own (active)

How will you wait?	Tolerating delay (passive)	Self-timing (for another) Active ===>
How will you separate inside and outside?	(Outside ===> Inside) Getting - Taking Precising ==>	(Inside ===> Outside) Holding on - Letting go Giving and Giving Up
How will you be a self?	Self-object differentiation	What is me and not-me? What is animate, what inanimate?
How will you be one person?	Total fusion	Hold on
How will you be two?	Total separation	Let go

Adult Illness	Psychosis or Borderline
	  Psychosis
		Obsessive-Compulsive
		  Neurosis

PROJECTIVE (Urethral)	INTRUSIVE (Phallic)	GENITAL (Oedipal)	
Bladder - Genitals	Genitals - Muscles	Interpersonal	
"I will plan for myself"	"I will go out into the world"	"I will be 'big' " ⟨ male / female	
Fear of being shamed	Fear of loss of body part	Fear of loss of place in gender - generations	
Ambition	Confidence	Love Jealousy Hate ⎫⎬⎭	⎧⎨⎩ Love Identifi- cation and anti-iden- tification
Abstraction - concept - plan	Body language and limits	Gender and genera- tional limits	
Self-timing (plans) Active	"Real time"	Generational future	
Inside ==⁚ Outside Projection	Inside ===> Outside Projection	Outside ===> Inside (Identification)	
Mastery (Personal power over self and world)	Identification (pre- genderal)	Identification (genderal) (male problem)	
	Anti-identification ("I am *not* that") ("I am different from that")	Genderal Anti-identifi- cation (female problem)	

Male and female physiologically differentiated ====>

Sociopathy	Hysteria	Neurosis	

12 | After Oedipus

Even during the oedipal crisis, each child makes an individual answer to the universal riddle of finding one's right place in the matrix of genders and generations. Each child arrives at a pattern of identifications and separations and loves and hates that is completely permeated with nuance and personal style. Hence it is hard to generalize about individuals' oedipal experiences. It is even harder to generalize about the still more variable experience after oedipus.

Despite the difficulties, Erik Erikson succeeded in extending the psychoanalytic idea of infantile stages into the period beyond oedipus. After what might be called the oedipal decision, the child enters on latency, a period characterized by Peter Blos as one with no *new* instinctual demands. The sudden burgeoning of sexuality that led the child and his parents to confront the questions of gender and generationing subsides. The questions and answers of the oedipal period remain stable. "He has experienced," Erikson says, "a sense of finality regarding the fact that there is no workable future within the womb of his family, and thus becomes ready to apply himself to given skills and tasks" (1963, p. 259).

Work is the key. The culture says, "This is how *we* work," and asks, "How will *you* work?" In all cultures, the children at this stage get some systematic instruction in the fundamentals of their culture's technology, its symbols, and its *ethos*. Erikson sees the child in this phase as facing outer and inner hindrances to doing adult work and trying to overcome a feeling of inferiority through a sense of successful industry.

Adolescence brings a new upsurge of hormonal change, sexual urgency, and family crisis, a recapitulation, typically, of the stages of infancy, a second chance to work out answers to the oral, nomic, intrusive, and gendering questions of infancy (Blos, 1968). The question, How will you enter the adult community? becomes immediate. The near-adult must arrive at a choice of career (a word that means road, etymologically echoing the earlier choice of Oedipus where three roads met.) Erikson has suggested that the wise society allows the adolescent to live in a moratorium, hovering between child and adult, enjoying the certain, all-encompassing answers of the young before accepting the need for the compromised wisdom of the adult. Erikson's idea suggests to me that this stage poses such questions as: Who will you be? What will you do? Whom will you love? The adolescent's task is to find for himself answers that will integrate his experience up to that point in such a way as to satisfy him and those inner and outer incarnations of the meaningful people in his life. There will be much lurching, much over-identification, much over-separation, until those whom Russell Baker calls "the big new people" find the paths or answers by which they can negotiate adult lives.

Crucial to those lives are the answers for the next stage. Erikson calls it "intimacy vs. isolation." With whom will you mate and have children—and how? At this stage, a young adult has to act out his or her answers to questions about the nature of love and sexuality, answers that build on but go beyond the body models of the intrusive or genital stages and the childish answers of penetration and grasping. Erikson speaks of the coregulation of two human beings through a sexuality of mutual orgasm so as to provide children with that same mutual regulation. Failure to find this answer leads to "isolation," a lack of intimacy that mere sexual "contact" cannot make up. In the last twenty years in America, this stage has become painfully iffy, as we have begun to accept new kinds of intimacy: "open" marriage, homosexuality, serial monogamy, or the extended family of divorce. The existence of more choices, many with more immediate appeal than long-term commitment to a not-always-satisfying other, makes it difficult to arrive at a stable social or personal intimacy.

Yet the hope of the next stage, generativity, rests on just that intimacy. It is here, Erikson suggests, that the human being becomes "the teaching and instituting as well as the learning animal" (1963, p. 266). Erikson treats this stage as the establishing and guiding of the next generation, either one's own children or young people in a working relationship, or more distantly, through work on which a later generation can rely. As a question, I would state it, "How will you conduct your life (at work and in your family) so as to extend yourself into the generation after you?"

This is, in effect, the complement to the oedipal question. There the child had to learn how to be a child. Here the adult has to learn how to be a parent in at least a metaphorical sense.

In our society, with its electronic immediacy of gratification, this stage becomes especially problematic. The question surfaces, Why reach out toward the next generation? and the answer often becomes, Why indeed? leading to escape, divorce, workaholism, the midlife crisis, and other ills that beset and isolate adults in midlife today.

Finally, the wheel of the generations turns once more, and parenthood becomes grandparenthood. Erikson visualizes this final stage as a closing of the circle in which the aging adult learns to accept the life cycle as part of a comradeship with his or her own parents and more distant times and work and cultures. As a question, I would put it, "How will you accept aging and death?" Failure to find an answer that brings one's life toward a wholeness leads to "despair." An answer that allows for a creative relation with one's forebears, one's agemates, and one's descendants constitutes "integrity." Erikson brings his eight stages to a complete cycle by defining, "Trust (the first of our ego values) . . . as 'the assured reliance on another's integrity.' " "Healthy children will not fear life if their elders have integrity enough not to fear death" (1963, pp. 268–69.

I have not tried to chart the questions that would detail the individual patterns of a life in an epigenetic plan like Erikson's. One can, however, imagine five basic themes (see the chart on pp. 244–45) persisting all through life, transformed and transforming, yet presenting the same issues again and again: fearing, loving, and hating; symbolizing; time; inside and outside; self and other. One could imagine, for example, a sense of time and timing that grows from the infant's earliest learning to tolerate delay through the various timings learned in early childhood through the oedipal imagining of oneself as a parent and as a child into the adolescent's sense of a now! that can integrate his own past as a child into his future as an adult. The next stage, the question of establishing intimacy, involves a sense of time as long-term commitment, and making that commitment into generativity involves the acceptance of the next generation, while the final stage requires us to accept, really accept, the very idea of generations.

Our first symbolic achievement was to imagine a nurturing other in her absence. Later symbolic abilities added rules, concepts, genders, and generations. The latency child learns techniques, while the adolescent acquires ideals and ideologies. Through intimacy we learn to give up the boundaries of symbols, indeed of our own egos, so that later, as parents, we can conceptualize the mind and feelings of a child again. Late in life that ability to give up one's boundaries can grow into the ability to give up self entirely.

One question that runs all through life is, How will you be separate from but united with your fellow human beings? It takes many different forms, yet they follow a cyclical pattern. The child's first great task was self-object differentiation, and we all went on to create a self who could rule a self, accepting rules from others or making rules oneself. Similarly we achieved a self who could plan for a self, who could become a self who was male or female, a child who could become a parent someday. This self takes still other forms in relation to others: the peers of latency become complicated into the adolescent's separation from parents and fusion with the peer-group. That fusion becomes the maturer intimacy of the young adult and the new version of fusion and separateness, parenting, for midlife, just as fusion and separateness took the form of being a child in early life. At the end, the acceptance of death means ultimate separation from one's fellows and fusion with—what? Dylan Thomas put it,

> . . . I must enter again the round
> Zion of the water bead
> And the synagogue of the ear of corn.

—a rich phrasing of Freud's death instinct or Lichtenstein's fusion with a stage prior to identity.

Cyclic, too, is the emotional climate in which we work out these major themes of timing, separation, inside-outside, and symbols. At the beginning, it was, How will you integrate your love and your resentment? The baby faced the problem of resolving its feelings of love and frustration so as not to split mother into an inner good and an outer bad, but rather to integrate love and hate into a total relationship. Obviously this is a task we face in different forms all through life: toward the rule-givers, toward those who ask us to project and plan, toward the sexual parents who ask that we accept our status as children and not try to be their mates or rivals. In adolescence we face the task of breaking free from our parents without rejecting them wholly, but instead integrating their inner presence with our new adult selves. Intimacy involves one more acceptance of another person who will inevitably give us both joy and frustration. How will I shape that mixture of love and occasional anger into a long-term relationship? Generativity involves the inverse of one's love and hate of parents: the love and resentment of one's own children. Ultimately there is the love and resentment of the generational process itself which, precisely by giving us birth and childhood, requires of us old age and death.

We can trace our passage through the generations by means of such essentially human questions. How do you set yourself in time? How do you symbolize? How do you relate self and other? How do you resolve conflicting feelings? These questions are posed us, however, in a particular way in a particular situation.

These situations are utterly particular, while the questions are splendidly general. Everyone who has engaged in psychoanalysis, however, knows how childhood continues into adult life. It seems to me that a full-scale biography could work out a whole life as the dialogue the individual had made from these questions that all humans are asked. Rare is the biography, though, that can trace the child in the adult or the adult in the child, for, even in psychobiography, we seldom find in public, sharable sources the data about childhood that would enable us to relate the child's answers to the answers the adult worked out in a career or marriage. Hence we have to rely almost entirely on accounts of psychoanalyses to make such connections.

We are fortunate, then, to be able to turn to a famous, perhaps the most famous case of a child in psychoanalysis. Now, moreover, we can trace the connections between a sixty-eight-year-old man and the four-year-old boy who was Freud's case of

Little Hans

It is quite literally a dialogue (1909b, 10:3–149).

In January 1908, at the age of four and three quarters, Hans developed a phobia. He became terrified of going out into the street. His father, who was one of Freud's first disciples, consulted the master, and Freud suggested that the father carry on the treatment by asking questions of his son and interpreting the answers the boy gave. Freud knew the boy and was evidently fond of him, for he had bought him a rocking-horse (fateful gift!) on his third birthday and carried it himself up four flights of steps to the parents' apartment. Only once, however, did the father take Hans to see "the Professor" for some especially powerful interpreting. From my point of view, however, Freud's and the father's careful observations and interpretations are of even more interest than the diagnosis and cure of Hans's phobia.

In 1908 the psychoanalytic theory of child development rested entirely on reconstructions from the analyses of adults. Freud had therefore urged his students (including Hans's father) to jot down their observations of their own children as a way of confirming and enlarging the theory. Hence we can read a great many details about Hans's upbringing before his phobia.

At the time Freud treated him, Hans had achieved training for both bowels and urine. Indeed, he took pleasure in showing off these accomplishments. He had developed a mastery-game in which he would go into a cupboard ("my W.C.") and take out his "widdler" (the English translators' solution for the German *wiwimacher)* and pretend, "I'm widdling."

That is, Hans had mastered one function of his penis. It makes *wiwi.* He had also found in his penis a satisfying symbol for his intrusion into the parental space (literally their bed) and the outer, adult world in general (for example, the loading dock across the street from their apartment). He had yet to learn, however, the genital function of his "widdler," namely, how he might one day use it to locate himself in a world of male and female, parents and children. Indeed, even at five, when he completed his "analysis," he had not solved that later problem.

Until the age of four Hans had slept in his parents' bedroom. They then moved to a larger apartment, and he slept in a separate room. All through his fourth year, however, he found ways of being taken into the parental bed.

At the age of three and a half, his mother had warned him that if he continued to touch his widdler, she would send for the doctor to cut it off. Hans unconcernedly responded that then he would widdle with his "bottom."

Also at the age of three and a half, Hans's baby sister Hanna was born, engendering considerable envy and resentment in the boy. Moreover, Hans happened upon the basins of blood and water in the bedroom where his mother had just given birth. Surprised, he commented, "But blood doesn't come out of *my* widdler."

Then, in January, when he was four and three-quarters, he saw a horse pulling a bus fall down. That frightened him. "That was when I got the nonsense," he said later. His "nonsense" was an unreasoning fear of going out into the street because a horse would fall down and bite him. Hans had developed, in short, a phobia.

In a question-and-answer model of development, Hans was being asked, How will you adapt the skill you have acquired in controlling your *lumf* and *wiwi* to your long-range goals so as to put yourself into the world of "big" things and people? How will you learn that the world is significantly divided into males, females, parents, and children?

Consider, then, these fragments of dialogue as variations from which to infer a theme or themes. Hans is speaking with his father ("I"):

I: "You'd like to have a little girl."
Hans: "Yes, next year I'm going to have one, and she'll be called Hanna too" (87).

[Father:] So on April 26th I asked him why he was always thinking of his children.
Hans: "Why? Because I should so like to have children; but I don't ever want it; I shouldn't like to have them" (93).

I: "Have you always imagined that Berta and Olga and the rest were your children?"
Hans: "Yes, Franzl, and Fritzl, and Paul too" (his playmates at Lainz), "and Lodi." This is an invented girl's name . . . (93).

Hans: "And really I was their Mummy."
I: "What did you do with your children?"
Hans: "I had them to sleep with me, the girls and the boys" (94).

I: "When you sat on the chamber and a lumf came, did you think to yourself you were having a baby?"
Hans (laughing): "Yes, Even at _____ Street, and here as well" (95).

Hans: "This morning I was in the W.C. with all my children.
First I did lumf and widdled, and they looked on. Then I put them on
the seat and they widdled and did lumf, and I wiped their behinds with
paper. D'you know why? Because I'd so much like to have children;
then I'd do everything for them—take them to the W.C., clean their
behinds, and do everything one does with children" (97).

In what he said, Hans showed three tactics of response to the projective,
intrusive, and genital questions he was asking and being asked. First, he
would frame hypothetical answers and act them out. Lest that seem like too
grand a way of describing the thought processes of a four-year-old, it is
worth noting that he could generalize, as from one horse to all horses or one
baby to all babies. He could also analogize from one entity to a very different
one on the basis of a common property: from a big animal to a big person to a
big widdler, for example, or from a box to a bathtub to a cart, all being
containers.

Second, he developed complexes, that is, clusters of ideas that were
consciously or, in particular, unconsciously linked. He used his cognitive
skills and his hypotheses to develop three main complexes. One was a set of
ideas about horses and the various carts and buses they pulled. Another was
a group of ideas connected with urinating and defecating and watching or
being watched while doing so. The third cluster had to do with containers
like boxes, bathtubs, the carts again, his own or his mother's belly and *lumf*
or a baby coming out.

Third, as the press of his own development and the increases in his
knowledge brought him into threatening territory, he developed defenses.
Typical for him were denial (refusing to perceive the threat) and identification. Just as he acted out his hypotheses, he would act out his defenses. He
would deny or identify in quite literal, physical terms. He would, as it were,
"do" them. Thus watching and being watched again became important, but
in another way: as doing or not doing, seeing or being seen.

If we focus on what knowledge Hans brings to the questions of the
intrusive (or phallic) phase, he has solved, as it were, one anal problem:
What is a living part of me and what is a dead part, non-me, and to be thrown
away? What is not living is what does not excrete. He now tried to translate
his solution to that problem into the imagery of the next phase, his widdler.
At age three and three quarters, Hans was at the railroad station and
watched some water being let out of an engine. He then remarked thought-
fully, " 'A dog and a horse have widdlers; a table and a chair haven't' " (9).
At this time he had actually spoken of a horse's and a lion's penis, a cow's
udder, a monkey's tail, the draining locomotive, and a doll's nongenital.
Despite this confusing evidence, Freud noted, "by a process of careful

induction he had arrived at the general proposition that every animate object, in contradistinction to inanimate ones, possesses a widdler" (11n). "The presence or absence of a widdler made it possible to differentiate between animate and inanimate objects. He assumed that all animate objects were like himself, and possessed this important bodily organ" (106).

Hans also "knew" (because he had seen) that his mother did not have a widdler. At this point, however, like the earlier time when she had threatened him with castration, this knowledge had no effect on him because it did not fit his world at this stage of development either cognitively or emotionally. Indeed, he had told his mother, "I thought you were so big you'd have a widdler like a horse" (10). As Freud puts it, "Hans had observed that large animals had widdlers that were correspondingly larger than his; he consequently suspected that the same was true of his parents, and was anxious to make sure." Hans now began asking his parents to let him see their widdlers so he might compare theirs with his (107).

In effect, he had arrived at a phallic answer to a phallic question. How shall I enter the world of the big people? By being big. By having a big widdler. But was he big enough? The world of the big people, moreover, had its dangers. Hans showed he knew them by his surprise at the bloody containers after his sister's birth: "But blood doesn't come out of *my* widdler" (10).

Hans went on hypothesizing nevertheless. Seeing his baby sister in the bath, he commented, " 'But her widdler's still quite small. When she grows up it'll get bigger all right' " (11, 14). He had continued and refined his earlier theory. There are degrees of widdlers: big beings have big widdlers; little beings have little widdlers; little beings and little widdlers grow into big ones.

Emotionally, his theorizing was accompanied by positive feelings about his penis. He frankly acknowledged the pleasure he felt when his mother touched him there. He played his mastery-game of widdling. He was also something of a show-off: "Last year when I widdled, Berta and Olga watched me." This year, however, he was (according to his father) more repressed. He would ask his father to take him behind the house to urinate so that no one should see him (20–21).

It was within this particular cognitive and emotional network that Hans developed his phobia. He became terrified of going out into the street lest a horse bite him. Freud read the primary meaning of Hans's phobia as his feeling in the street that he missed his mother from whom he did not wish to be separated and whom he wanted to caress (impossible on a street in 1905 Vienna even when she was with him). Fascinating as the ups and downs of Han's therapy are, I want to focus on just those episodes that shed some light on every boy's pattern of questions and answers.

One of those episodes (and a key to the treatment) was the answering of Hans's own questions. Freud arranged with Hans's father that he was to tell Hans certain things: that he knew Hans was very fond of his mother and that Hans wanted to be taken into her bed; that his fears had nothing, really, to do with horses; that he was afraid of horses because he had taken so much interest in their widdlers. Freud also suggested that the father tell Hans (when Hans had given him the lead, as by a question) that female beings had no widdler at all.

When Hans's father told him that neither Hanna, his mother, nor any little girls nor any women had widdlers, Hans apparently absorbed this information. Indeed, several months previously he seemed to acknowledge that Hanna's widdler was amusingly different from his own. Nevertheless, he revealed his persisting confusion by immediately asking his father, "Have you got a widdler?" The next morning he reported a dream in which he saw his Mummy's widdler. Evidently he had not (at least in fantasy) believed what his father told him (31-32). Later he completed his hypotheses: " 'And everyone has a widdler. And my widdler will get bigger as I get bigger; it's fixed in, of course' " (34). Freud took that last remark to be Hans's attempt to reassure himself against the real fear he was feeling. If there were living beings who did not possess widdlers, then his mother's castration threat of a year ago could come true. Someone "could take his own widdler away, and, as it were, make him into a woman!" (36)

That is Freud's statement, but if we think of Hans's various hypotheses about widdlers as his answers to the questions pressed on him by his culture and physiological growth, we can see why not having a widdler faced Hans with terrors that the phrase "make him into a woman" does not quite suggest. Without a widdler Hans would never be big enough to enter (break into, intrude upon) the world possessed by the grown-ups. Hans's future would have been taken away. Without a widdler, Hans could never be sure of delaying impulses, turning them into plans, and carrying them out in long-range goals, like growing up. He would be helpless, driven, impotent. Without a widdler, he could become inanimate, a dead un-self that could be flushed away like excrement—a nullity. Widdlerlessness, in Hans's intrusive, projective, or nomic fantasies, becomes total annihilation. Against such a threat, Hans mobilized a characteristic defense. He denied the possibility in physical terms: " 'It's fixed in, of course.' "

Still more questions were coming, notably the central genital (or oedipal) problem: How would Hans fit himself into a world divided into male and female and a parental generation and a children's generation? Here again, he would try to answer the cultural and biological question in the language of body and relationship he had at the time the question came up. At that point, however, horses had gotten all mixed up with widdlers and fathers and mothers and boys and girls.

The birth of Hanna combined with his own intrusive curiosity to involve Hans in another new question, Where do babies come from? For all their Freudian sophistication, his parents told him that the stork brought them! Hans wisely didn't believe them.

Hans's father realized that it was only heavy vehicles pulled by horses that frightened Hans. Hans himself interpreted the loading platform across the street from their apartment: the horses were lumfs coming out of a behind, the gates to the warehouse. In effect Hans had made an analogy between a heavily loaded wagon and a body loaded with feces (55, 68, and 127).

He went further with his anal analogy: heavily loaded wagons represented his mother's pregnancy. Hence Hanna was a lumf, and buses, furniture vans, and coal wagons were "stork-box carts," enclosures from which Hans had guessed babies could come, as well as his mother's belly (68, 81, 128, 131). There was still another link between horses and Hans's deep fears. When Hans's friend Fritzl was playing horsy, he hit his foot on a stone, fell, and bled. Hans concluded he got his "nonsense" (his phobia) because they kept on saying, " 'cos of the horse' " (*wegen dem Pferd*, echoing *Wägen*, vehicles). There were very bloody links indeed that connected falling down, bleeding, making a row with one's feet, horses, wagons, lumfs, and the birth of Hanna, all to the absence of a widdler (58–59).

Hans from the age of three and three-quarters to four had not treated these questions of gender and generations as real issues. Having no siblings of an age he could play with, he fell violently in love with any children he met at the skating-rink or on summer holidays. Once asked which of the girls he had met on his summer holiday he was fondest of, he named Fritzl, a boy. He would speak of two ten-year-olds he met as "my little girls," and he would hug a five-year-old boy cousin. He proclaimed, " 'I want Mariedl to sleep with me,' " the landlord's fourteen-year-old girl (15–16). In effect, Hans was trying to re-create parent-parent or parent-child relations at the child-child level as though distinctions between male and female or parent and child did not exist or matter—just as the early castration threat meant nothing to him at first. He would simply refer to the landlord's daughters as "my children," or proclaim, "Next year I'm going to have one [a little girl], and she'll be called Hanna too." In this connection, he even evolved a theory of parentage: " 'Boys have girls and girls have boys' "—a primitive way of responding to those two genital (or oedipal) distinctions (87).

We can regard Hans's phobia as his way of trying to use a frightening and inappropriate language of horses, carts, and even storks to deal with the cultural and biological questions of the intrusive and genital phases. How will you enter the world? How will you put yourself into gendering and generationing? By being a horse and falling down and spilling a cart. But that is a dangerous and terrifying prospect. Emotionally, Hans's answers involved his whole existence up to that time, so that a mistake would be catastrophic. It is in this framework that I read the confusing history of Hans's complexes. Hans's answer was to avoid (in the literal, physical sense of not going out of the house) those things with which he had symbolized the questions and answers of this stage of his development.

At age four, Hans had reached a phase where he was intent upon intruding into the large world of adults. Literally, he had tried to force his way into his parents' bed, but he also explored all phases of that adult world by his careful watching and listening and experimenting with bodily activities (various people's widdlings), the activities of lions, giraffes, locomotives, and activities of the horses and carts at the loading platform across the street.

In two situations involving his father, he seems to have imaged his curiosity quite physically, as a penetration of barriers. Once, he butted his head into his father's stomach, expressing his hostility. Earlier, however, he fantasied crawling through ropes marking off a forbidden place in the park. He did this *with* his father, and then both were apprehended by a policeman. Right after the visit to Freud, Hans reported another fantasy in which his father helped him penetrate barriers: "I went with you in the train, and we smashed a window and the policeman took us off with him." Hans was seeing his father intrusively, as a loving ally in penetrating barriers or as himself a barrier to be aggressively penetrated (42, 40, 41).

Hans's beginning the genital (or oedipal) phase introduced new questions that greatly intensified the problem of his ambivalence toward his father. In the pregenital stages of development, he had only to straighten out his ambivalence toward his parents one at a time. Now, in this triangular situation, he had to take into account his own rivalry with his father for his mother's affection and his own hostile rejection of Hanna and her kind of genital.

According to Freud, Hans's experience with the birth of a baby sibling was quite common. Watching his mother take care of Hanna, he revived his own feelings and memories about the pleasure he had felt as a baby when his mother took care of him. His present feelings of envy reenacted his earlier ambivalence toward his mother, and his ambivalent feelings toward the other members of his family (Hanna, his father) intensified the sense of risk he felt. It gave new and frightening importance to the knowledge that some animate beings did not have widdlers.

So far, I have treated Hans's phobia cognitively, in terms of what he did or did not know and the hypotheses he formed to deal with his inner development and his outer world. Emotionally, he was suffering in the phobic situation the dreadful terror that he would himself be wounded in the most awful way imaginable. Classical, that is, first- and second-phase psychoanalysis, introduced the idea of a continuum among the fearful fantasies of bodily harm characteristic of children in different phases of development. The phallic fear of helplessness, impotency, or castration derives from an earlier anal fear of being robbed of the body's contents, which is itself a transformation of the earliest oral fear of being eaten.

In third-phase terms, treating as central the early self-object separation and subsequent reunions, one would see these anxieties as the child's symbolizations, through his body, of fears about losing the self or the objects who love the self or whom the self loves. The earliest fear would be the total loss of either self or world (and therefore the other as well), a dread of annihilation that Hans symbolized by biting. The nomic (or anal) phase would be marked by fear of the loss of love, separation from the loved world or from the world's loving the self. A child might symbolize such a fear as the body being robbed of its contents. A child might say, there is something in me which is not me, and that is what the person I love desires. Or a child might say, I am not loved: I am to the person I love a not-human who will be thrown away in disgust. At the intrusive stage, the boy-child might fear the loss of his penis. That might symbolize a more global fear: I have lost the means whereby I can enter the big world. Oedipally, the boy might symbolize as castration the fear of losing a place in the world of parents and the world of adult gender identities (Fenichel, 1945, pp. 77, 276).

Deeper than the terrors Little Hans so painfully demonstrated lies still another affective problem. Hans's task, necessary for the first self-object differentiation, was to tolerate a mingling of love and hate for the mothering person who inevitably both gratified and frustrated his needs. Clearly, the happy, responsive four-year-old we read about had done that. Moreover, he had continued to tolerate his own ambivalence in the different idioms of subsequent stages. Nomically, he threw tantrums and stamped his feet, but he also proudly achieved an ability to follow the rules set down by his parents and his culture. So too he had learned bladder control and with it the power to turn his impulses into plans of longer range—his frequent remarks about the future he imagined for himself as a parent as well as his more immediate plans for his daily amusements.

In psychological jargon, Hans at age four was suffering from a combination of cognitive dissonance with affective overload. He was terribly loving and angry and afraid, all at once. Hans's father spoke of "the violence of his anxiety" (Freud, 1909b, 10:110). But his ideas were conflicted as well, and interestingly, Freud chose to deal directly with the ideas only.

He gave Hans "enlightenment," recognizing, of course, "It was not to be expected that he should be freed from his anxiety at a single blow by the information I gave him; but it became apparent that a possibility had now been offered him of bringing forward his unconscious productions and of unfolding his phobia" (10:41, 43). That is, Freud would help Hans's father to help Hans unravel his symbolizations and false hypotheses through free association. He would also give him new information with which he could build more realistic hypotheses about the world. It was almost as though Freud were using this very question and answer model: if Hans is stymied by the emotional and cognitive questions at the crossroads of the genital phase, let's give him answers he can use.

Accordingly, on Freud's instructions, Hans's father told him that women and girls do not have widdlers. He was (finally!) told what he already knew, that babies grow inside the mother's belly and are then pressed out like a "lumf" (87). His father also acknowledged that he knew about Hans's fantasies of replacing him in his mother's bed, and he could tolerate that (90, 92). Hans was not told, however, about the part played by fathers in begetting a child, nor was he told that someday the begetting of children would be under his control, and these omissions left him asking questions about "what things are made of (trams, machines, etc.), who makes things, etc.," questions "characterized by the fact that Hans asks them although he has already answered them himself. He only wants to make sure" (99). He also kept asking, said his father, what a father has to do with begetting his child. "On the other hand," wrote the father, "I have no direct evidence of his having, as you [Freud] suppose, overheard his parents in the act of intercourse," this although Hans had slept for the first four years of his life in his parents' bedroom! (100).

Hans marked his return to health by rewriting, as it were, an earlier fantasy. In that earlier fantasy, "I was in the bath," he had thought, "and then the plumber came and unscrewed it [my widdler, to take it away to be repaired]. Then he took a big borer and stuck it into my stomach" (65). Hans associated the bath with childbirth, with the basins with blood in them after Hanna's birth, hence with his mother's belly and all the other containers from which he imagined babies might come (69). The plumber might represent his father or, more probably, Freud, at any rate, the kind of fatherly man who could bore into a mother's stomach from which a baby will come. Later, Hans pushed a small penknife into a little doll so it would fall out between the doll's legs, acting out literally his idea of the way a baby or his penis might emerge (84).

He rewrote the earlier fantasy: "The plumber came; and first he took away my behind with a pair of pincers, and then gave me another, and then the same with my widdler" (98). Now, however, the plumber is benevolent:

he gives Hans a bigger behind and a bigger widdler. In the intrusive stage, notes Freud, "it was as though the child's wish to be bigger had been concentrated on his genitals" (107). If they would grow as a baby grows, then he would be as big as his father. Freud calls this new fantasy "triumphant" and remarks, "With it he overcame his fear of castration." In other words, it marked Hans's simultaneous recovery from his phobia and his mastery of the developmental tasks of the intrusive stage—at least to the point where he could continue to develop.

Hans's second fantasy was a more familiar one. Freud also calls it "triumphant." Hans was playing with some imaginary children he had invented, and he announced to his father that, while he had been their Mummy before, "Now I'm their Daddy." Mummy was to be their Mummy, and Hans's father was now to be their Grandaddy. His father interpreted: "So then you'd like to be as big as me, and be married to Mummy, and then you'd like her to have children." Yes, replied Hans, "and then my Grandmummy [his father's mother] will be their Grannie." In effect, Hans granted not only his own but also his father's oedipal wishes. Father *too* was to marry his mother. As Freud sums it up, "Instead of putting his father out of the way, he had granted him the same happiness that he desired himself: he made him a grandfather and married *him* to his own mother too." Hans thus demonstrates a certain maturing. He shows both the wish to be and the wish to be *like* his father, and he grants the more realistic of the two to his father: his father can be like Hans (96–97).

What this fantasy says to me is that Hans was confronting directly the developmental task of the genital phase. He was trying to situate himself in a world divided into male and female, parents and children. The birth of Hanna had forced the genital question on him by intensifying his need to find his own place in the framework of gender and generation. Now, once the phobia had subsided and therapy had set him back on his previous course of development, Hans was ready to resume his version of the universal human task of finding solutions to the questions we hear from inner and outer reality.

In this vein, he had a number of fantasies in which he developed ways to acquire his mother from his father. He "gave" his father to his grandmother, as we have seen, or bought his mother (130) or proposed teaming up with God to get mother to have a baby by him (91). As Freud commented, "For Hans they were not mere repetitions, but steps in a progressive development from timid hinting to fully conscious, undistorted perspicuity." He now knew he was male, and he had some notions about what that meant. He had yet to solve the problem of, so to speak, becoming a child, that is, accepting himself as a child who was not now a parent but would be in some far-off future.

I have been trying to represent Hans's development by imagining him as answering questions posed him by his biological sequence of development and by his culture. I have said very little about Hans's individual style of hearing or "reading" those questions or framing his answers. He was, after all, only a four-year-old boy. Had he really achieved a personal style by that age? Margaret Mahler's group concluded, "Later examinations, especially psychological tests, show that whereas . . . the phallic-oedipal phase and its resolution may substantially alter the vicissitudes of the three-year-old's basic personality. . . . The three-year-old as we knew him at that stage would shine through the subsequent layers of development" (Mahler et al., 1975, p. 200n). They suggest the establishment of something like a persisting identity theme, and I agree. I think I can discern traits in Hans and a recurring style of defense and adaptation from which I can formulate an identity theme. To be sure, Hans being translated from the German and speaking like a four-year-old, I cannot provide the precision I would ask of a like theme for Scott Fitzgerald, but I can see a theme nevertheless.

For example, when Hans identifies with his father or mother, he does so in a particular way. Like most boys in the intrusive stage, Hans had incorporated his father as an ideal and also as a danger—in his phobia, as a horse. Yet Hans himself was a horse, as when he would prance about: "I'm a young horse," or when he would play horsy and then try to bite his father (Freud, 1909b, 10:52, 58). I think it significant that Hans achieved his identification with his father through physical action. He does not say, as I might perhaps have said at that age, I want to be (like) my father because he does important mysterious work that makes him absent. Hans says, I want to be like a parent by doing what a parent does for children, feeding them, putting them to bed, taking them to the bathroom, wiping them, and even biting them. He identifies with his parents through actions. I would word that as a theme: to be (like) a parent by *doing for* children (or parents).

Hans expressed himself through literal, physical actions, like crawling into his parents' bed or making a "row" with his legs when he was put on the potty to make a *lumf* (52). I am also thinking of the cured Hans's playing all day long at loading and unloading packing cases (96) or his direct wish to sleep with Mariedl as his father sleeps with his mother (16) or his playing at being a horse (58) or, like a horse or a lamb, butting and biting his father (42).

Similarly, in the fantasies with which he resolved his neurosis, he imagined actions: the penknife birth from between the doll's legs (84) or the plumber's giving him a bigger widdler quite literally, with his pliers and his screwdriver (65, 98). Here, of course, he is not "doing for" so much as "being done for."

I think, therefore, one key term in Hans's personal style should be something like "doing" or "doing for" or "being done for" (the plumber) or "enactment" or perhaps "reenactment," since Hans is so often repeating someone else's action and so identifying himself with that person—or animal. His first curiosity about having babies took the form of imagining himself as a mother—"I'd like so much to have children; then I'd do everything for them—take them to the W.C., clean their behinds, and everything one does with children" (97). The next year, he decided to have a little girl, as his mother had had Hanna (87, 93, 94); and in general he wanted to be a mother and have babies. In effect, he was equating his own imagination with his mother's act of giving birth, almost a thumbnail description of the process of his illness in which his wishes became physically embodied in horses and carts. Finally, at the end of the case, he achieved a more usual solution to his genital or oedipal aspirations: he wanted to become his father. He "identified" with him.

In tracing the themes of someone's identity, a word like "identified" is helpful in enabling me to say how Hans is like some other boys or all other boys. If, however, I want to get at the individuality of Hans, "identified" smooths off the uniqueness. I can combine the way Hans is a type with the way he is like no other boys by imagining a feedback in which his individual identity uses a cultural and biological mechanism like identification. To do so I need at least to try to get at the unique qualities little Hans had already begun to show at ages three and four. Here, from what Hans does and says, I can infer an identity theme: "reenactment" or, more fully, *to be (like) a parent by doing for children (or parents)*.

A theme of "doing for" leads me to much else in Little Hans's life. I am thinking of such episodes as his tapping on the sidewalk and wondering if someone were buried underneath, as in the containers (69), his wish to crawl under the rope blocking off a space in the public gardens (40), his impulse to smash through a window (41), or his butting his head into his father's stomach (42), all efforts to break into or through. I remember his prancing about, saying "I'm a young horse" (58) or his making a row with his feet when he sat on the potty to make a *lumf* (54). I am thinking, too, of his dream of the two giraffes (parents) in which sitting down on top of the crumpled giraffe (mother) meant taking possession of it (39). All these episodes involve action, but more particularly all involve breaking through or just crossing boundaries, especially those between the inside and outside of Hans's or someone else's belly or behind.

These enactments and reenactments, it seems to me, also served Hans as adaptations. They enabled him to control or master things, as his game of pretending to widdle in the cupboard or play at loading and unloading packing cases demonstrated his mastery of urination and defecation. What

Hans seemed to need to master was the general problem of things coming from the inside to the outside. He was particularly troubled by the birth of Hanna, but also by widdling, *lumf,* and his own dire imaginings coming physically into the world.

At the same time, however, Hans emphasizes the literalness of these things, their actual look and sound. I am thinking of the way he enjoyed watching and being watched while urinating or defecating, or his looking at his parents' and playmates' widdlers, or the way he observed the activities on the loading platform across the street. He carefully distinguished the kinds of flushing the W.C. made, perhaps also the different sounds of male and female urinating, and certainly his mother's "coughing" during childbirth.

Much of Hans's looking and watching took the form of penetrating into forbidden places. He wheedled his way into the bathroom to watch his mother going to the toilet. He coaxed his way into the parental bed. He blundered into the room containing the bloody evidences of Hanna's birth. He used his sensing and his "doing" to "get in" or to see how others got in. Most important, he got out on the dangerous balcony of the apartment to watch the loading dock across the street, the site of his phobia. I discern a personal style in Hans's tendencies to act things out, to try to crash through barriers, to "do for," or to try to get into places.

To explore that style, I can bring these various themes together into one central identity theme by means of a kernel sentence. One can transform such a kernel into an infinite number of other sentences by substituting various specifics for its general terms, yet never lose the essential structure represented by the kernel—like an identity theme. I could state Little Hans's identity theme this way:

$$\left.\begin{array}{l}\text{getting my body into a situation}\\\text{getting something into my body}\\\text{getting something out of my body}\end{array}\right\} \text{ by} \left\{\begin{array}{l}\text{being done for}\\\text{doing for}\end{array}\right\} \text{ as} \left\{\begin{array}{l}\text{a child}\\\text{a parent}\end{array}\right.$$

That is, Hans either got his body into situations or got something into or out of his body by either being done for or by doing for others in parent-child ways.

One can substitute into a term like "parent" not only Hans's literal father and mother but parental persons, such as "the Professor," Freud, or the all-powerful plumber. Similarly, "a situation" can be transformed into any of the forbidden rooms or places Hans got into or his much larger effort to get into the family matrix of male-female and parent-child. "Getting something out of my body" could refer to doing "lumf" or getting rid of his "nonsense." "Getting something into my body" could be sitting on a dreamed giraffe or imagining a plumber attaching a new widdler or in a much larger sense taking in the affection and admiration Hans wanted from his parents.

I can read Hans's modes of identification as subtle combinations of the basic terms of his identity theme. He got something into his body when he identified with his mother (a baby) and when he identified with his father (a bigger widdler). He got his body into the dialectic of parent and child and male and female by acquiring a bigger widdler from the plumber or the Professor-doctor (being done for) or by getting his fantasies out of his body in his characteristically energetic way (reenactment).

In the same way, I can understand his "choice of symptom" as a function of his identity. Action being his way of forcing himself into the world, when that possibility became dangerous, he met the danger by inhibiting action. He feared lest something be done to him by the biting horse (father) or the loaded horse (mother). Conversely, he feared lest he do to father or mother something that would get him into a dangerous situation—and he stayed home.

Perhaps I have strayed too far. After all, any normal four-year-old boy becomes preoccupied with phallic intrusion and babies going into and out of the body and the rules about urinating and defecating. Couldn't the things I am saying about Little Hans be said about any typical boy his age? Or perhaps about any Viennese boy in 1905? Every child is like all other children, like some other children, and like no other children, and one can model this combination of individual, social, and bodily resources by a hierarchy of feedback networks. The child decides how he or she will put cultural resources to work, and they in turn give direction to the body that will actually do the work.

Little Hans faced cultural problems: a Vienna of Freud and horses. The latter he could see on summer holidays or from a Secessionist balcony facing a loading platform. He also confronted challenges all children face: establishing an identity; controlling hunger, excretion, or lust; finding a place as male or female, parent or child.

These we all face and we hear and respond to these challenges in our individual ways—as Little Hans did. He translated his problems into a spatial language of barriers to be broken through or controlled. He found that actions were his way to answer the issues his environment was posing him, where some other child might have arrived at passivity or thought or avoidance.

What is difficult to represent in this model is not this individual but generalizing at the level of many individuals. Already Hans has made clear that the individual oedipus complex varies so much that generalizations, even at this early stage, the third and fourth years of life, become unreliable. Mahler's group, for example, found that by twenty-one months, her toddlers were "changing so rapidly that they were no longer mainly phase specific" (1975, pp. 101–02).

On the other hand, if we could read back from the adult, we should be able to see these early themes in retrospect as Little Hans answers the questions of later development. We are fortunate, then, that a gifted man's generous candor allows us to look at the four-year-old boy through the sixty-eight-year-old man who was

Not So Little Hans

On February 5, 1972, *Opera News* published a memoir in which the former stage director of the Metropolitan Opera House, Herbert Graf, stated that he had been Freud's Little Hans (Graf, 1972).

Graf was the son of Max Graf, a writer, musicologist, professor of music history, and newspaper critic, who was one of Freud's first adherents. Originally, in Vienna, the career of opera director being unknown as such, young Herbert Graf had tried to become a singer, but he switched and established himself as a director, traveling here and there as he was invited to stage various productions. After directing a number of operas in Europe, he came to the United States in 1934 to escape Nazi persecution. He first made his mark here with a series of ten strikingly novel and controversial productions in the Philadelphia Orchestra Series of 1934–35. (He was told to take his work to Hollywood, where it belonged.) From 1936 to 1965, he worked with the Metropolitan Opera in New York, retiring to Switzerland. At the time of his death, he was general manager of the Grand Théâtre, the opera house of Geneva. Twice married, he had a son by his first wife and a daughter by his second. He died on April 5, 1973, five days before his seventieth birthday.

In a very broad way, one could say that the circumstances of Graf's American career posed him the question, How will you transfer your ability to produce operas from a European to an American context? This question in turn derives from his answers to earlier questions. What career will you choose? Where will you work? With whom will you share your adult life? We can imagine, then, Graf's life as a series of choices responding to the general questions that all humans face about time, intimacy, ambivalence, or work, and the particular questions that faced him as a a young Viennese Jew who had musical talent, a psychoanalytically inclined father, Nazis ruling his homeland, and a position at the conservative Metropolitan Opera. From his answers, his choices in life, I can picture patterns and I can infer an identity theme and the variations he worked out on it.

It would be delightful to infer an identity theme from Graf's operatic productions, but difficult because they might be too fugitive or collaborative to record clearly his individual choices. Nevertheless the psychohistorian Melvin Kalfus has resolutely begun interviewing Graf's coworkers and researching accounts of Graf's stagings for a promising study of "The Man Who Was Little Hans."

There is another route, however. As an adult, Herbert Graf left behind a record of many choices from which one could infer an identity theme and variations. He left the long personal memoir in *Opera News* and three books on the production of opera. For a psychoanalytic literary critic like me, such writings record thousands of words he chose, and from those choices I can represent an identity theme for a "not so little" Hans.*

As Kalfus's work recognizes, the most important choice Graf made was opera. In his memoir, he describes himself as a student in Vienna standing in line for half a day to get tickets for standing room. "Most of the time we were content to close our eyes and imagine ideal productions. . . . Even the most makeshift productions were enough to fire my imagination, and before long I began to try my hand at duplicating the wonders I'd seen in the opera house—first with a toy theater I built with my sister's help at home, and later in school productions." Graf spent one summer in Berlin, where Max Reinhardt was directing three theaters: "That Reinhardt summer was the turning point in my life. I felt it was my mission to do for opera what Reinhardt had done in the spoken theater" (1972, i, 26, 27).

Once Graf had fixed on opera for his efforts, he made his subsequent choices within the framework established by that first, basic choice. He developed a characteristic personal style, for which opera provided the medium and the limits, both giving him freedom and restricting that freedom. Having made his American reputation by his innovative Philadelphia productions, for example, he chose to exist for more than two decades under the stifling Metropolitan administration. "New productions, in the sense of new costumes and scenery, were very rare indeed" (1972, iii, 27).

As in his wish to be the Reinhardt of opera, Graf always longed for the new, and this trait lends his writings a sort of juvenile, wide-eyed enthusiasm. "I had been in New York for a short visit during the summer of 1930 and had marveled at the wonders of America," he wrote in 1951. "What could be more desirable for a young stage director who had experimented on new opera productions in prc-Hitler Europe for nine years, than this highly interesting opportunity to put his experience to work in a big city of the fabulous New World?" (p. 6). It was not all easy, of course.

During times of stress, one of the newspaper interviews reports of the Grafs, they would relax by taking out road maps and planning trips, some-

* Herbert Graf, *The Opera and Its Future in America* (New York: Norton, 1941). *Opera for the People* (Minneapolis: Univ. of Minnesota Press, 1951). *Producing Opera for America* (New York and Zurich: Atlantis, 1961). I will refer to Graf's works hereafter simply by date: (1941), (1951), and (1961). The memoir is (1972). In addition, I am grateful to Melvin Kalfus for providing me with a number of newspaper interviews and accounts of Graf's life and work.

times real, sometimes imaginary. Graf's wife, Liselotte, said he would rather go for an automobile trip than anything else except produce an opera. "Each name is a mystery to him," she said. "He begins to imagine what the town will look like. He sees the road and the scenery and the countryside. He travels there in his head in a minute."*

Perhaps it was this adventurous side of Graf that saw America as the New World, while claiming, "Opera in Europe is solidly entrenched in historic tradition" (1961, p. 70). He held a view of American opera so romantic as to border on fantasy:

> Here, in the first decades, were simple vigorous people, struggling to conquer the physical wilderness around them and achieve a measure of security and wealth. They were building their new world without the chains of old concepts and with pride in their personal freedom. In their minds, in their busy days, there was no place for the elaborate, glamorous entertainment of European kings and dukes, grand opera, which still bore traces of its aristocratic origin. They were content with their simple folk songs, in church and home.
>
> Later, when their material existence had been made secure and they could enjoy music in concert hall and theater, they listened to simple operas in English, stemming from the English ballad operas of the eighteenth century (1951, p. 12).

"The new folk opera," he wrote of the late eighteenth century, "was ultimately an enormously creative force in the development of later opera. It had new blood in its veins; it stemmed from the people. It replaced the stagnant artificiality of aristocratic Baroque opera, which was decaying. The pompousness of antique gods and heroes gave way to realistic portrayals straight from the hearts of a simple people" (1941, p. 139).

This romantic belief in a *Volk* had come with his first enthusiasm for Max Reinhardt's productions. "What impressed me most was the realistically detailed handling of the crowd scenes in such epic plays as *Julius Caesar* and Rolland's *Danton*." "As soon as I got back to Vienna I begged permission to stage the forum scene from *Julius Caesar* in the school gym, but since I paid a good deal less attention to the nuances of the big speeches than to the howling and whistling of the Roman mob, the dean soon called a halt to the whole venture" (1972, i, 27).

In the contrast Graf draws between wealthy, older aristocrats, associated with pomposity, chains, deans, and museums, and a more vital, primitive, poorer *Volk* associated with simplicity, freedom, boisterousness, and a New

---

* Elliott Arnold, "Temperament for Breakfast," *New York World-Telegram*, Nov. 24, 1939, p. 25.

World, I hear an artistic version of the struggle of the generations. As part of that struggle, Graf set out in his new world career to make young American and old European opera equal in the eyes of the world:

> In the end American opera will not be an unimaginative imitation of opera in Europe, but rather, as an integral part of American community life, it will become a new and even more exciting art form. The American opera of tomorrow will embody the dynamic, creative spirit of the American people in a cultural achievement recognized and honored not only in the United States but throughout the world (1961, p. 270).

I sense two themes in what I have so far quoted from Graf: a deep commitment to the new plus a strong wish for equality between the new and the old, but based on a firm recognition of the differences, even aggression, between them. In the signs "European," "American," "old," "new," "aristocratic," and "folk," I read more universal meanings: child and parent. That is, I hear Graf trying to answer an oedipal question, How will you deal with your resentment of the parental generation? His answer was, By developing in America an opera both European and free of European influence.

> If the past is any guide to the future, it would seem that the present situation of grand opera here makes the time nearly ripe for the development of native American opera which, combining the technique of European grand opera with a content and a style truly expressive of the American people of the present day, will become a rich and complete art form (1941, p. 270).

I hear Graf's continuing emphasis on cooperation and sharing as another continuation of this rivalrous reconciliation of young and old. He translated this theme of cooperation into a production style for the "young" opera: "The more true-to-life approach of folk opera called for natural acting, scenery, and costumes. This opera centered around a dramatic idea, of which every element now became the servant—not, as formerly, the master" (p. 143). Graf idealized this cooperative approach to production and proposed it for all opera:

> In its original form, the music drama comprised words, song, orchestral music, action, scenery, costumes, lighting, and a theater plan. It was a unique alliance of *all* arts—poetry, music, the dance, painting, sculpture, and architecture. Although each of these was a brilliant prima donna in her own right, none tried to overshadow another. Instead, they worked together as a perfect ensemble in the service of a common purpose (p. 79).

> By keeping the dramatic idea in place as the focal point, all the elements of opera (words and music) and its performance (singing, acting, dancing, scenery, costumes, make-up, lighting, and theater-building) become functional, unified means for its expression. Opera is then true "musical drama." But if the dramatic concept is abandoned, these several elements split apart as independent, self-centered star effects created by singers, dancers, conductors, stage directors, designers, and architects. Opera then becomes "grand opera" (1951, p. 21).

—a genre of which he thoroughly disapproved and had described a few paragraphs before as a "dream world." Old Europe and new America, star and crowd, parent and child, mob scene and "star effects," all are to be equal.

In Graf's efforts to tone down prima donnas, he also minimized his own role: "I've always felt that the stage director is opera's 'invisible man,' or should be. It's the very nature of his job to stay behind the scenes and leave the spotlight to the work itself" (1972, i, 25). Not only was he no genius, neither was the director he most admired:

> Look, I'm not a "brilliant" stage director in the style of a Reinhardt or a Zeffirelli, and even though I can appreciate that sort of virtuosity, it's neither part of my nature nor my aim. I'm a professor's son, an earnest worker, a know-how man who believes that certain aspects of operatic know-how can be passed along to others. People say Toscanini was a genius, but for me his ideas, his artistic insights, weren't the stuff of "genius," *that* came out in his amazing power to put his ideas across—simple, straightforward common sense, conveyed with the thrust and impact of revelation. In that sense he trained everyone who ever worked with him (1972, iv, 27–28).

It was a combination of the exalted and the common that satisfied Herbert Graf. Yet elsewhere in his memoir, he reminds us that his own "professional life runs parallel to the emergence of the director as prime mover of the production," and he speaks of "the czar producers of today," just as his own democratic encouragement of young singers like James McCracken, Reri Grist, Gwyneth Jones, or Robert Kerns created the very "stars" he warned against. Graf's theme of cooperation embodies ambivalence toward those cooperated with and those cooperated against—to the degree that they either become or began "above" the crowd. In effect, he would like to deal with the rivalry of parents and children by having us all be children playing—creating—together.

Graf conveys something of the same way of dealing with his ambivalence when he describes his father. Interestingly, he does not refer at all in the memoir to his mother. According to Freud, his parents divorced and each remarried some time after Little Hans's therapy, but Hans remained on good terms with both.

Max Graf was "an extraordinary man, the most extraordinary I've ever known" (and Graf's acquaintances included Toscanini, Furtwängler, and many other musical greats). Graf describes his father as a failed composer but a "formidable scholar" of literature and aesthetics, "equally at home in philosophy and science and quite capable of talking mathematics with Einstein, which he did." But he was also part of the crowd: "One of my most vivid boyhood memories is seeing him on the crowded footboard of a trolley headed for the Sunday soccer match at the Hohe Warte, one hand on the railing, the other clutching his most cherished book, a well-worn, annotated copy of Kant's *Critique of Pure Reason*." He was also a sexual being, "a true Viennese, in every sense: he knew how to enjoy a glass (or more) of wine and the company of pretty women" (1972, i, p. 25).

I can see these same personal themes in Graf's operatic ideology. He quite explicitly symbolizes the competing traditions of opera in family images (giving us, perhaps, a glimpse of his mother):

> Opera was a child born with a silver spoon in its mouth. Taken about to the parties of the nobility, it soon became spoiled and precocious. Its patrons used it to show off their wealth and social position. Like any spoiled child, it soon lost control of its qualities. The elements of opera became ungoverned prima donnas, each working for its own aggrandizement rather than for the sake of the whole—the music drama (1941, p. 83).

I detect in another of Graf's analogies a certain malicious pleasure in seeing this spoiled child or ungoverned woman in the New World. After 1929 in America, "opera, scion of the European aristocracy, has had to take off its top hat and go around among the great public seeking support" (1941, p. 15). More positively, because of radio, "opera has become the adopted child of the rank and file of music-lovers" (p. 16).

In order for ordinary Americans to enjoy opera, Graf wanted performances in English (despite a lot of rather snobbish opposition). "If opera is to reach the people, it will have to speak the language of the people" (1961, p. 193). Frustrated in getting the Metropolitan to do opera in English, however, Graf wrote, "My greatest professional satisfaction in the United States is associated with things I did away from the Met, with productions to bring opera to the people" (1972, iii, 29).

With the same aim, Graf devoted himself to producing opera for radio, movies, and television, even going so far as to copyright a design for a television opera theater, which would permit "an actual performance with a regular public which could be simultaneously videotaped. This would require the same 'liberated' theater, we spoke of earlier'' as contrasted to the illusionistic picture-frame stage (1972, iv, 29). Again, it was a matter of balance so as to make everybody equal:

> Opera production for television, therefore, requires sufficient knowledge and ability to strike the proper balance between operatic tradition and modern showmanship, between financial practicabilities and technical possibilities. . . . The artistic, technical, and economic problems are great, but they fade almost to nothing in comparison with the opportunity of bringing opera to bigger audiences than ever before. . . . Television can be the most decisive medium for forcing opera to take off its top hat and enter the American home (1951, p. 231).

Graf was as much concerned with "financial practicabilities and technical possibilities" as with the practical details of theater and set design or television production. He devoted whole pages of his first book, published in 1941, to the dollar sums achieved (or not) by this or that fund-raising scheme. His figures of speech also ran to the practical:

> I looked again at my blueprint of the people's opera. No, it was no impossible dream; it was the inevitable result of existing forces. There can be no further doubt about its eventual realization. The site and the tools for building the people's opera are ready; the time is ripe. Let us start production.

He used this building metaphor to conclude *Opera for the People*. He used a similar figure to end his program for *Producing Opera in America:*

> Our proposed program for opera in America lies before you. I hear some voices saying, "Dreams!" I can only reply that the real fantasy is in thinking that opera can establish itself successfully in America in any other way. It must build solidly on the foundations already in existence, and take advantage of the forces presently at work in America. These foundations and these forces are not dreams—they are the only real facts. From these foundations opera in the United States will rise and find its proper place in American cultural life.

Both the metaphors and the book titles testify to Graf's concern with practicality and realization—doing it.

Graf, however, was not an unambivalent doer. Victoria Hattam, my onetime associate at the Buffalo Center for the Psychological Study of the Arts, has written for me her own theming of Graf. She too calls him a "man of action" and points out how energetic he was throughout his career, even during periods of unemployment. At the same time, despite Graf's energy, Hattam points to the many times in the memoir that he uses words like "luck" and "good fortune." He describes all the major events in his career this way, she points out: his first directing job, his first associations with Toscanini and Bruno Walter, and his first engagement at the Met. For example, at the beginning of the interview, Graf says, "As luck would have it, my professional life runs parallel to the emergence of the director as prime mover . . ." (1972, i, 25). After the Philadelphia experiment of 1935–36, "That left me without a regular engagement for the coming year— a gap luckily filled by Walter's invitation to stage *Fidelio* in Paris" (ii, 29). His engagement at the Met: "As luck would have it, [Edward] Johnson's spring trip to Europe coincided with my own directorial wanderings. Wherever he went . . . there it was on the theater posters: 'Stage Director: Herbert Graf.' Poor Johnson, he must have thought it was a conspiracy! Finally he offered me a Met contract for the 1936–37 season" (ii, 29). "Others," suggests Hattam, "might have spoken of their efforts being finally recognized and rewarded, but these are not characteristic expressions for Graf."

In the same way, Graf externalizes his helplessness and frustration when confronted with the conservative "system" of the Metropolitan. Although there were marvelous singers, "the dismal look of their surroundings, plus lack of onstage rehearsal, . . . gave most of our performances a dusty, museum-like appearance" (1972, iii, 28–29). Yet he stayed with the Met for twenty-five years! In the interview, he describes himself as not much of a "fighter," and I have heard stories of his being tyrannized by Rudolph Bing, the director of the Met. Truly, he was "opera's 'invisible man.' " Evidently his tendency to "do" was balanced by a tendency not to do—by passivity. Hattam sums this trait up more precisely: "He sets a discontinuity between the action and the externalizing."

To act or not to act—Hattam is not the only student of Little Hans to catch this discrepancy. Melvin Kalfus, in his unpublished monograph, concludes that the boy developed, as a result of Freud's therapy, a True Self and a False Self (as theorized by Winnicott, 1960). The True Self was a "rather feminine desire for creative individuality," and the False Self was his need to identify and comply with an idealized, fantasy father. Graf's submission to Bing and other ogres, his minimizing his own talents in relation to Zefirelli and other more glamorous directors, in general, his making himself into the "invisible man" of opera—all these were his False Self. His True Self could listen to the creative unconscious and design impressive stagings, but the True Self always ran up against limits imposed by the False Self.

Perhaps because of this conflict, Graf prized a quality that would undo the gap between internal wish and external circumstances: not fighting, not anything "brilliant" or devious, but what Hattam calls "straightforward action." Graf, for example, applauded the new generation of " 'well-rounded' performers" who could act. "But the more we stress surfaces and rely on technique to make a point the more we risk losing the real expressive power opera has to offer." We can laugh at the poor acting of the older singers, but they had "clear, meaningful delivery," not just sheer beauty of voice, but "the affective power of their singing" (1972, iv, 28).

From boyhood he recalled a single phrase sung by Schmedes. It lingered "because, like Caruso, he knew how to act through the medium that was central to his artistic personality—the singing voice" (1972, iv, 28). The key value for Graf is "the ability to sing meaningfully," "personal expressiveness," the same thing he prized in Toscanini, "his amazing power to put his ideas across." "He had a direct, I might almost say primitive, grasp of what was artistically valid, rather like a peasant's shrewd awareness of what will and what won't work. . . . His insights were much closer to common sense than genius, and irresistible for that very reason" (ii, 29).

I hear Graf valuing the ability to take something from inside, a feeling, an idea, and concretize it, first through the physical voice, then through the responses of ordinary people who love opera. By contrast, Graf criticizes "surfaces" or "an operatic dream world" that is "just an exhibition" (1951, p. 20). "In all great periods of opera . . . it has had its roots in the hearts of its audience, and has crystallized their innermost, inarticulate feelings" (1941, p. 270).

I hear in the mature Graf's artistic values something like the boy Hans's need to act out his inner fantasies, giving them reality and testing them against reality: blueprints and foundations, what will work, "clear, meaningful delivery," "crystallized." I would like to be more precise, however, about the best way to read back

From Adult to Infant

When we talk about trying to portray an individual's psychological development over a lifetime, we are in the realm of psychobiography and psychohistory. Both try to reason from the child or adolescent to the adult.

For example, here is a statement about Abraham Lincoln: "Such men [great men] have an especial tendency to suffer from the loss of a beloved woman. . . . A very great mind, with an intense mental energy invested in its beloved images cannot easily, if at all, accept the loss of the most beloved image. . . ." The author goes on to say that the death of Lincoln's mother when he was nine led to an identification with the dead which can be traced in the adult Lincoln's speeches and dreams. The logic, I take it, goes something like this:

Some great men with early losses identify with the dead.
Lincoln was a great man.

Lincoln had early losses.
Lincoln identified with the dead (?).

Logically, the most that one can say is that Lincoln *may have* identified with the dead. Since one will decide that question by looking at the adult Lincoln, it is difficult to see what was gained by the psychobiographical excursion into childhood and the "Some people" generalization. Indeed, by resorting to generalization, the biographer conceals what might have been Lincoln's individual way of dealing with loss in the categorical term.

A somewhat different approach emerges in this analysis of the childhood recollections of the explorer and translator of the *Arabian Nights,* Richard Burton:

> The special interplay of these old memories, with the primitive themes of temptation, denial, smashing, poisoning, and decapitation— all having to do with his mother—are no less remarkable than the light-hearted tone of the writing, and the haste with which he dispatches a description of what may well have been the most awesome spectacle of his life [a guillotining]. . . . Sometime early in his life Burton had learned to detach himself from anxiety by assuming the role of observer.

Here the psychobiographer proceeds by generalizing a trait, a defense, really, detachment, from recollections of childhood, that can then be applied to adult actions. This is another kind of if-then procedure: If he defends by detachment as an adult, then he must have learned to do so as a child. If he defended by detachment as a child, then he will do so as an adult. But in fact we began simply by noticing that Burton wrote detachedly as an adult.

These if-then reasonings fail because the psychobiographers are trying to reason forward in time from what they do not know to what they do. Either they must be diffuse, because they have to draw on vague materials from infancy, or they will have to claim a rigor of cause and effect that, even with a patient on the couch, few psychoanalysts would assert. One can justly read Lincoln's dark sense of death or Burton's indifferent flamboyance as *consistent with* what we know of their early lives. Let cause and effect wait for that millennium when psychology will have become a "mature science." For now, the biographer committed to cause and effect will seem either impressionistic or overcertain, and for this style psychobiographers and psychohistorians have been, I think, justly censured.

Biographers almost always begin by being interested in the adult. Only later do they discover the facts or pseudo-facts of their subject's childhood. Identity theory would suggest that the psychological biographer work with, not against, this natural pattern of discovery. The adult's writings, speeches, and choices will all amply evidence a style which one can interpret as a theme and variations. Once one has inferred the adult's identity, it becomes possible to search infancy for its origins. One can then write the biography either in chronological order or in any other order that suits the themes one has inferred. Psychological if-then, cause-effect principles become ways of uniting themes rather than attempts at predicting an already known adult from a child we will (almost) never know.

Little Hans is the exception that requires that "almost." We know him better than most famous children, and the child is as intriguing as the man. We can use Hans to explore the "consistency" or the "it fits" on which the history of an I rests.

I can think of three ways to relate the man Herbert Graf to the boy Little Hans. In the first, I could connect between specific events in the adult's life and specific events in the child's. For example, I might see Graf's statement that he is or should be "opera's 'invisible man' " outside the playing space as an adult version of the boy perched on the balcony of his parents' apartment watching the carts going into and out of the loading dock across the street. I could read Graf's championing of the young American folk opera against the old aristocratic European opera as an adult version of the boy's wish to take his father's place in his mother's bed.

Obviously, however, such connections are speculative. How much more speculative I should be, then, if I were to draw them from written evidence alone (as most psycholiterary and psychohistorical biographies have to). And they are reductive. I may not want to say that Graf's campaign to Americanize opera is "no more than" a child's effort to legitimate himself into his parents' bed, but, given this approach, how can I say it is "more" than the only thing I have to compare it to? Even if Herbert Graf were associating away on the couch before me, I would hesitate to draw this kind of one-to-one conclusion.

I can do somewhat better with a second strategy. I can consider not specific actions but the adult's *traits* in relation to the child's. I might regard the adult Graf's preoccupation with the practical details of production, indeed his whole career as a director, as an extension of Little Hans's tendency to deal with his fears and fantasies by enactment. He wanted to appeal to people in general, to the various "stars" in an opera to cooperate toward a shared musical idea, and to create an American opera separate from European—I could read all those as continuations of Little Hans's generous impulses to "do for" the other children or to let his father marry his father's mother. Clearly, when I graduate from the one-to-one approach toward larger traits like "activity" or "generosity," I become both less reductive and less speculative. I am coming closer to a third, still larger way of tracing the development from Little Hans to Herbert Graf, opera director.

We can use the concept of identity to see both individual incidents and larger traits as parts of a whole person whom we can read as a theme and variations. We have considered many particulars: Graf's ideals for opera, his view of his own career, his choice of occupation, and his activities as a theater designer. We can describe these particulars over much of his adult life as variations on certain basic themes. Five occur to me.

1. Graf commits himself to the new against the old, contrasting the "dusty, museum-like," the "antique" or "stagnant artificiality," "pompousness," aristocrats, chains, and bad parents (or a spoiled child) with the young, "free," "new blood" of a "folk." He is committing himself, I think, to child over parent.

2. He perceives the world in competing pairs: old-young, rich-poor, aristocrat-peasant, Europe-America. At the same time, he wants to reconcile these pairs in an "alliance," "combining" them to become "rich and complete." His father is a "universal man" who nevertheless has the common touch. Toscanini is a genius because he has a peasant intelligence.

3. He stresses cooperation toward a "common purpose." In a production, every element is to be the servant, none the master, so as to form a "perfect ensemble." There are to be no "stars."

4. He concerns himself with practical details: roots, blueprints, foundations, buildings, to be contrasted with "surfaces," "exhibitions," dreams, or a "dream world."

5. He values in singers, conductors, directors, or himself the direct, immediate transformation of inner, inarticulate feelings into outer realities: personal expressiveness, voicing.

To read Graf's identity more fully I would want to bring these five themes together into a closer unity by means of a centering "theme of themes." I can bring themes 1-3 together under the general idea of uniting competitive groups of old and new into a common whole. Themes 4 and 5 seem to me to come together as the transformation of inner feeling to outer work. I could phrase a total identity theme for the adult Herbert Graf, then, as: *to unite competitors into a common whole by directly transforming inner feelings to outer realities.* If the theme is to be truly helpful, I should be able to unfold each of the key terms, like "competitors" or "common," into the details of Graf's behavior from which I abstracted the several themes. We should be able to see these various themes in the passages I have quoted, and we do.

Conversely, I can test such a theme by seeing how well it fits some episode that did not enter into its formulation. Graf provides one striking instance, his recall at the age of sixty-eight of a (perhaps the) key episode in his early childhood:

When I was still very young, I developed a neurotic fear of horses. Freud gave me a preliminary examination and then directed treatment with my father acting as go-between, using a kind of question-and-answer game which later became standard practice in child psychiatry. Freud documented my cure in his 1909 paper, "Analysis of the Phobia of a Five-year-old Boy," and as the first application of psychoanalytic technique to childhood neurosis the "Little Hans" case, as it's popularly known, is still a classic study in the field.

I remembered nothing of all this until years later, when I came upon the article in my father's study and recognized some of the names and places Freud had left unchanged. In a state of high excitement I called on the great doctor in his Berggasse office and presented myself as "Little Hans." Behind his desk, Freud looked like those busts of the bearded Greek philosophers I'd seen at school. He rose and embraced me warmly, saying that he could wish for no better vindication of his theories than to see the happy, healthy nineteen-year-old I had become (1972, i, 25–26).

Graf's thematic concern with outer manifestations and work shows in his attention to "names and places," to Freud's "Berggasse office," and his immediate resort to action to express his inner feelings: "In a state of high excitement I called . . ." Graf makes two other characteristic progressions in the first paragraph. He moves from "neurotic fear" to "standard practice," from inner feeling to outer work. He also moves from "very young," "preliminary examination," and "first application" to a "classic study," "popularly known," including all the age groups, Hans, his father, and "the great doctor" and "standard practice."

The second paragraph likewise develops an age-group contrast between the "high excitement" of "myself as 'Little Hans,' " and Freud, "like those busts of the bearded Greek philosophers I'd seen at school." Unconsciously, I think, Graf is putting Freud on the same side as the older, "dusty, museum-like" or "antique," operatic styles. He makes him dead. Then, as in the first paragraph, the language shifts from inner thought ("his theories") to external affirmation ("the happy, healthy nineteen-year-old"), from Freud as bearded philosopher to Freud warmly embracing.*

---

* A comparison of Freud's recollection of the interview with Graf's shows a different identity differently perceiving the same event.

One piece of information given me by Little Hans struck me as particularly remarkable [wrote Freud in his Postscript to the case]; nor do I venture to give any explanation of it. When he read his case history, he told me, the whole of it came to him as something unknown; he did not recognize himself; he could remember nothing; and it was only when he came upon the journey to Gmunden that there dawned on him a kind of glimmering recollection that it might have been he himself that it happened to (p. 148).

Freud treats Hans's reappearance in terms of information (for both Freud and Hans) which is to be explained scientifically (Freud's characteristic need to investigate and confirm reality). In

Once we have read Hans's behavior and Graf's as themes and variations, the continuities between the two become almost anticlimactically obvious. Each identity theme has two components that match the components of the other theme. Hans's doing for others or being done for by others becomes the adult Graf's need for sharing and cooperation. The adult, with a career, however, has a sense of *external* purpose while the child focuses on his body and family. Similarly, the boy's excremental and exploratory efforts to get his body into situations or to get something into or out of his body become the adult's concern with personal expressiveness, transforming inner feelings into outer work, to be sure, a work that much involved Graf in getting into and out of special spaces. We can relate discrete events such as Hans watching the cars loading and horses working from his parents' balcony and Graf's being the "invisible" director outside the acting space, not just in some simple one-to-one way but within the context of a total identity represented by such themes as the transformation of inner feelings into outer work.

It is tempting to see in Graf's statement that Freud "directed treatment" (specifically questions and answers between father and son) the prototype of Graf's later choice of a career as a similarly behind-the-scenes, "invisible" director of actors in dialogue. I would be making an incident-to-incident, reductive speculation, however. We do better to keep in mind the whole man, theme as well as variations. We would remember his tendency to make himself over into the great figures of his childhood, like his father or Reinhardt. We would remember his wanting to be an actor and the way a director also has to follow a double script as he acts out the actor acting the part, and we might agree, Yes, in his own way, Graf did model himself after Freud.

With a concept of identity it becomes possible to rethink specific elements of childhood in the light of the adult life, as one would do in an actual psychoanalysis. For example, after the trauma of his sister's birth, Hans was suddenly taken ill with a sore throat (10:10–11). He had interpreted the birth (partly) by his mother's coughing. One can understand his sore throat, then, through the identity themes as his "unit[ing] competitors" (identifying himself and his mother—adult theme) or "getting his body into a situation" in which he does as a parent does (child theme). His subsequent tonsillec-

---

the same way, responding to criticisms of analysis being applied to a child, Freud wrote, "But none of these apprehensions had come true. Little Hans was now a strapping youth of nineteen," shifting from fancies to facts, from the fears of others to the evidence. Freud's testing is a different move from Graf's expressive one: from Freud's ideas to Freud's work. Freud speaks of Hans's "glimmering recollection" that "dawned on him," resorting, again characteristically, to an explanation by means of a decisive moment (as in his theories of traumatic repressions, the boy's crucial sight of female genitals, and the primal murder of the father).

tomy gives the enactment (or variation on the theme) yet more meaning: he will have major treatment for his cough just as his mother did.

Reading from adult to infant through identity thus leads to a theme not touched in the original interpretations, Hans's identification with his mother through his own actions (as by making a row with his feet or having a "lumf" baby). The identity-governing-feedback model leads to a theory of Herbert Graf with which I can relate the experience of Little Hans's childhood to the achievements of Herbert Graf, opera director. I can even read back from the adult to surmise how the boy might have felt about experiences of which we know very little. An imitation of his mother must have had an importance for this future actor that it might not have had for another little boy. Conversely, creating and controlling young "stars" must have had a special value for a man who, as a boy, fantasied so much about giving birth and "doing for" children.

Life posed Little Hans/Herbert Graf questions, and he built a life by answering them. The history of his answering is the classical psychoanalytic form of explanation, a narrative or (to retitle a famous movie)

The Story of I

The I provides a theory for that story, something that will transform it from one kind of meaning (case history, autobiographical justification, or prescription for producing opera) to another: the arc of a life.

We can refine that meaning still further by bringing to bear the concept of identity governing a relatively fixed feedback. That is, Little Hans, "agent," grew and acted on his environment. His environment, in turn, his culture, family, and biology, posed Little Hans certain questions much like the questions they posed other little boys living in Vienna in 1905. To them he evolved answers, and he became, in effect, the sum or the style of those answers. In that sense, he was not only the agent triggering these feedbacks but also their consequence. Finally, you and I, by reading and interpreting Graf, have created a narrative and a theory of his life. In that sense we have "represented" him as a biographer or historian might.

Thus, the concept of identity (as agency, consequence, and representation) governing cultural and physiological feedbacks offers help for psychobiography, which is so often stymied in its effort to derive the eminent adult from the skimpy anecdotes of a half-remembered, half-invented childhood. You could not read ahead from four-year-old Hans's phobia to the adult's career as a director of opera, creating emotionally loaded spaces. No causality would hold. Using identity theory, however, you can analyze the adult's style in great detail, arriving at a theme and variations model of his I. With it, you could read even a quite limited history of infancy so as to phrase a continuity between child and adult.

Similarly, the literary critic can trace the hand of a Shakespeare (about whose personality we know next to nothing) from play to play. Each play offers his answers to the aesthetic problems posed by that plot, that audience, that cast, or that theater. The answers are the variations on the I that runs through all his plays. If we knew more about his personality or his childhood, as we know more about, say, Fitzgerald's, we could relate the works to the life in a new and to me far more convincing way than trying to relate trait to trait or childhood episode to an episode in a play by the adult.

In effect, the question and answer model of a life opens up the potential space between the individual and the historical reality he inhabited. Graf described his analysis as "a kind of question-and-answer game." Winnicott's squiggle game with Iiro offered a visual image of that process. The doctor drew a line that posed a question to the boy. The boy drew answers with a line that was both an answer to the question posed by the doctor's squiggle and an expression of his unique situation and identity. Even earlier, we began this book in the potential space between Freud and a young man on a park bench who was trying to express his frustration at being Jewish in an anti-Semitic society. In effect, his society was saying to him, "We are blocking you—what are you going to do about it?" His answer was, "I will—I won't—have descendants who will avenge me," and he tried to put this into the free space between himself and Freud. His answer expressed his unique situation and identity, this time willy-nilly.

Herbert Graf, like Iiro or the young man on the park bench, demonstrates how we can understand the little and the big events of a life as constituting a dialogue between questions posed by the historical reality and answers arrived at by a unique I. The questions are sometimes universal. Every human being has to answer the question that was so important for the boy Hans and the director Graf: How will you relate what is inside you to the physical reality outside you? Other questions are common, but not universal: How will you adapt your European values to the America to which you have had to flee? Others are wholly individual: How will an innovative director like you cope with the conservative system of the Metropolitan?

By contrast the answers, even when they seem universal, are all highly individual. Hans decided like most boys to grow up by identifying with his father. In deciding what to identify with, he singled out his father's directness, his common touch, his boyishness—which perhaps no one but Hans would have seen. In part Hans *created* the father he was going to identify with because even at the age of four he was the kind of person he was.

A life is "a kind of question-and-answer game" between an environment of questions that all or many people face and an I who arrives at individual answers. A psychology can include both the uniqueness of Herbert Graf and the universality of the oedipus complex Little Hans faced by imagining a human being in two modes. One is a unique, theme-and-variations identity that sets standards for the second mode: a hierarchy of feedbacks representing the culture we have internalized and the physiology we have been given as a sequence of questions. Identity is then three things: the agent that evokes the questions, the cumulating consequence of the answers, and the narrative by which an I can represent that cumulation.

I find this holistic model strong and useful, but I—this I—feel (characteristically) that it needs buttressing from another direction. Is it scientific? Classically, we have asked of a science that it deliver universals the way theories of gravity or evolution or quantum mechanics do. We have asked that a theory make statements about the one, the many, and the all with equal rigor. Can this psychology of the I do that?

Part IV | A Science of I

13 | Science and I

We are coming to conclusions. I need, therefore, to state, for you but for myself as well, what I have said and why I am asking you to believe it.

I have tried to "the" an "I." I am trying to make it possible to talk rigorously, even, in a sense, impersonally, about the inner, experiencing being whom you or I call "I." To do so I am suggesting a threefold concept of identity. I ARC. "I" is an agency, a representation, and a consequence.

As an agency, the I tries out on the world the guesses, hypotheses, strategies, or behaviors by which we create perceptions that we find satisfying. As a consequence, the I is what results when those hypotheses and strategies and behaviors feed back as perceptions onto—into—the self. The I as consequence is the sum or history of all that has happened to the I, everything the I as agent has shaped into a coherent self in response to the "feel" of those feedings back.

That coherent self is also, however, somebody's representation of a somebody. An I is not just something "there," inside us, which our descriptions come more or less close to. We do not "have" identities. Rather, identity is the way somebody represents an I, usually in words. Identity as I propose it is a relational term. Identity is between people, and because identity consists of words between people, identity presupposes a cultural realm of shared ideas and shared ways to represent them—language.

Specifically, by thinking of identity as a theme and variations (and the history of that theme and variations), we acquire a way to represent in words the wholeness and historicity of a person. A theme and variations can represent the dialectic of sameness and difference, the mingling of continuity and discontinuity, the dialogue of change and constancy which is a human life.

If we combine Heinz Lichtenstein's idea of identity as a theme and variations with identity as the agency and consequence of feedbacks, we can picture our minds as a chain of higher and lower networks, each lower loop answering to the standards of a higher, with a theme and variations identity setting levels throughout the whole network. With such a picture, we can interrelate either the small details of a life, one analytic hour during Freud's treatment of the Rat Man, for example, or cataclysmic changes, like the brainwashing of Dr. Vincent or Anna S.'s breaking out of her painful cycles of drunkenness and prostitution. We can picture how we share symbols with other humans, yet each use those symbols with a personal style. We can understand how we are able to perceive the world in ways common to other people who live in our culture or who have the same biological equipment as we, yet also show a distinctly personal style in our perceptions.

We can propose an answer to the ancient problem of the one and the many: How can one human individual, single and unique, come out of experiences all or many humans have? Why does each of us use our common human experience of being born, mothered, fed, cleaned, clothed, loved, frustrated, punished, challenged, and limited to become an individual with a unique history? Because we style what happens to us. Each of us shapes the experiences we share with other humans through an identity theme, its variations, and its unique history. Hence each of us experiences these events in our own personal way.

With this theme and variations concept of identity, we can add to Freud's monumental discovery of infantile stages like orality the dialectic by which they lead not only to human types but to human uniqueness. We can trace that dialectic throughout the individual's history from infancy to old age, the whole trajectory of a human life.

Experimental psychologists, however, will question the kind of explanation I am offering. To be sure, one can use identity to account for an astonishing range of human experiences, but are the explanations scientific? Or is all this no better than astrology? And does that matter? some humanists would reply. Since all ways of construing the world are fictions—human inventions—isn't one fiction as good as another?

No. I do not believe that all fictions are equal, and it does matter to me what claim I can make on you to believe what I have written. It matters terribly to me. Behind *The I* there is a real I, no fiction he, and his needs for certainty and consistency and confirmation are fierce indeed. This theory of I is very much a function of

This I

I am a student of literature. If I want to analyze the I who is writing *The I,* I turn to his books, as I did with Scott Fitzgerald and Herbert Graf. I think I could arrive at a fairly clear picture, although I hesitate at this point to inflict any more of this I's prose on you. Here is a paragraph from early in *The I* (quoted from my journal of 1951):

> I am glad to have kept this book, even as sketchily as I have. Someday I shall look back, and when I do I daresay the then-I will wonder what the now-I was like, just as the now-I wonders about the then-I. . . .

The passage proceeds by means of two sharply divided pairs, the now-I and the then-I, the then-I looking back to the past and the now-I looking forward into the future. At the same time, the prose doubles back on itself, as if to say, these seem different, but they aren't. The writer wants something that will resolve the dichotomy, an I or an end to wondering that will make the seeming two really one. The two mysteries he probes are time and the self, and the tactic that may provide an answer is *looking* at "this book."

I wrote my first published book out of my excitement at the then critical mode of looking "objectively" at texts not for some other reality they supposedly recorded but simply as words-on-the-page with a unity. In *The First Modern Comedies* (1959), I analyzed eleven plays of the late seventeenth century, using the close reading that was yielding so many rich interpretations of literature in the late fifties. I developed a unity for each play by showing how its several plots, characters, and figures of speech could be made mutually significant around a central theme (in much the same way that I have "made sense" of the Rat Man, Dr. Vincent, or Scott Fitzgerald in this book). I went on to put these themes themselves into a still larger unity and claim that Restoration comedy in general dealt with one basic theme, the tension between social surfaces and inner nature and the mastering of that tension—another dichotomy, between inside and outside. I thought I had discovered a truth.

Shortly thereafter, I began a television series teaching Shakespeare in the same straightforward, words-on-the-page, unpsychological way as, in an earlier series, I had analyzed current movies. I was continuing to focus objectively on surfaces and appearances, as I had with Restoration comedy. I was treating Shakespeare as a surface, as simply the words on the page, a verbal artifact to be analyzed as one would analyze a painting or a piece of music, or as a film makes people and things into a surface on a screen. I was interpreting the plays in what I thought was a rigorous, quasi-scientific way, arriving at *the* meaning from a surface that was undeniably *there*.

In the series and the book it gave rise to, *The Shakespearean Imagination* (1964), I prized "objective" and scientific truths, the safe ones, and I contemned what I perceived as fuzzy terms, vague boundaries, or unverifiable intuitions and values. I wanted either to see just a clear, daylit surface that we could all agree on or to make all of whatever I was observing into such a surface (as, in a strange, almost deconstructive way, by this very act of self-exhibition, I am still trying to do). I had a powerful curiosity about the self as it related to literature but an equally strong inhibition against entangling myself with that self. Hence, I engaged in paradoxes, like confining myself to the analysis of literature as a verbal surface but searching the depths by using psychoanalysis to study literature.

I had always been interested in laughter, perhaps because it, too, is something undeniably there, a reassuring translation of something deeper and perhaps more dangerous to a behavioral surface. In writing and teaching about comedy, I had read many of the hundreds of theories of why we laugh. Of them all, only Freud's, I felt, encouraged me to look in detail at the surface text of a joke, which I, thriving on the critical methods of the 50s and 60s, thought the only valid procedure. I began to wonder whether I could adapt Freud's theory of amusement to make a general theory for all of literary response. The more psychoanalysis I read, the more wondering became belief. One could, I was sure, understand—master, really—our responses to literature by a psychoanalytic analysis of the text one was responding to.

In 1966 I published *Psychoanalysis and Shakespeare*. Mostly the book continued my study of texts as objective, isolable words-on-the-page, but the last chapter dug under the firm boundaries with which critics of those days marked off author from text from reader. Rather, I urged, the literary transaction forms a continuum. Characters become real because we endow them with our own psychic reality. Readers give literary events a part of the readers' own psychic functioning. Hence the critic needs to accept his own role in the literary experience he creates, and for "the" critic, read "I"—this I.

Partly *The Dynamics of Literary Response* (1968) treated texts as the words-on-the-page with built-in conscious and unconscious meanings to be discovered. Partly the book acknowledged that the reader—this I—contributes to the experience of the text. We put something of ourselves into the "out there" of *Romeo and Juliet*. Yet I grounded my argument on the "scientific" Heider-Simmel experiment, which showed that people interpret all kinds of experiences, even those of little triangles, as acts of human beings. I was still on the side of a self that could be seen, proven, made certain and scientific, and so mastered.

When I began to test the theories of *Dynamics* with actual readers, I found that these real, live readers edited what they read as much as any Maxwell Perkins. They interpreted, remembered, and even perceived according to their own lights. I became more and more convinced intellectually that the personal style in which we transact literature is also a style that permeates every aspect of our being. *Poems in Persons* (1973), *5 Readers Reading* (1975), and *Laughing* (1982) all rest on the careful observation and interpretation of actual readers or laughers. All deal with surface behaviors: words-on-the-page or at least on the tape. All begin with at least an aspiration to the "scientific." Yet all led to the same conclusion: that we transact the world by means of our identities, that therefore interpretation, either of books or people, indeed the very isolating of words-on-the-page, is a function of somebody's identity. Certainty led to uncertainty.

Here are some concluding paragraphs from the last of these books before *The I:*

Laughing involves its theorists in their whole philosophy or in my case (yes, "case") my whole psychology. And I use *that* word too in a double sense: the psychology of me and the psychology I believe in. How, according to identity theory, could it be otherwise? In explaining, we slowly and strugglingly re-create our identities.

In laughing, we suddenly and playfully re-create our identities. "Slowly," "strugglingly," "suddenly," "playfully," and "identities" themselves, however, are functions of our identity, and our identity in turn is a function of the identity of the person (even a moment of ourselves) construing that identity.

Identity, then, offers but one small step in a dialectical understanding of many laughings. Nevertheless, I "know"—or at least I think I know— more than I did when I began my long inquiry into laughing twenty-five years ago.

Lo and behold, we have come back to the style of that early journal. Again we can find the dichotomies, from the double sense of "case" to the contrast of "know" with "think I know." We can find the same doubling back, the play on "case," the balancing off of "slowly and strugglingly" against "suddenly and playfully," and the return (as in the "now-I" and the "then-I" and this very sentence) to the self of long ago. We can find now an explanation (identity) that resolves the dichotomies in an overriding unity, but seeing and understanding and knowing certainties remain paramount values. We can find the same wonderment at the passage of time ("twenty-five years ago," "a moment of ourselves"), and it too is rendered in a dichotomy.

My I of 1984 can read continuities between my I of 1951 and my I in 1982. I still think the careful observation and analysis of verbal surfaces is the best way to understand the personal depths. I still use that divided way of thinking about the world, surface and depth, although the very identity theory I advocate renders it obsolete.

That is, identity theory says we take in the other—literature, people, society, politics, culture, even our own genders and selves—through our identities, which are themselves representations. That is the thesis of this book, and I believe it is true. Emotionally, however, I find that a very hard position to hold. I still want a firm and reassuring division between the I and what the I looks at, what I once would have called reality and now would call otherness. My prose sometimes, even with editing, lapses into that older mode of an I definitively and dichotomously different from a not-I.

I find identity theory emotionally hard to believe because of these paradoxes. That which is most our own to have or to be, our essential wholeness, is not our own, because the minute we review that wholeness, either we must divide ourselves into an observing self and a self observed and so cease being whole, or our supposed wholeness is something someone else must provide us.

No philosopher, I cannot resolve these paradoxes. I find them deconstructive, provocative, hard to take, but intellectually necessary. Hence, when I use these ideas of identity and knowledge and development and objectivity, they give me control and mastery but they also control me. That is, I feel helpless as I try to work with the between-ness of a self I once thought autonomous. I feel weakened by intrinsic limitations to science and human knowledge. I feel split if one me is really two, a self I feel immediately and a represented self. I can almost taste my need for a more traditional kind of certainty.

Identity, however, calls into question the basic polarities around which we have up to now defined certainty and the "scientific": self and other, "in here" and "out there," the invented and the discovered. These are the very polarities I characteristically favor as a base for making a reassuring sense of the human transactions around me. Identity says that we each transcend those seeming opposites, however, even when we are doing science. Identity throws everything into between-ness, leaving us no mooring outside or beyond the sea of human relations. Identity offers only itself as the ultimate reality, the kind of thing a self, a *cogito,* was, but identity is, precisely, relationship and therefore requires other realities for it to be between.

Hence, I think this theory of "the I" has shifted the usual debate. No longer is it enough to ask, Is psychoanalysis "scientific"? Is identity "scientific"? And then I would parry with, What do you mean by "scientific"? The question has become, Is physics "scientific"? Is biology? Is anything? If minds construe the world in individual ways, if this is the way it is and nothing is going to change that personal style of perception, then what do we mean by

"Scientific"?

As a non- or ex- or semiscientist, I carry around in my head a notion of science as rigorously confirmed, numerically exact, predictive, "objective," and unblemished by the jealousies, ambitions, and institutional politics that afflict less disciplined occupations. I suspect that most nonscientists share this idealistic picture. Scientists themselves, however, have no such illusions.

Theirs is a world of Murphy's Law and the Fudge Factor. They are willing to race ahead of the evidence and the rules drawn up by philosophical or psychological bystanders. They have to be—if we are to have discoveries. Nor do scientists accept or reject ideas for purely, "objectively" rational reasons. As Max Planck lamented, "A new scientific truth does not triumph by convincing its opponents and making them see the light, but rather because its opponents eventually die, and a new generation grows up that is familiar with it" (1949, pp. 33–34). A reading of *The Double Helix* will quickly dispel the illusion that scientists live by impersonal rigor, as will the occasional scandal of forged and fraudulent results among medical researchers.

Psychologists and others who rattle off criteria for something's being "scientific" often speak of prediction as a necessary condition for science. That may be true for the statics and dynamics customarily studied in freshman physics, eighteenth-century science, really. Prediction does not come about as easily in more modern fields, such as quantum physics, fluid mechanics, strength of materials, or, most notably, twentieth-century biology. In general, says the Nobel-winning biologist Jacques Monod, "The biosphere does not contain a predictable class of objects or of events but constitutes a particular occurrence, compatible indeed with first principles, but not *deducible* from those principles and therefore essentially unpredictable" (1970, p. 43).

The world of living organisms is unpredictable because the base from which we understand it, evolution, is unpredictable. Natural selection involves two intrinsically random and unpredictable processes: mutation and survival. Indeed, much of the scientific (as contrasted to religious) resistance to Darwin's theory in the nineteenth century came from the demand that a theory, to be scientific, yield predictable results. Much of twentieth-century biology, of course, like much of our physics, deals with the random and the probabilistic, making prediction impossible (Mayr, 1978, pp. 48–51).

As a layperson, I tend to think of scientists as proudly possessing a broad consensus about "the way things really are." Here again, this is not a view shared by scientists. Another Nobel laureate, Percy Bridgman, remarks, "I believe that in society as at present constituted the possibility of consensus, except with respect to the simplest situations and as a first approximation, is a mirage. There is no such thing as true consensus, and any ostensible reality supposed to be revealed by the consensus does not exist" (1959, p. 246).

I have to rely on quotations like that from Bridgman's book because I am not a scientist and I do not know how things look and feel from inside, so to speak, the society of science. Obviously, however, I do not mean to suggest by these quotations that science has lost its awesome coherence, only that what we of the laity tend uncritically to believe about science is not what scientists themselves believe. In particular, the real world of working scientists is not governed by a few simple rules that can be easily set down.

Jacques Lacan, who in this respect is as laic as I, writes, "Science is an ideology of the suppression of the subject" (1970, p. 89). Again, this idea is something that we laypeople carry around in our heads. Scientists themselves know that science rests on several personal, "subjective" elements. Science to scientists is simply not an "impersonal" or "objective" activity.

Mathematician Jacob Bronowski develops this human element in science by drawing on the psychology of perception: "We are not able even to receive visual impressions except by a process of indirect inference. Inferences are, therefore, at the root of all our mental processes, even those exercised directly through the senses" (1967, p. 22). Brain physiologist Ragnar Granit warns, "We must not underestimate what the interpreting brain itself adds to make the seen world more intelligible" (1977, p. 128). And philosopher Stanislav Andreski spells out the necessity of personal perceptions to the scientist still more bluntly:

> If you ask a physicist to tell you how he tested a hypothesis he will say: 'I did this, I did that; I saw this and that. . . . If you disbelieve him and he invites you to take part in experimenting you will say: 'Ah, now I see . . . this moves here and that moves there . . . now I see such a colour or line or what have you.' Thus you cannot give an account of the evidential foundations of physics without hearing and uttering 'I.' And what kind of meaning can you attach to this word without . . . introspection; and without postulating the existence of other minds within which processes are taking place which are similar to those which you alone can observe?

In other words, you cannot express physics in the language of physics alone because its theories rest on the evidence of the senses. Scientific research takes place within the frame of human perception, dependent on an I (1972, pp. 21–22) and also on a theory of the I.

Just as important as perception are our processes of belief and especially commitment to our beliefs. Scientific laws are made as much as they are discovered, because laws rest on human beliefs and human self-knowledge. Bronowski develops the position this way:

> If I write a paper and it goes to China and Czechoslovakia and South America and Los Angeles everybody in all these places who reads it believes that I am telling the truth as I see it. Nobody assumes that what I am saying is true. It is not given to us to know what is true in that sense. But everybody knows that I write the scientific paper on an implicit, unwritten understanding among scientists that it can be absolutely believed to be what I believe.

It is from this trust between persons that science proceeds, and science has been so successful only "because it is based on perfect trust in the truth of statements." "You cannot take the simplest statement in science without having to believe a lot of people." Hence, the constant increase of knowl-

edge in science rests on an *ethical* base (1967, pp. 125, 131, 130, 129).
The biologist Monod makes the same point:

> In an objective system . . . any mingling of knowledge with values is
> unlawful, *forbidden*. But [the] . . . "first commandment" which en-
> sures the foundation of objective knowledge, is not itself objective. It
> cannot be objective: it is an ethical guideline, a rule for conduct. True
> knowledge is ignorant of values, but it cannot be grounded elsewhere
> than upon a value judgment . . . (1970, p. 176).

In other words, the "is" of science rests on the "ought" of scien*tists*.

The ethical imperative "Report only what you believe to be true" is itself
absolute, but it can by no means be as clear-cut as the actual observations the
chemist or the biologist makes. Do you report the room temperature and the
barometric pressure (as we were required to do when I was an undergradu-
ate in chemistry lab), the color of the paint on the wall, the Dow Jones Index
for that day, or the biorhythm readings for the experimenter? It is simply not
possible to report *everything* about an experiment. One has to select, and
what one selects depends upon various prejudgments. What we believe
relevant enough to be reported and even what we believe to be true inevitably depend on our own values. Even more important, what we believe to be
true depends on what we understand to be our beliefs. The report of
scientific observations depends on self-knowledge and introspection.

Depending on introspection, however, does not mean that scientific
observations are "merely" subjective. We need to be able to distinguish my
observation of clock time from my belief in disarmament or my love for my
wife. They are all "subjective" but differently so. How?

The biologist-philosopher Michael Polanyi begins "by rejecting the ideal
of scientific detachment. In the exact sciences, this false ideal is perhaps
harmless, for it is in fact disregarded there by scientists. But . . . it exercises
a destructive influence in biology, psychology and sociology, and falsifies
our whole outlook far beyond the domain of science" (1958, p. vii).

Science, says Polanyi (like Bronowski and Monod), rests on commitment.
So, probably, does all knowledge. Polanyi speaks of "the *personal participation* of the knower in all acts of understanding." "Into every act of knowing
there enters a passionate contribution of the person knowing what is being
known, and . . . this coefficient is no mere imperfection but a vital component of his knowledge" (pp. vii–viii). He titles his book *Personal Knowledge*.

This personal, passionate contribution does not, however, make our
understanding, scientific or otherwise, subjective. It does just the opposite.
It distinguishes what is only subjective from what is truly knowledge. It is
precisely the act of commitment "that saves personal knowledge from being

merely subjective." When I commit myself to a belief or a fact, I do so because I responsibly submit to "the compelling claims of what in good conscience I conceive to be true." Thus, personal commitment is an act of hope and a striving to fulfill an obligation that goes beyond the personal, that indeed has a "universal intent" (p. 65). Such comprehension is not therefore simply subjective. It is "neither an arbitrary act nor a passive experience, but a responsible act claiming universal validity" (pp. vii–viii).

Consider two beliefs, one that astrology is true, the other that everybody goes through a "nomic" phase in childhood. You cannot separate the supposed truth of astrology from the personal, passionate commitment that says it is a truth. If you do not share that commitment, the belief in question will simply seem "subjective" (or, worse, delusional or faked). I believe, however, that you and I went through a nomic stage. Therefore I am puzzled when I meet people who do not share my belief, because when I say that everyone goes through a nomic stage, I also and inevitably am saying my belief that any sensible person, given the evidence I have seen, should come to the same conclusion.

Conversely, it is not possible to believe that some claim about the world is true and think that believing it is true is merely subjective. You can't believe in the truth of astrology or of a nomic phase and not be committed to that belief, because you can't be both committed and not committed at the same time—so runs Polanyi's argument. "Subjective," then, refers to an uncommitted contemplation of somebody else's "personal," that is, committed, believing knowledge (pp. 303–06). Or, as the bishop of Gloucester said, "Orthodoxy is my doxy—heterodoxy is another man's doxy." Hence we observe the politics of science and the painful truth of Planck's complaint that new ideas establish themselves not by virtue of their correctness but by the demise of their opponents.

The philosopher of science Nicholas Rescher offers yet another perspective on this relation between our minds and what we think lawful in a scientific sense. We make, he points out, a distinction between *accidental* and *lawful* generalizations. Consider these:

1. All the oak trees on my street are dying.
2. All the oak trees on my street are deciduous.
3. All oak trees are deciduous.

All three are generalizations. All three are factual. That is, they generalize about the world as it is. The phrase "on my street," however, limits the first two to generalization about the world as it is. The third goes further, making a claim about the world as it *must* be. The first two are accidental generalizations, the third is not limited that way.

We will accept the third generalization as an explanation in ways that we will not accept the first two. Rescher suggests that the difference comes from the lawfulness of "All oak trees are deciduous," and he isolates, as the key to that lawfulness, the sense of necessity, of must-ness. A law goes beyond simply saying, "All Xs are Y." It claims "All Xs *must be* Y." All oak trees *must be* deciduous. If you ask me, "Why is that oak tree shedding its leaves?" and I answer, "Because all oak trees are deciduous," that is a "scientific" explanation. But, Rescher points out, if I answer, "Because it is on my street and all the oak trees on my street are deciduous," I sound a bit confused. "Because it is on my street and all the oak trees on my street are dying" seems even weaker. We will accept generalization 3 as an explanation, but not 1 or 2.

In distinguishing kinds of generalization, Rescher illuminates one of the difficulties experimental psychologists have in being "scientific." Psychological experiments often depend on a particular questionnaire or a particular group of people being tested. As someone has said, experimental psychology is the scientific study of the college sophomore. Because the conclusions from psychological experiments are so closely tied to the methods and conditions of the particular experiment, results look more like type 1 or 2 generalizations than type 3.

Rescher points to another property of lawfulness. A law describes not only the world as it is and as it must be, but the world as it might be. "If all Xs are Y, then if Z (which is not an X) were an X, it would be Y." "If this pine were an oak tree, then it would be deciduous." "If there were a Santa Claus and if he were in orbit round the equator, he would obey the laws of planetary motion." That is why, says Rescher, laws are laws, because they apply not only to Mars or Venus but to Santa Claus also, even though he does not exist—indeed especially since he does not exist.

We do not extend ordinary generalizations to "contrafactuals" this way. "If this pine tree were on my street, it would be deciduous." "If this pine tree were on my street, it would be dying." The difference is that we believe a law applies to situations beyond those we have observed and beyond even those we could conceivably observe, but we have no such belief about the accidental generalization.

For me, trying to judge psychoanalysis and this theory of the I as sciences, the key point Rescher makes is that lawfulness can never be simply or wholly based on observation. Laws generalize about the world as it must be and as it might be. Hence, lawfulness rests on *imputation,* a mental act, an act by an I.

To be sure, we want that imputation to be well-founded, and Rescher gives two key factors for well-foundedness. One is correspondence to fact.

The other is the "systematic coherence" that fits the generalization into a fabric of other generalizations to build a rational, integrated body of knowledge which makes up "science."

Beyond those familiar tests, however, "laws are therefore in significant respects not discovered, but made. A law, unlike a simple assertion of regularity, involves claims . . . that are mind-dependent and cannot be rested simply upon objective matters of observed fact" (Rescher, 1970a, pp. 178–183, 195, see also 1970b). I would add that if laws depend on mind—on belief, really—they depend on I's.

In short, the scientist is an I, and science rests on the ethics of an I, the perceptions of an I, the customs, the modes of inquiry, the procedures, the methods of interpretation, the sense of relevance, and the audience of that I, in short, on a lot of people's mental "set." Science rests on the ethical and other commitments of the I's who do science. Science even, arguments like Polanyi's and Rescher's show, relies on a belief —a faith, really—that I can extend my generalizations from the observed beyond the observable to that which I could not possibly observe. To claim that science is only objective is to befuddle, because science builds not only on disciplined observation but also on personal faith and personal imagination.

To admit that is to show how much our ideas of science have changed since the time of Freud's great discoveries, based on his own Helmholtzian faith in a world of "objective" forces and energies. Today, the "hard" sciences are still quaking (or quarking) from the advent of quantum physics and relativity. These new disciplines, notes Nobelist Percy Bridgman, brought into the subject matter of physics, "the problem of the role of the observer to which quantum theory has devoted so much attention and regards as so fundamental" (1959, p. 6). "It was not possible to formulate the laws of quantum mechanics," writes Eugene Wigner (another Nobelist), "in a fully consistent way without reference to the consciousness. . . . Even though the dividing line between the observer, whose consciousness is being affected, and the observed physical object can be shifted towards the one or the other to a considerable degree, it cannot be eliminated" (1967, p. 172).

Hence Bridgman, developing a theory of science as operations, can insist:

> When I make a statement, even as cold and impersonal a statement as a proposition of Euclid, it is I that am making the statement, and the fact that it is I that am making the statement is part of the picture of the activity. In the same way, when you quote a proposition of Euclid the fact that it is you who quote it is part of the picture which is not to be discarded (1959, p. 4).

He is saying that science and scientist are inseparable, much as his predecessor Werner Heisenberg did: "The laws of nature which we formulate mathematically in quantum theory deal no longer with the particles themselves but with our knowledge of the elementary particles" (1958, pp. 99–100). "The familiar classification of the world into subject and object, inner and outer world, body and soul, somehow no longer quite applies, and indeed leads to difficulties. In science, also, the object of research is no longer nature in itself but rather nature exposed to man's questioning, and to this extent man here also meets himself" (pp. 104–05).

Philosopher of science Karl-Otto Apel points out that before there can be data, there has to be an understanding to describe the data and know what it is. Do we include the Dow-Jones Index in our daily lab report? This preunderstanding of data rests on our understanding of human language and the forms of our life (1972, p. 19). As the novelist E. M. Forster is said to have said, "How can I tell what I think until I see what I say?"

In this vein, another distinguished scientist, Edwin Land of Polaroid fame, speaks of the "polar partnership" between the self and the world, between mind and matter. If you ask about the existence of a tree,

> In many ways the tree certainly does not exist in the physical sense without the observer. The tree does not exist for radio waves of a certain wavelength [longer than the tree is tall], nor does it exist for neutrinos [to which matter is transparent]. The tree exists as part and parcel of the interaction between that part of the cosmos and our part of the cosmos, namely the "We" that has evolved over many centuries to be a partner with the tree.

Similarly, if you ask about redness or a red object,

> In fact there is no exterior red object with a tremendous mind linked to it by only a ray of light. The red object is a composite product of matter and a mechanism evolved in permanent association with a most elaborate interlock—so that there is no tremor in what we call the "outside world" that is not locked by a thousand chains and gossamers to inner structures that vibrate and move with it and are part of it.

> Not only is there a unity between matter and being, internally, but the end product of the process is, so to speak, the process itself.

> In the gradual acceptance of the hypothesis that the processes involved in exercising the polar partnership are themselves reality, I find it helpful to think of a symphony in which the opening theme asks a question and the closing theme states that the question is itself the answer (1978, pp. 25–26).

Land's image of the symphony reminds me of how close the scientist's idea of the way we humans understand our world can come to the artist's picture of that understanding. The literary critic Alfred Kazin notes, "Just as philosophers discovered the nature of thinking by realizing that we do not really 'see' anything that does not resemble the innate forms in which we think, so achievement in any art lies in the ability to recreate the 'world' into something that the mind feels totally at home with, that it ultimately welcomes as a further aspect of itself" (1980, p. 56). Similarly the classicist Norman O. Brown rephrases Alfred North Whitehead's philosophy this way: "Whitehead says the reality is unification: reality is events (not things), which are prehensive unifications; gathering diversities together in a unity; not simply *here* or *there*, but a gathering of here and there (subject and object) into a unity" (1966, p. 155; Whitehead, 1925, pp. 66–72).

Land suggests the way that the scientists' answers depend on the scientists' questions. Physicists these days often question their values and theories about reality. *Newsweek* quotes one well-known physicist who compares the present situation in the "hard" sciences to the game of twenty questions.

> "What is so hard," argues physicist John Archibald Wheeler of the University of Texas, "is to give up thinking of nature as a machine that goes on independent of the observer. What we conceive of as reality is a few iron posts of observation with papier-mâché construction between them that is but the elaborate work of our imagination."
>
> Wheeler has devised an ingenious "thought experiment" to suggest how the observer himself helps determine the reality that he perceives. Imagine, he says, a game of "twenty questions" in which one player leaves the room while the others select a word he is to guess when he returns. While he is gone, the other players decide to alter the rules. They will select no word at all; instead each of them will answer "yes" or "no" as he pleases—provided he has a word in mind that fits both his own reply and all the previous replies. The outsider returns and, unsuspecting, begins asking questions. At last he makes a guess: "Is the word 'clouds'?" Yes, comes the answer, and the players explain the game.
>
> When the questioner begins, he assumes a word already exists, just as physicists beginning an experiment think reality already exists. Yet the word comes into being through the questions raised, and the physical world emerges from the observations made. If the player asks different questions, he finds a different word, and if scientists perform different experiments they find different realities. Just as the word does not exist until it emerges from the questions asked, says Wheeler, no phenomenon is a phenomenon until it is observed. "For our picture of the world, this is the most revolutionary thing discovered," says Wheeler. "We still have not come to terms with it" (Begley, 1979, p. 62).

Scientific laws rest on nature, yes, but also on human belief, human intellect, human imagination, and human ethics. Wheeler and Land show in a more concrete way than Rescher how laws are made as much as they are discovered.

Some philosophers of science have come to the same conclusion that the twenty questions image for physics leads to: that how it is depends on what you ask. Traditionally, philosophers have said that the sciences deal with explanations of the causes of things by means of covering laws: if this, then that. If you drop something, then it will accelerate at a constant rate. If you frustrate someone, then they will show aggression.

The humanities deal with meanings and intentions: understanding, as opposed to explanation. I understand the logic of Rescher's argument. I understand *Hamlet*. Explanation being different from understanding, the humanities and the sciences are supposed to be two separate cultures.

In fact, they are not, philosopher Apel argues, particularly when the science is trying (as psychology and psychoanalysis do) to look at human beings. There, understanding is crucial, and you cannot test your understanding of a person's reasons by the methods that would work with an if-then law. Suppose you are trying to understand why a certain group of farmers left a certain stretch of land. There is no way that observing the operation of if-then, covering laws in this case and others like it will decisively answer the question. At most that kind of testing, writes Apel,

> can give hints, on the assumption that these hints can be integrated into the very attempt of *understanding*. For it is not just *observation of data* . . . but *communication* by language with so-called *objects* as *co-subjects* which would provide the best test of one's having understood somebody's reasons for action (1972, p. 17).

It is not only the psychologist or the historian who necessarily mixes the sciences and the humanities, however. This involvement of the understanding of reasons with the explanation of events holds true for all the sciences. The reason is that the scientist's idea of an "event" or "data" has profoundly and radically changed.

The older, positivistic idea was that data preceded all understanding or explaining. The more modern, "twenty questions" view has to be that whenever a scientist calls something "data," he has already engaged in an act of understanding. He has already built on his fundamental ideas of what the world is like and how science is conducted. "Data," "event," "the way it was," "what really happened"—all these rest on preexisting assumptions of what counts as an event or data or "really."

Where did these assumptions preexist? Among the community of chemists, biologists, psychologists, or literary critics. These communal assumptions are in our minds whenever—as professionals—we frame a hypothesis, decide something is a "fact," or agree that some idea has been "confirmed." They are in our minds when we judge how much of the personal we will allow in a "scientific" procedure. In short (as we saw in part II), each of us, when we DEFT a new fact, DEFTs it by means of the guidelines of our particular profession and the customs of our culture and, at an even more basic level, the capacities of our physical senses. I come back to the model of chapter 6. An I governs cultural and physiological feedbacks.

The twenty questions game would take us that far. Apel adds another chain to the argument, however, drawing on a well-known thesis of the later Wittgenstein. One person alone cannot follow a rule (because a rule requires language, and language requires someone spoken to as well as a speaker). Thus one person alone cannot practice science (despite all the "mad scientist" horror movies). "From this [it] follows that understanding and interpretation as means of communication fulfil a *complementary* function to describing or explaining" (1972, pp. 17, 19, 22).

That is, we can know an event by objectifying it. We can also know it by relating ourselves as human beings to the human elements in the event—or in our explanation of the event. A scientist or historian tests his "objective" explanation against the responses of his culture, other scientists or historians. These two ways of knowing, explanation or describing and interpretation or understanding, add to each other and exclude each other at the same time so as to give us a more total vision, much the way our eyes work as a pair. Each eye sees differently, but each is equally valid. To see in depth, we need both and we need their *difference*. Two eyes that both saw the same thing would not give us perspective. Neither would one eye alone.

So with the understanding of reasons between I's and explanations through if-then, covering laws. Apel's argument suggests that to set up understanding through identity as an alternative to explanation through if-then laws would be as false as to set up the right eye as an alternative to the left. The challenge is to see the world with both and to understand how both work together. Then, when we combine the two, we achieve a new richness. Explanation and understanding complement each other, as do description and interpretation.

In short, the scientist is an I, perceiving and DEFTing and building laws from a personal understanding and evaluation of those perceptions. As Bridgman concludes:

> If one is reconciled to the inevitability of describing the world from himself as center, a unity is thereby automatically restored to the world, the unity conferred by the necessity of seeing everything from a single origin. This is not the illusory unity which we formerly thought we had, but is the only unity we can use, the only unity we need, and the only unity possible in the light of the way things are (1959, p. 248).

This quotation, like the others, is this nonscientist's appeal to a scientist's authority. I believe that these practicing scientists, unlike some nonscientists or social scientists, frankly acknowledge that science rests on the ethical and other commitments of the very human I's who do science. Because it rests on human mental processes, scientific knowledge is no simple matter of passively observing the world and drawing the inevitable logical conclusions.

Let me return, then, to the question with which I began this section, How "scientific" is science? What do we mean by "scientific"? Whatever science means in a positive sense, I am content to leave to the philosophers of science. In a negative sense, however, one thing is clear. Science is *not* impersonal, objective, independent of its social setting or of the I's who create science and are its audience. Science is, like the I, between. There are no doubt many possible models for science with a capital S, but I would claim that the picture I gave in chapter 6 of an I using cultural and physical hypotheses will serve for one. It provides an idea of science that one can carry about in one's head, against which to read the various claims and statements that people make, in particular, those of humans scientifically studying humans, the psychologists and the psychoanalysts.

14 | The State of the Arts

"Hard" scientists recognize that no matter how objective a science's aims, it rests on the beliefs, ethics, customs, imagination, and commitment of some I. Can there be a science of the I then? Can there be a science that studies the very origin of science, or is that necessarily an art? In other words, can there be such a thing as a scientific psychology?

Despite the problems and paradoxes built into psychology, the staunchest statements of a nineteenth-century scientific position nowadays come from

The Experimental Psychologists

They wish to assure us—and presumably themselves—of the validity of what they are doing. The usual experimental paper in psychology takes great care with its procedures (and its prose) to qualify itself as "scientific." Often an early paragraph will glance disparagingly at pre-twentieth-century or psycho-analytic psychologists who fail to meet the experimenter's standard. Yet to turn from today's physicists and other "hard" scientists to today's psychologists is to walk back into an earlier, Victorian time, at least so far as conceptions of science are concerned. "The scientific man has above all things to strive at self-elimination in his judgments." Thus wrote one of the founders of modern psychological methods, Karl Pearson, in 1892 (p. 11). Many, I think virtually all, experimental psychologists would say the same today.

Seymour Fisher and Roger Greenberg, for example, have written a masterful survey of experimental tests of psychoanalysis. They considered "scientific" only those observations "secured through procedures that are repeatable and involve techniques that make it possible to check on the objectivity of the reporting observer" (1977, p. 276). Theirs is the kind of remark that every experimental psychologist I know or have read makes. Their easy use of terms like "scientific" or "objectivity," however, contrasts strikingly with the recognition by a Bronowski or a Land of the interrelation between the observer and the observed.

Of course, they did not consider a report of what happened in the clinic or on the couch as allowing a check on the "objectivity" of the observer. Not

300

unreasonably. Often "scientific" psychologists accuse therapists and clinicians of letting their wishes and fears color their case reports. "Research has . . . demonstrated," say Fisher and Greenberg, "that when an observer enters into transaction with the object of his observations, as in psychotherapy, he is likely to create the behavior he is looking for in a manner analogous to a self-fulfilling prophecy" (p. 276). Joseph Masling and Murray Schwartz would agree: "Such psychoanalytic descriptions as 'libido,' 'oral needs,' and 'castration fears' are constructs that transform their subjects in the act of defining them" (1979, pp. 264–65).

Yes, the phenomenon is well known, but it happens with experimenters as well as clinicians. Psychologists have done a great deal of research on it as the "Rosenthal" effect or (so Masling suggests) the "screw you" effect—referring perhaps to some hypothetical sophomore who gets tired of pushing a button hundreds of times and decides to do in both the experiment and his professor's hopes of promotion (Rosenthal, 1966; Masling, 1966; Friedman, 1967). The experimenter's needs, his subject's "set," the mythology of the profession, all color the supposed "objectivity" of experiments. Most experimental psychologists hope to "control for" this interference, because they assume that it is possible to isolate the observer from the observed. The physicists, as we have seen, do not. They say that you have to rely on the experimenter's (and the subject's?) ethical commitment to truth or intellectual premises. It seems to me that that must be even more true in psychological than physical experiments.

One can create the illusion of an impersonal objectivity by defining a psychological experiment as just the part that some computer or a graduate assistant carries out, but that tactic only moves the experimenter's personal influence to another, less obvious place in the experiment. He sets it up, decides what shall be controlled for, programs the computer or the graduate assistant, and settles what constitutes success and significance.

Other psychologists recognize, as the physicists do, that the person and the experiment intertwine. It was in 1954, for example, that the distinguished psychologist Gardner Murphy wrote, "A dozen years ago, it was becoming clear that the process of perceiving was soon to be brought into relation to the entire personality of the perceiver" (p. xvii). If perception is a function of personality, then an experimental psychologist ought to ask how he or she can take into account the personalities of both the subject S and the experimenter E. Despite the passage of four decades, however, few do. Most experimentalists assume that they can reach objectivity by "controlling for" personality, averaging it out of the picture.

An easy "objectivity" may be hard to believe, but the rest of Fisher and Greenberg's criterion, "procedures that are repeatable," seems reasonable enough—until we lean on the terms a bit. What is "repeatable"? Is having

Scott Fitzgerald answer a questionnaire the same as having Dr. Vincent do it? Typically, psychologists assume that one "subject" can be substituted for another in repeating an experiment or in adding up the number of times a certain question is answered a certain way. Yet doesn't that assume a great deal about human beings? Is the assumption that subjects are interchangeable "scientific"? More scientific than a clinician's careful observation of either Scott Fitzgerald or Dr. Vincent?

You cannot step into the same river twice. No events, if we are to be microscopically exact, are "repeatable." Listened to precisely enough, no two beats of a heart or ticks of a clock or throbs of an engine are the same. What constitutes repeating, then, is a question of degree and involves the experimenter's judgment as to what matters. Often, an experimental psychologist will assume that two different people pushing the same buttons counts as repeating, but the same person pushing a different arrangement of the same buttons would not. That seems to me a debatable, even "subjective," decision.

Different subjects do not read the same instructions the same way, write two psychologists about experimental "controls." Tasks "do change, even in the course of a single experimental session." "People can be found responding in different ways at different times within a single problem" (Cole and Means, 1982, pp. 134–41, 175). Subjects may be frightened, distracted, or bored. These background factors are hardly neutral, and I know of no way an experimenter can control them out of the experiment so as to make the task imposed on the subjects independent of the subjects' feelings.

Nevertheless, Fisher and Greenberg ruled out clinical reports because "there is no way to gauge which clinical reporters are telling it the way it really happened and which are wishfully seeing things in a way that supports their favorite theoretical stance." Here again, the decision may have been wise, but the phrasing states an attitude toward science more characteristic of the late nineteenth than the late twentieth century. First, there is the easy assumption that someone can tell it "the way it really happened," quite different from a Monod or a Bridgman. Then there is the contrasted position of those who are wishfully seeing things so as to support their pet theory. Yet surely most experimenters are heavily involved in shoring up their favorite theories. Otherwise why would they be experimenting? On their experiments, their grants, contracts, and promotions depend. Yet Fisher and Greenberg are seeking "objectivity" someplace other than in the ethical commitment of which Bronowski and Monod speak.

Most striking to me is their assumption that the writers of the papers they are examining are either one way or the other, either wishfully seeing or "telling it the way it really happened." Surely psychologists as sophisticated as Fisher and Greenberg want to be able to take into account the probability that both are happening, both a commitment to truth and a belief in one's theory. Their well-meant "objectivity" is what Polanyi spoke of as "the destructive influence" of the ideal of scientific detachment.

In an earlier, also excellent survey of "scientific" tests of psychoanalysis, Paul Kline gives these three criteria:

1. *Observations* — which must be under *controlled* conditions (that is, eliminate the role of extraneous variables)
2. *Constructs* — which must be *operational* (that is, have clearly specified and identifiable empirical referents)
3. *Hypotheses* — which must be *testable* (that is, clearly disconfirmable)
(1972, p. 1).

Again, this all sounds reasonable enough until (as Bridgman prescribes) we press on the words a little.

The very idea of "extraneous" variables implies that Kline already knows what is and is not relevant. Moreoever, what a psychological experimenter typically excludes as extraneous are precisely the human factors, the differences between a Scott Fitzgerald and a Dr. Vincent. Imagine a college age Dr. Vincent as a resentful "volunteer" in some psychology department's pool, learning nonsense words for the experiment his professor is hoping to publish. Imagine Scott Fitzgerald as an amorous Princeton sophomore learning the same nonsense words for a beautiful research assistant on whom he has a hopeless crush. How does one "control for" such human factors?

Kline asks for "identifiable empirical referents," things you can see or hear and then count. I have heard attributed to Edward L. Thorndike, one of the founders of modern experimental psychology, this remark: "If a thing exists at all, it exists in some amount. If it exists in some amount, it can be measured." Again, that sounds commonsensical enough and, to me, with my own deep wish that we could understand human beings just by their surfaces, appealing. Yet what a colossal assumption it is. Suppose we substitute for Thorndike's "a thing" honesty or love. "If honesty exists at all, it exists in some amount. If it exists in some amount, it can be measured." Suppose we were to substitute some of the terms that currently exercise philosophers of mind: intention, understanding, or empathy. The seemingly simple assumption that a mental quality can be rendered as "a thing" (or as an "identifiable empirical referent") leads to a drastic curtailing of the psychologist's subject matter to exclude the feelings and experiences that most matter to us. Or it commits us to the Lear fallacy, that unhappy king's tragic effort to quantify his daughters' love.

Kline's third requirement restates the familiar idea that, to be "scientific," a theory or hypothesis must be falsifiable by some observation of fact. Yet this business of confirmation and disconfirmation has many wrinkles, as philosophers of science like Wesley Salmon point out (1973). Suppose we were testing the statement, "All crows are black." Should we check the color of herring? Well, perhaps we should, since a silver herring fits the statement about crows being black—because it confirms the converse, "If it is not black, it is not a crow." Yet, curiously, finding feathers on a crow is not evidence for the proposition, "All birds have feathers"—because that would be reasoning from the consequent to the premises, and the logic has to go the other way: (1) All birds have feathers. (2) This crow is a bird. (3) This crow has feathers. Salmon recalls a "facetious characterization of logic texts as books that are divided into two parts: in the first part [on deduction] the fallacies are explained and in the second part [on induction or scientific method] they are committed."

Surely the scientist is right to ignore the silver of herring when considering the blackness of crows and to generalize from the feathers of some birds to the principle that all birds have feathers. Finally, what counts as a legitimate confirmation and what doesn't depend partly on logic and reality, to be sure, but also on what the community of scientists have agreed. More exactly, as Thomas Kuhn has shown, confirmation depends upon the way the confirmations to which we have committed ourselves determine what we consider logical or real (1962).

Biologists of the 1980s accept all kinds of electrical procedures that biologists of the 1880s would have greeted with skeptical laughter. When I was an engineering student, we thought we were doing pretty well if we got within 10 percent of the answer we were supposed to get. Psychologists have agreed that confirmation will be a 5 percent disconfirmation of the null hypothesis. That is, let's assume that a boy's grades in school have no relation to the side of the street he lives on, a null hypothesis. Then we compare the grades of the boys who live on my street. If we find that the boys on my side of the street have, by and large, higher grades than the boys on the other side and if—here the mathematics get complicated—the difference is such that there is only a 5 percent probability of its happening by chance, then (so psychologists assume) we are entitled to assume that the null hypothesis is wrong, that there is some connection between the boys' grades and the side of the street they live on. Maybe the boys on the west side study together. Maybe they have daylight longer. Maybe they absorb smartness from their smart neighbor. Who knows?—but the psychological community would agree that the *absence* of connection had been *dis*proved.

Does 5 percent disprove a hypothesis? Suppose the "hypothesis" is that I have put into a drawer 95 white socks and 5 black ones. In the darkness of early morning I reach in and pull out a black sock. Should the 5 percent probability, the 19-to-1 odds against my doing that, make me doubt that I put in 95 white and 5 black socks? Even if I pulled out black socks twice in a row, odds 361-to-1 against doing so by chance (p < 0.0025), I would still be sure how many socks I had put in the drawer, and no mere statistics would shake my certainty about the number and color of the socks I own. On the other hand, I am less sure about the relation between boys' grades and where they live, and the statistical test, I agree, would make it seem possible that there is some connection. The disproof (and therefore proof) depend not just on the numbers but at least in part on my feelings about the hypotheses before and quite apart from the result of the experiment.

One basic problem for any psychologist is that his supposedly objective discoveries about mind themselves depend on mind, his own, his subjects', and his fellow experimenters'. A biophysicist, writing for a popular psychology magazine, arrives at the paradox by surveying the disciplines: physics, chemistry, biology, and psychology. First, psychologists believe that we can explain the human mind physiologically. Second, biologists believe that we can explain physiology by means of atomic physics, as so many movements of atoms of carbon, nitrogen, oxygen, or whatever. Third (as we have seen in chapter 13), physicists believe that atomic physics requires a mind as a basic part of the system (Morowitz, 1980, p. 16). More simply, it takes a mind to explain a mind. Either way, psychology—any psychology—involves a fundamental paradox.

Another basic problem for the psychological experimenter as for the biologist, but not the physicist, is that the subjects of the experiment vary considerably. Each rat's running of a maze will differ somewhat from every other rat's run. How can the psychologist deal with the variation and arrive at laws that apply uniformly? Some methods are, to be sure, taboo. One day, when I was walking through the psychology building of a large university, an agitated student came running down the hall. He scrambled from side to side of the corridor, stooping, grabbing, grabbing again, running some more. One of the gerbils in his experiment had escaped. After a few minutes, he stopped, stood up, shrugged, and walked off saying, "Oh well, that one didn't fit the curve anyway."

Perhaps we should invoke in that anonymous student's name what Nigel Calder calls "the Harvard law of animal behaviour: 'When the same stimulus is given repeatedly under carefully controlled conditions the animal will behave as it damned well pleases.' " The same thing is true of humans: "Even if one were only attempting to control the minds of a homogeneous group of psychiatric patients [sic] with a drug with which one had had considerable experience, the desired effect would not be produced in all patients, and one would not be able to plan specifically that any particular effect would be produced in a particular patient" (Calder, 1970, pp. 22, 76).

Statistics represent a valiant effort to deal with that variability. While the statistical laws themselves are pure and incontrovertible products of logic, the way they are used and the qualities they purport to measure are—inevitably, I think—problematic. One of the problems is whether smoothing off—cancelling out, really—the variability is the only or even the best strategy for dealing with it. In effect, when the student reports that nineteen gerbils traversed the maze or the professor of psychology writes that twenty sophomores (Ss) turned the knob to the right, whatever individual differences there were among the gerbils or the sophomores are gone.

Reporting the deviation in numerical terms acknowledges variation but loses the detail of it, precisely the detail that is essential to a concept like identity. If—and I realize that is a very large "if"—if identity governing lower-level feedbacks is a telling model, if it truly offers a way of talking about the way shared or "given" structures and individual choices coact to become behavior, then we need to be able to talk not only about countable behaviors but interpretable identity. Statistical methods, however, at least as we know them today, make it impossible to address the identity part of the model. Statistics can describe with great precision how a ship moves, but deliberately make it impossible to say anything about the captain who is steering her.

> This is the main reason [writes one of the discoverers of the helical form of DNA, Francis Crick] pure psychology is, by the standards of hard science, rather unsuccessful. . . . The basic difficulty is that psychology attempts to treat the brain as a black box. The experimenter studies the inputs and outputs and tries from the results to deduce the structure and operation of the inside of the box. . . .
>
> The difficulty with the black-box approach is that unless the box is inherently very simple a stage is soon reached where several rival theories all explain the observed results equally well. Attempts to decide among them often prove unsuccessful because as more experiments are done more complexities are revealed.

It is at this point, says Crick, that the brain physiologist wants to get inside the black box (1979, pp. 221–22). The assumptions of psychology, however, make it difficult, perhaps impossible, to combine physiological information with the usual methods of psychological experimentation (disconfirming a null hypothesis, for example, or correlating behavioral inputs and outputs). The difference in methods cuts the natural connection between psychologists and brain physiologists.

Psychology's reliance on if-then principles and statistical methods also causes trouble when psychology meets psychoanalysis. Textbooks in psychology customarily convert psychoanalysis into a set of testable general laws or principles. I am thinking in particular of Calvin S. Hall's *A Primer of Psychoanalysis,* widely used in American psychology departments and a principal reason why American psychologists have such odd ideas about psychoanalysis. It is rather as though one knew Shakespeare only in Chinese translation.

The problem is that psychoanalysis, a largely holistic discipline, cannot be rendered in if-then principles. Trying to do so produces either principles that can be tested but unrealistically rigidify psychoanalysis or principles that cannot be tested (leading to smugness among antipsychoanalytic psychologists).

I think many psychologists share my uneasiness about the methods of experimental psychology, at least unconsciously, to judge from the constant claims to being "scientific" that percolate the psychological journals. Paradoxically, however, all the talk of method and disconfirmation and repeatability is not itself "scientific." Hard scientists—should I call them unsocial scientists?—don't trouble themselves about such basic assumptions. They engage in what Thomas Kuhn has called "normal science," carrying on experiments within the established rules and procedures of the scientific game of today without much questioning or concern about them. It is only when some new discovery challenges this consensus that physical and biological scientists begin the kind of self-questioning that experimental psychologists seem constantly engaged in. As Kuhn says, "It is precisely the abandonment of critical discourse that marks the transition to a science" (1970, pp. 6–7).

Thus, experimental psychology, for all its scientific claims, indeed precisely because of them, shows that it has not yet reached the status of a science. The more psychologists assert that they are being "scientific," the more they tip us off that they aren't yet. "Once a field has made that transition [to a science], critical discourse recurs only at moments of crisis when the bases of the field are in jeopardy" (idem).

That commitment to a tidy, freshman-year science is an old-fashioned virtue in one sense. In another it may be a sacred cow. Noam Chomsky, for example, sees psychology's scientism as a stultifying limitation.

> The reader who undertakes the useful exercise of searching the literature will discover, I believe, not only that there is little significant scientific knowledge in this domain, but further that the behavioral sciences have commonly insisted upon certain arbitrary methodological restrictions that make it virtually impossible for scientific knowledge of a nontrivial character to be attained (Chomsky, 1972, p. ix).

Niels Bohr is quoted as saying, "There are the trivial truths and the great truths. The opposite of a trivial truth is plainly false. The opposite of a great truth is also true" (Waelder, 1963, p. 18). Experimental psychology as we know it today has cut itself off from the great truths, and that is a pity.

Modern psychology has received immense support from government, industry, and an inquisitive public. Work has been widely abstracted, circulated, and followed up for five sixths of a busy century. Yet I would be hard put to state more than one or two theories of real generality that have wide acceptance in the profession (a notable exception being the theory that perception and cognition are active). The introductions to psychology textbooks, textbook introductions being an index to the basics of any field, present grandmotherly truths or ingenious experimental methods but not general scientific principles.

Chomsky continues:

> To a considerable degree, I feel, the "behavioral sciences" are merely mimicking the surface features of the natural sciences; much of their scientific character has been achieved by a restriction of subject matter and a concentration on rather peripheral issues. Such narrowing of focus can be justified if it leads to achievements of real intellectual significance, but in this case, I think it would be very difficult to show that the narrowing of scope has led to deep and significant results.

> In all but the most elementary cases, what a person does depends in large measure on what he knows, believes, and anticipates. A study of human behavior that is not based on at least a tentative formulation of relevant systems of knowledge and belief is predestined to triviality and irrelevance (1973, pp. xi, ix).

A scientific pride goeth before a scientific fall.

Even though it is unlikely that psychologists will seize upon psychoanalysis, I would like to be able to report that

The Psychoanalysts

are ready and waiting to supply the general principles that would rescue the experimental psychologists from the fate of triviality that Chomsky describes. Unfortunately, that is not the case. Masling and Schwartz report the psychoanalytic situation itself is in something of a muddle.

"Psychoanalysts abstract qualities from the people they observe and then write about these qualities as though they had a life apart from the people in whom they were observed." ("Anality." "The" Oedipus complex. "The" superego.) "Psychologists come along and treat these statements as general laws, devising experiments" to test them. In effect, the psychoanalysts, by making "anality" or "the" oedipus complex or "the" superego into things, have created general laws (as they apply to those things) where perhaps there are none, at least where the psychologists' tests fail to show them (1979, p. 266).

Where, then, are the covering, if-then laws of psychoanalysis?

There may be none. They would have to rest on individual psychoanalyses, and perhaps one cannot generalize from these. In general, writes André Green, internationally renowned psychoanalyst, the analyst and the patient together construct a meaning which has never been created before the analytic relationship began. Therefore, the analyst and the patient are not dealing with truth in its scientific sense (1975, citing Viderman, 1970). To be sure, there are fragments of historical truth in what the patient says, but the aim of therapy is not to recover the truth but to arrive at the best mediation between the various agencies in the mind of the patient, id, ego, and superego (Loch, 1977, p. 228).

This is, however, a very different way of talking about the process than when I entered analysis in 1960. Then, most American psychoanalysts spoke of a psychoanalysis as an automatic, self-correcting process, working out the laws of psychoanalytic psychology. The patient lay on the couch associating away. The analyst from time to time interpreted. The truth or falsity of the analyst's interpretations came out as changes in the patient's free associations. An incorrect interpretation would simply be rejected. A correct interpretation might be resisted but would result in deeper, richer associations.

The content of an analysis would vary from patient to patient, to be sure, but the process of free association was self-correcting, independent of both the patient's and the analyst's personality. It made no difference to the process whether the analyst was a man or a woman, smart or stupid, warm or severe. This is very different from the idea that patient and analyst together create a meaning which depends upon the potential space unique to this patient and this analyst.

To grasp the change, we can think of the science of psychoanalysis as passing through three stages. At least, psychoanalysis has gone through three different ways of considering itself as a science.

At first, Freud set out to achieve a Helmholtzian psychology. It was to have all the rigor of physics or chemistry, and he often spoke about psychoanalysis as if he were creating an experimental science. From particular cases, one would hypothesize general laws, then test them out by particular interpretations to particular patients. In any one analysis, the analyst hypothesizes interpretations based on the general principles of psychoanalysis. If he says them to the patient (one does not, after all, communicate one's every interpretation), then the patient's subsequent free associations would show whether or not the interpretation was correct. The patient's free associations after the interpretation provide the "experiment" that proves or disproves the general law.

In 1959 two of the most distinguished American analysts were simply stating a widely held view when they insisted that psychoanalysis was just like any other science. Psychoanalytic therapy, said Jacob Arlow, "is by no means a perfect experimental tool, but it is, nevertheless, . . . governed by strict methodological considerations and operating within accepted canons of the scientific method." Heinz Hartmann maintained that the aim of psychoanalysis, besides therapy, was "to develop lawlike propositions which then, of course, transcend individual observations." To be sure, observations rely on the mental processes of the analyst, but they are "subject to the constant scrutiny of the analyst," and that is one reason the analyst has to be analyzed himself as part of his training. "Psychoanalysis has discovered potential sources of error and found a way to combat them."

A later view, also widely held, treats psychoanalysis as an observational science. The analyst engages patients in the same interpersonal way an anthropologist does when he moves his bedroll into the tepee or the kraal. He not only observes, he talks to the subject of his science. He actively synthesizes factual evidence like a Darwin comparing finches in the Galápagos. He observes the patterns of his patient's behavior just as the anthropologist observes the customs of a tribe or the biologist the behavior of an orang-utan. The interpretation is not so much an "experiment" as a making known: to the anthropologist, the analyst, the patient, the tribe.

A still later view treats psychoanalysis as a "hermeneutic," a system of interpretation. This is the current view among most analysts outside of the more conservative institutes in the United States. It makes language paramount, the patient's words or the analyst's. Rather than read through language to some inferred behavior or events, the analyst and patient take language itself as the event. The event (in the analysis at least) becomes the language it is reported in. Psychoanalytic principles then become ways of finding the meaning in that language, just as the techniques of literary criticism or biblical interpretation are ways of finding—or, better, assigning—a meaning.

That is, in interpreting one needs to go beyond the old-fashioned "conduit" metaphor of language in which somebody puts a meaning in at one end and somebody else takes it out at the other. Rather, meaning is something people actively create with their minds from a text, just as they actively perceive colors (chapter 5 above) or read symbols (chapter 4).

Most modern psychoanalysts, like Roy Schafer, would assert that the psychoanalyst is no longer committed (as Freud so deeply was) to determinism. For the modern analyst, "Determinism . . . is a way of putting questions to actions" (1976, pp. 228–29). It is a principle of inquiry, a way of insisting, Why? and again, Why?

The assumption is that actions have reasons. Actions do not occur without meaning. "The analyst's real commitment is not to determinism in a universe of mechanical causes, but to intelligibility in a universe of actions with reasons." "The essence of the psychoanalytic method is the exploration and understanding of personal paradigms," writes Louis Breger (1981, p. 48), by which he may mean something like identities.

Interestingly, Freud demonstrates all three of these modes, the "scientific," the observational, and the hermeneutic, in his well-known comparison of the method of the psychoanalyst to that of the archaeologist, the comparison with which we began this study of holistic method.

> Imagine that an explorer arrives in a little-known region where his interest is aroused by an expanse of ruins, with remains of walls, fragments of columns, and tablets with half-effaced and unreadable inscriptions. He may content himself with inspecting what lies exposed to view, with questioning the inhabitants—perhaps semi-barbaric people—who live in the vicinity, about what tradition tells them of the history and meaning of these archaeological remains, and with noting down what they tell him—and he may then proceed on his journey. But he may act differently. He may have brought picks, shovels and spades with him, and he may set the inhabitants to work with these implements. Together with them he may start upon the ruins, clear away the rubbish, and, beginning from the visible remains, uncover what is buried. If his work is crowned with success, the discoveries are self-explanatory: the ruined walls are part of the ramparts of a palace or a treasure-house; the fragments of columns can be filled out into a temple; the numerous inscriptions which, by good luck, may be bilingual, reveal an alphabet and a language, and, when they have been deciphered and translated, yield undreamed-of information about the events of the remote past, to commemorate which the monuments were built (1896c, 3:192; see also 1937d, 23:259–60).

In this fascinating passage, Freud is thinking in all three of the scientific modes of psychoanalysis. There is what the philosopher would call "correspondence" truth: the archaeologist will find out exactly what the rubbish and the ruined walls and the inscriptions consist of, and whatever the stones finally "say" has to correspond to what his picks, shovels, and spades uncover. There is also the participant-observer truth of the anthropologist. Freud's archaeologist has to *ask* the natives. He has to *dig* into the ruins. He has to *guess* at the alphabet. Finally, there is the hermeneutic effort. He has to try to build the fragments into one coherent narrative. He has to arrive at—give them—their "meaning." The archaeologist has to make all three of these scientific modes work together for him. So does the analyst.

These three views of the "science" of psychoanalysis (determinist, observational, interpretive) correspond to three stages in the intellectual development of psychoanalysis. At first the analyst sought explanations based on the polarity unconscious-conscious, when the analyst tried to dig out what was hidden. Then analysts used explanations based on the polarity ego-nonego, when the analyst worked (like a participant-observer) with the patient's ego in a "therapeutic alliance" toward the best outcome for that ego. Nowadays analysts seek explanations based on the polarity self-nonself, with the analyst acknowledging his own interaction with the patient, as Freud's archaeologist (particularly in 1937) acknowledges his own part in what he finds and how he interprets what he finds (Holland, 1976; see also Appendix, pp. 331–33).

You could state the psychoanalytic combination of strategies another way (as the philosopher Habermas does). The psychoanalyst uses causal generalizations, if-then laws, but in an analysis, the analyst must always be applying them in a given context. Theory gives rise to a narrative of an individual (the history of his identity, if you will), and conclusions about causes always refer to this narrative (1971, p. 273).

It is particularly true of psychoanalysis (although, as we have seen in chapter 13, Polanyi says it is true of all the sciences) that what general principles there are function within boundary conditions that are in principle unpredictable. Freud himself accepted the idea that psychoanalysis would never be able to predict. One could, he noted, trace in great detail an outcome back to its origins. One cannot go the other way, predicting an outcome from the determining origins. You cannot, said Freud, know beforehand which of the determining factors will prove the stronger. A small change in the unconscious forces can end in a much greater change in final behavior, just as a change in the vote of a small faction in an electorate can completely change the policy a whole nation finally adopts (1920a, 18:167–68).

Psychoanalysis in principle does not lead to predictions? From the point of view of the experimental psychologist, this is a damaging, perhaps fatal admission. (See, for example, Kline's third criterion on p. 303.) If you can't predict, then you aren't stating propositions that can be disconfirmed. Or are you?

A single experiment can falsify a determinist scientific principle. If you were to drop a billiard ball from the Leaning Tower of Pisa, and it didn't fall with uniform acceleration, Newton's laws would be in big trouble. They would not be covering the facts they are supposed to cover. How do you falsify an interpretation, though? Not by an experiment but, as we saw with Sherlock Holmes, by new data. If the old interpretation will not deal with the new facts, then a new interpretation is needed.

Isn't this the same way an if-then law is defeated? You show that it does not cover the new data, like the billiard ball that does not accelerate uniformly. I would say the same holds true for experiments as for interpretations. If new facts do not fit the old hypothesis, then the old hypothesis is defeated *because* a new hypothesis is called for. So far as falsification or disconfirmation is concerned, I think experiment and interpretation do not fundamentally differ. Finally, the old hypothesis is only defeated by a better one—and better is a matter of degree, of the ethics of the scientist, and of the customs and values of the scientific community.

Indeterminacy, narrativity, relationship, the irrelevance of prediction—each looks as though it prevents psychoanalytic therapy and hence the psychoanalytic theory built on it from being "objective" in ways that would suit the experimental psychologist. That is, they do not allow the (to me) questionable assumption that it is possible to isolate the observer from the observed.

If, however, such hard sciences as optics and quantum mechanics are taking the self into account, surely it is time the human sciences free themselves from the posture of what Weston LaBarre irritatedly calls "the invisible man desperately trying not to be seen seeing other men" (1967, p. viii). Georges Devereux, in his cogent book *From Anxiety to Method in the Behavioral Sciences* (1967), seeks to get his fellow social scientists to "abandon—at least in a naive sense—the notion that the basic operation in behavioral science is the observation of a subject by an observer." "The behavioral scientist cannot ignore the interaction between subject and observer in the hope that, if he but pretends long enough that it does not exist, it will just quietly go away" (pp. 295, xviii). And LaBarre: "A basic datum of all social science . . . is *what happens within the observer*—in the large sense his own 'countertransference' reactions as a specific human being" (p. ix).

LaBarre's word "countertransference" reminds me that he and Devereux come from the clinical tradition of psychoanalysis. I would like to think, obviously, that psychologists, conscience-struck by LaBarre's and Devereux's strictures, will rush to psychoanalysis, particularly to this theory of identity. It seems unlikely, though. The American Psychological Association has 56,000 members. There are perhaps 100,000 psychologists in and out of the APA in America alone, probably half of whom are experimentalists. Many have talent, some genius. All, so far as I can tell, are committed to a nineteenth-century model of science that rules the person of the scientist out of the game.

It does not help to hear psychologists proclaim that *they* are "objective and scientific" (defined in a pre-twentieth-century way) while "psychoanalysis is subjective and humanistic." Weston LaBarre expresses both the intellectual trouble with the position and the animosity that such smugness evokes: "Self-designated 'social sciences,' yearning for the prestige of exact physical sciences from the seventeenth century onward, solemnly continue to pattern themselves on a seventeenth-century mechanistic Newtonian model, quite as if Einstein and Heisenberg had not revolutionized physics in the three-century interim" (1967, pp. vii–viii).

As we have seen from the hard scientists, all science involves both the subjective person and the objective world, both if-then explanation and interpretation or understanding. Indeed all modern science is concerned at one or another level with precisely the relation between them. So is psychoanalysis. So, I think, is psychology.

It would be as much of an error to assume that psychoanalysis is only interpretation as it is to assume that psychology is only "objective" experiments. Indeed the two errors—each common—mesh to create the deadlock that we have today. The psychologist dismisses the psychoanalyst as "unscientific." The psychoanalyst dismisses the psychologist's experiments. "That has nothing to do with analysis." Each claims to be a general psychology that excludes the other. Seeing experimental psychologists and psychoanalysts at such odds is very frustrating for anyone so passionately (and ambivalently) committed to making sense out of human beings as I am.

Crucial to breaking this deadlock and crucial to the status of psychoanalysis as a science is the problem of generalizing from Tom, Dick, or Harry to you and me. Where do the covering, if-then laws, which are so important to the hard sciences, fit in psychoanalysis? Psychoanalysis always begins with a case study of some one person in all the uniqueness and particularity of which humans are capable. The general law, as we have seen, reaches out by Rescher's "nomic necessity" not only to all known cases, all possible cases, but even to impossible cases, contrafactuals like Santa Claus in orbit. How does one move from a unique and individual case like Herbert Graf or Paul Lorenz or Scott Fitzgerald to that kind of "nomic necessity"? If Santa Claus were in orbit round the earth, he would obey the laws of planetary motion. Would he also have an oedipus complex?

15 | An Idea of Psychology

To the achievements of either science or psychoanalysis, the notion that 'Science is objective, psychoanalysis subjective,' is too simple a response. Rather, each involves both that "subjective" person and that "objective" world. It is not enough to ask, 'Which shall we believe?' We need to ask ourselves, 'How can we understand their coming together?' In the same way, I do not think it sophisticated enough to say simply, 'Experimental psychology is objective and scientific, psychoanalysis subjective and human-istic.' Each involves both "subjective" person and "objective" science, and the real question is, How can we use both the personal and the impersonal to understand the coming together of personal and impersonal? How can we combine, rather than oppose, the strategies of the two sciences?

So far, we have seen that experimental psychology tries deliberately to exclude the individual and that psychoanalysis tends not to address the problem of general laws. I would like to find a psychology that will interre-late the individuality that psychoanalysis studies with the general laws which the natural sciences derive and which experimental psychologists seek.

"Anybody who studies personality theory, anthropology, or history," writes D. E. Berlyne, one of the most intense of experimentalists, "is inevitably impressed with the dissimilarities between human beings and human societies that are revealed to him." He might understandably greet any attempt to generalize about all or most human beings with skepticism. "But as soon as any two human beings are compared with, say, a tree, their similarities will appear immense and their differences minor" (1971, p. 29). From this point of view, all that interests the psychologist are general laws that apply to all or just about all human beings.

I believe that psychology can do more, represented, for example, by that maxim of Kluckhohn and Murray which has served us before. All humans are in some ways like all other humans, in some ways like some other humans, and in some ways like no other humans. The idea of identity as a hierarchy of feedbacks responding to positive and negative emotions sug-gests ways of rendering that idea more tellingly than simply as some, some, and some.

In the two-level picture (p. 145), identity, the reference standard set at the top and working its way down through two—or many—levels, states the way in which one person is like no other person. The combination of theme and variations at any given moment which cumulates the history of that theme and its variations is unique.

In the lower loop, the feedback through reality at the physical level is fixed. Every person shares about the same physiology and the same physical reality—at least as compared with a tree. Further, every person in the same place at the same time as this person would tend to share that same loop: anyone looking through the same microscope, for example. In that sense the lower levels articulate the way in which one person is like every other person.

As for one person's being like some other people, consider this sentence, "The book is ready for the printer." At the general level of physical reality, it is the same for everybody. You see the serifs on T or the downstroke of y just about as I do. In another sense the sentence is quite unique. "Book" brings a picture to my mind of a leatherbound copy of *Poems in Persons* that I have been wondering where to keep. I am sure "book" brings some entirely different picture to your mind, and I can never create exactly the same picture in my mind. Nevertheless, despite the different identities at the tops of our hierarchies, we communicate through the shared physical reality of the sentence and the reality in our minds of the culture on which it rests.

It is by virtue of that inner cultural set governing our essentially similar physical perceptions that we read or hear that sentence the same way. Yet that cultural set operates in two different modes. In one, it has an almost physiological force. "Book" cannot begin with an h or a t. "The" cannot go after its nouns, "book the" or "printer the." In that sense cultural standards function in the feedback loops to say, This cannot be otherwise. If it is, you will get garbled or zero feedback. You will feel bad: anxious, unfulfilled, or frustrated. If you tried to spell "book" with hieroglyphs or cuneiform, you couldn't. Conversely, if the only writing you knew were ideograms or kana, you couldn't read "book." In that sense some of your inner cultural reality operates like a physical ability or limitation. It is like having absolute pitch or being tone deaf.

In less elementary contexts, however, your cultural set operates much more loosely. When I hear "book" I think of the word as meaning something about like what you are holding now: lots of pages, few pictures, no ads, protective covers (either hard or soft), uniform page formats, one-time publication, just the opposite of a magazine. You probably hear the word much the same way. If you and I were in the advertising business, however, "book" would be the normal word for the upcoming issue of *Playboy* or *Cosmopolitan*. On Madison Avenue, "book" can mean "magazine."

The dictionary meaning of a word does not constitute the same kind of "it can't be otherwise" cultural standard as the necessity of beginning "book" with a b. Among the same people who understand that you have to begin "book" with a b, the word can nevertheless have quite different meanings (magazine or, so my dictionaries tell me, a life sentence in prison or a record of bets or a bundle of tobacco leaves or the words of a musical comedy).

The meaning of a word, then, does not have the same limiting power as the spelling. The common answer is that the context "determines" the meaning, but that again oversimplifies. If I am talking to an advertising account executive and I hypothesize that when he says "book" he means magazine, I may be able to make sense of what he says. My hypothesis may yield satisfying feedback. I may feel good. If I am talking to an English teacher and I hypothesize that "book" means a bundle of tobacco leaves, very likely my hypothesis will yield no useful feedback and leave me feeling bad. "Context" means bringing a cultural "set" to bear. One's cultural "set" in this sense does not impose a standard on the comparator of the level below. Rather it means a ready-made hypothesis that I bring to bear on what I hear.

My cultural "set" affects my behavior in at least two quite different ways, then. One is to impose a limitation: this rule cannot be otherwise. The other merely says: this rule might be otherwise, but this is the one to try first. If we use the two-level feedback picture for an idea of my mind, my cultural values can occupy two different places in it. One is as a standard that sets limits on lower levels: being unable to read "book" as other than book. The other is as a store of ready-made hypotheses to try out on the world. "Book" probably means printed pages, bound on one side, between covers, and not published periodically—probably.

All people are in some ways like all other people, in some ways like some other people, and in some ways like no other people. When I talk about identity in the particular I ARC sense that this book develops, I am addressing the unique individual who is like no other person. When people talk about the ways an individual is like all other people, they are usually talking about the physical or physiological human who has two legs, two arms, two ears, and who speaks, laughs, or dies as every human does.

When psychologists show how some individual fits a statistical generalization, they are talking about the ways that person is like some other people. In effect, they are fitting him into a cultural group. It may be a real culture—Southerners behave this way—or it may be an ad hoc culture—the people on whom I tried this experiment behaved this way. In either case, the generalization functions in one of the two ways we read "book." Either it sets an absolute standard on lower level loops or it serves as a ready-made hypothesis that people try out. If it is a standard, then the psychologist is likely to find it among all people in the culture because "the rule could not be otherwise." If it is a hypothesis, then the psychologist will find it only among some people in the culture.

Thus the two-level feedback picture gives us a way to imagine the relation between the conclusions the psychoanalyst draws and the results the experimenter gets. The experimental psychologist tests the human world by projecting hypotheses into it. Then experiments confirm or deny the hypotheses in particulars, as the results of the experiments feed back into the psychologist's perceptions. The subjects behave the way they were supposed to, or they don't. The experimenter feels satisfied or puzzled accordingly.

The lower, the more precise the hypothesis, the closer it is likely to be to sensory reality, the more likely it is to be some process that all humans share, and the more it will lend itself to experimental methods. Experiments that test the way our eyes jump around a scene are more likely to work than experiments on the way we feel toward politicians. Conversely, the larger, the higher the hypothesis, the more likely it will be a function of the subject's identity, the less likely it is to repeat itself in an experiment, and the more an explanation for it will require the interpretations of a psychology like psychoanalysis.

The psychoanalyst is talking, one way or another, about an identity that *uses* the rules the psychologist describes. Those rules may apply totally, to all people in a given culture (like syntax), or they may apply flexibly and probabilistically (like meanings). Either way, however, in an aphorism of H. J. Home that deserves to be more widely known, "Mind is the meaning of behavior" (1966, p. 46).

If there is an element of interpretation that governs the if-then laws that psychologists seek, could this be a basis for Noam Chomsky's disturbing hypothesis that "some possible sciences lie beyond human grasp, perhaps the science of causation of behavior among them" (1972, p. 157)?

The feedback model can shed some light on the limitations that Chomsky points to. A psychology asks, How do my needs shape what I see and know and believe? A theory of human identity offers an explanation—at the same time that that very theory is shaped by human need and subject to the same sort of explanation as the ideas it would explain! Thus, one can trace in the theories proposed by theorists of personality the influence of their own personalities (Stolorow and Atwood, 1979).

One aspect of the question that Chomsky raises is that the making of a psychological theory is the kind of event that a psychological theory ought to be able to explain. A psychology ought to be able to account for its own coming into being. No mere if-then laws, however, can explain the framing of the if-then laws themselves. Hence a psychology cannot consist simply of if-then laws.

There is something to psychology beyond statistical correlations, then. Admittedly, the feedback model is oversimple. Nevertheless it offers a glimpse of what that something beyond is: identity or, in the broadest sense, some intention or purpose that has to be interpreted rather than reduced to an if-then, cause-effect, ground and consequence, or independent and dependent variable. "Mind is the meaning of behavior."

If we can model the mind as a hierarchy of feedbacks, then the psychologist faces two quite different operations. Going up that hierarchy requires an act of interpretation, but going down it one can discover if-then rules. Going down the hierarchy of mind one can discover rules of the like-all-people or like-some-people type. If, however, one wants to discover how those rules are applied or not applied, if one wants to discover why the experiment did not yield a 100 percent, uniform result, then one has to look upward, and this is true of both like-all-other-people and like-some-other-people principles. In effect one has to look upward to find what Polanyi identifies as "boundary conditions" (1968) and Herbert Simon calls "the thin interface between the natural laws within it [the artifact] and the natural laws without" (1969, p. 57).

For example, "All humans have two ears," a like-all-others principle. Once it is established, you learn about the application of such a principle even more by considering the cases where it does not apply—injuries, abnormal births, diseases—than by simply accumulating cases where it does. Another like-all-others principle: "All humans pass through an oedipus complex" (including Santa Claus). Again, having once established the principle, you learn about the oedipus complex by seeing it in action. You learn about the limits of the oedipus complex (its boundary conditions, so to speak) by looking at the cases where the generalization does not hold: autistic children, psychotics, or one-year-olds.

The same holds true for like-some-other principles. "Most human beings are between five and seven feet tall." You would learn one kind of thing by studying the distribution of heights. You would learn another kind, boundary conditions perhaps, by studying children, pygmies, Watusi, the circus's people, and professional basketball players. "Men like aggressive jokes more than women do." Again, the exceptions are as interesting as the laughers who justify the rule. One could, in fact, learn relatively little about male aggression by studying only the men who like aggressive jokes compared to studying both those who do and those who don't.

To study the negatives and limits to the type of principle that regular psychologists propose, one needs to look up the hierarchy and find uniqueness and like-no-other behaviors. One has to interpret holistically, and this requires a different kind of intellectual maneuver from the experiments devoted to if-then, covering laws that psychologists conventionally rely upon. One cannot check a holistic interpretation by experiment, only by rating it against another interpretation.

One person, some people, everybody—these three levels of psychological principle claim different kinds of truth. Everybody principles are often intuitively obvious, at least the biological ones. Everybody has two legs, two arms, two ears. These are the obvious truths that show how we humans are like humans and not like frogs or trees. Principles about some people claim a different, a scientific truth: the building and scrupulous testing of carefully wrought hypotheses. The one-person principles of identity theory seem to me yet a third kind. They account for (provide narrative accounts of the inner dynamics of) what actual people do in actual situations.

In effect one could imagine the human being that the psychologists study, *homo studiandus,* by means of the two-loop diagram:

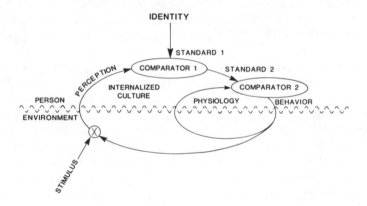

A personal identity like *no other* person's uses cultural and other values that are like *some other* people's to govern a physical body and world that are about the same for *all other* people.

As Paul Diesing shows, when working with a holistic explanation, you test a certain level of explanation, not as an if-then by itself, but in relation to the levels above and below it. You discover and improve low-level descriptions from theory. You test high-level theories by the adequacy of the low-level statements they yield. You test a whole case description such as my analysis of Shaw's identity "by its success in organizing and explaining its constituent themes." "Only a theme, at the lowest level, is tested by direct empirical criteria, such as specific . . . predictions, frequency counts, and statistical operations" (1971, pp. 229–34).

The low-level themes, the pawns in the game, came in the first place from theory. Having noticed Shaw's preoccupation with the mouth, I looked in

Shaw's life for a preoccupation with skin (and noticed his woolly suits) because I knew "orality" includes stimulation of the skin.

If case descriptions, taken together, yield a theory of types of cases ("nomic" or "intrusive" character-types, for example), you can test that typology only "by the adequacy of the case descriptions it makes possible." If the typology yields a yet more general theory, such as the psychoanalytic theory of child development, still one tests the "general theory only indirectly, by testing the usefulness of its associated typology" (Diesing, 1971, pp. 229–34).

I would sum these testings up and down the levels of generality by saying that these levels are in a dialectical or feedback relation to each other. The general defines the specific and the specific the general. Interpretation of meaning and mind situates the general law, and the general law guides interpretation. If I say, "Intrusive personality traits give rise to symptoms of hysteria," that is partly a way of asking, What was this man like before the hysteria? How did he walk and move and act on the physical world? How are the symptoms from which he suffers related to breaking into a physical or interpersonal world?

In effect, the general statement guides particular inquiries by which I can refine the general statement and learn just what "phallic" or "hysteric" entails. In studying particular cases, then, it is not enough simply to generalize cases into an overall law like, "Intrusive personality traits give rise to symptoms of hysteria." One uses the generality to discover data and data to modify the generality.

"One uses. . . . " There has to be a "one"—somebody who does it. This dialectic of testing and exploration demands human participation at every step.

An older way of thinking about science assumed that the general law was the end point. You collected data, framing laws of greater and greater generality, hoping to arrive at some scientific Utopia with THE law of laws that covered everything. A more modern view would be that there is no end point. Science is a process that will never stop. Data enable us to propose theories which enable us to discover more data. Conversely, new technology opens up new data for us so that we can make new kinds of theories. A theory is but a way station, for at any moment people may take a new slant on theory and so change the kind of data we would search out.

In particular, so far as psychology is concerned, I think experimentalists should no longer regard the general principle or the correlation between dependent and independent variable as the end product of research. We should reverse the traditional roles. Instead of using the individual case only to make a hypothesis to be tested, we can use the test to provide a guide to inquire into the case—and then use the case to build generalizations which one can test and then apply to the case and so on around and around through a continuing feedback.

Interestingly, in imaging this process, the feedback diagrams suggest that the experimenters' correlations may be functioning in different places. If the correlations are very high, 100 percent or 90 percent, the experimenter may have demonstrated some "real" or hard-wired loop that strictly determines the feedback a given behavioral output will have. If the correlations are low, the experimenter may simply have demonstrated a preference for a certain behavioral output or hypothesis. In short, I am suggesting that we use this feedback picture of an identity controlling perceptions to replace the merely numerical concern with $p<.05$ or $p<.01$ or $p<.001$. Instead, *we can try to understand where in the feedback process the generalization formulated by the psychologist fits and functions.*

I am suggesting that psychologists seek significance not in abstract, arbitrary statistical criteria but in the kind of actual payoff one gets by applying the hypothesis. What counts is not methodology but what we can learn. Does the experimental result enable me to enlarge my inquiry by setting up a dialectic between the principle and the case? Fundamentally, we are really trying to understand some event and understand it more and more as we study it more and more. Whatever method enables us to do that is the more scientific.

The nineteenth century imagined a science of more and more comprehensive laws culminating in some universal law that applied to everything, at which point the scientists could all close down their laboratories. Today, one might define the aim of science more simply: the understanding of what is not yet understood. In that sense, a covering law can be useful either to deduce facts or to ask questions. One could treat a generalization like "Intrusive personalities are likely to have hysterical symptoms" as the occasion for testing and measuring the likelihood of hysterical symptoms. One could also use it simply to inquire into the next case to be understood. Are the symptoms hysterical? Is this person intrusive? What is the relation between the symptom and the total personality? This kind of science seeks a continuing relationship between case and law rather than finding a law and stopping.

For example (I am particularly indebted to Theodore Mills for this demonstration), a sociological study of the Nixon tapes combined General Inquirer content analyses, measurement of the I/We quotient, verb/adjective quotients, and other experimental or statistical techniques to enrich an already sensitive case study of one group's disintegration. One could use a countable increase in "I" and decrease in "we" to demonstrate that the White House "plumbers' group" was losing its cohesion. That insight, however, enabled Mills's team to turn back to the tapes and look for other, less regularizable signs, metaphors of things coming apart, for example, or changes in the figures of speech applied to the group leader, Nixon. These insights in turn led back to other sociological tests, for instance, leadership indicators. The numbers could show a positive or negative or nominal change, but the precise size of the numbers proved not as useful as the insights they gave rise to in the particular case. In general terms, the "experimental" or "survey" techniques and the interpretive ones stood in a dialectical relation to each other, each adding to the other (1977).

That is, Mills and his group used them dialectically, in an exploratory feedback of the kind that diagrams of the I illustrate. In general, in twentieth-century science an active scientist has replaced the neutral observer of the nineteenth century. As Stephen Toulmin points out, such a conception of science is *more,* not less, scientific than that traditional one, for "a physical world described in terms of *order* and *information* . . . is a world within which human perception, communication, and interaction can find the natural place they lacked, both in Descartes' world of *matter* and *machines,* and in Helmholtz's world of *energy.*" Such a science "will be capable of embracing not only the world of nature, as human beings experience and interpret it, but also the activities and experience by which humans perceive, think about, and deal with that world" (1978, pp. 332–33). Psychology—any psychology—ought to be that kind of science, not one that tries to blink away the human element, since a psychology is trying to explain just that, the human element.

The most stringent criteria for science have come from realist philosophers like Karl Popper. They have insisted that the only knowledge worthy of the name scientific or indeed of the name knowledge consists of propositions that have successfully resisted disconfirmation (1972). Popper asks for two things: first, disconfirmable propositions, and second, processes of disconfirmation. "The method of science is the method of bold conjectures and ingenious and severe attempts to refute them." He is describing, in effect, the feedback that I believe defines an I.

To apply Popper's test to identity theory, one must recognize that identity theory does not rest on the proposition, "Identity is a theme and variations," but on the claim, "*I can* represent so-and-so's identity as a theme and variations." Then there are clear procedures for judging that claim or disconfirming it (as by a more inclusive or more direct interpretation). So understood, a psychology based on I ARC DEFTly meets Popper's criterion.

A difficulty, however, would come about if Popper were to insist that these processes of disconfirmation be independent of the disconfirmer. If one insists on that dissociation, then I cannot reconcile what I am suggesting as a science of I with such a notion of realism or objectivity, nor do I think such a notion truly realistic or objective. It leaves out the human element so demonstrably there. If, however, one accepts the role of the human being in disconfirming, then it seems to me that the kind of psychology I am suggesting in this chapter fits both our strongest criteria for what is scientific and also the realities of human experimentation, a science in the full sense of one that includes the activities by which humans perceive, think about, and deal with a real world.

We can put that another way. If we could not talk about people rigorously, then to maintain rigor in a scientific inquiry we would try to keep the personal element out. Suppose, however, we can talk about individuals rigorously (and I am claiming that any psychology must try, and identity theory enables us to do just that). Then we lose no rigor by including the personal influence. In fact, we would lose rigor by leaving it out. An experimenter who claims objectivity because a computer or a graduate assistant can carry out the experiment only obscures the true state of affairs.

We come back to the basic paradox that limits what we can hope for from psychology. Any psychology that tries to describe human thoughts and actions must explain humans doing psychology. A theory of human identity governing if-then laws offers an explanation and a way of describing and interpreting that I, even if it is an I doing psychology. *But* that very theory is shaped by my human needs and subject to the same sort of explanation as the ideas it would explain. This is both the limitation and the achievement of identity theory. It does not turn a blind eye to the role of the person in science, and the price it pays for that inclusion is the illusion of objectivity and the hope of finality.

"Objectivity" in a theory built on identity means accepting that knowledge is knowledge by persons. At some point we have to give up hopes of finding absolute laws separate from persons and accept a continuing dialogue among different persons formulating laws. You could read that result as the deconstruction of science. I prefer, having my needs, to see it as a way toward unity and a kind of certainty, this book's

Conclusions

I am proposing a model for the way we act on the world. We push trials out from ourselves into the world, and we take in the results in what one kind of engineer would call an information-processing feedback loop and another a generate and test sequence. These feedback loops embody the if-thens and the correlations that regular psychologists discover which are the principles by which our bodies and our cultural values function.

These principles do not run themselves. Something above and beyond them supplies the standards they seek, and I call that something identity. It initiates the loops. It is what results when, in the history of the individual, the world responds to his trials. It is somebody's representation of that individual as a theme and variations.

In I ARC and DEFT, I am suggesting a picture that we can carry around in our heads with which to think about experiments and psychologies and readings and interpretations and the relation between mind and body. Identity (an agency, a consequence, and a representation as theme and variations) governs the if-thens and correlations of our bodies and our cultural values as they function in feedback loops when we feed actions into the world and it feeds responses back to us. Ultimately what decides what we will accept as truth is how that feedback feels: clear or muddied, congenial or dissatisfying, culturally coherent or bizarre.

I DEFTly ARC provides a very general theory that is in itself neither true nor false but a general organizing idea that tells us what to look for. I would like to think "the I" is that kind of large idea of which Bohr said, its opposite is also true. Given such a picture, we can think with some cogency about the way a person has a certain style.

By means of the I and ARC and DEFT we can understand better why a Scott Fitzgerald writes the way he does or a Charles Vincent changes and unchanges under brainwashing or the way an Anna S. renews but continues herself by being psychoanalyzed. We can understand how identity governs such familiar mental processes as using symbols or perceiving. They answer to a picture in which identity is the agency that sets the standards for symbolizing or perceiving in lower-level feedback loops.

That picture in turn lets us write the classic psychoanalytic story of the way children become adult types into a dialogue. Culture and family pose the infant certain general questions (five, in my thinking) which the infant hears and answers in its own individual body language. We can trace this kind of a dialogue all through a life, from a four-year-old Little Hans up to a sixty-eight-year-old Herbert Graf. In this framework we can even speak of Santa Claus's oedipus complex. Nomic necessity applies to the loops and questions, while the language in which they are heard and answered is unique.

Given such a picture, we can begin to grasp some of the paradoxes that I broached in the preface. My I seems realer than anything else I know, yet it is completely intangible. It is so because it is the reference level for the systems by which I sense. I can no more touch or sense my identity than my house can set its own thermostats. The I is what I sense with. It cannot be sensed itself, yet I experience my I directly and immediately. Then, the minute I think about it, it becomes other, not-me. Why? Because thinking of an identity, especially one's own, cannot include the identity doing the thinking. I can only approximate my I by phrasing it, but never completely and never "correctly," because it was first and foremost a bodily identity, a thing of touch and smell and taste, too deep for words. It came into its ghostly being before I knew words.

The I ARC DEFTly picture of an I offers a thread through humanistic, deconstructive paradoxes like these. It also offers the hope of a psychology which is scientific in a twentieth-century rather than a nineteenth-century sense. I intend two things by that distinction between the centuries. First, in twentieth-century science, facts don't come into our senses naked and innocent from the world around us. They come from hypotheses. The familiar phrases of the psychologists use certain shibboleths—"bias," "distortion," "control the variables," "get something to count," "replicability," "reliability," "validity"—in order to criticize psychoanalysis for not providing raw facts. Yet these shibboleths proceed from hypotheses about what counts as a fact just as much as the psychoanalyst's "orality" or "oedipus complex" does.

Second, because facts come from hypotheses, facts ultimately depend on people because hypotheses do. Science is not a set of abstract laws, devoid of human intervention. People give rise to science, and science carries its ancestry in its principles.

Hence it is, in this century, no longer possible to draw a neat line between subjective and objective, between situations the person is in and situations the person is out of, between science and humanities. Certainly, numbers do not make such a shibboleth, nor can we say simply that science seeks out "covering laws" while the humanities deal with uniqueness and the individual case.

One simply cannot divide the way we know things into scientific and interpretive, personal and impersonal, objective and subjective. This is the idea on which *The I* is built, and on it the book must stand or fall.

Rather, this feedback picture suggests, science involves both numbers and ideas, both covering laws and the individual case. Science consists precisely of the dialectic or feedback between them. Numbers improve the idea, and the idea improves the numbers. The covering law helps us better understand the individual case, and our better understanding of the case lets us improve the covering law. Both the humanities and the sciences share this pattern, differing not in kind but in the degree to which each emphasizes covering laws. Both ask us to use our skills both to generalize laws and to interpret persons.

As you must have surmised by now, I have a deep and permeating need to see a unity and consistency in things. Since my education first took me along a technological route, through electrical engineering, and only later to the study of literature, two of the things that I seek to unify are the sciences and the humanities or, I could say, certainty and beauty, fidelity and desire.

Science requires a community of scientists to establish the rules of the game. Hence, science and the humanities are not two opposed cultures. Rather each fulfills and complements the other. Measured data about the world (the traditional material of science) presuppose communication between people (the traditional material of the humanities).

I see psychoanalysis, particularly if it combines identity theory with modern feedback theories of the brain, perception, cognition, and memory, as a science that gives reasons for such a synthesis, making it possible. Such a psychoanalysis means we can talk about "the I" with precision. Hence we can unite the psychological and the physical sciences and both with the humanities. "It is only the modern formulation of the mind-body problem which prevents us from unifying psychology and physics in an all-encompassing world-picture" (Ricoeur, 1978, p. 337).

Instead of "two cultures," then, I see a continuum of intellectual activities. Some stress individuality, others generality. Some accent the feedback we get from reality, some the hypotheses we bring to reality, but all take place within a relationship of feedback between a theme-and-variations self and the world that begins at the ends of our fingertips. All presuppose a theory of the I. It is impossible to make a statement in any science or any of the humanities without making some assumptions about human beings.

This theory of the I codifies a set of such assumptions that I like to think works better than most. Identity theory lets us represent an I with precision, as a theme and variations. Further, we can add to that theme-and-variations representation the concept of identity as feedback system. Identity-as-agent sets the standard for a feedback through our cultural resources, our bodies, and our environment, and the feedback itself sustains and creates identity-as-consequence. The I uses eyes and ears, memory, ego (in a psychoanalytic sense), and gender (in a feminist sense) to create and re-create itself. Such an ARCed I fits not only with psychoanalysis but with late twentieth century thinking about perception, memory, cognition, and the architecture of the brain. It is a theory of the I that any humanist or scientist can use.

We need not, as some distinguished modern philosophers and psychoanalysts have claimed, dispense with the idea of "mind." Rather we can think about mind quite precisely, and we can use that concept to explain behaviors. Mind is the meaning of behavior. With identity we can find that meaning in a child's triumphant growing or in the achievements of a Darwin, a Shakespeare, or a Freud. We need not choose between sciences and humanities. At the heart of the study of life, no matter what we call it, there is—am—an I.

Appendix

The I, the Ego, and the *Je:* Identity and Other Psychoanalyses

In this appendix,* I am trying (to use a word literary critics have found useful) to "situate" identity theory in relation to other versions of psychoanalytic theory. As I see psychoanalysis, it has gone through three phases (Holland, 1976). It was, first, a psychology of the unconscious, second of the ego, and today, I believe, of the self. All three psychoanalyses base themselves centrally on Freud's original discoveries, but each successive phase moves outward, going beyond the phases that preceded it by framing them in a larger, more inclusive human psychology.

The earliest stage grew out of Freud's discoveries of latent and manifest content in a variety of phenomena: dreams, neurotic symptoms, jokes, forgetting, and slips of all kinds. As he came to realize that this polarity between manifest and latent or conscious and unconscious applied in so many different spheres of mental activity, he understood that he had arrived at a general psychological principle of explanation: the dynamic tension between conscious and unconscious, thought of as "the" unconscious or "the" conscious, as systems, structures, forces, or even places in the brain.

We can date the second phase, ego psychology, from Freud's positing a superego, an ego, and an id in 1923. Ego psychology balances the mind's synthesizing functions against external reality or some other internal psychic structure. Its basic polarity for explanations thus poises ego against nonego, that is, the mind's control and balance of the agencies acting on it against those agencies themselves. Hence, although therapy in the first phase sought to make "the" unconscious conscious, therapy in the second aims at enlarging and strengthening the ego. Indeed, as Freud himself concluded, one can no longer speak of "the" unconscious as an isolated system. One

---

* I wrote this appendix primarily for readers proficient in psychoanalytic theory who are curious about the relation between this theory of an I ARCing DEFTly and established psychoanalytic concepts. In comparing the two, however, I found it necessary to summarize a certain amount of general psychoanalytic knowledge. I believe therefore that the appendix might also prove useful to readers *not* familiar with psychoanalytic theory, as an introduction to this or that psychoanalytic concept sufficient for reading *The I*. Since, then, this appendix is meant to serve both the expert and the not so expert, I have made my summaries somewhat fuller than if I had been writing for experts alone.

can only use the word in phrases like "unconscious ego" or "unconscious superego."

In the third phase, the tension whose dynamics will explain things is between self and nonself. As early as 1930, in the first chapter of *Civilization and Its Discontents,* Freud had embarked on this third phase. He stated that, in the earliest months of life, the infant's ego includes the world around it, in the way we adults experience falling in love or mystical experiences. "Originally the ego includes everything; later it separates off an external world from itself" (1930a, 21:68). He had, in effect, recognized that for at least the beginning of an individual's life span, the wholly intrapsychic model of the first two phases of psychoanalysis had to give way to an interpsychic model, one that included both the individual mind and its surround.

This is a monumental change in psychoananalytic theory, and Freud was not overstating it when he compared the discovery of this early developmental phase to the unearthing of Minoan and Mycenaean civilization beneath the classical and archaic Greece that the West had known since the Renaissance. Oedipus was a classical drama directed to the Olympian father-gods. Now Freud, by describing this early fusion, had found the ancient mother-goddess who had to be before Oedipus could be.

Once Freud had put forward the idea that at the beginning of life the ego is a permeable interface between self and outer world, later psychoanalysts have found a steadily increasing body of evidence that that is true all through life. Thus the third phase of psychoanalysis grows from work done during the fifties and sixties by theorists like Erik Erikson, Jacques Lacan, Heinz Kohut, Heinz Lichtenstein, Otto Kernberg, and (especially) English object-relations theorists like W. R. D. Fairbairn, Harry Guntrip, D. W. Winnicott, and Marion Milner. Now, in the 1980s, a great many psychoanalysts are thinking and explaining by means of a dynamic tension between self and other that includes but goes beyond the earlier dynamics of ego and nonego, conscious and unconscious. Often, these psychoanalysts describe themselves as "going beyond" ego psychology, and sometimes they contrast what they see as their more advanced view to what seems an unduly conservative commitment on the part of some psychoanalytic institutes to ego psychology.

Freud himself said, however, that our egos lose their boundaries when we fall in love or when we have mystical experiences, and subsequent psychoanalytic writers have argued that what Freud theorized for special cases is a general phenomenon of adult life. For example, I asserted (in 1968) that the same thing happens when we become "absorbed" in literary or artistic works. Long before I came along, Lacan had suggested his *stade du miroir* in infancy and D. W. Winnicott had developed his even more powerful concept of a transitional space between self and other in which all cultural experience takes place. One can read Erik Erikson's large concepts of adaptation, mutuality, and psychosocial development as building this interpersonal model of the mind. So does Charles Rycroft when he updates the old-fashioned symbolic decoding to treat psychoanalytic symbolism as an active way of relating oneself to the world. So, in a way, does Hans Loewald in rethinking the traditional concepts of id, ego, and superego or Roy Schafer in developing an "action language" of self and other that will get psycho-analysis beyond those second-phase constructs. Heinz Kohut, by addressing therapeutically a self that includes id, ego, and superego but is not limited to them, develops a third-phase psychoanalytic therapy parallel to classical psychoanalytic treatment.

One can remember these three phases by the parts of speech they make the word "unconscious" into. Always, Freud used the word to mean whether or not one was aware of some idea or feeling. In the first phase, however, "unconscious" could also be a noun, referring to a thing, a system, or even a place. In the second phase, when Freud announced that "uncon-scious" was no longer a system, only "descriptive," the word became an adjective only. Now, Roy Schafer ingeniously suggests, "unconscious" ought to be an adverb: we should think of a whole person doing this or that unconscious*ly* (1976, pp. 241–43).

This three-phase capsule history of psychoanalysis gives us a frame for sorting out theories and situating identity theory within them. To each phase, identity theory brings a concept of identity which is very like the second-phase psychoanalytic concept of "character." The classic definition is Otto Fenichel's: "the habitual mode of bringing into harmony the tasks presented by internal demands and by the external world" (1945, p. 467; see also the discussion of characterologies on pp. 160–64 above).

"Character," in turn (as Victor Rosen pointed out in 1961), is much akin to "style." (Etymologically, both words have to do with scribing marks on a surface.) Style is a literary critic's word, but the concept works in much the same way for a copy editor, a fashion columnist, or a sportswriter. Style is someone's distinctive or characteristic mode of doing something, and you can therefore use the word for boxing or business or brewing, for any one or all aspects of a life, as in *life-style*. It is, for all practical purposes, identity, shorn of the theoretical niceties that cling to the later term.

By thinking in terms of style, then, we can connect identity theory to other concepts in psychoanalysis. Usually, *identity is a way of saying that a certain concept from elsewhere in psychoanalyis is carried out with such and such a style*. For example, in

Classical Psychoanalysis

the central concepts are conscious and unconscious. Sometimes, in question periods after lectures on identity theory, people ask me, "Where is the unconscious in all this?" "The" unconscious is where it always was. The concept of identity does not change it.

Freud first defined the unconscious descriptively, as all those contents of the mind that are at any given moment outside of conscious awareness and that can only be brought to consciousness with special efforts or under special circumstances (like dreams or free associations). This is the unconscious as adjective, and none of Freud's revisions of theory changed this basic definition.

The unconscious in this sense is completely private. That is, only I can know what I am aware of (and, I suppose, what I am unaware—unconscious—of). You (or my analyst) might infer that I am unconscious of this or that, but only I can really know.

Identity is representation, and there are two possibilities. Identity can be perceived by the person in question, the one "inside" the identity (so to speak), or identity can be perceived by another from "outside." This distinction between an "inside" and an "outside" interpreter is important because, in it, a theme-and-variations concept of identity poses and preserves the classical psychoanalytic polarity of conscious and unconscious.

Even with empathy, we on the outside will never feel exactly the pleasure another mind feels, never know things, even knowledge we share, in the same way, never love as that other person loves. On the other hand, we can see and even measure behavior from outside as accurately as we please.

Behavior is "outside" as a literary text is. Both present visible surfaces, both spring from an intention, and with both one infers an intention from the surface. Presumably any given intention is conscious or unconscious or both, but one cannot infer which—from outside.

If you write, "To be or not to be," I can legitimately conclude that you intended to write "To be or not to be." I could be mistaken, however. You may have actually intended to write "To see or not to see" and, like the young man with *aliquis,* slipped. There is no way I could tell from what you say alone that you had made a slip of the tongue. There is no way I can infer from a text alone what of your intention was conscious and what unconscious.

I pick up a Fitzgerald story, and I find that it is about an idealized woman and something being withheld from the hero. Every other story by Fitzgerald that I read has the same themes. Is this a conscious choice for him or unconscious?

The idealized woman and the hero withheld from are not unconscious in the sense that he was unaware of them—Fitzgerald was certainly aware of what he was writing as he wrote it. Standing outside Fitzgerald, however, considering his identity, how can we know what he was aware of in his recurring choice of theme and what not—what was unconscious, what conscious?

So with behavior. You stub your toe. For all I know, you deliberately intended to kick that rock (like Dr. Johnson). Whether you did or did not, though, the data for thinking about identity could be no more than your stubbing your toe.

To the outside observer, the distinction between conscious and unconscious is invisible. Freud saw through the forgetful young man in a way the young man himself could not. Only the person observed can demonstrate the distinction between conscious and unconscious, as the young man showed by his surprise that he had not been consciously aware of the connection between his wish for avenging descendants and his worry about his mistress's pregnancy. In therapy or in conversation Fitzgerald might let us infer something about how much he knew of his own patterns, but even then we would be relying on his word.

At the same time, however, the young man knew all kinds of sensations, feelings, memories, information, and intentions opaque to Freud outside and on which Freud's inferences depended. Hence Freud's discovery of the young man's motive in forgetting depended precisely on their being two of them, one inside the identity, the other outside it, being able to talk back and forth.

In psychoanalytic therapy the therapist is outside, and the patient inside. The patient associates and says what he feels. The therapist infers the unity of what he hears, but that understanding can only become therapeutic when the patient takes it "inside." Conversely, the therapist can only function as a therapist if the patient will bring what he has inside, outside. One way of thinking about therapy, then, would be: the combining of outside insights and inside experience in an identity-creating relationship, namely, the verbal space in which the interpreter and interpretee act together that Freud described in his 1937 paper on "Constructions in Analysis" (23:258–59). In this way psychoanalysis mingles a self defined by both a feeling of wholeness and an observation of it, a therapeutic alliance between an inside, experiencing, associating ego and an outside, observing, analyzing ego.

Whether you free associate on the couch or stub your toe or misquote Virgil or write stories about all-powerful women and deprived heroes, identity need say nothing about your intention and can say nothing about whether it was conscious or unconscious. Identity has nothing to do with "conscious" or "unconscious" in the exact, descriptive sense: what you are subjectively aware of. There is, however, another sense.

In the first phase of psychoanalysis, "unconscious" is also "the" unconscious, a noun and a system with its own forces and energies. In his early clinical work Freud concluded that an unconscious thought was "dynamic," with forces (like physical forces) pushing either toward consciousness or unconsciousness, expression or repression.

Identity does not change the idea of a dynamic unconscious any more than the descriptive, but for a different reason. "The" unconscious no longer exists as a concept. Freud eliminated it when he introduced the id, ego, and superego and began the second phase of psychoanalysis. "We will no longer use the term 'unconscious' in the systematic sense" (1933a, 22:72). "The" unconscious has no place in second- or third-phase psychoanalysis.

I have been addressing the question, How does identity theory relate to the classical distinction between conscious and unconscious? There is a parallel question: How does identity relate to the distinction between primary and secondary process?

By secondary process, Freud intended the mental processes that psychology had traditionally studied: problem solving or rational, goal-directed thought governed by the reality principle. In dreams, jokes, symptoms, and free association, however, he had found forms of thought that were completely irrational and directed to immediate pleasure, that simply did not follow such rules of secondary process thinking as the axiom against logical contradictions, the principle of cause and effect, or the laws of time and place. This "primary process thinking" was, he thought, earlier, childish, something one grew out of in waking life if not in dreams.

I prefer a concept of primary and secondary processes that matches the picture of mind put forward in chapter 6, a hierarchy of feedbacks in which the higher levels govern the lower. The secondary processes are those aimed outward, at encountering reality, while the primary processes are attuned to the feelings that tell us whether the secondary processes are succeeding in their feedbacks through reality. The primary processes are those the ego must use for all the functions aimed inward, at preserving the continuity and identity of the self and assimilating (in Piaget's sense) new experiences to the way the self schematizes reality (as in chapters 4 and 5). Hence, the secondary processes depend upon a constant feedback of information from the outside world, while primary processes are independent of feedback from outer reality. Primary processes take over in dreaming and mental illness, because something (like sleep) interrupts the feedback needed to sustain the secondary processes.

If we think of primary and secondary process thinking as arranged in a hierarchy of higher and lower (as in chapters 5 and 6), then secondary process thinking must be the lower, tied to our sensory contacts with the outer world. Animals would have rather highly developed secondary processes. Primary process would be higher, associated in one direction with identity, in the other with governing secondary processes to sustain and enhance the self. Hence, we need not think of either primary or secondary processes as "primitive" or "infantile" with respect to the other. Both develop progressively all through life. Both serve in the adaptation of the human organism to its social and biological surround (Noy, 1969). Nor would one think of a "regression" from secondary to primary process. Art, which reverses the balance of the primary and secondary processes in life, is not childlike or primitive but simply a shift in modes.

We carry on both these kinds of thinking with a certain style: quickly or slowly, skipping steps or plodding, carefully or uninhibitedly. Since identity is a way of putting these stylistic features into words, it applies equally to primary and secondary processes. One dreams with a certain personal style of dreaming, hence as a function of one's identity. One pays one's income tax within a certain style which is, if not the same, at least like the style with which one dreams.

In my picture, then, identity uses both primary and secondary processes, with primary governing secondary. A person uses those processes as one might use the processes of language or arithmetic. We can imagine the primary and secondary processes as a smorgasbord of strategies that all people share but from which each person chooses in an individual way, with a certain style. A Shaw will choose those strategies of either primary or secondary process that fit his general need to find a significant other. A Fitzgerald will tend not to use strategies that do not enable him to find a large, withholding other. Any person will prefer some strategies and perhaps avoid others entirely. Identity theory thus gives us a way of understanding how primary and secondary processes can be the same for everyone yet my primary processes be *my* primary processes, just as my English is my English. The concept of an I ARCing and DEFTing through a hierarchy of feedback loops seems to me to enlarge the classical psychoanalytic concept of primary and secondary process quite usefully.

A third question likely to be asked about identity by those steeped in classical psychoanalytic theory is, Where are the drives in this? Is identity consistent with the classical psychoanalytic theory of the drives? If I were to answer in a word, I would say, "Yes," but the question is a complex one because Freud evolved his theory of the drives gradually over a whole lifetime (Bibring, 1936/1969).

In his last formulations, Freud wrote of two kinds of drive, libidinal and aggressive, life-instincts and death-instincts. Freud generalized the sexual instinct and the self-preservative into Eros, which he defined as seeking "to combine organic substances into ever larger unities," "to force together and hold together the portions of living substance." "The aim of the first of these basic instincts is to establish ever greater unities and to preserve them thus—in short, to bind together; the aim of the second is, on the contrary, to undo connections and so to destroy things" (1920g, 18:42–43 and 60n).

Freud speculated that if he were to generalize the aggressive drive as he had the libidinal one, its final aim would be to lead what is living into a state of inertia prior to organic life. It would be a death instinct. To generalize it that way, however, requires reversing the drive from active to passive, from a self undoing the connections in something external to a self undoing the connections in the self. No one, so far as I know, has found any evidence of such a reversal.

Ethologists translate Freud's assumption of an aggressive drive into an innate human drive to war. Intellectual (as opposed to clinical) fans of psychoanalysis rhapsodize about a "death instinct" or "Thanatos." In general, people tend to get romantic about the drives, they sound so much like love and hate. Few clinicians have found much in a death instinct that corresponds to human experience, however, and the idea appeals today mostly to the philosophical or to the idolaters of Freud.

Most Anglo-American analysts have accepted Freud's dual instinct theory in its less generalized form: one drive to form unities and another to split them apart into nullity. In life, any given instinct combines elements of both. "The sexual act is an act of aggression with the purpose of the most intimate union" (1940a, 23:149). In eating, one establishes a unity with the object but destroys it as a separate entity.

In relating the drives to identity, I find it helpful to return to Freud's original, clear definitions. It is certainly not easy, for drive is a frontier concept bridging mind and body. Sometimes Freud wrote about it as wholly physiological. Sometimes he included the *Triebrepräsentanz,* the mental representation or psychical representative of the bodily force. It is perhaps, as Freud suggested, neither necessary nor wise to try to eliminate that ambiguity.

One can distinguish four components of any given drive. It has a source (*Quell*), that is, some process located in a particular organ or part of the body. It has an aim (*Ziel*), namely, a satisfaction obtained by balancing the organic tension, as food, up to a point, satisfies hunger. The drive usually, but not always, has an object (*Objekt*) by means of which satisfaction is to be achieved—often a person but sometimes a thing, like food. Finally, it has a "pressure" or "impetus" (*Drang*) by which Freud seemed to mean a quantitative measure of the amount of action required to satisfy the drive (Freud, 1915c, 14:111–15 and 117–23).

One can use identity, it seems to me, to make "drive" more precise and useful; one can use "drive" to make identity precise. That is, one could speak of a quantitative factor in a person's identity from drives. One person has more drive than someone else or less: that would be Freud's *Drang.* Similarly, one could compare the balance of aggression and libido in different people. Some, obviously, are more aggressive than others. Certainly different people accent different *Quelle.* Shaw was an oral character, more so than Fitzgerald, although he was oral too. Also, different people seek different objects. Shaw sought a purposeful other. Fitzgerald sought one that would withhold. As for *Ziel,* Fitzgerald sought saturation, while Shaw was abstemious. One could regard the various components of Freud's concept of drive—aggression, libido, source, aim, object, and impetus—as ways of inquiring into and making more precise a statement of identity. A statement of identity, conversely, would be a way of understanding these various components as a whole.

There is, however, one fundamental difference between drive and identity. Freud located the drives in the biological self, while identity is a representation of that self in someone's mind. In this sense, I think of identity as freeing the concept of drive from a nineteenth-century cosmology.

Freud thought of actual, physiological drives, but modern biologists and later analysts are more reluctant to posit physiological entities than he was. With identity, we need not imagine those drives as part of our inherited physiology. Identity simply asks, Can we sort out behavior into two logically exhaustive quests, one to unite and preserve unity, the other to divide unities and so destroy? Identity makes the drives into a representation of self by means of drives.

Psychoanalysis is often said to be a psychology of conflict, for example, in the conflict between libidinal and aggressive drives. Identity, however, which so stresses unity, might seem to ignore conflict. One might well ask (and people do), Where in identity theory is conflict?

Conflict refers to two or more competing impulses or perhaps a conflict between reality and an impulse. Identity describes the style of the adversaries. To the extent that an impulse is a part of the psychology of the individual, identity describes the style of the impulse: hasty, inexorable, displaceable, peremptory, reversible, splittable—whatever. Presumably, if one has read identity well, one would be able to see in each aspect of the conflict the same identity. That does not imply, of course, that there is no conflict, only that the scene of battle is lit all in the same hues.

Freud addressed the matter of conflict, however, more precisely in the second phase of his thought than in the first.

Ego-Psychology

is the psychoanalysis that deals most directly with conflict, and it is the relation of identity to ego-psychology that will be of greatest concern to most American analysts. Let me proceed step-by-step, then, with what I take to be some of the fundamental theses of ego-psychology. If I linger on what will seem elementary to most American analysts, it is because French psychoanalytic theory, in its sudden growth, is deeply questioning some of these postulates.

In 1915 (in a mere five months between March and August!), Freud wrote a series of twelve papers hoping to clarify his basic concepts so as to provide a firm theoretical foundation for his new science. Seven of these papers, however, he never published and apparently destroyed. Evidently, he had already begun to have doubts about first-phase theory, based on "the" unconscious versus "the" conscious. Beginning with *Beyond the Pleasure Principle* in 1920, he began to unfold a quite different system designed to account for two clusters of clinical evidence with which earlier theory had not dealt.

First, it was clear from the outset that one can observe and so split oneself, as the double appearance of "self" in that sentence suggests, but there are subtler forms of self-splitting. From the first Freud had spoken of a "censor" for whom the ideas in dreams had to be disguised. Obsessional neurotics and paranoiacs had delusions that they were being observed, and such an observer would have to be some form of their own selves. People mourning for a lost loved one typically reproached themselves for inadequacies toward that lost other.

In general, people have a sense of guilt: they inwardly criticize themselves for not living up to some ideal or for breaking certain taboos. This sense of guilt is often unconscious, as the adulterous young man's thinking of a group of saints might consciously express unconscious feelings of guilt. Hence "the" unconscious of first-phase theory was not just repressed impulses striving toward consciousness. Something critical and repressive was also unconscious.

The young man's guilt might be momentary, but the self-observation of an obsessional neurotic or a paranoiac person could go on for years. In dreams there is *always* a censor to be evaded. Freud therefore began to posit a self-critical entity that persists in time, a "structure" in Anglo-American usage, although Freud himself tended to speak of a "psychical apparatus" (*seelischer Apparat*) that included a certain "system" (*System*) or "agency" (*Instanz*—a judicial metaphor, as in the phrase, "a Court of First Instance" [1953–74, 1:xxiii–xxiv]). Whatever the terms, the point is, something in the mind shows a constancy and consistency in its workings like an organ in the body. The key, in other words, is time—duration.

Finding long-lasting, unconscious self-critical tendencies, Freud posited in 1923 an unconscious, censorious structure embodying the sense of guilt (particularly in the symptoms of obsessional neurosis), the normal conscience, self-reproaches during mourning, and paranoid delusions. The patient senses an agency holding sway in his ego which measures his self and each of its activities against what Freud had earlier called an "ideal ego" that each of us has created for ourselves in the course of development. In 1923, Freud named this agency the "superego."

This book, like most Anglo-American analytic writings, treats the superego (as a structure) as having two functions. First, it includes an ego ideal derived from the earliest identifications with parents and associated with values and ideals, one's sense of what one must be to "be somebody." Failure to live up to one's ego ideal leads to lost self-esteem or a sense of inferiority or inadequacy or depression—the fifty-year-old's question: Is *this* all I am going to be? Second, we have a superego properly so called, a "thou shalt not," derived from a later identification with the parents as they criticized, prohibited, or punished (as in our phrase "the voice of conscience"). Fear of punishment, guilt, or anxiety are the penalties exacted for a breach of these superego demands. Conversely, living up to both one's superego and ego ideal should lead to feelings of mental well-being, security, and, occasionally, humor.

Speaking loosely, people sometimes call the superego the basis of morality. Certainly, a person's ego ideal and superego will embody the values of society to the extent and in the way that person experienced them as a child through parents. These values may, however, be quite childish and as a result not moral at all (Schafer, 1974). The ego ideal's imperative may be truly imperial: you must control all evil impulses in the world; you must be omnipotent. The superego may say, Thou shalt not be dependent, for that is effeminate.

I think the tone, intensity, and maybe even the style of my moral impulses come from my experience of my parents, but their content does not. What I think moral at fifty-six has to do with what I now think, read, and know more than with the values I held as a boy. I rejected most of my parents' values in my twenties. As against the older psychoanalytic view, which treats morality as a residue carried over from childhood, contrast what I have learned since: my experience of authorities as (sometimes) reasonable, my ability to grasp their reasonableness, my assuming positions of authority myself, my capacity for empathy, my experience of moral models, and my ability to reason through the consequences of different moral positions. I deem it best, in thinking psychoanalytically about morality, to interpret the ego ideal and the superego as general rather than particular imperatives: Thou shalt be good. Thou shalt not do wrong. These imperatives command in the same style one's parents once did, gently, furiously, relentlessly, or lovingly, but the content of that "good" or "wrong" is likely to be more adultly thought out.

So far as identity is concerned, it refers to precisely that style of the superego and ego ideal, their recurring patterns, their rhythm, flexibility, intensity, persistence, and the like. An interpretation of identity would also consider patterns in the virtues and vices the superego rewards and punishes. For one person, sexual fidelity might be an important virtue and failings in fidelity would be the occasion for deep guilt. Another might care more about verbal honesty, monetary nicety, or personal loyalty. Such commitments would be part of identity.

The superego, however, dealt with only part of the clinical evidence that the earlier topographic (Cs.-Ucs.-Pcs.) system had not accounted for. In his psychoanalytic practice, Freud had also encountered unconscious resistance to the treatment. For example, the young man who forgot his *aliquis* commented, "I hope you don't take these thoughts of mine too seriously, if indeed I really had them." Questioning his thoughts is certainly resistance (since he obviously did have these thoughts), but he probably would not consciously accept it as such. More typically, a patient continues, say, to antagonize his boss although he knows (from his psychoanalysis) he does so in the self-defeating belief that his boss stands for his father. He acts out instead of interpreting and controlling—and he can't control it.

If there is unconscious resistance, then, Freud concluded, the agency that represses (the former Cs.) is not wholly conscious and the former division into Cs. and Ucs. is again too simple. There must be an unconscious ego as well as an unconscious superego. This is the reasoning that led Freud to replace his earlier division of the mind into "the" conscious, "the" unconscious, and "the" preconscious with a more complex picture, made up of superego, ego, and id, which included the earlier one. From my point of view, identity is like the coloring or the steadiness of line in this larger picture.

Opposite the superego Freud set what he called *das Es*, literally, "the it," a term taken from Nietzsche *via* Groddeck. By it, Freud intended "whatever in our nature is impersonal and, so to speak, subject to natural law," the sensation we have of being " 'lived' by unknown and uncontrollable forces." " 'It shot through me,' people say; 'there was something in me at that moment that was stronger than me.' " For *das Es*, Freud's early English translators chose the Latin *id* to parallel the already well established *ego* (1923b, 19:23, 23*n*, 7, 7*n*; 1926e, 20:195).

Oldest of the psychic structures, the id "contains everything that is inherited, that is present at birth, that is laid down in the constitution— above all, therefore, the instincts" (1940a, 23:145). It is the agency that— somehow— spans body and mind, soma and psyche. In some never specified way, it lets me sense the chemistry of my stomach walls as hunger, the pressure on my seminal vesicles as sexual desire. I do not think of it as an organ so much as a logical necessity: there has to be something like an id to bridge from body to mind.

"It is filled with energy . . . but it has no organization." "We call it a chaos, a cauldron full of seething excitations." It follows primary process thinking. The laws of logic, above all, the law of negation or exclusion do not apply. "Contrary impulses exist side by side, without cancelling each other out or diminishing each other: at the most they may converge to form compromises." The id has nothing to do with ideas of space or time and "most remarkable," its own mental processes do not change in time. "Wish-ful impulses [in the id] are virtually immortal; after the passage of decades they behave as though they had just occurred" (1933a, 22:73–74).

As with the superego, identity would include the content of the id: What impulses are dominant? Oral? Intrusive? Aggressive? Identity also refers to the style of the id. How strong is it? How inflexible, inexorable, and peremptory? How distractible?

Between the id that "lives us" and the thou shalt and thou shalt not of the superego, stands *das Ich,* the ego or "I." Originally synonymous with self, ego came to mean something considerably more complicated when Freud posited "the" ego, superego, and the structural hypothesis in 1920. In the structural view, only the id is wholly unconscious. Superego and ego are partly conscious (or preconscious) and partly unconscious.

Possibly the safest (if least useful) way to define the ego is: self minus id and superego. More usefully, one could say that the ego is the repository of consciousness, judgment, memory, intelligence, affects, perception, motor control, defense mechanisms, self-preservation, instinct control, one's sense of time, identifications with early objects, but most particularly perception, motility, and consciousness, which Freud called the "nucleus of the ego" (1923b, 19:28; 1940a, 23:145–46; see also Fenichel, 1945, p. 468). Key to all these transactions, although Freud does not single them out, are relation-ships to other people, and the effort to take other people into account led to an early and fruitful offshoot from ego psychology: object-relations theory.

In relation to identity, the most important thing the ego does is unify. "The ego is an organization characterized by a very remarkable trend towards unification, towards synthesis," said Freud (1926e, 20:196), and Hermann Nunberg summed up this unifying force in his classic phrase, "the synthetic function of the ego" (1931). The ego, precisely by virtue of its integrating power, takes even symptoms and makes them "useful in asserting the position of the self . . . more and more closely merged with the ego and more and more indispensable to it" (1926d, 20:99). Symptoms, in my terms, are functions of identity just like other kinds of behavior—and that is one reason they are difficult to cure. At the same time, however, in the process of cure, "as we analyse it [the neurotic patient's 'torn mind'] and remove the resistances, it grows together; the great unity which we call his ego fits into itself all the instinctual impulses which before had been split off and held apart from it" (1919a, 17:161). In identity terms, cure means keeping the same identity but changing its manifestations and the balances within it, for example, among various instincts and controls of instinct (as with Anna S.)

From the point of view of identity, the ego brings together various forces in a way that may not appear completely adaptive to an observer outside the I but feels to the person "inside" the I the best possible balance for his particular identity. Each of us will have a dream, choose a vocation, or even arrive at a neurotic symptom in such a way as to enable us to feel, think, and act in a way that feels coherent, that maximizes satisfactions and minimizes pains (except—perhaps—for the most crazed among us). Someone watching from outside can trace a coherence, an identity.

In short, when one represents an identity for Dr. Vincent, it includes representations of the styles of his id, ego, superego, and the balances among them. Identity theory includes an assumption that the style of Dr. Vincent's id will make sense alongside his ego style. Identity theory is consistent with the structural view.

In general, identity refines the second-phase concept of character, Fenichel's "the ego's habitual modes of adjustment to the external world, the id, and the superego, and the characteristic types of combining these modes with one another" (1945, p. 467). Since Fenichel bases his concept of character on Robert Waelder's "principle of multiple function," we need to look at the relation of that cornerstone of ego-psychology to identity.

Cause and effect, in psychoanalysis, become very complicated indeed. One can analyze many free associations into a single latent thought (like Freud's wish in the *table d'hôte* dream to enjoy a love that cost nothing). A single latent thought evidently gives rise to many manifestations: dream images or, in associations, memories, phrases, or pictures. Conversely, a single manifest idea like Freud's spinach can express guilt toward parents, reversal of preference, or *beaux yeux* (love) contrasted to money. "Not only are the elements of a dream determined by the dream-thoughts many times over," remarks Freud, "but the individual dream-thoughts are represented in the dream by several elements" (1900a, 4:283–84). For example, Freud's *table d'hôte* dream served not one but several purposes: it preserved Freud's sleep, it expressed a wish for love, and it warded off guilt. Further, had Freud continued to free associate he would no doubt have arrived at still other latent thoughts that apparently entered into or caused the dream. In principle, according to Freud there are no limits to the determinants.

The phrase psychoanalysis uses for this special kind of indefinitely large causation is "overdetermination" or, more recently, "multidetermination." Freud was probably most accurate of all when he suggested simply, "the principle of the complication of causes" (Moore and Fine, 1967, s.v. "Over-determination"; Freud, 1901b, 6:60–61).

Historically this multidetermination led to a major psychoanalytic concept: Robert Waelder's "principle of multiple function," first published in Vienna in 1930 and in the United States in 1936. "I found the notion of over-determination difficult to accept logically," wrote Waelder three decades later. "If a_1, a_2, ..., a_n were factors which were both necessary and sufficient to bring about a certain result A, I saw no room for another factor a_{n+1}." Accordingly Waelder proposed a characteristic psychoanalytic strategy: turn the problem around and look at it from the opposite point of view. "It seemed to me to be more satisfying to say that behavior served several functions, or, as one might also say, that it was at once responsive to many pressures, or was a solution for many tasks" (1960, p. 56).

From the very beginning, Freud had recognized that dreams, hysterical symptoms, slips of tongue or pen, forgettings, or jokes all represented compromise formations. The individual makes some kind of a deal among two or more competing wishes, needs, or fears, or, more technically, the ego mediates between the superego and the id.

Given id, ego, and superego, Waelder could have formulated his principle that way. Had he done so, however, he would have neglected two other ideas being talked about in Freud's Viennese circle in the late thirties.

The first was adaptation, not in the crude sense of "adjusting to reality." Any changes in the world as we sense or act on it constitute tasks for the ego, because the ego is what senses or acts on reality. Sometimes, as in work or politics, the ego copes alloplastically, by changing the environment. Sometimes, as with a death or with changes in one's own body, the ego can only cope autoplastically, by changing the self. Either way, the ego fits the self and the environment together. It adapts them.

A second idea percolating psychoanalysis in the 1930s was the so-called repetition compulsion. Freud ultimately combined it with the aggressive drive to make a death instinct, but at first he conceived it simply from clinical evidence.

People repeat. Having once found an adaptive solution, we try that solution again before trying to invent another (like the hypotheses in a feedback picture). After a trauma, the victim will relive the event in repeated nightmares. In transference, an analysand re-creates in his analyst the figures of his childhood. Some people have "destiny neuroses," getting themselves into the same predicament over and over: they "fall" for unsuitable lovers, they always manage to say just the wrong thing, or they blunder just at the moment of success. What is striking about these repetitions is that they do not give pleasure—indeed, they are often exceedingly painful. Logically enough, Freud entitled his 1920 exploration of this enigma *Beyond the Pleasure Principle.*

We repeat these particular unpleasures and also our pleasures (as in the scripts and scenarios I discussed in chapter 10). Accordingly, Freud concluded that he had discovered a "conservatism" intrinsic to the very nature of biological drives. "It seems, then, that an instinct is an urge inherent in organic life to restore an earlier state of things . . . " (1920g, 18:36). The compulsion to repeat represents something very like the definition of a wish or the persistence of impulses in the id or the perpetuation of parents in the superego. It is generalizable, therefore, if not to all organic life, at least to many—I would say all—human drives and structures. Taken that way, it makes for a considerable neatening of theory. Waelder could analyze multi-determination into id, ego, superego, repetition compulsion, and reality (as related to the mind through perception and action).

A second book provided other bases for Waelder's principle: Freud's *Inhibitions, Symptoms and Anxiety.* Some call it the first book of ego psychology because it firmly asserted the ego's executive role in psychic organization. Published in 1926, it was no doubt discussed in the Vienna circle well before that. In this book, Freud gave up his older idea that anxiety resulted from a chemical transformation of unrelieved desire (sexual, usually) which overtook a relatively defenseless ego.

The new theory, as Waelder sums it up, holds that "in a situation of danger . . . the ego may anticipate the latter in the form of anxiety and that this anticipation then becomes the immediate signal which tends to induce the organism to adjust itself so as to avoid the danger—for example, [by] flight." In other words, the ego gets "affect signals" of pleasure and unpleasure, particularly anxiety and guilt, and in response to these signals the ego sets in motion ways of coping with the problem (or, if we think of this as feedback, of zeroing the signal).

Waelder speaks of the tasks that arise for the ego because of the id, the superego, reality, and the repetition compulsion. One can group the four agencies facing the ego symmetrically along two axes. The id presses for drive satisfaction while the superego inhibits it. Reality constantly demands new solutions while the repetition compulsion wants to cling to old ones. Try something new. Do what worked before. Do it! Don't do it!

As these four inevitably conflict, they present the ego with problems, but they also give the ego resources with which to solve them. The ego can act on the real world to gratify the id. The repetition compulsion guarantees a kind of efficiency in the search for adaptations. The superego can warn the ego away from conduct that would elicit pain or punishment. Hence the ego is active as well as passive toward the four agencies. The ego actively, as it were, sets itself problems of overruling one or another of the four agencies, balancing them, assimilating them to its own tasks, and so on.

With this theoretical armamentarium, Waelder was in a position to develop what seems to me the cornerstone of ego-psychology and second-phase psychoanalysis, the principle of multiple function. Every attempted solution to one problem by the ego, says Waelder, is at the same time an attempt to solve all the others. Each act by the ego serves a multiple function within the mind as a whole.

The ego's active and passive relations to the other four agencies make a total of eight types of problems facing the ego at any one time. Thus, when the ego tries to solve one problem, it necessarily tries to solve up to seven others. Clearly a given transaction may be—must be—more successful in one of its eight aspects than another. It is impossible that one solution could enact with equal success all eight tactics, for they embody fundamental inconsistencies (do it, don't do it, try something new, follow the tried and true).

In the ego's serving so many taskmasters, Waelder sees "that sense of perpetual contradiction and feeling of dissatisfaction which, apart from neurosis, is common to all human beings." Conversely, multiple function suggests the unique importance of the act of love, "as that psychic act which comes nearest to a complete solution of all the contradictory problems of the ego."

Also built into this model of psychic functioning are basic concepts like psychological time (as wishes, the quest for a former perception, and as old and new adaptations). Emotions, particularly pleasure and unpleasure, not only provide basic motivations but also feed back signals as to whether a given solution by the ego has been successful (see chapter 6).

Finally, understanding the multiple functions of psychic acts leads to a hermeneutic or method of interpretation. If each psychic act attempts a solution of all other problems which are found in the ego, then every psychic act must have a multiple meaning. To interpret it, one must look along the various axes about which the ego makes its multiply functioning syntheses. As Waelder says, "A multiple meaning corresponds to a multiple function."

For example, consider the young man's forgetting *aliquis* in relation to the four agencies. On the one hand, the young man harbored an aggressive wish for avenging descendants (aggression from the id, and presumably a solution he had often proposed to himself before). Balancing it was a wish for no descendants, possibly under pressure of guilt from the superego—all those saints!—certainly because of his conscious knowledge of what a child would mean to him in his present reality. Similarly, Freud's *table d'hôte* dream represents a compromise between Freud's id-wish to have love even though he is selfish and his superego hesitations about that wish, expressed as a need to deserve love by being unselfish. He himself remarks that the dream repeats an episode in his courtship of Martha, while it also represents a response to his current financial needs in reality.

The two axes along which ego meets nonego—id and superego, reality and repetition compulsion—suggest a structural basis for the dualism we so often see in dreams, slips, of symptoms. At the same time, each psychic act "is to be understood as the expression of the collective function of the total organism," or, as I prefer to say, as a unity or convergence from four different directions.

Waelder's shift from determination toward interpretation marks, in a way, the beginning of the third phase of psychoanalysis, but within the second phase Waelder's principle provides a broad theory of psychoanalytic causality. As such, it represents a major rebuilding of the conceptual frame around the first, basic data of psychoanalysis, like Freud's interpretation of his dream. The frame becomes both larger and simpler, eliminating the need for subordinate concepts like, for example, "neurosis." They become permutations and combinations of the eight possible relations of the ego to id, superego, reality, and the compulsion to repeat.

Among the problems that the principle of multiple function clarifies is the psychoanalytic concept of character. It becomes almost anticlimactic, given multiple function. Fenichel writes, "The mode of reconciling various [ego] tasks to one another is characteristic for a given personality. Thus the ego's habitual modes of adjustment to the external world, the id, and the super-ego, and the characteristic types of combining these modes with one another, constitute character." Essentially what Fenichel adds to ordinary multiple functioning is the "habitual." "The term character stresses the habitual form of a given reaction, its relative constancy. Widely differing stimuli produce similar reactions" (1945, p. 467).

Because it is so long-lived, character in ego psychology almost becomes a structure like ego or superego. Fenichel speaks of it as an "ego function," analogous to walking, I suppose. That phrasing marks a difference between ego psychology and identity theory. In ego psychology (in Erikson's writings, for example), identity would be a function of the ego. In identity theory, the ego would be a function of identity.

Nevertheless, of all the psychoanalytic concepts we have considered, character comes closest to identity. By focusing on the recurrence of themes and patterns, identity accents the habitual in Fenichel's definition. Indeed the theme-and-variations aspect of identity provides a way of precisely defining and conceptualizing the habituality implicit in "character," and the hierarchy of feedbacks makes it possible to imagine how character is learned and how character is consistent with what we know of the brain.

Long before and long after Fenichel's phrasing, psychoanalysis had been addressing the unity of the personality. In 1908, Freud had written: "The sexual behaviour of a human being often *lays down the pattern* for all his other modes of reacting to life." If he pursues the object of his love energetically, he will probably pursue other aims with equal vigor, but if he inhibits himself sexually, he will probably inhibit himself in other areas of life as well (1908d, 9:198). Freud is describing a unity at any given time. Erikson reports that play constructions by a given individual vary but also show continuity from childhood into the early forties (1972). That is a unity over a life span.

Either synchronically, then, or diachronically, psychoanalytic observations lead to a sense of unity in a personality and to ways of thinking about it. Ego-psychology had, in Heinz Hartmann's words, "sharpened our eyes to the frequent identity of patterns in often widely divergent fields of an individual's behavior" (1951, p. 38). In 1966, Anna Freud spoke of "a general cognitive and perceptive style of the ego" as though it were a psychoanalytic commonplace, an extension of notions of defense "to include besides the ego's dealings with danger, anxiety, affects, etc., also its everyday functioning such as perceiving, thinking, abstracting, conceptualizing." Such a "style," said Heinz Hartmann, would embrace a person's moral behavior (his superego, therefore) as well as his characteristic defenses and instinctual drives (1960, p. 53). Ideologies, values, and all systems projected on the world would express total personality (Kardiner, 1945)—even a person's prose style would (Holland, 1968b). One of the best studies of style in this sense of a unity pervading a person's behavior is Victor Rosen's 1961 article, reprinted in his book of 1977. Rosen makes the important point that style must include the "meaningful collaborative response from another individual," in an artistic situation, "a collaboration in effect between the producer and the observer" (pp. 452, 298). Rosen had recognized the necessity, as in this book, of including other-ness in the essence of self.

By 1966, however, when Miss Freud was speaking of a general ego style, Erik Erikson had already set the magical word "identity" on the lips of the world, enlarging and changing Fenichel's "character" in three ways. First, where character is something observed by someone else, Erikson's identity is one's own inner sense of continuity and coherence. Second, this inner sense coincides with one's meaning for others. There is mutuality. The individual's identity depends upon the supportive understanding of his human environment. Third, for Erikson, because of this mutuality, identity is achieved only in adolescence, "before which it cannot come to a head" (1975, p. 19) because the community has not yet granted its part of identity to the individual. Final identity, however, is "fixed at the end of adolescence" (1968, p. 161) and is more or less unchangeable after that. "Therapy and guidance may attempt to substitute more desirable identifications for undesirable ones, but the total configuration of the ego identity remains unalterable" (1946, p. 26).

People have found Erikson's concept of identity richer than earlier psychoanalytic theories of character because it talks about the individual's mutuality with his community. Hence Erikson's "identity" has led to important work in psychohistory and psychosociology.

The problem I find with this version of "identity" is that one is always trying to talk about someone else's inner sense of identity from outside. How can you know how I feel about my own wholeness or my sense of solidarity with my university, with other literary critics, or the political life of my country? Hence I turn from what is properly a person's "sense of identity" to "identity" *tout court*.

I ARC, including identity as representation, makes a necessary departure from Fenichel's "character" or Erikson's "identity." Identity as developed in *The I* stands alongside and apart from the structural description of character as id, ego, and superego, much as identity stands alongside the division of awareness into conscious and unconscious.

I have heard both Anna Freud and Robert Waelder say at lectures that the psychoanalytic ideas that grew up in the 1930s in Vienna evolved around and with Freud, although he encouraged their publication by others. Such ideas, presumably, included character and the principle of multiple function on which it is based.

Freud himself believed in something very like an innate character or an identity formed very early: "original, innate distinguishing characteristics of the ego," in effect, a personal ego style that operates from the beginning of life. "Even before the ego has come into [separate] existence, the line of development, trends and reactions which it will later exhibit are already laid down for it" (1937c, 23:240). What he is describing is now called "temperament" as, for example, Stella Chess has observed it in infants (Thomas, Chess, and Birch, 1968, 1970), and Burks and Rubenstein have traced it in adults (1979).

Freud was developing these ideas in a Vienna that still included the brilliant group of students that surrounded him in his last years, among them Heinz Hartmann. Hartmann began addressing this question: How can one bring into psychoanalytic thought the way human beings live in the world, both the physical world and the world of human relationships necessary for human survival? He answered by dividing the human ego into two "spheres." One sphere, the primitive, driven, dreaming, unconscious ego, was the traditional subject of psychoanalysis and only haphazardly adaptive. The other sphere was conflict-free, autonomous, and more or less automatically adapted from birth to survive in an "average expectable environment." We are either born knowing or we learn to see, stand, walk, talk, remember, read, write, and so forth, free of the conflicts associated with, say, multiple functioning (1939).

Autonomy presupposes (to me, at least) style-less-ness. Hartmann seems to me to be saying that there are various things we do like seeing or remembering which everyone does the same way. They are automatic or autonomous. In a sense, they do themselves. If that were true, then the idea of a conflict-free sphere would conflict with the everyday observation that we all have different styles of seeing, walking, remembering, or handwriting.

Further, others following Hartmann (and, to some extent, Hartmann himself) began to talk as though there were two kinds of ego, the old unifier and the new autonomous ego. Analysts began to assign rather complex acts like driving a car or writing a letter or rhyming to this new structure.

Clearly, this version of autonomous ego is a considerable extension. No matter how firmly the young man on the park bench had learned his Virgil in school, a distracting thought of his mistress drew this seemingly "autonomous" activity back into conflict, and he forgot his *aliquis*. It is well to remember Hartmann's original definition of a conflict-free ego sphere: "that ensemble of functions which *at any given time* exert their effects outside the region of mental conflicts." Any such "sphere" is not a "structure" in the psychoanalytic sense for it is not long-lived. It is a limiting condition, a balance that can be upset by any transient thought.

In terms of ego-psychology, it seems to me neater theoretically to think of just one kind of ego with the primary function of unifying the demands of the other structures. One can discuss conflict (or lack of it) as a separate issue, even while recognizing that there are ego functions which operate free of conflict most of the time.

Identity theory gives us a hierarchy of feedbacks as a way of imagining "autonomous" functions. That is, we can think of processes like walking, talking, seeing, or remembering as lower-level feedback loops. They get their standards from higher levels that more closely reflect a personal style or identity. Most of the time, however, there is no need to change the standards. We hear or walk without thinking about doing so. We are like the driver of a car who leaves it on "cruise control" to hold a set speed. The driver only steps on the brake to change the set speed if he wants to pass or to turn, that is, if a higher level of his mind perceives conditions that require a new cruising speed. We only pay attention to the way we walk if the terrain is rough or slippery. We only pay attention to the way we hear English if we are hearing it spoken with an accent or over a faulty telephone. "At any given time," walking and hearing language and even driving are likely to be autonomous in Hartmann's sense, although embodying a personal style and governed by upper levels of a hierarchy that are themselves always involved in conflict. A conflict-free sphere in the sense of lower levels of feedback not only fits with but forms an essential part of identity theory.

In general, then, one can derive the concept of identity and an identity principle from ego-psychology or mesh the two quite neatly. At the same time, however, there is a profound ambiguity in ego-psychology that justifies the transition of psychoanalysis to a third phase. It has to do with drives. Freud called the id a seething cauldron but not completely chaotic. "Contrary impulses exist side by side. . . . They may converge to form compromises." Indeed, drives in life take highly particular forms—for caviar, for Mozart, for a certain beloved redhead.

When a drive seeks a specific aim like that, psychoanalysis would speak of a "wish," and it is one of the earliest and most important definitions of classical theory. A wish is based on a previous satisfaction; it is "a psychical impulse . . . to re-evoke the perception itself, that is, to re-establish the situation of the original satisfaction . . . a repetition of the perception which was linked with the satisfaction of the need" (1900a, 5:565–66).

I find two important ideas in this definition. First, it puts any given wish into a framework of history and development. In theory, even the most adult of wishes could be traced back through a long series of similar (but not identical) perceptions of satisfaction to some early, infantile gratification. Yet the id, Freud tells us, is timeless and immortal. A wish thus bridges from the timelessness of the id to the here and now of the ego. Second, a wish has an aim. It has, so to speak, a picture in mind. Hence, the id has to have some structure in order to imagine such a satisfaction, to have an aim. The id thinks, but in ego-psychology thinking is a function of the ego, and the id is not supposed to think. Finally, then, Freud's definition of a wish cuts across his seething cauldron image for the id.

The point is not that an idea of Freud's from 1900 is inconsistent with an idea from the 1920s—that would scarcely be surprising. Rather, the concept of a wish or of the aim of a drive says (to me, at least) that one cannot draw sharp lines between id and ego. Their relationship is profoundly ambiguous, and one can read Lacan, for example, and much of third-phase theory as trying to express that ambiguity. A transition, not a boundary, separates id from ego. If so, then we must take the structures of id, ego, and superego more freely and metaphorically than many American psychoanalysts currently do.

Freud apparently did, or so Waelder reported in a paper he left unpublished at his death. "Ego, superego, and id were, for Freud, more imagery than theory and . . . he continued to think in terms of living beings and living processes rather than in terms of these concepts" (Guttman, 1969, pp. 272–73; see also Waelder, 1964, p. 84*n*).

Freud's attitude suggests that he would have favored Roy Schafer's extremely important critique of ego-psychology (1976, 1978). Schafer is not objecting to the facts of psychoanalysis, but hc wants to change the rules of the language for discussing them. Following the reasoning of such analytic philosophers as Wittgenstein, Hampshire, Austin, and Ryle, Schafer tries to make logical sense out of such sentences as, "I tried to control myself," where the "self" at the end of the sentence apparently refers to something different from the "I" at the beginning. Intention involves infinite regress: "I intended to intend to intend . . . to buy a microcomputer." Similarly, to say an action was caused is to assume that there was a cause for that cause and a cause for the causing cause and so on.

Schafer says that many statements by psychoanalysts get into logical trouble, some because they lead to infinite regresses, some because they use nouns like "ego," "force," "mind," or "self" to describe what are essentially processes that should be described with verbs. Hence Schafer prescribes an "action language" which does away with both motivation and self terms. Instead one should speak of a "person" or some equivalent doing something—verbs and adverbs. Instead of "There was a repressing force," say, "Hannah repressed." Instead of "I failed to control myself," say, "I did X, but reluctantly" or "I did X, but I wanted to avoid Y."

Most important, actions have interpretations rather than causes. Schafer wants to move psychoanalysis out of the language of determinism and the natural sciences and into a language of interpretation, significance, and meaning (as the feedbacks I develop in chapters 4-6 become the dialogue of chapters 7-12). From Schafer's point of view, then, multiple function is not four entities interacting but multiple ways of looking at an action. In a way, then, he would agree with Waelder that "a multiple meaning corresponds to a multiple function," but he would mean 'a multiple function is *really* a multiple meaning.'

Similarly, Schafer suggests that "unconscious" today should be an adverb, not an entity. "Unconscious" refers to the way a person does something: "I unconsciously admired him."

One of the entities that Schafer jettisons is, inevitably, identity, defined as "the theme of significant personal actions" (1976, p. 114). He rejects identity as a thing one can "have" or "acquire" or "lose" (*pace* Erikson). One should really regard identity, he says, as a way of thinking about a person, of pointing to some feature.

It seems to me that Schafer is saying just what I mean by identity as representation, as a way of pointing to the enduring aspects of a person. I must admit, that definition would involve us in nouns again. Nouns are perhaps not all bad, though, since the model of mind as a hierarchy of feedbacks helps resolve just those verbal paradoxes that led Schafer to posit an action language.

That is, if the mind is a hierarchy of feedbacks, then one can make sense of a sentence like "I failed to control myself" or even "There was a repressing force." If we picture the mind as higher loops prescribing reference levels for lower loops, we can think of those reference levels as a repressive force but also as an act of a person. "I failed to control myself" would mean that an upper level of the mind tried to assert some standard for a lower loop, but the lower loop ran on regardless. One can sort out sentences that refer to the self as different segments of the hierarchy. "Non-self" would be clear enough, too, as the world outside those hierarchies.

Nevertheless, Schafer rejects concepts like "self" or "identity" as subjects for his action verbs. I don't see why. That is, I don't see why a carefully defined verb and adverb describing an action must preclude a carefully defined subject for the verb. Why can't the subject be an identity understood as agent, representation, and consequence? The two approaches seem to me to dovetail nicely, although together they involve the by-now familiar paradox that the identity who is the subject of the action is also a representation of the actor by someone else (Schafer's "way of thinking about"). Identity is a function of the interpreter as well as the interpretee (but Schafer seems to accept this).

I have another suggestion in relation to Schafer's action language. In a way, we could think of identity (in *The I*) as an adverbial of manner. I, for example, read and write Norman N. Hollandly, I teach Norman N. Hollandly, and so on. One could fit my concept of identity into Schafer's action language by thinking of the identity of a person as a long string of adverbs that refer to the way that person does things: lovingly, impulsively but guardedly, unifyingly, fearfully, unconsciously, or however. If we were to take that long string of adverbs and seek the recurrences in them (Schafer's "theme of significant personal actions"), we would arrive at an identity in my sense.

One can read Schafer's proposal for an action language, I think, as a reaction to ego-psychology. Most such reactions, however, have taken a direction opposite to Schafer's, not toward behavior and actions, but toward

A Psychology of the Self

These psychologies of the self seem to me to mark the third phase of the history of psychoanalysis. Many analysts, particularly in England and on the Continent, have declared themselves to be beyond ego-psychology. They have in common, it seems to me, the explaining of psychological events by means of the dynamic tension, not between conscious and unconscious or between ego and other-than-ego, but between self and not-self or self and "Other."

Erikson, it seems to me, belongs in this camp, although he calls himself (and most others call him) an ego-psychologist. Where Hartmann stressed adaptation to the physical and biological world Erikson emphasized adaptation to the social environment. Extending the original, classical sequence of child development into adulthood, maturity, and old age made human growth include growth in society as well as in the family. Each of Erikson's stages was therefore not just psychological but psychosocial. Erikson enlarged, particularized, but most of all humanized the idea of adaptation as Hartmann had left it (1963, p. 65; see also 1959).

Conceptually, if not historically, one can regard the English object-relations theorists as particularizing Erikson. I am thinking of Harry Guntrip, W. R. D. Fairbairn, Charles Rycroft, and especially D. W. Winnicott (also, in their somewhat different ways, R. D. Laing and M. Masud R. Khan). They concentrated their attention on both child and adult patients in their individuality and particularly the individual kind of relationship or "space" they created between patient and therapist or child and parent or patient and society. Where Erikson rested his observations in the large word "mutuality," these English writers went on to detail how different individuals differently created mutuality in different settings and phases of development. They did so through concepts like "transitional object," "adequate mothering," "schizoid condition," or the contrast between a "false self" that obeys the world and a "true self" the false self hides.

The most decisive rejection of first- and second-phase psychoanalysis, I think, is W. Ronald D. Fairbairn's. He replaces entirely Freud's innate instincts and their vicissitudes in favor of a theory of the personality conceived in terms of the infant's relations to objects (1963).

Such a theory derives ultimately, as I read it, from the work of Melanie Klein. One of the first to specialize in the analysis of children, Klein had considerable influence in England, and as a result English psychoanalysis focused on the early relationship of mother and child sooner and more intensely than American or French.

Klein explored the child's ambivalent first relationship with the mother (for Klein, mother's breast) and concluded that the child dealt with that ambivalence by splitting the breast into good and bad parts and fantasying the biting, emptying, and annihilation of the bad part. (The ability to split, of course, implies the existence of a functioning ego many months before classical or second-phase theory would.) From this "schizoid" position the child progresses to a "paranoid" position, the child's projection of its own hostility onto the mother and the resulting fear that the mother will retaliate. At a still later stage, the child introjects its mother and directs its rage inward. The result is a "depressive" position. Finally, if all goes well, the child is able to separate its representation of its mother from its self-representation, to accept its own rage, and to realize that its own feelings are what threaten its internal world. If all does not go well, the child or adult falls into the psychosis associated with the early position associated with the failure. All of this, clearly, lays much greater stress on early object relations than Freud did or than the ego psychologists tended to. Clearly, it is somewhat different from the picture I have developed in chapter 8.

Klein's theories rested on her work with older children who had regressed. Inevitably her ideas could be corrected or replaced by direct observation of children, and that is the way I read Spitz, Mahler, Stern, and the other baby-watchers. Their careful observation of children tends to prove the part of Klein's theory that most psychoanalysts thought wrong: early ego functions. Observation alone, however, cannot confirm her speculations as to the child's inner strategies of splitting, projection, and introjection.

Of the many analysts who today concentrate on the mother-child relation, the one who speaks most directly to me is D. W. Winnicott. I have referred to him many times in this book in connection with his concept of "potential space," which seems to me so like the way I imagine identity interacting with the world around it. It is well to remember, however, that Winnicott himself thinks of "potential space" and the "transitional object" in terms of the child's relation to a mother (Grolnick and Barkin, 1978, pp. 539–49).

Nevertheless, it seems to me, the ideas that I associate with identity build on object-relations theory and enhance it—with one major difference. Typically object-relations theory gets stated in terms of category or type: depressive position, schizoid position, false self, introjection, or rapprochement phase. I read this as a habit of mind retained from medicine or nonpsychoanalytic psychology, not essential to the ideas of object-relations psychoanalysis, only the most familiar way of generalizing from one individual to many. Identity theory, by contrast, uses thematic analysis, as do the object-relations theorists when they are talking about individuals: Mahler's Bruce or Winnicott's Iiro.

The key to identity theory is the precise use of words to phrase an identity theme. Although verbal precision has always mattered in psychoanalysis, so far as I know, Franz Alexander was the first to use this kind of verbal precising of a theme with his "emotional syllogisms" in the 1930s. He would use a sentence like "I give so much and therefore I have the right to receive" as a way of bringing together a wide range of a patient's behavior (1935). We see the same kind of thing in the 1970s as "script analysis" in the popularization of psychoanalysis usually called "TA," transactional analysis (Berne, 1971). But these formulas embrace only a part of someone's behavior, thus following in the tradition of Freud's descriptions of character-types (1916d). In the same way, Lacan's *scenario* or *mythe familial* for the Rat Man deals only with the love and money parts of his life (1953).

The first theorist I know who explicitly set out a method for finding a theme for all of someone's behavior was the French literary critic Charles Mauron. He would "superimpose" all of a writer's writings to find a single *mythe personel* which would sum up "networks of associations or groupings of images" which in turn expressed "both . . . the troubles of the living man and the obsessive metaphors of the author" (1964, pp. 141–42). Mauron was in turn anticipated by Sartre in *l'Etre et le Néant* (1943) in his concept of the For Itself, *l'être pour soi,* the self who is for itself, but continually projecting itself toward future possibilities. Sartre, in his 1947 study, shows how Baudelaire exemplifies such a *projet*. Indeed, Sartre's last words in that book could serve as a motto for *The I:* "The free choice that a man makes from himself becomes absolutely identified with what we call his destiny."

Object-relations theory, it seems to me, needs the careful phrasings of identity themes. The inability of category, class, or type to express the individual theme becomes more telling in object-relations theory than elsewhere in psychoanalysis because an individual's life space is even more individual (so to speak) than his or her biophysical makeup. Life space would include both the biological person and the social person in all the individuality of both. Therefore, it seems to me, treating childhood phases from the first year of life on as a dialogue instead of classes of events has unusual promise for object-relations theory. Development as dialogue may provide object-relations theory a useful way of generalizing unique themes over many cases without rubbing off the individuality of the case to fit a category drawn from outside or before the event.

Where the not-self is for Erikson society and for the object-relations theorists the mother or her successors, for Jacques Lacan the Other, as he calls it, is language. They use human relations. Lacan uses puns. More exactly, Lacan uses the undoubted fact that the Others of Anglo-American theory come to the child in a prepackaged world of either images (in the early, prelinguistic months) or language (for all the rest of life). In a way, one can read all of Lacan as dealing with the ambiguity inherent in Freud's definitions of id and ego. The id is the mind's representative of desire—chaotic, peremptory, unthinking—yet it images what it desires. Hence it must have some of the structure that Freud attributes to the ego. Lacan deals with the ambiguity by replacing the concepts of id and ego with the *moi* and the *je*—or at least we can say that for the purpose of comparing Lacan's ideas with identity theory (1966).

At first the helpless infant cannot deal with the flood of perceptions his environment provides. A baby achieves only a jumble of fragmentary signifying networks of association. During what Lacan calls "the mirror stage," the infant senses the discrepancy between the integrated image of itself it would see in a mirror (or which a mother would reflect) and the chaotic jumble within. In an effort to achieve that unity, the infant identifies with the integrated Other (mother). In a third stage, the infant seeks to keep up that fusion against the competition of the father and the alienating effect of language. (Language cannot render the inner chaos of the *moi* and hence becomes paradoxical, an instrument of understanding that always misunderstands.) Lacan's *moi* (as I understand it) is unconscious, the agent of desire (and hence of lack), and therefore the embodiment of the "truth" of a person, their "signified" (their meaning, so to speak).

Such a *moi* corresponds reasonably closely, I think, to the idea of identity that the body of this book puts forward. The child's original push (continued all through life) toward a convergence of signifying networks corresponds to the theme-and-variations aspect of identity. The *moi*'s desire and the sense of lack on which it is based corresponds to identity as feedback, ever perpetuating a difference between the standard and the actual.

Lacan seems to think of the *moi* in almost geometric terms, as a network full of holes and gaps, which the *moi* seeks to close. The *moi* relates to the real world (another Other) by perception, cognition, primary and secondary processes, the subjective experience of reality, all of what Lacan designates as the Imaginary. Various ways I have thought about Lacan's Imaginary are: as what language theorists would call a person's "referents," as Freud's "thing-representations," or as the representations of desire in the id. The crucial thing is the absence of symbols.

Unaided by the Symbolic, the realm of language, these functions of the *moi* in the Imaginary would remain chaotic and disorganized. With language, the individual replaces a dyadic relation to reality with a triadic. "I see what I want" or "I feel what I want" becomes "I can say what I want" or "I can generalize about what I want." Yet language, Lacan says, alienates and misdirects by the very promise of understanding.

Against the *moi* is the *je,* the agent of language, operating in the Symbolic as a mediator between the desires and the perceptions of the *moi* and the fully real world. If the *moi* is what is signified, the *je* consists of the network of signifiers, always shifting and sliding into one another, each signifier defined by the next, never attaining to meaning and the *moi.* The *je* does what an American analyst would describe by defense mechanisms: it denies, opposes, negates, shows off, lies, flees. It does these toward outer reality, the Real, and toward the inner reality of the *moi*. The *je,* by contrast, is unreal, the mere "I" of my sentences that takes on life only as the *moi* gives it. The *je* misrecognizes and denies the *moi,* where the truth of the individual resides, his identity.

In 1953, Jacques Lacan did do an analysis of the identity of one famous patient, the Rat Man, or as he termed identity, *le mythe individuel.* (Curiously, his term corresponds to the "personal myth" of the ego-psychologist Ernst Kris.) In seeking one central myth, he did something very like my own quest for an identity theme.

In the actual interpretation, however, Lacan does not try to find a style for the Rat Man that permeates all his acts. He looks for a pattern in only a few: the Rat Man's crisis over paying the postage; his fear of the rat torture; his inability to make up his mind about his lady.

Further, because Lacan sees the human determined by the prepackaged reality presented him by society and the family, he lays great importance on Rat Man's father's failing to pay gambling debts, on the mysterious friend who lent the senior Lorenz money, and on the father's choice between women. To fit Lacan's theory of the individual's entering a preestablished symbolic realm, the Rat Man's myth must derive from his father's myth. Inevitably, as Lacan's editor admits, since that is the prehistory of the case, "there are times, especially in his elaboration of the flashiness and bravado of the Rat Man's father, when Lacan does seem to invent details rather than interpret them" (Evans, 1979, p. 391; Lacan, 1953, 1979).

There are thus both similarities and differences between Lacan's ideas and identity theory. Certainly Lacan's sense that the methods of symbolic analysis, be they scientific or linguistic, yield *savoir*—knowledge—but not *verité*—truth—corresponds to my belief in identity as representation rather than something in an individual waiting to be discovered like buried treasure. Similarly, I resonate to Lacan's blurring of the lines between id and ego, fantasy and reality. My image of feedback accords with his sense of the dialectic relationship between the individual and society, particularly the symbolic structures of a culture. Often, I find, if translated out of their pixilated jargon, Lacan's ideas sound like familiar and quite sensible concepts from ego-psychology or identity theory.

On the other hand, Lacan offers much that is different, not only from my thinking but from Freud's. Lacan introduces the *je* to rid himself of the ego as a mediator, indeed to get rid of the ego entirely. With the ego go such familiar concepts as defense mechanisms (especially the idea of regression) and character. In fact, so far as I can tell, the idea of "character" does not exist at all in French psychoanalysis. Similarly, Lacan reintroduces "the" unconscious, despite Freud's having written it out of psychoanalysis. Indeed, Lacan jettisons all of post-1923 Freud.

Hence, I think Lacan is kidding when he claims a "return to Freud." Poor dignified Professor Doctor Freud. Lacan's ministrations make him look as though, on his morning constitutional around Vienna's Ring, he had stepped into a clothing store, and the clerk sent him on his way in purple espadrilles, a cowboy hat, and wraparound sunglasses. Surely the clerk ought not also to proclaim, "See? This is the *real* you!" Lacan is more a Freudian prophet than a Freudian fundamentalist.

Where Lacan innovates out of a wish to bring linguistics and metaphysics into psychoanalysis, the two major innovators of the last two decades in America, Otto Kernberg and Heinz Kohut, are trying to expand the clinical base of psychoanalysis. Partly, I think, because so many senior American psychoanalysts worked as general psychiatrists in the Second World War, American analysts have long been interested in using psychoanalysis for psychotics and borderline patients, who are more disturbed than the classical psychoneurotics. In treating these cases, analysts report patients' perceiving themselves as grandiose, magnificent, absolutely entitled to the best, or alternatively as useless, worthless, and beneath contempt (presumably these two feelings are opposite sides of one pathological coin). In a psychoanalytic setting, patients may seek in their analysts simply approving mirrors of themselves or ideals into which they can merge.

Kernberg deals with these phenomena in terms of object-relations theory (1975, 1978). The individual develops by internalizing interpersonal relations, particularly in the form of persistent constellations. Each of these consists of a self-image, the image of a significant other bound in a relationship to the self (one of the parents, presumably), and the emotions associated with that relationship. These self-object-affect configurations evolve, says Kernberg, into the libidinal and aggressive systems and ultimately into the familiar adult structures of ego and superego.

Various forms of pathology can affect this development. For instance, in order to cope with a painful self-object-affect system, the individual may divide it into a part all good and a part all bad. An overuse of this kind of splitting develops a borderline character. Kernberg has described many other phases in the child's differentiation and integration of self- and object-images, but I have not tried to include them lest I further complicate my own already complicated picture of development in chapters 7–12.

Kohut begins with much the same data: the borderline cases, the idealizing or grandiose behavior toward others or in the patient's transference toward the psychoanalyst. Like Kernberg, Kohut sees narcissism as critical in the process of separation and individuation (particularly Mahler's "practicing subphase"). Like Kernberg, Kohut sees the child using external objects (originally the parents) to solve this problem. Kohut calls these "self-objects," someone (or something) used in the service of the self and the maintenance of its instinctual investment. Such an object may provide a way for the individual to say, "I am perfect" (the grandiose self) or "You are perfect but I am part of you" (the idealized image of the parent) (1971, 1977; see also Kohut and Wolf, 1978; Ornstein, 1974).

Kohut adds frankly to Freud and ego-psychology in a way that Kernberg does not. For Kohut, for example, the self is a structure. (It is invested with libidinal and aggressive energy. It endures in time.) The self is also represented in the mind: the familiar psychoanalytic concept of self-representations. One apprehends the self, as an analyst or a patient or simply a person living, through empathy, which occupies a central role in Kohut's methods and thought.

Kohut adds to the familiar oral, anal, phallic sequence of development another track describing the energy directed toward objects, particularly those self-objects from which the nuclei of the ego are formed. Furthermore (and this has created a considerable flap in American psychoanalytic circles) Kohut feels that one must loosen classical psychoanalytic treatment for these narcissistic disorders. The narcissistic disorders represent failures in development (not, as Kernberg would say, pathological regression or other defense). Hence the analyst's job is to promote that development. The analyst needs to become a self-object for the patient, a real person who delivers praise or blame as progress is or is not made. In general, a person needs self-objects all through life, and the analyst may be only one of many performing that role.

By contrast, Kernberg takes a more traditional view. A narcissistic disorder represents a defense against both early, massive feelings of love and hate (the ambivalence of the first year) and later, mature acceptance of object-relations and their limits. In treatment, Kernberg would analyze the narcissistic disorders as one would analyze any other defense, seeking insight and maintaining analytic neutrality. Rather than meet and sustain a need for idealized or grandiose self or others, Kernberg would analyze it away.

These differences in therapy are only secondarily relevant to "the I" and its theory, however. Kernberg's and Kohut's theories impinge on the theses of this book primarily as they suggest other aspects of development to be added to the developmental dialogue of chapters 7–12. In particular, both Kohut and Kernberg address grandiosity, idealization, and splitting—whatever the situation, an exaggerated view of self or other as all-powerful, all-good, all-bad, or simply all. I could therefore translate the clinical data on which they agree into another question to be traced through the developmental dialogue or landscape: How will you deal with the fact that you (or, in a symbiotic phase, you and your nurturing other together) are not all?

What objects will you find to sustain your need to idealize yourself and others? Kohut traces the pathological answers to early arrest. Kernberg finds that individuals answer, then lose their answer under later stress. Which is correct and which, if either, needs to be added to this picture of identity depends on the evidence which the next decade will see developed in therapy.

I am less comfortable with Kohut's inclusion of a separate track for the development of narcissism. Even so, I think it could be added to the diagram of pages 244–45 as another series of questions and answers parallel to the more or less traditional sequence I have given. It also seems to me that that diagram could include either Kernberg's self-object-affect structures or Kohut's self-objects as features of the developmental landscape or dialogue.

Kohut's use of self-representations corresponds to my treatment of identity as representation. In addition, however, Kohut introduces the self as a structure. That seems to me parallel to my treatment of identity as an agency and as the consequence of that agency as it acts through feedbacks. By insisting on the self as a structure in the psychoanalytic sense, however, Kohut seems to me to make it a thing "in" a person (like the traditional view of an ego), and that is not consistent with my view that one must think of identity at all times as a representation.

When I make that representation of identity out of a theme and variations, I think I am being consistent with both Kernberg and Kohut, although I am not relying (as much as Kohut would) on empathy but rather on observation and interpretation. Obviously, though, empathy has its place in the theme-and-variations interpretation of an identity, too.

In general, it seems to me, identity theory is consistent with the rest of psychoanalytic theory as we know it today. Certainly the concept of identity includes and builds upon first-phase, conscious-unconscious psychoanalysis. Similarly, identity includes and builds upon the second phase and ego-psychology, especially the concept of character to which identity closely corresponds and the concept of multiple function which provides a basis for the leap from multiple agencies to a single style. Identity enlarges second-phase psychoanalysis by repersonalizing—positing individual styles for—such abstractions in ego-psychology as "multiple function" or "superego" or, indeed, "ego" itself.

Identity theory is itself, however, a form of third-phase psychoanalysis. It also enhances other third-phase theories by offering a precision for, for example, such concepts from object relations theory as potential space or true and false selves or Erikson's psychosocial identity. To be sure, this concept of identity differs from Erikson's later thinking (although it is very close to his early ideas about "ego identity"). It does, however, offer a precise way of interpreting Erikson's mutualities (by reading them as ARCing and DEFTing a theme and variations).

Identity is more problematic in relation to Lacan. Certainly it offers a way of thinking about the *moi* and the *je* (like the true and false selves of English theory) which is not inconsistent with Lacan's thinking. One could say that Lacan's networks of signifieds and signifiers simply arc identity, although a phrasing of identity would be less concerned with verbal details and more with large themes. Identity theory accords with Lacan's blurring of the lines between ego and id, and Lacan's distinction between *savoir* and *verité* parallels the insistence in identity theory that identity is somebody's representation of identity. Lacan's insistence on "the" unconscious and his abandonment of Freud's concept of an ego do not touch identity theory directly. What is difficult, however, is the absence in his thinking of the idea of character and its replacement by gaps and leaks in a linguistic network otherwise formulated by the surrounding culture or by a family myth. To be sure, one can accommodate this scheme to identity or identity to this scheme but only by turning one or the other inside out.

The American theories of Kohut and Kernberg mostly do not impinge on identity theory. They deal closely with what the therapist is to say in the therapy, while identity is useful to the therapist primarily as a way of thinking the patient through. If, after some years of clinical experience, one or the other of these two theories becomes established, it would be possible, so to speak, to "write it into" identity theory, particularly the identity picture of development.

For the time being, however, I would prefer to relate identity theory to psychoanalysis as a sixth metapsychological principle (as at the end of chapter 3). For the past twenty years, analysts have agreed that any psychoanalytic interpretation or theory should admit of five kinds of statements: about forces, about energies, about structures, about genesis and development, about coping with reality. In relation to psychoanalysis, it is my purpose in this book to urge a sixth such principle, the personal. It follows from the fifth. Since any given psychological phenomenon involves the interaction of self and reality, it is just as essential to talk about what the individual personality, the I, does in a given psychological transaction as to talk about the effect of reality. Any psychoanalytic theory or interpretation should include statements about the continuing identity of the I's involved.

This sixth metapsychological principle applies two ways. Were we to discuss the effect on you of reading this book, it would be essential to take into account your personality. That seems obvious enough. Less obvious, perhaps, is that we *also* need to take into account the personality of the person analyzing the effect of this book on you. Writer and reader, experimenter and subject, interpreter and interpretee—in any psychological venture the I is finally you *and* I.

Bibliography

In the bibliography I have included only texts that relate to the study of the theory of the I, not, for example, biographical materials for the study of Fitzgerald or Shaw.

Abraham, Karl (1921). "Contributions to the Theory of the Anal Character." *Selected Papers on Psychoanalysis*. New York: Basic Books, 1953.

Alexander, Franz (1935). "The Logic of Emotions and its Dynamic Background." *International Journal of Psycho-Analysis*, 16, 399–413.

American Psychiatric Association (1968). *Diagnostic and Statistical Manual of Mental Disorders*. 2d ed. Washington, D.C.

Andreski, Stanislav (1972). *Social Sciences as Sorcery*. London: André Deutsch.

Apel, Karl-Otto (1972). "Communications and the Foundations of the Humanities." *Acta Sociologica*, 15, 7–26.

Arlow, Jacob (1959). "Psychoanalysis as Scientific Method." In Hook, ed. (1959), pp. 202–11.

Aslin, Richard N., Jeffrey R. Alberts, and Michael R. Peterson, eds. (1981). *Development of Perception: Psychobiological Perspectives*. Vol. I: *Audition, Somatic Perception, and the Chemical Senses*. Vol. II: *The Visual System*. New York: Academic Press.

Atkinson, Janette, and Oliver Braddick (1981). "Acuity, Contrast Sensitivity, and Accommodation in Infancy." In Aslin et al., eds. (1981), Vol. II, pp. 245–77.

Barr, Harriet Linton, Robert J. Langs, Robert R. Holt, Leo Goldberger, and George S. Klein (1972). *LSD: Personality and Experience*. New York: Wiley Interscience.

Bateson, Gregory (1972). *Steps to an Ecology of Mind*. New York: Ballantine Books.

Begley, Sharon (1979). "Science: Probing the Universe." *Newsweek*, March 12, p. 62.

Belsky, Jay, ed. (1982). *In the Beginning: Readings on Infancy*. New York: Columbia Univ. Press.

Belsky, Jay, and Robert K. Most (1982). "Infant Exploration and Play: A Window on Cognitive Development." In Belsky, ed. (1982), pp. 109–20.

Bergman, Anni (1978). "From Mother to the World Outside: The Use of Space During the Separation-Individuation Phase." In Grolnick and Barkin, eds. (1978), pp. 147–65.

Bergson, Henri (1896). *Matière et Memoire. Matter and Memory*. Trans. Nancy Margaret Paul and W. Scott Palmer [pseud.]. New York: Macmillan, 1911.

Berlyne, D. E. (1971). *Aesthetics and Psychobiology.* New York: Appleton-Century-Crofts.

Berne, Eric (1971). *What Do You Say After You Say Hello?: The Psychology of Human Destiny.* New York: Grove.

Bever, Thomas G. (1973). "Language and Perception." In Miller, G. (1973), pp. 149–58.

Bibring, Edward (1936). "Zur Entwicklung und Problematik der Triebtheorie." *Imago,* 22, 147–76. *Almanach der Psychoanalyse* (1937), pp. 230–51. "The Development and Problems of the Theory of the Instincts." *International Journal of Psycho-Analysis,* 22, 102–31 and 50 (1969), 293–308.

Bloom, Kathleen, ed. (1981). *Prospective Issues in Infancy Research.* Hillsdale, N. J.: Lawrence Erlbaum.

Blos, Peter (1968). "Character Formation in Adolescence." *Psychoanalytic Study of the Child,* 23, 245–51.

Bower, T. G. R. (1974). *Development in Infancy.* San Francisco: W. H. Freeman.
——— (1975). "Infant Perception of the Third Dimension and Object Concept Development." In Cohen and Salapatek, eds. (1975), Vol. II, pp. 33–50.

Bowlby, John (1951). *Maternal Care and Mental Health.* Geneva: World Health Organization.
——— (1958). "The Nature of the Child's Tie to His Mother." *International Journal of Psycho-Analysis,* 39, 350–73.
——— (1969). *Attachment and Loss.* Vol. I. *Attachment.* New York: Basic Books.

Brazelton, T. Barry (1973). *Neonatal Behavioral Assessment Scale.* Philadelphia: Lippincott.

Breger, Louis (1981). *Freud's Unfinished Journey: Conventional and Critical Perspectives in Psychoanalytic Theory.* London: Routledge and Kegan Paul.

Bretherton, Inge, Sandra McNew, and Marjorie Beeghly-Smith (1981). "Early Person Knowledge as Expressed in Gestural and Verbal Communication: When Do Infants Acquire a 'Theory of Mind'?" In Lamb and Sherrod, eds. (1981), pp. 333–73.

Bridgman, P. W. (1959). *The Way Things Are.* Cambridge: Harvard Univ. Press.

Bronowski, Jacob (1967). *The Origins of Knowledge and Imagination.* Silliman Foundation Lectures, 1967. New Haven and London: Yale Univ. Press, 1978.

Brown, Norman O. (1966). *Love's Body.* New York: Vintage Books.

Bruner, Jerome S., Jacqueline J. Goodnow, and George A. Austin (1956). *A Study of Thinking.* New York: Wiley.

Bruner, Jerome S., and David Krech, eds. (1949–50). *Perception and Personality: A Symposium.* Durham, N.C.: Duke Univ. Press.

Burks, Jayne, and Melvin Rubenstein (1979). *Temperament Styles in Adult Interaction: Applications in Psychotherapy.* New York: Brunner/Mazel.

Buxbaum, Edith (1959). "Psychosexual Development: The Oral, Anal, and Phallic Phases." In Levitt, ed. (1959), pp. 43–55.

Calder, Nigel (1970). *The Mind of Man: An Investigation into Current Research on the Brain and Human Nature.* New York: Viking.

Campos, Joseph J., and Craig R. Stenberg (1981). "Perception, Appraisal and

Emotion: The Onset of Social Referencing." In Lamb and Sherrod, eds. (1981), pp. 273–314.

Chasseguet-Smirgel, Janine, ed. (1970). *Recherches psychanalytiques nouvelles sur la sexualité féminine*. Paris: Payot, 1964. *Female Sexuality: New Psychoanalytic Views*. Ann Arbor: Univ. of Michigan Press, 1970.

—————(1976). "Freud and Female Sexuality: The 'Dark Continent.' " *International Journal of Psycho-Analysis*, 57, 275.

Chodorow, Nancy (1978). *The Reproduction of Mothering: Psychoanalysis and the Sociology of Gender*. Berkeley: Univ. of California Press.

Chomsky, Noam (1972). *Language and Mind*. Enlarged Edition. New York: Harcourt, Brace, Jovanovich.

—————(1975). *Reflections on Language*. New York: Pantheon.

Cohen, Leslie B., and Philip Salapatek, eds. (1975). *Infant Perception: From Sensation to Cognition*. Vol. I, Basic Visual Processes. Vol. II, Perception of Space, Speech, and Sound. New York: Academic Press.

Cole, Michael, and Barbara Means (1981). *Comparative Studies of How People Think: An Introduction*. Cambridge: Harvard Univ. Press.

Condon, William S. (1976). "An Analysis of Behavioral Organization." *Sign Language Studies*, 13, 285–318. Reprinted in *Nonverbal Communication: Readings with Commentary*. Ed. Shirley Weitz. 2d ed. New York: Oxford, 1979, pp. 149–67.

Condon, William S., and W. D. Ogston (1966). "Sound Film Analysis of Normal and Pathological Behavior Patterns." *Journal of Nervous and Mental Diseases*, 143, 338–46.

Crick, Francis H. C. (1979). "Thinking About the Brain." *Scientific American*, September, pp. 219–32.

Deregowski, Jan B. (1968). "Difficulties in Pictorial Depth Perception in Africa." *British Journal of Psychology*, 59, 195–204.

Dervin, Daniel (1975). *Bernard Shaw: A Psychological Study*. Lewisburg, Pa.: Bucknell Univ. Press.

Devereux, George (1967). *From Anxiety to Method in the Behavioral Sciences*. The Hague: Mouton.

Diesing, Paul (1971). *Patterns of Discovery in the Social Sciences*. Chicago: Aldine-Atherton.

Dillon, George L. (1978). *Language Processing and the Reading of Literature: Toward a Model of Comprehension*. Bloomington: Indiana Univ. Press.

Eckerman, Carol O., Judith L. Whatley, and Stuart L. Kutz (1982). "Growth of Social Play with Peers During the Second Year of Life." In Belsky, J., ed. (1982), pp. 157–66.

Ehrenzweig, Anton (1965). *The Psycho-Analysis of Artistic Vision and Hearing: An Introduction to a Theory of Unconscious Perception*. 2d ed. New York: George Braziller.

Eimas, Peter D. (1975). "Speech Perception in Early Infancy." In Cohen and Salapatek, eds. (1975), Vol. II, pp. 193–231.

Erikson, Erik (1946). "Ego Development and Historical Change." *Psychoanalytic Study of the Child*, 2, 359–96.

—— (1956). "The Problem of Ego Identity." *Journal of the American Psychoanalytic Association*, 4, 56–121.

—— (1958a). *Young Man Luther*. New York: Norton.

—— (1958b). "The Nature of Clinical Evidence." In Erikson (1964), pp. 47–80.

—— (1959). *Identity and the Life Cycle: Selected Papers by Erik H. Erikson. Psychological Issues*, Vol. I, No. 1, Monograph 1.

—— (1963). *Childhood and Society*. 2d ed. New York: Norton.

—— (1964). *Insight and Responsibility: Lectures on the Ethical Implications of Psychoanalytic Insight*. New York: Norton.

—— (1968). *Identity: Youth and Crisis*. New York: Norton.

—— (1972). "Play and Actuality." Reprinted in Lifton, ed. (1974).

—— (1975). *Life History and the Historical Moment*. New York: Norton.

Evans, Martha Noel (1979). "Introduction to Jacques Lacan's Lecture: The Neurotic's Individual Myth." *Psychoanalytic Quarterly*, 48, 386–404.

Evarts, Edward V. (1979). "Brain Mechanisms of Movement." *Scientific American*, September, pp. 164–79.

Fairbairn, W. Ronald D. (1963). "Synopsis of an Object-Relations Theory of the Personality." *International Journal of Psycho-Analysis*, 44, 224–25.

Fantz, Robert L., Joseph F. Fagan III, and Simon B. Miranda (1975). "Early Visual Selectivity as a Function of Pattern Variables, Previous Exposure, Age from Birth and Conception, and Expected Cognitive Deficit." In Cohen and Salapatek, eds. (1975), Vol. I, pp. 249–345.

Farrell, B. A. (1962). "The Criteria for a Psycho-Analytic Interpretation." *Proceedings of the Aristotelian Society*, 36, 77–100. Reprinted in *Essays in Philosophical Psychology*. Ed. Donald F. Gustafson. Garden City, N.Y.: Anchor, pp. 299–323.

Fenichel, Otto (1931). "Specific Forms of the Oedipus Complex." In Fenichel (1953), pp. 204–20.

—— (1935). "The Scoptophilic Instinct and Identification." In Fenichel (1953), pp. 373–97.

—— (1945). *The Psychoanalytic Theory of Neurosis*. New York: Norton.

—— (1953). *Collected Papers: First Series*. New York: Norton.

Ferenczi, Sandor (1916). "The Ontogenesis of Symbols." In *Six in Psychoanalysis: Contributions to Psychoanalysis*, ed. Richard C. Badger (Boston, 1916), pp. 276–81.

Fish, Stanley (1980). *Is There a Text in this Class?: The Authority of Interpretive Communities*. Cambridge: Harvard Univ. Press.

Fisher, Seymour, and Roger P. Greenberg (1977). *The Scientific Credibility of Freud's Theories and Therapy*. New York: Basic Books.

Fodor, Jerry A., Thomas G. Bever, and Merrill F. Garrett (1974). *The Psychology of Language: An Introduction to Psycholinguistics and Generative Grammar*. New York: McGraw-Hill.

Fodor, Jerry A. and Jerrold J. Katz, eds. (1964). *The Structure of Language*. Englewood Cliffs, N. J.: Prentice-Hall.

Fraiberg, Selma (1969). "Libidinal Object Constancy and Mental Representation." *Psychoanalytic Study of the Child*, 24, 9–47.

——— (1977). *Insights from the Blind*. New York: Basic Books.

Freedman, Alfred M., Harold I. Kaplan, and Benjamin A. Sadock (1972). *Modern Synopsis of Comprehensive Textbook of Psychiatry*. Baltimore: Williams and Wilkins.

Freedman, David A. (1981). "The Effect of Sensory and Other Deficits in Children on Their Experience of People." *Journal of the American Psychoanalytic Association*, 29, 831–67.

Freud, Anna (1966). "Obsessional Neurosis: A Summary of Psycho-Analytic Views as Presented at the Congress." *International Journal of Psycho-Analysis*, 47, 116–22.

Freud, Sigmund. *The Standard Edition of the Complete Psychological Works*. Trans. and ed. James Strachey in collaboration with Anna Freud, assisted by Alex Strachey and Alan Tyson. 24 vols. London: The Hogarth Press and the Institute of Psycho-Analysis, 1953–74. All subsequent references to Freud's works are to volume and page in this edition. The letters after the date refer to the "Freud Bibliography" in volume 24 of the *Standard Edition*, pp. 47–82, which gives complete bibliographical information for English and German editions.

——— (1895). See Freud (1950 [1895]).

——— (1896c). "The Aetiology of Hysteria." 3:129–221.

——— (1900a). *The Interpretation of Dreams*. 4–5:1–627.

——— (1901a). *On Dreams*. 5:633–85.

——— (1901b). *The Psychopathology of Everyday Life*. 6:vii–279.

——— (1905d). *Three Essays on the Theory of Sexuality*. 7:125–243.

——— (1908b). "Character and Anal Erotism." 9:169–75.

——— (1908d). " 'Civilized' Sexual Morality and Modern Nervous Illness." 9:179–204.

——— (1908e). "Creative Writers and Daydreaming." 9:143–53.

——— (1909b). "Analysis of a Phobia in a Five-Year-Old Boy." 10:3–145.

——— (1909d). "Notes upon a Case of Obsessional Neurosis." 10:155–320.

——— (1911b). "Formulations on the Two Principles of Mental Functioning." 12:215–26.

——— (1912b). "The Dynamics of Transference." 12:99–108.

——— (1912–13). *Totem and Taboo*. 13:1–162.

——— (1913h). "Observations and Examples from Analytic Practice." 13:193–98.

——— (1913i). "The Disposition to Obsessional Neurosis." 12:313–26.

——— (1915c). "Instincts and their Vicissitudes." 14:111–40.

——— (1915e). "The Unconscious." 14:161–215.

——— (1916–17). *Introductory Lectures on Psycho-Analysis*. 15:3–16:476.

——— (1916d). "Some Character-Types Met with in Psycho-Analytic Work." 14:311–333.

——— (1918b). "From the History of an Infantile Neurosis." 17:3–60.

——— (1919a). "Lines of Advance in Psycho-Analytic Therapy." 17:159–68.

—— (1920a). "The Psychogenesis of a Case of Female Homosexuality." 18:147–72.

—— (1920g). *Beyond the Pleasure Principle*. 18:7-64.

—— (1921c). *Group Psychology and the Analysis of the Ego*. 18:69–143.

—— (1923b). *The Ego and the Id*. 19:3–66.

—— (1923c). "Remarks on the Theory and Practice of Dream-Interpretation." 19:109–21.

—— (1925j). "Some Psychical Consequences of the Anatomical Distinction between the Sexes." 19:243–58.

—— (1926d). *Inhibitions, Symptoms and Anxiety*. 20:77–175.

—— (1926e). *The Question of Lay Analysis*. 20:179–258.

—— (1930a). *Civilization and its Discontents*. 21:59–145.

—— (1931b). "Female Sexuality." 21:223–43.

—— (1932a). "The Acquistion and Control of Fire." 22:185–93.

—— (1933a). *New Introductory Lectures on Psycho-Analysis*. 22:3–182.

—— (1937c). "Analysis Terminable and Interminable." 23:211–53.

—— (1937d). "Constructions in Analysis." 23:257–69.

—— (1940a). *An Outline of Psycho-Analysis*. 23:141–71.

—— (1950). *The Origins of Psycho-Analysis: Letters to Wilhelm Fliess*. New York: Basic Books, 1954, 1977.

—— (1950 [1895]). "Project for a Scientific Psychology." 1:283–397. Also in Freud (1950), pp. 347–445.

—— (1965a). *Sigmund Freud/Karl Abraham. Briefe 1907 bis 1926*. Ed. H. C. Abraham and E. L. Freud. Frankfurt am Main: S. Fischer. Trans. Bernard Marsh and Hilda C. Abraham. *A Psycho-Analytic Dialogue. The Letters of Sigmund Freud and Karl Abraham, 1907–26*. London and New York: The Hogarth Press and the Institute of Psycho-Analysis, 1965.

Friedman, Neil (1967). *The Social Nature of Psychological Research: The Psychological Experiment as a Social Inter-Action*. New York: Basic Books.

Frye, Northrop (1963). "Literary Criticism." In *The Aims and Methods of Scholarship in Modern Languages and Literatures*. Ed. James Thorpe. New York: Modern Language Association of America, pp. 57–69.

Geschwind, Norman (1979). "Specializations of the Human Brain." *Scientific American*, September, pp. 180–99.

Gibson, James J. (1977). "The Theory of Affordances." In Shaw and Bransford, eds. (1977), pp. 67–82.

Gill, Merton M., and Philip Holzman, eds. (1976). *Psychology versus Metapsychology. Psychological Issues*, Vol. 9, No. 4, Monograph 36. New York: International Universities Press.

Gilligan, Carol (1982). *In a Different Voice: Psychological Theory and Women's Development*. Cambridge: Harvard Univ. Press.

Gouin Décarie, Thérèse (1965). *Intelligence and Affectivity in Early Childhood: An Experimental Study of Jean Piaget's Object Concept and Object Relations*. Trans. Elisabeth Pasztor Brandt and Lewis Wolfgang Brandt. New York: International Universities Press.

Graf, Herbert (1972). "Memoirs of an Invisible Man." *Opera News,* 36, i, 25–28; ii, 27–29; iii, 27–29; iv, 26–29.

Granit, Ragnar (1977). *The Purposive Brain.* Cambridge and London: MIT Press.

Green, André (1975). "The Analyst, Symbolization and Absence in the Analytic Setting (On Changes in Analytic Practice and Analytic Experience)." *International Journal of Psycho-Analysis,* 36, 1–22.

Gregory, Richard L. (1968). "Visual Illusions." In Held and Richards, eds. (1972), pp. 241–51.

————, ed. (1981). *Mind in Science: A History of Explanations in Psychology and Physics.* Cambridge: Cambridge Univ. Press.

Grolnick, Simon A., and Leonard Barkin, eds. (1978). In collaboration with Werner Muensterberger. *Between Reality and Fantasy: Transitional Objects and Phenomena.* New York: Jason Aronson.

Guttman, Samuel A. (1969). "Obituary: Robert Waelder, 1900–67." *International Journal of Psycho-Analysis,* 50, 269–73.

Habermas, Jurgen (1968). *Erkenntnis und Interesse.* Frankfurt am Main: Suhrkamp Verlag. *Knowledge and Human Interests.* Trans. Jeremy J. Shapiro. Boston: Beacon Press, 1971.

Halle, Morris, and Kenneth N. Stevens (1964). "Speech Recognition: A Model and a Program for Research." In Fodor and Katz, eds. (1964), pp. 604–12.

Hampshire, Stuart (1962a). *Thought and Action.* New York: Viking Press.

————(1962b). "Disposition and Memory." *International Journal of Psycho-Analysis,* 43, 59–68.

Hartmann, Heinz. (1939). "Ich-Psychologie und Anpassungs-Problem." *Internationale Zeitschrift für Psychoanalyse,* 24, 62–135. *Ego Psychology and the Problem of Adaptation.* Trans. David Rapaport. *Journal of the American Psychoanalytic Association,* Monograph No. 1. New York: International Universities Press, 1958.

————(1951). "Technical Implications of Ego Psychology." *Psychoanalytic Quarterly,* 20, 31–43.

———— (1959). "Psychoanalysis as a Scientific Theory." In Hook, ed. (1959), pp. 3–37.

———— (1960). *Psychoanalysis and Moral Values.* The Freud Anniversary Lecture Series, The New York Psychoanalytic Institute. New York: International Universities Press.

Heisenberg, Werner (1958). "The Representation of Nature in Contemporary Physics." *Daedalus,* 87, 95–108.

Held, Richard (1965). "Plasticity in Sensory-Motor Systems." In Held and Richards, eds. (1972), pp. 372–79.

———— (1981). "Development of Acuity in Infants with Normal and Anomalous Visual Experience." In Aslin et al., eds. (1981), Vol. II, pp. 279–96.

Held, Richard, and Whitman Richards, eds. (1972). *Perception: Mechanisms and Models.* San Francisco: W. H. Freeman.

Hendrick, Ives (1958). *Facts and Theories of Psychoanalysis.* 3d. ed. New York: Dell.

Henry, Jules (1972). *Pathways to Madness.* New York: Random House.

Holland, Norman N. (1968a). *The Dynamics of Literary Response.* New York: Oxford Univ. Press.

———— (1968b). "Prose and Minds: A Psychoanalytic Approach to Non-Fiction." In *The Art of Victorian Prose,* eds. George Levine and William Madden. New York: Oxford Univ. Press, pp. 314–37.

———— (1973). "Defense, Displacement and the Ego's Algebra." *International Journal of Psycho-Analysis,* 54, 247–57.

———— (1975a). *5 Readers Reading.* New Haven and London: Yale Univ. Press.

———— (1975b). "An Identity for the Rat Man." *International Review of Psycho-Analysis,* 2, 157–69.

———— (1976). "Literary Interpretation and Three Phases of Psychoanalysis." *Critical Inquiry,* 3, 221–33.

———— (1977). "Literary Suicide: A Question of Style." *Psychocultural Review,* 1, 285–303.

———— (1978). "Human Identity." *Critical Inquiry,* 4, 451–69.

Holt, Robert R., ed. (1967). *Motives and Thought: Psychoanalytic Essays in Honor of David Rapaport. Psychological Issues,* Vol. 5, No. 2/3, Monograph 18/19. New York: International Universities Press.

Home, H. J. (1966). "The Concept of Mind." *International Journal of Psycho-Analysis,* 47, 42–49.

Hook, Sidney, ed. (1959). *Psychoanalysis, Scientific Method, and Philosophy.* New York: New York Univ. Press.

Horney, Karen (1932). "The Dread of Woman." *International Journal of Psycho-Analysis,* 13, 348–60. In Horney (1967), pp. 133–46.

———— (1967). *Feminine Psychology.* New York: Norton.

Hymes, Dell (1973). "Speech and Language: On the Origins and Foundations of Inequality Among Speakers." *Daedalus,* 102, 59–85.

Irigaray, Luce (1977). "Women's Exile" (interview). *Ideology and Consciousness,* No. 1 (May), pp. 62–76.

Ittelson, W. H., and F. P. Kilpatrick (1951). "Experiments in Perception." *Scientific American,* August. In *Frontiers of Psychological Research: Readings from Scientific American.* Ed. Stanley Coopersmith. San Francisco and London: W. H. Freeman.

Jackendoff, Ray S. (1972). *Semantic Interpretation in Generative Grammar.* Cambridge: MIT Press.

James, William (1890). *The Principles of Psychology.* 2 vols. New York: Henry Holt. Reprint. New York: Dover, 1950.

Jones, Ernest (1916). "The Theory of Symbolism." In Jones (1948), pp. 87–144.

———— (1918). "Anal-Erotic Character Traits." In Jones (1948), pp. 413–37.

———— (1948). *Papers on Psycho-Analysis.* 5th ed. London: Baillière, Tindall, and Cox.

———— (1953–57). *The Life and Work of Sigmund Freud.* 3 vols. New York: Basic Books.

Kagan, Jerome (1972). "Do Infants Think?" *Scientific American,* March, pp. 74–82.

Kanzer, Mark (1952). "The Transference Neurosis of the Rat Man." *Psychoanalytic Quarterly,* 21, 181–89.

————, ed. (1971). *The Unconscious Today: Essays in Honor of Max Schur.* New York: International Universities Press.

Kaplan, Louise (1978). *Oneness and Separateness: From Infant to Individual.* New York: Simon and Schuster.

Kardiner, Abram, and Associates (1945). *The Psychological Frontiers of Society.* New York: Columbia Univ. Press.

Kazin, Alfred (1980). "Hopper's Vision of New York." *The New York Times Magazine,* September 7, p. 56.

Kernberg, Otto (1975). *Borderline Conditions and Pathological Narcissism.* New York: Jason Aronson.

———— (1978). *Object-Relations Theory and Clinical Psychoanalysis.* New York: Jason Aronson.

Klein, George S. (1970). *Perception, Motives, and Personality.* New York: Knopf.

———— (1976). *Psychoanalytic Theory: An Exploration of Essentials.* New York: International Universities Press.

Klein, George S., and Herbert Schlesinger (1949). "Where Is the Perceiver in Perceptual Theory?" In Bruner and Krech, eds. (1949–50), pp. 32–47.

Klein, Melanie (1930). "The Importance of Symbol-Formation in the Development of the Ego." *International Journal of Psycho-Analysis,* 11, 24–39. In Klein, M. (1975), 1:219–32.

———— (1975). *Complete Works.* 5 vols. London: Hogarth Press.

Klein, Melanie, Paula Heimann, and R. E. Money-Kyrle, eds. (1957). *New Directions in Psycho-Analysis.* New York: Basic Books.

Kline, Paul (1972). *Fact and Fantasy in Freudian Theory.* London: Methuen.

Kluckhohn, Clyde, and Henry A. Murray (1948). "Personality Formation: The Determinants." In *Personality: In Nature, Society, and Culture.* Eds. Clyde Kluckhohn and Henry A. Murray. New York: Knopf, 1961, p. 53.

Kohut, Heinz (1971). *The Analysis of the Self. Psychoanalytic Study of the Child,* Monograph 4. New York: International Universities Press.

———— (1977). *The Restoration of the Self.* New York: International Universities Press.

———— (1979). "The Two Analyses of Mr. Z." *International Journal of Psycho-Analysis,* 60, 3–27.

Kohut, Heinz, and Ernest S. Wolf (1978). "The Disorders of the Self and Their Treatment: An Outline." *International Journal of Psycho-Analysis,* 59, 413–25.

Kolers, Paul A. (1964). "The Illusion of Movement." In Held and Richards, eds. (1972), pp. 316–23.

Kris, Ernst (1952). *Psychoanalytic Explorations in Art.* New York: International Universities Press.

Kubie, Lawrence S. (1959). "Psychoanalysis and Scientific Method." In Hook, ed. (1959), pp. 57–77.

Kuhn, Thomas S. (1962). *The Structure of Scientific Revolutions.* Chicago: Univ. of Chicago Press.

———— (1970). "Logic of Discovery or Psychology of Research?" In *Criticism and the Growth of Knowledge.* Ed. Imre Lacatos and Alan Musgrove. Proceedings of the

International Colloquium in the Philosophy of Science, London, 1965, vol. 4. Cambridge: Cambridge Univ. Press, pp. 1–23.

LaBarre, Weston (1967). Preface, *From Anxiety to Method in the Behavioral Sciences*, by George Devereux. The Hague: Mouton.

Lacan, Jacques (1936). "Le Stade du miroir comme formateur de la fonction du Je, telle qu'elle nous est révélée dans l'éxperience psychanalytique." *Revue Française de Psychanalyse*, 13 (1949), 449–55.

——— (1953). "Le mythe individuel du nevrosé ou 'Poésie et Verité' dans la nevrose," *Ornicar?*, No. 17. "The Neurotic's Individual Myth." Trans. Jacques-Alain Miller. *Psychoanalytic Quarterly*, 48 (1979), 405–25.

——— (1956). "Fonction et champ de la parole et du langage en psychanalyse." *La Psychanalyse*, I. "The Function of Language in Psychoanalysis." In *The Language of the Self*. Trans. Anthony Wilden. Baltimore: Johns Hopkins Press, 1968.

——— (1966). *Écrits*. Paris: Editions du Seuil. *Écrits: A Selection*. Trans. Alan Sheridan. New York: Norton, 1977.

——— (1970). *Scilicet*. Vol. 2/3. Paris: Editions du Seuil.

——— (1979). *The Four Fundamental Concepts of Psycho-Analysis*. Ed. Jacques-Alain Miller. Trans. Alan Sheridan. New York: Norton.

Lakoff, George (1974). Interview with Herman Parret. In Fillmore, Charles, George Lakoff, and Robin Lakoff, eds. (1974). *Berkeley Studies in Syntax and Semantics I*. Berkeley, Cal.: Department of Linguistics and Institute of Human Learning, Univ. of California. Pp. XI.1–44.

Lakoff, Robin (1973). *Language and Woman's Place*. Rpt. Tokyo: Bunri Co.

Lamb, Michael (1981). "The Development of Social Expectations in the First Year of Life." In Lamb and Sherrod (1981), pp. 155–75.

Lamb, Michael, and Lonnie R. Sherrod (1981). *Infant Social Cognition: Empirical and Theoretical Considerations*. Hillsdale, N.J.: Lawrence Erlbaum.

Land, Edwin H. (1959). "Experiments in Color Vision." *Scientific American*, May, pp. 23–26. Reprinted in Held and Richards (1972), pp. 286–98.

——— (1978). "Our 'Polar Partnership' with the World Around Us." *Harvard Magazine*, 80, 23–26.

Laplanche, J., and J.-B. Pontalis (1968). *Vocabulaire de la Psychanalyse*. Paris: Presses Universitaires de France. *The Language of Psycho-Analysis*. Trans. Donald Nicholson-Smith. New York: Norton, 1973.

Lasch, Christopher (1974). "Freud and Women." *New York Review of Books*, 3 October, pp. 12–17.

Levitt, Morton, ed. (1959). *Readings in Psychoanalytic Psychology*. New York: Appleton-Century-Crofts.

Lewis, Michael (1981). "Self-Knowledge: A Social Cognitive Perspective on Gender Identity and Sex-Role Development." In Lamb and Sherrod (1981), pp. 395–414.

Lewis, Michael, and Jeanne Brooks-Gunn (1982). "Self, Other, and Fear: The Reaction of Infants to People." In Belsky, ed. (1982), pp. 167–77.

Lewis, N. D. C., and H. Yarnell (1951). *Pathological Firesetting*. Nervous and Mental Disease Monograph No. 82. New York: Coolidge Foundation.

Liberman, Alvin M. (1973). "The Speech Code." In Miller, G. (1973), pp. 128–40.

Lichtenstein, Heinz (1961). "Identity and Sexuality: A Study of Their Interrelationship in Man." *Journal of the American Psychoanalytic Association,* 9, 179–260. In Lichtenstein (1977), pp. 49–122.

—— (1964). "The Role of Narcissism in the Emergence and Maintenance of a Primary Identity." *International Journal of Psycho-Analysis,* 45, 49–56. In Lichtenstein (1977), pp. 207–21.

—— (1973). "The Challenge to Psychoanalytic Psychotherapy in a World in Crisis." *International Journal of Psychoanalytic Psychotherapy,* 2, 149–74. In Lichtenstein (1977), pp. 345–68.

—— (1974). "The Effect of Reality Perception on Psychic Structure: A Psychoanalytic Contribution to the Problem of the 'Generation Gap.' " *Annual of Psychoanalysis,* 2, 349–67. In Lichtenstein (1977), pp. 323–44.

—— (1977). *The Dilemma of Human Identity.* New York: Jason Aronson.

Lifton, Robert J. (1961). *Thought Reform and the Psychology of Totalism: A Study of "Brainwashing" in China.* London: Penguin, 1967.

—— ed. (1974). *Explorations in Psychohistory: The Wellfleet Papers.* New York: Simon and Schuster.

Lloyd, Barbara B. (1972). *Perception and Cognition: A Cross-Cultural Perspective.* London: Penguin.

Loch, Wolfgang (1977). "Some Comments on the Subject of Psychoanalysis and Truth." In *Thought, Consciousness, and Reality.* Ed. Joseph H. Smith. Psychiatry and the Humanities, Vol. 2. New Haven and London: Yale Univ. Press.

Loewald, Hans (1978). *Psychoanalysis and the History of the Individual.* New Haven and London: Yale Univ. Press.

Lyons, John (1977). *Noam Chomsky.* Penguin Modern Masters. Rev. ed. Harmondsworth: Penguin.

MacNeill, Ian, producer (1959). Guy Glover, director. *Four Families.* National Film Board of Canada. Dist. McGraw-Hill Co. 161 min.

Mahler, Margaret, Fred Pine, and Anni Bergman (1975). *The Psychological Birth of the Human Infant: Symbiosis and Individuation.* New York: Basic Books.

Marx, Karl (1844). "Economic and Philosophical Manuscripts of 1844." In *Early Writings.* Trans. Rodney Livingstone and Gregor Benton. The Marx Library. New York: Vintage Books, 1975, p. 350.

Masling, Joseph (1966). "Role Related Behavior of the Subject and Psychologist and its Effects upon Psychological Data." In *Symposium on Motivation.* Ed. D. Levine (1966). Lincoln: Univ. of Nebraska Press, pp. 67–103.

Masling, Joseph, and Murray M. Schwartz (1979). "A Critique of Research In Psychoanalytic Theory." *Genetic Psychology Monographs,* 100, 257–307.

Matas, Leah, Richard A. Arend, and Alan Sroufe (1982). "Continuity of Adaptation in the Second Year: The Relationship between Quality of Attachment and Later Competence." In Belsky, ed. (1982), pp. 144–56.

Mauron, Charles (1964). *Psychocritique du Genre Comique.* Paris: José Corti. Appendix 1 A.

May, Robert (1980). *Sex and Fantasy: Patterns of Male and Female Development.* New York: Norton.

Mayr, Ernst (1978). "Evolution." *Scientific American,* September, pp. 47–55.

Mazlish, Bruce (1975). *James and John Stuart Mill: Father and Son in the Nineteenth Century.* New York: Basic Books.

McCluskey, Kathleen S. (1981). "The Infant as Organizer: Future Directions in Perceptual Development." In Bloom, K., ed. (1981), pp. 119–36.

McDougall, Joyce (1964). "Homosexuality in Women." In Chasseguet-Smirgel, ed. (1970), pp. 171–212.

——— (1972). "Primal Scene and Sexual Perversion." *International Journal of Psycho-Analysis,* 53, 371–84.

Mead, Margaret (1974). "On Freud's View of Female Psychology." In Strouse, ed. (1974), pp. 116–28.

Meissner, W. W. (1966). "The Operational Principle and Meaning in Psychoanalysis." *Psychoanalytic Quarterly,* 35, 233–55.

——— (1971). "Freud's Methodology." *Journal of the American Psychoanalytic Association,* 19, 265–309.

Michaels, J. (1955). *Disorders of Character: Persistent Enuresis, Juvenile Delinquency, and Psychopathic Personality.* Springfield, Ill.: Charles C. Thomas.

Miller, George A., ed. (1973). *Communication, Language, and Meaning: Psychological Perspectives.* New York: Basic Books.

Miller, George A., Eugene Galanter, and Karl H. Pribram (1960). *Plans and the Structure of Behavior.* New York: Holt, Rinehart and Winston.

Miller, Jonathan (1978). *The Body in Question.* New York: Random House.

Mills, Theodore M. (1977). "The Disintegration of the Nixon Group in the White House." Presentation at the meeting of the Group for Applied Psychoanalysis, 16 November 1977. Available from the Center for the Psychological Study of the Arts, State University of New York at Buffalo, Amherst, N. Y. 14260.

Milner, Marion (1952). "Aspects of Symbolism in Comprehension of the Not-self." *International Journal of Psycho-Analysis,* 33, 181–95.

——— (1957a). "The Role of Illusion in Symbol Formation." In Klein, M., et al. (1957), pp. 82–108.

——— [Joanna Field] (1957b). *On Not Being Able to Paint.* 2d ed. New York: International Universities Press.

——— (1969). *The Hands of the Living God.* New York: International Universities Press.

Mitchell, Juliet (1974). *Psychoanalysis and Feminism: Freud, Reich, Laing, and Women.* New York: Pantheon.

Money, John, and Anke Ehrhardt (1972). *Man and Woman Boy and Girl.* Baltimore: Johns Hopkins Press.

Monod, Jacques (1970). *Le Hasard et la Necessité.* Paris: Editions du Seuil. *Chance and Necessity.* Trans. Austryn Wainhouse. New York: Knopf, 1971.

Moore, Burness E. (1976). "Freud and Female Sexuality: A Current View." *International Journal of Psycho-Analysis,* 57, 287–300.

Moore, Burness E., and Bernard D. Fine (1967). *A Glossary of Psychoanalytic Terms and Concepts.* New York: American Psychoanalytic Association.

Morowitz, Harold J. (1980). "Rediscovering the Mind." *Psychology Today,* August, pp. 12–17.

Muller, John P., and William J. Richardson (1978–79). "Toward Reading Lacan." *Psychoanalysis and Contemporary Thought,* I (1978), 323–72, 503–29; II (1979), 199–252, 345–435.

——— (1982). *Lacan and Language: A Reader's Guide to "Écrits."* New York: International Universities Press.

Munroe, Robert L., and Ruth H. Munroe (1975). *Cross-Cultural Human Development.* Monterey: Brooks/Cole.

Murphy, Gardner (1949). Discussion of Klein and Schlesinger (1949). In Bruner and Krech, eds. (1949–50), pp. 51–55.

Nauta, Walle U. H., and Michael Feirtag (1979). "The Organization of the Brain." *Scientific American,* September, pp. 88–111.

Neisser, Ulric (1967). *Cognitive Psychology.* New York: Appleton-Century-Crofts.

Norman, Donald A., David E. Rummelhart, and the LNR Research Group (1975). *Explorations in Cognition.* San Francisco: W. H. Freeman.

Noton, David, and Lawrence Stark (1971). "Eye Movements and Visual Perception." *Scientific American,* June, pp. 35–43.

Noy, Pinchas (1969). "A Revision of the Psychoanalytic Theory of the Primary Process." *International Journal of Psycho-Analysis,* 50, 155–78.

——— (1973). "Symbolism and Mental Representation." *Annual of Psychoanalysis,* 1, 125–58.

Nunberg, Hermann (1931). "The Synthetic Function of the Ego." *International Journal of Psycho-Analysis,* 12, 123–40.

Nunberg, Herman, and Ernst Federn, eds. (1962). *The Minutes of the Vienna Psychoanalytic Society, Vol. I: 1906–08.* Trans. Herman Nunberg. New York: International Universities Press.

Olson, Gary (1981). "The Recognition of Specific Persons." In Lamb and Sherrod (1981), pp. 37–59.

Ornstein, Paul H. (1974). "On Narcissism: Beyond the Introduction; Highlights of Heinz Kohut's Contributions to the Psychoanalytic Treatment of Narcissistic Disorders." *Annual of Psychoanalysis,* 2, 127–49.

Papoušek, Hanuš, and Mechtild Papoušek (1981). "How Human is the Human Newborn, and What Else Is to Be Done?" In Bloom, ed. (1981), pp. 137–55.

Parsons, Anne (1964). "Is the Oedipus Complex Universal? The Jones-Malinowski Debate Revisited and a South Italian 'Nuclear Complex.' " *Psychoanalytic Study of Society,* 3, 278–326.

Pearson, Karl (1911/1892). *The Grammar of Science.* London: Dent.

Peckham, Morse (1965). *Man's Rage for Chaos: Biology, Behavior, and the Arts.* Philadelphia: Chilton.

Penfield, Wilder (1975). *The Mystery of the Mind.* Princeton, N.J.: Princeton Univ. Press.

Peterfreund, Emanuel (1971). *Information, Systems and Psychoanalysis.* New York: International Universities Press.

Piaget, Jean (1970). *The Moral Judgment of the Child.* New York: Harcourt, Brace.

Planck, Max (1949). *Scientific Autobiography and Other Papers.* Trans. Frank Gaynor. New York: Philosophical Library.

Polanyi, Michael (1958). *Personal Knowledge: Towards a Post-Critical Philosophy*. Chicago: Univ. of Chicago Press.

——— (1968). "Life's Irreducible Structure." *Science*, 160, 1308–12.

Poole, Roger (1972). *Towards Deep Subjectivity*. New York: Harper and Row.

Popper, Karl (1972). *Objective Knowledge: An Evolutionary Approach*. Oxford: Clarendon Press.

Popper, Karl, and John C. Eccles (1977). *The Self and its Brain*. Berlin: Springer International.

Powers, William T. (1973a). *Behavior: The Control of Perception*. Chicago: Aldine.

——— (1973b). "Feedback: Beyond Behaviorism." *Science*, 179, 351–56.

——— (1978). "Quantitative Analysis of Purposive Systems: Some Spadework at the Foundations of Scientific Psychology." *Psychological Review*, 85, 417–35.

Pribram, Karl H. (1969). "The Neurophysiology of Remembering." *Scientific American*, January, 73–86.

Pritchard, R. M. (1961). "Stabilized Images on the Retina." In Held and Richards, eds. (1972), pp. 176–82.

Rapaport, David (1960a). "On the Psychoanalytic Theory of Motivation." In *Nebraska Symposium on Motivation*, 8. Ed. M. R. Jones. Lincoln: Univ. of Nebraska Press.

——— (1960b). *The Structure of Psychoanalytic Theory: A Systematizing Attempt*. *Psychological Issues*, Vol. 2, No. 2, Monograph 6. New York: International Universities Press.

Rapaport, David, and Merton M. Gill (1959). "The Points of View and Assumptions of Metapsychology." *International Journal of Psycho-Analysis*, 40, 153–62.

Reich, Wilhelm (1949). *Character Analysis*. 3d ed. New York: Noonday.

Requin, Jean, ed. (1978). *Attention and Performance VII*. Proceedings of the Seventh International Symposium on Attention and Performance, Sénanque, France, August 1–6, 1976. Hillsdale, N.J.: Lawrence Erlbaum.

Rescher, Nicholas (1970a). *Scientific Explanation*. New York: The Free Press.

——— (1970b). "Lawfulness as Mind-Dependent." In *Essays in Honor of Carl G. Hempel*. Ed. Nicholas Rescher et al. New York: Humanities Press.

Ricoeur, Paul (1970). *Freud and Philosophy: An Essay on Interpretation*. Trans. Denis Savage. New Haven and London: Yale Univ. Press.

——— (1978). Discussion of Toulmin (1978). *Annual of Psychoanalysis*, 6, 336–42.

Rodrigué, Emilio (1956). "Notes on Symbolism." *International Journal of Psycho-Analysis*, 37, 147–57.

Rosen, Victor (1961). "The Relevance of 'Style' to Certain Aspects of Defence and the Synthetic Function of the Ego." *International Journal of Psycho-Analysis*, 42, 447–57. Reprinted as "The Psychology of Style." In Rosen, *Style, Character, and Language*. Ed. Samuel Atkin and Milton E. Jucovy. New York: Jason Aronson, 1977, pp. 285–307.

Rosenblueth, Arturo, Norbert Wiener, and Julian Bigelow (1943). "Behavior, Purpose, and Teleology." *Philosophy of Science*, 10, 18–24.

Rosenthal, Robert (1966). *Experimenter Effects on Behavioral Research*. New York: Appleton-Century-Crofts.

Rubinstein, Benjamin (1976). "On the Possibility of a Strictly Psychoanalytic Theory: An Essay in the Philosophy of Psychoanalysis." In Gill and Holzman (1976), pp. 229–64.

Rycroft, Charles (1968). *Imagination and Reality*. New York: International Universities Press.

—— (1974). "Is Freudian Symbolism a Myth?" *New York Review of Books*, 24 January, pp. 13–15.

—— (1975). "Freud and the Imagination." *New York Review of Books*, 3 April, pp. 26–29.

—— (1979). *The Innocence of Dreams*. New York: Pantheon.

Ryle, Gilbert (1949). *The Concept of Mind*. New York: Harper and Row.

Salapatek, Philip (1975). "Pattern Perception in Early Infancy." In Cohen and Salapatek (1975), Vol. I, pp. 133–248.

Salmon, Wesley C. (1973). "Confirmation." *Scientific American*, May, 75–83.

Sander, L. (1969). "Regulation and Organization in the Early Infant-Caretaker System." In *Brain and Early Behavior*. Ed. R. Robinson. London: Academic Press.

Sartre, Jean Paul (1943, 1956). *L'Être et le Néant: essai d'ontologie phénoménologique*. Paris: Gallimard. *Being and Nothingness: A Phenomenological Essay on Ontology* (1956). Trans. Hazel E. Barnes. New York: Washington Square Press, 1966.

—— (1947). *Baudelaire*. Paris: Gallimard.

Schafer, Roy (1970). "An Overview of Heinz Hartmann's Contributions to Psychoanalysis." *International Journal of Psycho-Analysis*, 51, 425–46.

—— (1974). "Problems in Freud's Psychology of Women." *Journal of the American Psychoanalytic Association*, 22, 459–85.

—— (1976). *A New Language for Psychoanalysis*. New Haven and London: Yale Univ. Press.

—— (1978). *Language and Insight*. New Haven and London: Yale Univ. Press.

Schank, Roger, and Robert P. Abelson (1977). *Scripts, Plans, Goals, and Understanding: An Inquiry into Human Knowledge Structures*. Hillsdale, N.J.: Lawrence Erlbaum.

Schimek, Jean G. (1975). "A Critical Re-Examination of Freud's Concept of Unconscious Mental Representation." *International Review of Psycho-Analysis*, 2, 171–87.

Schramm, Wilbur (1973). "Mass Communication." In Miller, G., ed. (1973), pp. 219–30.

Segal, Hanna (1957). "Notes on Symbol-Formation." *International Journal of Psycho-Analysis*, 38, 391–97.

—— (1978). "On Symbolism." *International Journal of Psycho-Analysis*, 59, 315–19.

Segall, Marshall H., Donald T. Campbell, and Melville J. Herskovits (1966). *The Influence of Culture on Visual Perception*. New York: Bobbs-Merrill.

Serebriany, Reggy (1976). "Dialogue on 'Freud and Female Sexuality.' " *International Journal of Psycho-Analysis*, 57, 311–13.

Shaw, Robert, and John Bransford, eds. (1977). *Perceiving, Acting, and Knowing: Toward an Ecological Perspective*. Hillsdale, N.J.: Lawrence Erlbaum.

Shengold, Leonard (1971). "More about Rats and Rat People." *International Journal of Psycho-Analysis*, 52, 277–88.

Sherrington, Sir Charles (1963). *Man on His Nature*. The Gifford Lectures. Edinburgh Univ., 1937–38. 2d ed. Cambridge: Cambridge Univ. Press.

Sherrod, Lonnie R. (1981). "Issues in Cognitive Perceptual Development: The Special Case of Social Stimuli." In Lamb and Sherrod (1981), pp. 11–36.

Sherwood, Michael (1969). *The Logic of Explanation in Psychoanalysis*. New York and London: Academic Press.

Simon, Herbert A. (1957). *Administrative Behavior: A Study of Decision-Making Process in Administrative Organization*. 2d ed. New York: Macmillan.

———— (1969). *The Sciences of the Artificial*. Cambridge: MIT Press.

Smirnoff, Victor (1968). *La Psychanalyse de l'enfant*. Rev. ed. Paris: Presses Universitaires de France. *The Scope of Child Analysis*. Trans. Stephen Corrin. New York: International Universities Press, 1971.

Smith, Frank (1971). *Understanding Reading: A Psycholinguistic Analysis of Reading and Learning to Read*. New York: Holt, Rinehart, and Winston.

Smith, Joseph H., ed. (1978). *Psychoanalysis and Language*. Psychiatry and the Humanities, Vol. 3. New Haven and London: Yale Univ. Press, 1978.

Smith, M. Brewster, Jerome S. Bruner, and Robert W. White (1956). *Opinions and Personality*. New York: Wiley.

Spelke, Elizabeth S., and Alexandra Cortelyou (1981). "Perceptual Aspects of Social Knowing: Looking and Listening in Infancy." In Lamb and Sherrod (1981), pp. 61–84.

Spieker, Susan (1982). "Early Communication and Language Development." In Belsky, ed. (1982), pp. 121–32.

Spitz, René (1965). *The First Year of Life: A Psychoanalytic Study of Normal and Deviant Development of Object Relations*. New York: International Universities Press.

Spitzer, Leo (1948). *Linguistics and Literary History: Essays in Stylistics*. Princeton, N.J.: Princeton Univ. Press.

Stayton, Donelda J., Robert Hogan, and Mary D. Salter Ainsworth (1982). "Infant Obedience and Maternal Behavior: The Origins of Socialization Reconsidered." In Belsky, J., ed. (1982), pp. 194–203.

Stern, Daniel (1977). *The First Relationship: Mother and Infant*. The Developing Child Series. Cambridge: Harvard Univ. Press.

Stoller, Robert J. (1968a). "The Sense of Femaleness." *Psychoanalytic Quarterly*, 37, 42–55.

———— (1968b). *Sex and Gender*. New York: Science House.

———— (1972). "The 'Bedrock' of Masculinity and Femininity: Bisexuality." *Archives of General Psychiatry*, 26, 207–12.

———— (1974). "Symbiosis Anxiety and the Development of Masculinity." *Archives of General Psychiatry*, 30, 164–72.

———— (1975). *Perversion: The Erotic Form of Hatred*. New York: Pantheon.

Stolorow, Robert D., and George E. Atwood (1979). *Faces in a Cloud: Subjectivity in Personality Theory*. New York: Jason Aronson.

Strouse, Jean, ed. (1974). *Women and Analysis: Dialogues on Psychoanalytic Views of Femininity.* New York: Laurel Editions.

Suomi, Stephen J. (1981). "The Perception of Contingency and Social Development." In Lamb and Sherrod (1981), pp. 177–203.

Thomas, Alexander, Stella Chess, and Herbert G. Birch (1968). *Temperament and Behavior Disorders in Children.* New York: New York Univ. Press.

——— (1970). "The Origin of Personality." *Scientific American.* August 1970, pp. 102–09.

Tolman, Edward (1932). *Purposive Behavior in Animals and Men.* New York: Appleton-Century.

Toulmin, S. (1978). "Psychoanalysis, Physics, and the Mind-Body Problem." *Annual of Psychoanalysis,* 6, 315–36.

Trilling, Lionel (1950). "Art and Neurosis." In *The Liberal Imagination.* New York: Doubleday Anchor, pp. 159–78.

Turnbull, Colin (1961). "Some Observations Regarding the Experiences and Behavior of the BaMbuti Pygmies." *American Journal of Psychology,* 74, 304–08.

Turvey, Michael T., Robert E. Shaw, and William Mace (1978). "Issues in the Theory of Action: Degrees of Freedom, Coordinative Structures and Coalitions." In Requin, ed. (1978), pp. 557–95.

Vaillant, George E. (1977). *Adaptation to Life.* Boston: Little Brown.

Verbrugge, Robert R. (1977). "Resemblances in Language and Perception." In Shaw and Bransford, eds. (1977), pp. 365–89.

Viderman, S. (1970). *Le construction de l'espace analytique.* Paris: Denoël.

Von Bertalanffy, Ludwig (1952). "Theoretical Models in Biology and Psychology." In Krech, David, and George Klein, eds. (1952), *Theoretical Models and Personality Theory.* Durham, N.C.: Duke Univ. Press. Reprint. New York: Greenwood Press, 1968, pp. 24–38.

Waddington, C. H. (1957). *The Strategy of the Genes: A Discussion of Some Aspects of Theoretical Biology.* London: George Allen & Unwin.

Waelder, Robert (1930, 1936). "Das Prinzip der Mehrfachen Funktion." *Internationale Zeitschrift für Psychanalyse,* 16, 286–300. "The Principle of Multiple Function: Observations on Over-Determination." *Psychoanalytic Quarterly,* 5 (1936), 45–62.

——— (1960, 1964). *Basic Theory of Psychoanalysis.* New York: International Universities Press; Schocken Books, 1964.

——— (1963). "Psychic Determinism and the Possibility of Predictions." *Psychoanalytic Quarterly,* 32, 15–42.

Wallach, Hans (1959). "The Perception of Motion." In Held and Richards (1972), pp. 310–14.

Weatherick, N. E. (1980). "Why Not Psychological Psychology?" In Chapman, Antony J., and Dylan M. Jones, eds. *Models of Man.* Leicester: British Psychological Society, pp. 348–53.

Weinstein, Fred, and Gerald M. Platt (1973). *Psychoanalytic Sociology: An Essay on the Interpretation of Historical Data and the Phenomena of Collective Behavior.* Baltimore: Johns Hopkins Univ. Press.

Wellek, René (1960). "Closing Statement." In *Style in Language*. Ed. Thomas A. Sebeok. Cambridge: MIT Press, pp. 408–19.

Werner, Heinz, and Bernard Kaplan (1963). *Symbol-Formation: An Organismic-Developmental Approach to Language and the Expression of Thought.* New York: Wiley.

Whitehead, Alfred North (1925). *Science and the Modern World. The Lowell Lectures.* New York: Macmillan.

Wigner, Eugene (1967). "Two Kinds of Reality." *Scientific Essays of Eugene P. Wigner.* Bloomington and London: Indiana Univ. Press, pp.185–99.

Winnicott, Donald W. (1951). "Transitional Objects and Transitional Phenomena." *International Journal of Psycho-Analysis,* 34 (1953), 89–97. In Winnicott (1958), pp. 229–42, and Winnicott (1971a), pp. 1–51.

———— (1958). *Through Paediatrics to Psychoanalysis.* London: The Hogarth Press and the Institute of Psychoanalysis, 1975. First published as *Collected Papers: Through Paediatrics to Psycho-Analysis.* London: Tavistock, 1958. Also published as *Through Paediatrics to Psycho-Analysis: The Collected Papers of D. W. Winnicott.* New York: Basic Books, 1975.

———— (1960). "Ego Distortion in Terms of True and False Self." In *The Maturational Processes and the Facilitating Environment.* New York: International Universities Press, 1965, pp. 140–52.

———— (1966). "The Location of Cultural Experience." *International Journal of Psycho-Analysis,* 48 (1967), 368–72. In Winnicott (1971a), chap. 7, pp. 95–103.

———— (1971a). *Playing and Reality.* London: Tavistock.

———— (1971b). *Therapeutic Consultations in Child Psychiatry.* New York: Basic Books.

Witkin, Herman A. (1959). "The Perception of the Upright." *Scientific American,* February. In Stanley Coopersmith, ed. *Frontiers of Psychological Research.* San Francisco: W. H. Freeman, 1966, pp. 186–92.

Witkin, Herman A., et al. (1954). *Personality Through Perception: An Experimental and Clinical Study.* New York: Harper.

Wolff, Peter H. (1967). "Cognitive Considerations for a Psychoanalytic Theory of Language Acquisition." In Holt, ed. (1967), pp. 300–43.

Wollheim, Richard (1979). "The Cabinet of Dr. Lacan." *New York Review of Books,* 15 January, pp. 36–45.

Yarrow, Leon J., Judith L. Rubenstein, Frank A. Pedersen, and Joseph J. Jankowski (1982). "Dimensions of Early Stimulation and Their Differential Effects on Infant Development." In Belsky, ed. (1982), pp. 183–93.

Young, John Zachary (1978). *Programs of the Brain.* Oxford: Oxford Univ. Press.

Zetzel, Elizabeth Rosenberg (1966). "An Obsessional Neurotic: Freud's Rat Man." In Zetzel (1970), pp. 216–28.

———— (1970). *The Capacity for Emotional Growth.* New York: International Universities Press.

Zinberg, Norman E. (1974). *"High States": A Beginning Study.* Washington, D.C.: Drug Abuse Council, Inc.

Index

Fodor, Jerry A., 116, 120
Forster, E. M., 295
Fraiberg, Selma, 190, 193
Free association, 3–7, 13–22
Freedman, Alfred M., 208
Freedman, David A., 180, 181
Freud, Anna, 349, 350
Freud, Sigmund: *aliquis* man, 3–7, 279;
    archeological analogy, 7, 12, 311–12;
    art, 104; character, 159–61, 205,
    208–09, 350; child development,
    159–60, 163, 166, 177, 191, 203,
    208–09, 237; death instinct, 75; dream
    of Pope, 107, 126; dream of table
    d'hote, 13–16, 344, 348; drives, 179,
    337–39; early psychoanalysis, 331;
    ego-boundaries, 163; ego-psychology,
    331–32, 336, 339–53; feedback,
    113–14; femaleness, 209, 220–27;
    fetishism, 228; holistic reasoning, 7,
    12; imagination, 91–92; interpretation,
    335; Lacan and, 360; laughter, 286;
    Little Hans case, 250–63, 268, 275–76,
    276n; maleness, 222–23; oedipus
    complex, 215–16, 222–23; perception,
    107–10; prediction, 312; psychoanalytic
    principles, 73–75, 79–80; Rat Man
    case, 37–50, 93, 123–25, 283, 285, 357;
    reconstruction, 48; repetition
    compulsion, 74–75; scientist, 79–80,
    128, 294, 309; Shaw on, 57;
    symbolism, 85–106; third-phase
    psychoanalysis, 332; unconscious,
    "the," 104, 331–32, 333, 334, 342;
    unity, 15–17, 48, 349; wish, 91, 113,
    352
Friedman, Neil, 301
Frye, Northrop, 11–12

Galanter, Eugene, 138
Garrett, Merrill F., 116, 120
Gender, 209, 217–28, 240–45
Geschwind, Norman, 133
Gibson, J. J., 117–19
Gill, Merton M., 79–80, 161, 163
Gilligan, Carol, 220
Gogol, Nikolai, 205
Goodnow, Jacqueline J., 138
Gordon, David J., 56n, 77–78
Gouin Décarie, Thérèse, 182
Graf, Herbert, 264–80. *See also* Little Hans

Granit, Ragnar, 127, 137, 138, 139, 140,
    143, 152, 290
Green, André, 309
Greenacre, Phyllis, 172
Greenberg, Roger P., 187, 220, 300–03
Gregory, Richard, 111
Grolnick, Simon A., 356
Guntrip, Harry, 332, 355
Guttman, Samuel A., 353

Habermas, Jurgen, 312
Hall, Calvin S., 306–07
Halle, Morris, 116, 118
Hampshire, Stuart, 153, 353
Hartmann, Heinz, 74, 128–29, 162–63, 166,
    172, 310, 349, 350–52, 355
Hattam, Victoria, 270–71
Heider, Fritz, 286
Heisenberg, Werner, 294–95, 314
Held, Richard, 115, 179
Hemingway, Ernest: 210; "The Battler,"
    99–102
Hendrick, Ives, 235
Henry, Jules, 168, 172
History, 297–98. *See also* Psychohistory
Holistic analysis, 3–22, 23; and experi-
    mentation, 12; and feedback, 80–81;
    of individual, 175–76; in psycho-
    analysis, 7, 23; science and, 12–13;
    symbols in, 16–21
Holland, Norman N., 38, 144, 201, 284–88,
    331, 349
Holmes, Sherlock, 8–9, 12, 23
Home, H. J., 318
Hopkins, Gerard Manley, 81
Horney, Karen, 226
Humanities, and science, 327
Husserl, Edmund, 126
Hymes, Dell, 146
Hysteria, 245

I. *See* Body, Identity, Mind, Science
Id, 148, 342–43, 352–54. *See also*
    Ego-psychology
Identity: as adverbial, 354; as agency, 34,
    283, 327; ARC concept of, 49, 137,
    154–55, 176, 279, 283, 323, 325–27;
    behavior and, 306, 334–35; brain-